SAVING THE SAVED

An Exposition of 1 Peter

David R. Anderson, Ph.D.

GRACE THEOLOGY PRESS

Saving the Saved: An Exposition of 1 Peter

© 2020 David R. Anderson

Published by Grace Theology Press

The website addresses recommended throughout this book are offered as a resource to you. These websites are not intended in any way to be or imply an endorsement on the part of the author or publisher, nor do we vouch for their content.

eISBN: 978-1-7336223-9-4 | ISBN: 978-1-7336223-3-2

Printed in the United States of America

First Edition 2020

DEDICATION

To my incredible wife, Betty,
without whom most of my life would have been lost.

CONTENTS

INTRODUCTION

Most of us would like to have a life with some meaning, some significance. But how can you measure the significance of one's time on earth? What is the best way to measure the value of a human life? Some people would have us believe it is our physical stats that really count. Well, *USA Today* once published the vital statistics of Miss America contestants and came up with an average for each category. Let's see how you girls measure up.

1. The average Miss America is 23 years old.
2. All the contestants are single.
3. The majority of contestants have brown hair.
4. Most contestants also have brown eyes.
5. The average height for Miss America is 5'6".
6. Her average weight is 114 lbs.
7. The average dress size is 6.
8. The average waist size of a Miss America is 24 inches.
9. Her average shoe size is 7 1/2.
10. Miss America doesn't smoke.

Interestingly enough, when these contestants were asked to rate their beauty on a scale of 1-10, they gave themselves an average of

SAVING THE SAVED

8.62. So, even 23-year-old beauties with the 24-inch waists and size 6 dresses don't see themselves as 10s. If ever there were measurable vital statistics you would think might mean something, it would have to be those of the Miss America or Miss Universe contestants. But most of us don't measure the value of our human life by physical statistics. There must be a better way with an equal opportunity for everyone.

Not surprisingly, the One who created us also made a way for us to measure the meaning of our lives. Peter learned this lesson the hard way. It was a lesson he learned by flunking. And he never forgot his embarrassment at flunking this test. I'm the same way. I don't remember the questions I get right on a test. It's the ones I miss. I'm thinking right now about a question I missed from a test I took decades ago. I won't miss it again. We can learn from our mistakes. That's what Peter did. And he wrote a whole book about it.

What test did Peter flunk? Our minds immediately rush to his denial of Christ. No doubt that was his greatest recorded failure. But he didn't write a book about that. No, he wrote a book of the Bible about his failure at Caesarea Philippi recorded for us in Matthew 16. He had just moved to the top of the class. He has just confessed that he believed Jesus was "the Christ, the Son of the living God." (16:16). Jesus patted him on the back and said, "You got it. You are blessed. I will give you the keys of the kingdom of heaven." With each word, Peter's head grew a size larger. Talk about puffed up. He struts around, polishing his fingernails on his robe.

Then, Jesus suddenly lets the wind out of Peter's sails. He tells the disciples that He is going to suffer and die. "Then Peter took Him aside and began to rebuke Him" (16:22). Can you imagine rebuking Jesus? But wait a minute. Don't we do that every time we tell God we are not happy with how things are going in our lives: that rebellious child, that spouse who left me and the children, that investment where a friend took all my money, that inflamed cell that turned into cancer and is eating away at my body, and so on? My preferred future for my life just isn't working out. Neither was Peter's. He was planning on sitting at the right hand of Jesus when He set up His kingdom.

But now Jesus tells Peter and the others he is going to be killed in Jerusalem. Peter isn't having any of this. How can a dead king set up a kingdom?

Now Jesus does the rebuking. "Get behind me, Satan!" Sterner words have never been spoken. Jesus actually reveals that the devil is speaking through Peter. Jesus goes on to say Peter is only concerned with his own kingdom and his own glory, "the things of men." So, he corrects Peter in 16:24-27. In these verses, Jesus tells His disciples how to save their lives or how to lose them, how to have meaningful and significant lives or how to waste the very purpose for which they were created. He even told them how God will measure the significance of our lives. Peter never forgot the lesson. He wrote a whole book about it: 1 Peter, a book about "Saving the Saved." It is a book about how people who are already guaranteed of a place with God forever by the death of Christ (they are saved) can actually save their time on earth (their lives) forever.

In my years of disciple-making, I know of no other truth outside the gospel itself that has transformed more lives than Jesus' lesson to his disciples on "Saving the Saved." He wants people to know that having our sins forgiven through Christ's death on the cross and receiving the free gift of eternal life is the most important truth we will ever believe, but that is only the starting block of an exciting race; it is not the goal line. When we trust Christ as our Savior, we've only just begun, as Karen Carpenter used to sing. Now we are in a race. The starting gun has gone off. How we run that race will determine how much of our time on earth is either saved with an eternal significance or lost forever, never to be retrieved. To see how Peter developed this idea, read on.

1

"SENSE AND SENSIBILITY"

1 Peter 1:1-2

INTRODUCTION

Dr. Richard Selzer writes in his book *Letters to a Young Doctor* that most of us are shielded early in life by some sort of imaginative protective membrane. This membrane shields us from the horror of life much as the immune system of the body guards us from harmful bacteria. But it seems that somewhere down the road, as the years roll by, the membrane becomes porous or has some sort of tear, and horror slips in. For many believers this poses a theological dilemma. As James Dobson says in his book by a similar title, God doesn't make sense.[1]

Sometimes even little children get confused about God when things go wrong in their lives. One little boy named Chris, whose face had been burned in a fire, sent this note to his psychotherapist: "Dear Dr. Gardner. Some big person, it was a boy about 13, he called me a

---

[1] James Dobson, *When God Doesn't Make Sense* (Wheaton, IL: Tyndale House Publishers, 1993).

1

turtle. And I know he said this because of my plastic surgery. And I think God hates me because of my lip. And when I die, he'll probably send me to hell. Love, Chris."[2]

Chris naturally concluded that his deformity meant God had rejected him. Why else would an all-powerful, all-knowing Creator make him in such an awful way? He must be a reject. It is a logical conclusion. To say God made him this way because He loves Chris may make sense to us, but not to Chris. We are able to endure the most extreme circumstances, even death, if the circumstances make sense. Before he was hanged, Nathan Hale said to his British executioners, "I only regret I have but one life to give for my country." Yes, we can hang on if the suffering makes sense. Meaning in the midst of dire circumstances does not knock us down; it is the absence of meaning—senseless suffering—that becomes intolerable.

The key problem is our expectations. Unbelievers have no expectations. But believers with a personal relationship to the Creator of the universe Who claims to love them and to have a wonderful plan for their lives have high expectations. As Ron Dunn, the Dallas pastor whose son committed suicide in his teenage years, says in his book *When Heaven is Silent,*

> The truth is, I felt I deserved better treatment. Position ought to merit some consideration. After all, if a person is living for God, that ought to count for something, shouldn't it? I mean, there ought to be some fringe benefits, right? A few perks go with the job. Special treatment, preferential consideration? Hey, I'm a child of God. I devoted my life to serving Him— He ought to keep that in mind when He starts handing out calamities and catastrophes. That's only fair.
>
> Fair. That's all I ask, Lord. Just be fair. Is that too much to ask? How can it be fair when the children of my friends are graduating from college, starting careers, getting married,

---

[2]   Ibid., 12.

having children while my son lies in a grave. A little justice, Lord. A little justice.[3]

These failed expectations bring disillusionment to our doorstep. Like a pushy sales person, they come in uninvited, sit down, and make themselves right at home in my living room, dining room, in the library of my soul. When I ask them to leave, they sneer. When I inform them they have outstayed their welcome, they won't move out.

These are the people Peter writes to: hurting believers who can't make any sense out of their circumstances. These are people who feel like they have been abandoned by God. So, let's look at the text itself to get a better grip on the specific problem.

THE PROBLEM   1:1-2

> Peter, an apostle of Jesus Christ, to the pilgrims of the Dispersion in Pontus, Galatia, Cappadocia, Asia, and Bithynia, elect according to the foreknowledge of God the Father, in sanctification of the Spirit, for obedience and sprinkling of the blood of Jesus Christ:
>
> Grace to you and peace be multiplied.

Peter claims to be writing to pilgrims of the **"Dispersion."** That word doesn't mean a whole lot to Gentiles, but it did to the Jews living in the Christian era, who had put their faith in Christ as their Messiah. After Stephen was martyred, these newly minted Jewish Christians scattered throughout the Mediterranean world to avoid the persecution of people like Saul of Tarsus and others who were trying to kill them. There was suffering on several fronts:

1. Rejection by other Jews because of their faith in Christ.

2. Rejection by the Gentiles because they were Jews.

---

[3]   Ronald Dunn, *When Heaven Is Silent* (Nashville: Thomas Nelson Publishers, 1994), 96.

3. Hurting economically because they left their businesses behind.

4. They were foreigners living in Turkey (all the areas mentioned were part of modern day Turkey).

Now Peter confounds the problem with his choice of the word **"elect."** That means these people were "chosen" by God. But chosen for what? A life of suffering? They appear to be suffering because they are Christians, not because of sin in their lives. It doesn't make sense.

But now things go from bad to worse. Peter says these believers are chosen **"according to the foreknowledge of God the Father."** You mean God chose me for this kind of suffering before the suffering ever began? And you tell me this is a loving Father Who cares for His children? There seems to be something very warped about all this.

Maybe we can find some help from the word translated **"according to."** It is the Greek word *kata*, which (according to *BDAG*)[4] can mean either "in accordance with" or "based on, because of, with the result that." One option not listed is "in spite of." The Arminians claim that God looked down through the corridors of time and knew those that would receive Christ as their Savior, and as a result of this foreknowledge, He chose (elected) them.

The Calvinists don't like that approach because they claim the prior knowledge of those that would believe makes faith a condition for election, and one of their main points (among Five Point Calvinists) is Unconditional Election. So, some of them like the late R. C. Sproul say that God looks down through the corridors of time and, knowing that no one will receive Christ on his/her own, drags certain

---

[4] We will refer to *BDAG* from time to time. It is the best one-volume English dictionary on the Greek of the New Testament, *A Greek-English Lexicon of the New Testament and other Early Christian Literature*, Bauer, Danker, Arndt, and Gingrich, 3rd ed. (Chicago: University of Chicago Press, 2000).

members of the human race (the elect) into His kingdom kicking and screaming all the way. I was teaching this passage in Almaty, Kazakhstan, around the turn-of-the-century. One of the students, who was a devout Five Point Calvinist, objected by saying that R. C. Sproul would never teach such a heinous doctrine. I simply referred him to *Chosen But Free* and Sproul's discussion of *helkuō*,[5] where he teaches that John 6:44 means no one can come to Christ except the Father drags him. It is true that in a hostile context like when Paul and Silas were dragged (Acts 16:19) before unbelieving magistrates *helkuō* means precisely that: to drag. But in a family context of love the word means "to draw," as it is properly translated in most English versions.

Many of us prefer "in accordance with" for the translation of *kata*. This translation allows us to walk arm in arm with the Holy Spirit into the kingdom. God does not force the elect to believe in Jesus. As C. S. Lewis points out, God can never ravish; He can only woo. Just as a man (in the normal dating ritual for the last hundred years in our western culture) selects the woman he would like to pursue as a life partner, God initiates the election process (He woos us—John 6:44). But He doesn't force us. We can reject His wooing (as every man or woman that rejects the light brought to him by God does—Romans 1:20ff and John 1:9). But after a period of "dating" God pops the question: "Will you marry Me?" He gives us a choice: "Whosoever will." Why? Because without a choice He would never know we love Him. In our culture, why don't men just find a woman that appeals to them and knock them over the head with a club and take them off to their cave? Obvious. They would never know if they are loved. Take away choice; take away love. You mean God has a choice (election) and humans have a choice (election)? Exactly. He chose us of His own free will, and we chose Him of our own free will.[6]

---

5   R. C. Sproul, *Chosen but Free* (Wheaton, IL: Tyndale House Publishers, 1986), 69-72.

6   David L. Allen and Steve W. Lemke, editors *Whosoever Will* (Nashville,

He elected us, and we elected Him. We walk arm in arm into the kingdom. We prefer this meaning for *kata* ("according to").

But doesn't "foreknowledge" mean predetermination? No, that was something introduced by Augustine (died AD 430). No church father before Augustine equated foreknowledge with predetermination. Augustine did it by importing pagan religions into Christianity: Stoicism, Neo-Platonism, and Manichaeism. He spent ten years as a Manichaean before becoming a Christian. Manichaeism was the highest developed form of Gnosticism. They are the ones that taught Augustine that regeneration precedes faith, something he then introduced to Christianity and something R. C. Sproul claims to be the foundation of Five Point Calvinism.[7] All these philosophies were deterministic. Hard determinism. Foreknowledge simply means a prior knowledge of everything that will actually come to pass. But this does not mean knowing something will happen predetermines that it will happen. What Augustine missed was the difference between foreknowledge and omniscience.[8]

Whereas foreknowledge is prior knowledge of what actually will come to pass, omniscience includes what will actually come to pass but also takes into account what could come to pass. In other words, it includes the "woulda, coulda, shoulda." In English grammar we would say that foreknowledge is in the indicative (the mood for reality), whereas omniscience includes the subjunctive (the mood for potentiality). Foreknowledge is what really will come to pass; omniscience includes foreknowledge but adds to it what

Tennessee: B&H Academic, 2010) and Robert J. Kerrey, *How Does God Draw People to Believe in Jesus? A Biblical Analysis of Alternative Answers and Why it Matters* (Grace Theology Press, 2019).

7 R. C. Sproul, *Willing to Believe* (Grand Rapids: Baker, 1997), 193.

8 See Ken Wilson, *The Foundation of Augustinian-Calvinism* (Regula Fidei Press, 2019) and *A Defense of Free Grace Theology: With Respect to Saving Faith, Perseverance and Assurance* (Grace Theology Press, 2017), 33-65.

could have come to pass, or what might have come to pass, or what would come to pass. See I Samuel 23 for great interplay between the foreknowledge of God and the omniscience of God and how David made one decision based on God's foreknowledge and another based on His omniscience.[9]

So, when we come to a fork in the road with three choices on which direction to take, God in His foreknowledge knows we are going to choose option B. And we do. He knows what actually will come to pass. That's knowledge of future reality. But He also knows what would happen if we chose option A or option C. That's what keeps foreknowledge from being predetermination. With human choice we always have options. Take choice away, and people are no longer people; they are robots. Volition or human choice is essential to personhood. We are created in God's image. Part of His image is having volition. Augustine's determinism destroyed human choice. And make no mistake: Augustine was the first Church Father to introduce determinism into orthodox Christianity. That is one reason why the Eastern Church never accepted Augustine as a Church Father. They knew he was introducing pagan religions into the *Regula Fide* (Rule of Faith held by the orthodox Church Fathers until Augustine). The result of determinism? No choice; no love. If anything, the Bible is a love story between God and man, not the story of a divine sadist that creates creatures for the express purpose of torturing the vast majority of them in hell or Lake of Fire forever just to show the small minority that enjoy His mercy just how just He is.

Peter also says these elect believers of the dispersion are **"sanctified,"** which means to be set apart for a special purpose.

---

9   See Robert Duncan Culver, *Systematic Theology* (Geanies House Great Britain, Christians Focus Publications Ltd. Mentor Imprint, 2005), 86. "The term designates God's cognitive awareness. He has perfect, immediate, knowledge of all events and things, whether actual or conditional upon the acts of "free" beings; whether the events or things are only possible or actual and whether they are past, present or future."

There are four types of sanctification in the Bible: 1) Prospective (before physical birth—Jeremiah 1:5; Galatians 1:15); 2) Positional (at spiritual birth—Hebrews 10:10); 3) Progressive (after spiritual birth—Hebrews 10:14); and Perfective (when Christ returns and we no longer have a Sin(ful) Nature). Here in 1 Peter 1:2 we have Prospective Sanctification. But, again, this only adds to the problem. You mean I've been set aside for the purpose of suffering? Thanks a lot. It still doesn't make any sense.

Maybe the next phrase will help us out: **"for obedience and sprinkling of the blood of Jesus Christ."** This probably refers to obedience to the gospel and the purifying of the cross; in other words, to become a Christian. But that's just my problem. I wouldn't have these difficulties if I were not a Christian. It's because I am Christian (chosen, foreknown, and sanctified to be a Christian) that I'm suffering. It just doesn't compute; it makes zero sense.

And in the midst of this mess, Peter has the gall to close off his salutation with **"grace to you and peace be multiplied."** Really? How can I find peace in the midst of this mess? This salutation (Peter's "Hello" in these opening two verses) seems to be mocking me in the midst of my nonsensical suffering.

John of the Cross calls this "diaspora experience" the "dark night of the soul." I would suggest it is not a rabbit trail in the Christian life but a major highway. If so, what signs can we use to keep us from turning off God's highway into a dead end of disillusionment? The first sign is:

1. Construction Ahead.

This points to God the Father and His prior knowledge of our future problems. We are told that He has chosen us in accordance with His foreknowledge. And no matter how we want to interpret the relationship between election and foreknowledge, the fact remains that He knew the road ahead would be bumpy for us when He chose us to be in His forever family. Does that make Him a divine sadist? No more so than those of us that are parents and have brought children into a fallen world with foreknowledge that they would face suffering.

Such a concept can cause problems on the one hand, but on the other it is comforting. When I see a sign on the freeway saying, "Construction Ahead," I don't particularly like it, but it does tell me there is someone in charge of this freeway, and that someone has a plan. Obviously, they don't intend to destroy the freeway. They're working on it to improve it. They clearly have a Master Plan. Though there may be temporary displeasure for me, the long-range plan is good and beneficial for many people, and so, I'm able to endure the hardship without grumbling.

Likewise, just realizing that God the Father knows the future and therefore knew about the future in advance and chose me anyway can be a great comfort. It tells me there is a Master Plan. It tells me that though the road ahead may be bumpy, He would not lead me down it unless it is going to be beneficial in the long run.

You see, just because something does not make sense to me does not mean it doesn't make sense to someone that knows the future, someone that has foreknowledge. Perhaps they can see things I cannot. In my limited knowledge I can't make heads or tails out of the circumstances, but He is not limited by my limited knowledge. We must accept the fact that we are limited but He is not.

We aren't even capable of being absolutely sure of much of the universe we can touch, taste, smell, see, and hear. The scientific books of a hundred years ago read like joke books today. Even when I was in college, they were teaching that we have 48 chromosomes instead of 46. Black holes had not been discovered, and the concept of cloning was labeled science fiction. The point is, man's knowledge is constantly expanding and correcting. And if we can't get a comprehensive grip on the world around us that we can see, what are we going to do with one we can't see? When it comes to comprehending the inscrutable ways of God, man's mind soon runs out of hypotheses. And that is uncomfortable.

Does it seem strange to you that as we look through our dark glasses at the mysteries of this life, our little pea-sized brains can't seem to figure things out? And God is not under any obligation to explain it all at this point. As Solomon (Proverbs 25:2) says, "It is the glory of God to conceal a matter." Deuteronomy 29:29 says, "The secret things belong to the Lord our God." And Isaiah 55:8-9 teaches, "'For my thoughts are not your thoughts; neither are my ways your ways,' declares the Lord. 'As the heavens are higher than the earth, so my ways are higher than your ways and my thoughts higher than your thoughts.'"

Rather than disillusionment, we should find comfort in the fact that we cannot understand it all. After all, if we could figure God out completely, He wouldn't be any smarter than we are. And if there isn't someone up there a whole lot smarter than we are that can make sense out of chaos and order out of calamity, then we would all have reason to despair. Let us rejoice and be encouraged by knowing that God our Father had prior knowledge of the bumpy road ahead of us on our journey through life, and He still chose us to be in His forever family.

2. Yield.

Here we refer to the sanctifying ministry of the Holy Spirit. Even before the foundation of the world, we have been set aside for a special purpose. The very same prospective sanctification that set aside Jeremiah to be a prophet and Paul to be an apostle to the Gentiles has set us aside for something special.

And when we combine the Selection of the Sovereign with the Sanctification of the Spirit, the result is Design. You know, there're some things we can only see in the dark. Who of us hasn't had the experience of awe when we see the majesty of the stars on a clear, dark night? If you locate the Big Dipper, Orion, the North Star, and other fixed markers in the map of the heavens, these constellations function like loudspeakers echoing the message of design from all corners of the universe.

So, only in the darkness of life, the dark night of the soul, are we able to see these stars in God's heavenly dimensions: the stars of the election, foreknowledge, and prospective sanctification. This constellation comprising the work of the Father and the Spirit cry out the message of design and order, purpose and reason, and they bring hope. But we must yield to His special purpose in our life, or we'll get bumped off the highway as surely as a car speeding through a yield sign into an occupied lane. When we harden ourselves to His special purpose in our lives because it's so different from the script, we might have written for ourselves, then the clay is telling the potter what to do, and the work of the potter is frustrated.

3. Keep Right.

Here we mean we must keep the right view of God in mind. Lack of sense does not mean lack of sensibility. Concepts like election, foreknowledge, and sanctification before we were born can sound pretty cold and detached. But even when God doesn't make sense, He has sensibility. He does care; He does feel; when we hurt, He hurts. That's exactly what the work of the Son tells us in the rest of verse two. If we saw the Selection of the Sovereign and the Sanctification of the Spirit, now we look at the Sprinkling of the Son. The sprinkling which made us acceptable to the Father was done by means of the blood of the Son. And it's so easy for us to read quickly over that statement without pausing to catch its significance.

The blood of Christ tells us God cares. God so loved the world that He gave His only begotten Son . . . No greater love has any man than this, that he laid down his life for his friends. Though we were elected, foreknown, and sanctified in eternity past, simultaneously the decision was made between the Father and the Son to provide a sacrifice to extricate man from his horrible predicament. And through this sacrifice, not only was the path of reconciliation between God and man made possible, but the potential was also provided for a way to set straight all the inequities, the injustices, and the undeserved suffering of mankind on the planet. The cross cries out that God cares. Lack of sense does not mean lack of sensibility.

Dr. Tony Campolo described a boy named Jerry in one of his messages.[10] Jerry had been afflicted from birth with cerebral palsy. He walked and talked with great difficulty, yet he came to a Christian summer camp where Dr. Campolo was the principal speaker. It was apparent from the first day that Jerry would be rejected by the other junior highers, who immediately set about establishing a hierarchy of social power. An in-group emerged, as it always does, composed mostly of the good-looking guys and the cute girls. They were far too sophisticated and self-centered to mess around with a cripple–a loser like Jerry. They were also rude to the other outcasts–the kids that had been hurt and those that lacked confidence. They didn't stand a chance.

All week Dr. Campolo watched Jerry struggle to find his place. It was brutal to witness. The popular kids mocked the way he walked and talked. They would imitate his labored speech, saying, "Wwwhhhaaatt . . . tiiimmmmmmmmmme . . . issssssss . . . cccrrafffttt . . . ccclllaaassss?" Then they would all laugh hysterically as though Jerry were deaf. At other times, they avoided him like the plague.

A service was held on the final morning of the camp, during which the students were invited to give their testimonies about what Jesus Christ had meant them. One by one, the superstars came to the microphone—the athletes, the cheerleaders, and the popular kids. They delivered their little canned speeches, but there was no power in their witness. Their words were empty.

Then Jerry started making his way down the aisle from the back of the auditorium. The other students saw him too, and they began to whisper and point. Then a ripple of laughter passed over the crowd. Ever so slowly, Jerry came to the platform and then carefully and painfully climbed the three stairs at the side.

---

[10] Dobson, 173.

Finally, he reached the microphone. He stood for a moment looking at his peers, and then said with great effort, "I . . . loooo vvvve . . . Jeeeeessssssuuuussss . . . aaannnnnddddd . . . Jeeeeeeee ssssssssuuuuuuussssss . . . loooooooolvvvvveessssss . . . mmmmeeeeeeeeeee." Then Jerry turned to make his long journey back to his seat.

Jerry's simple testimony went through the crowd of teenagers like a bolt of lightning. His sense of the Savior's love for him in spite of the human cruelty around him and his own physical handicaps, exposed the sin and the self-centeredness in their lives. They began streaming into the aisles and down to a place of prayer at the front. The Lord had used the least capable spokesman of all those teenagers to accomplish His purposes.

No, lack of sense does not mean lack of sensibility. You see, God is just not as insensitive as most of us humans.

CONCLUSION

One of the incredible aspects of the salutation is the mention of the person and work of each member of the Godhead. Selected by the Sovereign, Sanctified by the Spirit, and Sprinkled by the Son. There is no other letter in the New Testament that mentions all three members of the Godhead in its salutation, let alone mentions the work of each one. I would suggest that this is one more way in which the Divine Author of this letter tries to bring comfort in the midst of chaos. This heavenly trio surrounds the suffering of the believer like a Divine Triangle of Care and Concern. It's the author's way of saying God is not asleep in the midst of our suffering; He's not detached and distant. Every member of the Godhead has His full attention in the human drama taking place on earth. None of them is out searching for life on other planets. Life on earth has their full attention. Even the angels, we read later on in the chapter, are down on their hands and knees, so to speak, watching the human drama unfold. Behind the fog of our suffering the three brightest stars in the universe are shining for us, the objects of His affection, the very ones He has selected and sanctified and sprinkled. And remember, faith walks in the light but flies in the fog. Fog faith never does understand; it simply trusts in a sovereign God's purpose and love.

And so, Peter writes, **"Grace to you, and peace be multiplied."** Why? Because we can trust this kind of God. Television once presented a docudrama on three families that were given the bad news of terminal illness. With approval from the three patients (two men and a woman), they captured on film the moment each of them learned he or she was afflicted with a malignancy in its latter stages. The initial shock, disbelief, fear, and anger were recorded in full and graphic detail. Afterwards, the documentary team followed these three families through the treatment process with its ups and downs, hopes and disappointments, pain and terror. Eventually all three patients died, and the program ended without comment or editorial.

There was so much that should have been said. What was interesting were the different ways these people dealt with their frightening circumstances. The two that apparently had no faith reacted with anger and bitterness. They not only fought the disease, but they seemed to be at war with everyone else. Their personal relationships and even their marriages were shaken. But the third individual had a different response.

He was a humble black pastor of a small, inner city Baptist Church. He was in his late sixties and had been a minister throughout his adult life. His love for the Lord was so profound that it was reflected in everything he said. On his final Sunday in this church he talked openly about his impending death: "Some of you have asked me if I am mad at God because of this disease that is taken over my body. I'll tell you honestly that I have nothing but love in my heart for my Lord. I'm going to a better place where there will be no more tears, no suffering, and no heartache. So, don't feel bad for me. Besides, our Lord suffered and died for our sins. Why should I not share in his suffering?"

Then he began to sing, without accompaniment, in an old, broken voice:

> Must Jesus bear the cross alone,
> And all the world go free?
> No, there's a cross for everyone,
> And there's a cross for me.
>
> How happy are the Saints above,
> Who once went sorr'wing here;
> But now they taste unmingled love,
> And joy without a tear.
>
> The consecrated cross I'll bear,
> Till death shall set me free,
> And then go home my crown to wear,
> For there's a crown for me.[11]

Yes, faith walks in the light, but flies in the fog. We trust in a God who may not always make sense, but always has sensibility.

---

[11] Ibid., 226.

2

"DEALING WITH DEPRESSION"
1 Peter 1:3-5

INTRODUCTION

Have you ever been depressed? Few, if any of us, would answer "no" to that question. According to Dr. Archibald Hart,[12] the average size church could have as much as 5% of its members experiencing a significant depression at any given time. Depression has been called "the common cold" of psychological problems. It's like a snarled rope, difficult to untangle and holding thousands of people in a bind of despair and discouragement.

The bonds of depression usually begin as threads while we are growing up. Pat Springle describes Susan, one of his clients, in his chapter "The Blob and the Abyss."[13] Susan had been neglected by her workaholic father, and her emotionally crippled mother had looked

---

[12] Archibald D. Hart, *Counseling the Depressed* (Dallas: Word Publishing, 1987), 11.

[13] Robert S. McGee and Pat Springle, *Getting Unstuck* (Dallas: Word Publishing, 1992), 7.

at her for comfort. In effect, Susan became her mother's parent, taking responsibility for mom's emotional state. Susan learned to cope with her pain by "being the best." In high school she made good grades, played on the varsity tennis team, and was voted most popular in her class. In college, being the best became more difficult because the level of competition was higher, but she was still driven to succeed. Susan got a good job after graduation, and three years later she got married. Her relationship with her husband reflected her success goals. As a couple, they were always on the go, filling their lives with fun and meaningful things. Even at church Susan was known as somebody that could be counted on to get things done.

Yet, as a sales representative in a highly competitive market Susan could no longer outperform everyone else. She began to experience failure—more than she could handle. Losing at the comparison game was a new experience for Susan. When she confronted the stark reality, she became depressed and withdrawn. Her exuberant confidence turned to despair. Her energy quickly withered into lethargy. Springle met her after she had been depressed for about a year. When he asked her to explain her childhood and her relationship with her parents, she told him the facts. Yet there was no hint of emotion as she spoke of being neglected by one parent and smothered by the self-pity and helplessness of the other. She matter-of-factly explained her rise to popularity in high school and college, her driven lifestyle, her superficial marriage, and her failure to excel at work.

Susan sounded more like the 6 o'clock news than a description of life filled with hurt and despair. There were no feelings expressed at all—just words. Sensing that her denial was thick and hard, Springle asked, "Susan, what generally makes you angry?" She answered confidently, "Nothing. I don't get angry. I guess I've grown past that." Then she sighed, "But I know something's wrong. I just don't know what it is."

Several months of weekly discussion followed, and slowly, very slowly—Susan began to feel again. Then she became suddenly overwhelmed by the enormity of her pain. She sobbed, "I've spent my life trying to be somebody . . . just wanting somebody to care about me . . . but now I feel so empty, so alone, like I've fallen into an abyss with no bottom to it—and nobody with me to hold onto."

The abyss . . . the black hole. That's depression. That's our subject in this lesson: **Dealing with Depression.** What does God have to say that might help us out of this black hole? Well, first of all, we must clarify that we are not addressing biological, physio genic depression. We are not talking about bipolar disorder. We're not addressing chemical imbalances. That realm belongs to the medical doctors. Here we are assuming their body chemistry is okay, but they're still depressed, perhaps on the verge of clinical depression, which would require hospitalization to get help in today's world. Furthermore, we're not dealing with depression that comes as a result of sin. No, in I Peter the Christians are not suffering because of sin, but because they're Christians. That's exactly where these people find themselves. As we read these verses you'll probably say, "It doesn't mention depression. How do you know they were depressed?"

Well, it doesn't take Sherlock Holmes to realize these folks we're depressed. Reactive depression forms in any normal human being in the face of a dramatic loss or cumulative losses. A normal wife will undergo some depression after her husband dies. And these people were facing losses all over the place. We mentioned them in our last lesson. They lost relationships (Jewish families who cut them off), finances, homes, and perhaps even immediate family members or friends due to the persecution from people like Saul of Tarsus. On the cumulative points for stress, these folks were off the charts. Knowing they were depressed wouldn't take divine revelation for Peter. That would be normal, expected. It would be abnormal if they were not depressed.

So, what can Peter share with these shell-shocked believers that could help lift them out of their black hole? What truth would you choose to share with people you care about that might be stuck in a black hole of depression? Peter makes a fascinating choice. He chooses to tell them how to save their lives, that is, how to redeem the time. He isn't sharing the gospel of justification salvation with them. He's not telling them how to get to heaven when they die. Verse 3 tells us they are already "born again." No, the good news Peter has to share is for people who are already believers but need some motivation to keep on going when the Christian life gets rough, and it gets rough precisely because they are Christians. They could avoid most of their problems if they just had not believed in Jesus.

In his introduction (1:3-12) Peter mines some of the most profound and valuable truths from God's mountain of truth. But in a way he is passing on what Jesus shared with him in Matthew 16:24-27. In that passage Jesus told his disciples how to save their lives or lose their lives. He was not talking about heaven or hell. Matthew 16:27 is connected to the previous three verses by the word "for" (*gar*), meaning He is explaining or giving a reason for what He said in those three verses, verses about self-sacrifice. Hold on to your time on earth (your life) for your own selfish kingdom building and you will lose the very purpose for which God created you. But throw your life away (lose it) in the eyes of the world, and you will discover the very reason why God created you. And not only that, but when Christ returns, He will reward you based on what you have done with your life (v. 27). That is the goal (1:9) of the Christian faith—to glorify God by living out our time on earth for His kingdom (Matthew 6:33), not ours.

So, in this letter Peter wants to tell us how to make our lives count for eternity. In this introduction he praises God for this plan to make our lives count forever (1:3-5), he sets forth (1:6-9) the process involved in this plan (undeserved suffering), and the paradox of this plan that would put suffering before glory (1:10-12). In this lesson we just want to look at 1:3-5 where Peter praises God for this incomparable plan. You might call it a plan for preservation. The word usually translated "saved" (a verb) or "salvation" (a noun) can also be translated "preserve" or "preservation." If you save some meat from spoiling, you preserve it. In 1:3-5 Peter talks about the preservation of our spirits, our securities, and our very selves.

19

I. PRESERVATION OF OUR SPIRITS 3

> Blessed be the God and Father of our Lord Jesus Christ, who according to His abundant mercy has begotten us again to a living hope through the resurrection of Jesus Christ from the dead,

The word for "begotten . . . again" (*anagennaō* = *ana* [again] + *gennaō* [to be born]) is used only twice in the NT. Both are in this chapter (1:3, 23). Peter is telling his readers to praise God because they have been born again. But these people are saying, "That's just the problem; if I were not born again, I wouldn't be having these problems. What's there to praise Him for?" Three things, answers Peter, which are only available to those who have been born again.

The first of these things is the salvation (preservation) of our spirits forever through resurrection. If God raised Jesus from the dead, then He's going to raise all those who believe in Jesus from the dead as well. Resurrection from the dead gives them a *living* hope to help counteract the prospect of losing their physical lives. They can never lose their spiritual lives. But not only can they never lose their spiritual lives; they can also never lose their spiritual "securities."

II. PRESERVATION OF OUR "SECURITIES" 4

> to an inheritance incorruptible and undefiled and that does not fade away, reserved in heaven for you,

The word here translated **"inheritance"** (*klēronomian*) is used consistently outside of Paul as a reward for faithfulness (Matthew 5:5; 19:29; 25:34; Hebrews 6:12; Revelation 21:7). Sometimes even Paul uses it that way: ". . . knowing that from the Lord you will receive the reward of the inheritance; for you serve the Lord Christ" (Colossians 3:24). Notice the word "reward."

One cause for the depression of these Jewish Christians was the loss of their possessions. Essentially, when they left Israel, they had to make a run for it. They left most of their physical possessions behind, including their inheritance that had been in the "family" for centuries: their plot of land. When Moses stood on Mount Nebo giving instructions to the slaves that had escaped from Egypt and had not died in the wilderness after forty years of wandering, he told them essentially to do two things: to enter the land and to possess the land. The Hebrew words for "possession" and for "inheritance" are used interchangeably in the Old Testament.[14] When they took over the land, they divided it into states; each tribe got its own state, so to speak. Those states were divided up among the families belonging to each tribe, respectively. Each family had its own plot of land. That was their inheritance, their possession of the land of Israel. If they got into financial trouble, they could mortgage their land or their inheritance, but it could not be foreclosed on. Every seven years debts were forgiven. In other words, as long as they were in the land they could not lose their inheritance. It was their source of security.

But now they have been dispossessed. It's the dispersion; they're out of the land. They have lost their inheritance. Or wait a minute; have they? Peter comes along and says they may have lost their physical inheritance, the land, but in its place God has given them a spiritual inheritance reserved in heaven just for them. This is a portfolio of securities no one can steal. Peter underscores the uniqueness of these "securities" with three adjectives:

1. **Incorruptible** = *aphtharton* = not subject to rusting away like metals

2. **Undefiled** = *amianton* = morally untainted, not subject to fraud

3. **Unfadable** = *amaranton* = flowers which cannot fade

---

[14] See Francis Brown, S. R. Driver, C.A. Briggs, *Hebrew and English Lexicon of the Old Testament* (Oxford: The Clarendon Press, 1966), *nahal*, 635, and *yarash*, 439.

No doubt his readers have never heard of such an inheritance. This is a million times better than the one they just lost. And to emphasize the permanence of their spiritual possessions Peter says they are **"reserved"** in heaven for them. This word "reserved" (*tetērnmenēn*) is in the perfect tense, which usually indicates action completed in the past with results extending to the present, all of which helps underscore the permanence of these heavenly possessions.

We live in an age of *Accidental Billionaires* like the founder of Facebook, Mark Zuckerberg, or even the Winklevoss twins Zuckerberg defrauded of their proprietary information. They took part of Zuckerberg's settlement money and became Bitcoin billionaires. When Bitcoin hit $20,000 a coin, they were worth two billion. The next week, when Bitcoin dropped to $10,000 a coin, they had lost half their net worth. So, it is with earthly treasure. As the Scriptures say: Money has wings (Proverbs 23:5). Not so in heaven. Peter's readers have reason to rejoice and praise God. They lost something temporal to gain something eternal. As Jim Eliot said, "He is no fool who loses something he cannot keep to gain something he cannot lose."

Peter's third reason for encouragement adds a whole new dimension to the "salvation equation." Not only can God save their spirits and their "securities," He can also save their very selves. We will develop this more fully in v. 9, but Peter gives us a sneak preview here.

III. PRESERVATION OF OUR SELVES   5

who are kept by the power of God through faith for salvation
ready to be revealed in the last time.

The meaning of "to save" or "salvation" in the NT refers to deliverance from drowning or disease just as often as it does salvation from our sins so we can go to heaven. When Jesus uses the word "save" in Matthew 16:24-27, the context is one of discipleship where His followers are asked to take up their crosses and follow Him, knowing they may be killed in the process. His motivation to move His followers to voluntarily sacrifice their lives? Rewards (24:27).

Peter is doing the same thing here. He did not forget his mistake at Caesarea Philippi. He wouldn't wear the dunce cap again. In theology we like to teach about the three tenses of salvation: 1) Salvation in the *past* from the Penalty of sin—justification; 2) Salvation in the *present* from the Power of sin—sanctification; and 3) Salvation in the *future* from the Presence of sin—glorification. Those distinctions are very helpful in getting people to understand that salvation in the Bible extends beyond going to heaven when they die. But helpful as these distinctions are, the use of "save" by Jesus in Matthew 16 is distinct from even these three tenses of salvation.

Here Peter (as Jesus taught him) speaks of a wasted life versus an eternally significant life, a life that is lost versus a life that is saved. It speaks of making each day count for eternity. It gives one a transcendent cause to live for, a reason to get up in the morning, an eternal purpose for existence that reaches beyond sitting on a cloud and strumming a harp.

But to live for this eternal cause requires faith. Peter's readers could not see the ROI, the return on their investment. That won't show up until Christ returns and reviews our lives at the Judgment Seat of Christ (JSOC). At that time, He will say, "OK, your time on earth since you received Me as your Savior have been X. Some of the time you lived selfishly for your own kingdom instead of mine. We will call that time Y. The time left that will count forever will be X – Y = Z. This much of your life will glorify my Father forever and ever. This much (Z) of your life (time on earth since knowing Me) will be saved."

Tim Dunn sits on the board of trustees of Grace School of Theology. Although he had been a believer for decades, it wasn't until his forties that he reoriented his life to living 100% for His glory. A gifted man both in terms of intellect and opportunity, Tim had done well in the oil industry. As a high school kid growing up near Midland, Texas, he had always wanted to be the president of an oil company. And he made it. He would never want for money. But what would he do with his life?

According to Tim, it was when Earl Radmacher, former founder and president of Western Seminary in Portland, OR, came to Tim's church in Midland and taught on spiritual gifts and rewards for serving that he began to see that the Christian life was about a lot more than getting one's stamp to go to heaven. As Tim began reading books by Jody Dillow such as *Reign of the Servant Kings*, he understood what it meant to save his life for eternity. He says he gave everything—all his wealth, all his talents, all his life—to glorify the Lord. The truths Peter opens up for us completely revolutionized Tim's life. What about yours?

You see, this "salvation of the self" deals with the third type of loss that produces depression: loss of meaning. We can lose our spirits or save them (v. 3); we can lose our "securities" or save them (v. 4); and we can lose our significance in life or save it. But what exactly are the steps that will help us deal with depression?

1. Recognize that normal depression is good (Matthew 5:5).

"Blessed are they who are they that mourn: for they shall be comforted" (Matthew 5:5). Dr. Thomas Hora says that "mourning is an opportunity to let go of attachments."[15] In the Beatitudes Jesus gave a special place of comfort to those who grieve. Usually we link mourning to only one loss—the death of a loved one. However, reactive depression is best understood and most effectively dealt with when it is perceived as a grieving process that follows loss or deprivation. Mourning is, therefore, a process that must be seen to apply to all losses, and God's comfort can be claimed for all times of grieving.

The loss that causes reactive depression must be seen in its broadest context. It can take many forms. For instance, it can be the separation of one person from another, or from a pet. It can be the theft of belongings, the receiving of a tax demand for past errors, or the criticism of a friend. It can be the loss of self-control when we

---

[15] Thomas Hora, *Existential Metapsychiatry* (New York: Seabury Press, 1977), 206.

get angry. These are all losses that can create reactive depressions.[16] Life is full of losses. Friends come and go; children grow up and leave home; every stage of life demands that we let go of that which is past. So, depression, in that sense, is normal and good. It's when these normal reactive depressions turn into clinical depression that we have a different problem.

Part of avoiding clinical depression over life's sudden or cumulative losses is learning that depression at this level is not only okay, it is good. It may seem paradoxical, but in reactive depression the more effectively we experience our loss, the more quickly we will recover. Fighting off depression or trying to minimize the pain of it only serves to prolong it. So, we must give ourselves permission to feel the pain. Find a trusted friend who can be a safe haven for you to feel this pain. You need someone that would just listen to your pain without trying to cut you off. You see, most people don't realize that your feelings of depression must intensify before you can begin climbing out of the black hole. Healing takes place when we allow grieving to run its course.

Small losses need small depressions, and large losses need more. For spilt coffee, maybe five minutes; a flat tire, perhaps one hour; a traffic ticket, maybe twenty-four hours; a disagreement with your boss, perhaps forty-eight hours; a fight with your spouse, you decide. Every loss has its "appropriate" depression period, and you should allow yourself an appropriate time of despondency. When you choose that appropriate time, you will "give in" to the depression, having given yourself permission to do so, experience your "low" faster, and snap out of the depression sooner. Doing this also removes inappropriate guilt many Christians tag onto depression because they think a victorious Christian is always supposed to be "up." Also, it avoids the compounding of losses that can only result in an extended down somewhere down the road.

---

[16] Hart, 73-86.

2. Avoid a Negative Mindset.

The grieving process I have described thus far is essentially a normal process in the sense that we all have the capacity to mourn and adjust to our losses, but there are ways in which this process can be sabotaged. When this happens, normal depression becomes clinical depression. Negative thinking is just such a saboteur. Some cognitive psychologists insist that thinking *always* precedes emotions and our feelings are just the product of our thoughts. In the world, negative thinking can be the cause of depression as well as one of its consequences, thus causing continued depression.

Aaron Beck is one of the major proponents of this cognitive theory. He contends that a "negative cognitive set" is primary and that the depressive emotion is secondary. In other words, the fact that we feel sad is not as important as the way in which our thoughts keep us feeling sad. Our errors in thinking about ourselves, the world, and the future can cause and maintain some depressions. Beck says these thinking errors, called cognitive sets, are invariably negative, causing the depressed person to interpret events in the world in a bleak manner.[17] The negative thinking style leads to self-depreciation and self- blame, which are taken as truth by the depressed individual. Errors of logic then follow.

Do you suppose that this is why Peter begins his introduction with praise? He immediately puts their minds on something positive. And notice he puts their minds on something besides themselves. He changes their focus. And perhaps that's exactly why Paul in Philippians 3:12ff and 4:8-9 wants us not to wallow in the past, but to focus and dwell on things that are positive. Sometimes a list of positive virtues can help us crystallize our thinking. When Philippians 4:9 tells us to dwell on these positive thoughts, the word "dwell" is *logizomai*, an accounting term that means to reckon a column of figures; to add

---

[17] Aaron Beck, *Cognitive Therapy and the Emotional Disorders* (Boston: International Universities Press, 1979), 263-306.

them up. So, we are to do this with positive thoughts. List them in a column. Add them up. Dwell on them.

3. Assess the losses (Philippians 3:13-14; Matthew 19:29).

a. **Identify the losses.** This can be a complex, complicated process. For example, if someone loses his job due to layoffs, downsizing, etc., there are really several losses involved besides just the loss of a job. There is, for example, the loss of income, the loss of status, the loss of friends at the job, the loss of face when telling friends and family that one has been "fired," the loss of familiar surroundings, the loss of routine, and on it goes. To assess the losses, one must identify the losses.

b. **Categorize the losses.** Some losses are real, some imagined, some concrete, some abstract, some physical, some spiritual. The most important thing for the Christian is to divide between that which is passing and that which is permanent. Paul said he actually took the things of this world that are passing and counted them as "loss" for the excellency of the full knowledge of Jesus Christ. In Matthew 19 the disciples realize they have voluntarily suffered the loss of their jobs to follow Christ. They asked what they could expect to get in return for such loss. Christ comforts them by telling them that they will have a promotion, although it won't come until the next world. And he tells all Christians who suffer loss of material things and even relationships that they will be more than compensated in the next life.

4. Get a new perspective (Romans 12:2).

That's really what Christ and Paul are doing in the former passages (Matthew 19:29 and Philippians 3:1-14). They are shifting their way of looking at what they have lost. And that's exactly what Peter is doing in this passage. He acknowledges that the believers of the Diaspora have had many losses. That is why they are depressed. But he is helping them gain a new perspective. Once again, remember Jim Elliot's words: "He is no fool who gives up what he cannot keep to gain what he cannot lose." These believers may lose their physical lives, but they cannot lose their eternal lives. These believers may have lost physical possessions, but they cannot lose their eternal possessions. These believers may have lost the meaning and significance they enjoyed in their former communities, but they cannot lose the meaning and significance of their lives on earth if they have used them to be faithful to Christ.

Romans 12:2 ("...be not conformed to this world but be transformed by the renewing of your mind") speaks of a transformation which comes about from the renewing of our minds. Coming out of depression involves a new perspective, a new way of thinking about things, and a new evaluation of the situation. Larry Crabb, the Christian psychologist, bases much of his counseling on Romans 12:2. He points out that the passage does not promise transformation from a renewing of our circumstances. Getting a new job, getting a new boss, getting a new wife or husband, or getting better health, won't necessarily make us happy. The transformation of Romans 12:2 comes not from the renewing of our circumstances, but from a renewing of our mind, or how we look at our circumstances. That's another way of calling for a change in our perspective. It's not our circumstances that determine our state of mind. It's how we look at our circumstances that determines our state of mind. Peter is trying to change how his readers look at their circumstances. He is trying to give them a new perspective. He's trying to switch their thinking from this world to the next, from physical loss to spiritual gain.

Crabb likes to tell the story of the college boy who needed a car to get around so he opened the want-ads and began looking for cheap cars, since that's all he could afford. He saw a Mercedes-Benz for sale for just $200. He looked at the year and saw that the car was only one year old. He thought he must be reading a misprint. But he decided to call the number and inquire. He said, "Is this car really for $200 dollars?" The woman said it was. "Is there anything wrong with the car? Has it been in a wreck? Is there water damage?" The woman replied that the car was in perfect, mint condition. Still incredulous, the college kid asked if he could come over to take it for test drive. "Of course," said the woman. So, the kid had a friend drop him off and wait for him while he drove the Mercedes around the block. It was just as the woman said. The car was in perfect condition. So, when he returned, he asked the woman if she had a clear title. She did. So, he pulled out two $100 bills and gingerly offered them to the woman in exchange for the title to the car. She took the $200 and signed the car over to him. The guy wanted to run before she changed her mind. He wondered if she was crazy. He turned to go and then looked back and said, "I'm sorry, the curiosity is killing me. Why are you selling this car for $200?" The woman said, "Well, I just got word from my husband that he has run off to Hawaii with his secretary. He needed some cash, so he asked me to sell his Mercedes and send him the proceeds. And that's what I'm doing."

You see, it's all a matter of perspective. From the college student's perspective, the sale made no sense at all, but from the perspective of the woman selling the car, it made all the sense in the world.

CONCLUSION

Martin Seligman has developed the concept of what he calls "learned helplessness."[18] This is the prolonged depression that has a battered woman divorcing and then going out to marry another abusive husband just like the one she left. It's the emotional state when one thinks "it is the end."

When you cannot control the outcome of a life event and nothing you do seems to make any difference, this feeling of helplessness

---

[18] Martin E. P. Seligman, *Learned Helplessness* (San Francisco: W. H. Freeman, 1975), 21.

causes the body to give up and puts it into a depression. One becomes passive, unresponsive, and will often repeat the same mistake over and over again in an endeavor to cope with the helplessness. Feelings of worthlessness and abandonment also occur.

For self-esteem to survive and for a sense of competence, one must feel in control of one's life. Without this control, helplessness and hopelessness set in. To some extent this accounts for the fact that loss generally leads to depression. One does not have any control over the loss. Something was taken away, and one cannot bring it back. These people believe the only escape from their life trauma is to get depressed. Some sense of control must be returned to the psyche of the depressed person for them to heal.

Paradoxically, the best remedy for the depressed person that is a Christian at this point is to actually surrender control to the One who controls the universe. If one cannot manage his own little world, then relinquish control to the One who controls a much bigger world, the universe.

This concept is the very nugget buried in the center of this passage. God is the One who's keeping us by His power. He is able. And if He is, then we can be certain that these present losses can be translated into eternal gain. The One who is keeping us will certainly keep our spirits, our "securities," and our selves. This is a new perspective, and a new perspective is the main way to deal with depression.

3

"LIFE SAVING 101"

1 Peter 1:6-9

INTRODUCTION

In 1905 an engineer in Europe whose hobby was physics published five papers of far-reaching significance. One of those papers dealt with the study of light and its constancy, so he called his results the "principle of invariance."[19] Later on, people called it relativity, so that was his paper on special relativity. He kept working on his theories, refined them, and pulling on every ounce of his genius, went on to create what is called his general theory of relativity in 1916. It dealt with the fact that the universe is expanding but also decelerating in the speed of its expansion.

The implications of these theories were immense. They were so immense they caused Albert Einstein, a former atheist, to believe in God. But he realized if the universe is expanding but also decelerating

---

[19] Most of this information about the universe comes from Hugh Ross's book *The Creator and the Cosmos* (Colorado Springs, CO: NavPress, 1993), chapters 3 and 6.

in the speed of its expansion, only one natural phenomenon could cause both features (the expansion and the deceleration): an explosion. If a hand grenade explodes, its particles expand outward, but the friction of the air as well as the force of gravity cause the particles to decelerate in their expansion. That's the nature of an explosion. So, Einstein was the first scientist to propose the big bang. Later on, they realized it had to be a hot, big bang.

But Einstein initially resisted the implication of his theories, that is, if there was an explosion that began expansion of our universe, there had to be someone there to pull the plug. The simple law of cause and effect says there has to be a Prime Mover. Einstein resisted this conclusion, so much so that he created a theory to counter-act expansion of the universe known as the steady-state universe. Later suggestions by scientists who followed Einstein were the static-state universe and oscillating universe. All of these suggestions were in an effort to provide enough time for evolution, which requires near infinite time. The thirteen to twenty billion years scientists claim for the current age of universe is only a drop in the bucket of time required for evolution to be a viable option to explain life as we know it.

All of the biological arguments for or against evolution are really moot at this point. The Hubble telescope and COBE (Cosmic Background Radiation Explorer) have proved to the satisfaction of most astrophysicists in 1992 the hot big bang to be a fact as sure as the law of gravity. Einstein was persuaded by Hubble himself that his original theory of relativity was true and that the static state universe was false. So that's when Einstein converted to become a theist, one who believes in God (1929). Being Jewish, rabbis living near him came to congratulate him on his new-found faith, but he interrupted them and said, "Wait a minute. Wait a minute. I'm not saying I believe in your God. And I certainly don't believe in the Christian God. I believe in a Supreme Intelligence that created everything, but in no way believe in the Judeo-Christian God, because that is a personal God." They responded, "Well, if He is intelligent and all-powerful and created people, that certainly means a personal God and a personal being is superior to an impersonal being. And that would mean that your Supreme Being is not supreme and therefore not God." Einstein retorted, "No, not so. For a personal God would not allow the kind of suffering we see in this world. It makes no sense whatsoever."

Einstein wasn't the first or last to be derailed from faith in a personal God by human suffering. I came to know Christ at a prep school in Chattanooga, Tennessee (The McCallie School). The founders of the school required everyone in the school to take a course in the Bible to graduate. It was through reading the Bible and conviction of my own sinfulness that I saw my need for a Savior and trusted Christ. One day, years after leaving the school, I was reading an article about one of its graduates that had gone on to become famous. I knew he used to be the head of the Christian Student Union at this little school and had intended on becoming a missionary. In his autobiography (*Call Me Ted*)[20] he claimed to have become a born-again Christian three times while at McCallie. However, watching his sister die a painful death while he was in college as well as the suicide of his father had shattered his faith, if he ever had it. And in an interview for a magazine article, Ted Turner said, "I was taught that God was a God of power and love. But a God of power and love would not allow the suffering I've seen in this world. It makes no sense."

So more than one great thinker has stumbled over the problem of human suffering in this world. It just doesn't seem to make sense. But for the unbeliever this suffering doesn't disillusion him. He can't be disillusioned because he didn't have any faith to begin with. But many Jews and Christians have been knocked off the rails of Judaism or Christianity by the suffering either they have personally encountered, or they have witnessed in this world. So, let's take a closer look at this paradox, the paradox of a loving, omnipotent God and human suffering. As we do, we shall see that human suffering is

---

[20] Ted Turner, *Call Me Ted* (New York: Grand Central Publishing, 2008).

actually one of God's paths to salvation, but not the kind of salvation we are usually have in mind.

The first book of the New Testament introduces us to different ways of understanding the biblical concept of salvation. Matthew does use the word "save" for forgiveness of sins in Matthew 1:21, but it goes on to use the word "save" in a number of other ways. Quite often it is about rescuing from physical death or healing from a physical disease. It is used of physical healing twice in Matthew 9:22 where a woman with an issue of blood for twelve years is healed (saved). But in Matthew 16:24-27 he talks about saving your life; being a life saver. The salvation comes through self-sacrifice. We don't get the picture here of a free gift. We don't get the picture here of grace, an undeserved favor. But we do get the picture of discipleship.

Jesus picked up His cross that I might receive the free gift of eternal life, and I pick up my cross that I might enjoy what we call the abundant life. Jesus picked up His cross that I might have heaven tomorrow, but I pick up my cross in order to enjoy a little of heaven on earth today, to whatever degree that is possible. For the ultimate end of this type of salvation is rewards given when Christ returns, as Matthew 16:27 makes clear: "For the Son of Man will come in the glory of his Father and his angels and will reward each according to his works." The first word in the verse ("for") ties v. 27 with what precedes. It is explaining what it means to save one's life. The salvation viewed in Matthew 16:24-27 is the salvation of our time on earth for His glory and His kingdom. The extent of that salvation will be revealed to believers at the Judgment Seat of Christ (1 Corinthians 3, 2 Corinthians 5, Romans 14).

The issue here is the salvation of our *psychē*, a noun used four ways in the New Testament. In this context it refers to our time on earth in our physical bodies or what we call our "life." This is your life. What are you going to do with your life? Jesus says this life (our time on earth in our physical bodies) can be saved or lost. It is lost through selfishness and saved through selflessness for the Savior.

Now Peter was so impressed with this teaching of our Lord in Matthew 16 that it haunted him the rest of his life. In a sense Peter's greatest triumph (his confession of Christ) and his greatest rebuke ("Get behind me, Satan") came on the same day in the same setting. We usually remember what we learn through embarrassing failures longer than other lessons. So, Peter never forgot the lesson of Matthew 16:24-27. He not only never forgot it, he wrote a letter about it–1 Peter. 1 Peter is an expansion on the lesson he learned at Caesarea Philippi (Matthew 16:24-27). And right after Matthew 16 comes, guess what, Matthew 17 (Mount of Transfiguration). Peter's second letter is about what he learned on the Mount of Transfiguration. But back to 1 Peter.

Let's go straight to 1 Peter 1:9. Here he says that the goal of our faith is the "salvation of our souls." But that word for "souls" is *psychē*, the same word we had in Matthew 16:25-26 (4x) where it meant "life" (your time on earth). It is the same subject matter as Matthew 16:24-27. In 1 Peter we have a message to people that are already "born-again" (1:3, 23), but after being born again (heaven is locked up), the issue for them is how much of their time on earth will be saved for eternity, will count for eternity. That is the goal of their faith after they have been born again. And Peter tells them in the body of this letter three general ways they can save their lives for eternity: 1) Through Personal Sanctification–their Character (1:13-2:10); 2) Through Personal Submission–their Conduct (2:11-3:12); and 3) Through Personal Suffering–their Courage (3:13-4:19). So, through their character, and/or their conduct, and/or their courage in this life after becoming believers they can make their lives count for eternity (save their lives).

If the "end of your faith" in 1 Peter 1:9 were a reference to getting into heaven when we die, then we only get into heaven through enduring the grief of various trials in our lives (1:6-8). That's what we call suffering. And most evangelicals would have to admit that if we only get in heaven because we have believed in Jesus and haven't endured personal suffering through our trials without faltering, then that is salvation by faith plus works. But if the issue here is not getting into heaven when they died (since we believe that is it is a guarantee to all who are born-again—1:3, 23), then the "end of their faith" must be something other than entrance to heaven.

Of course, this is where Augustine got off track. He saw the people born again in 1:3, but unless they endured faithfully through the trials and grief from these trials after being born again, they could not receive the end of their faith, the salvation of their souls, which for Augustine met entrance to heaven. Therefore, he concluded that born-again people could be lost in the end, that is, not elect. This is why he taught that justification is a life-long process of infusing the character Christ into the life of the regenerated believer, but we would not find out if the regenerated believer had been sufficiently justified (made like Christ) until end of his life. The goal of his faith was to get into heaven, the salvation of his soul, according to Augustine and those who followed him.

But what if "salvation of the soul" is being used just as it was in Matthew 16? Then "the end of your faith" for the self-denying follower of Jesus was explained in Matthew 16:27. It was to receive the rewards accorded by Jesus to the faithful believer when he returns. It is our proposal this is exactly what Peter's teaching, a lesson learned from our Lord himself. And this is what we call "life-saving" or "saving the saved."

Let's go back to the introduction to 1 Peter, his introduction to "life-saving." It says these were Jewish believers of the diaspora. These are the Jews who were living in the land, trusting Christ as Savior, and then through the persecution of believers that began with Stephen were scattered abroad around the Mediterranean world. They were cut off from their former business connections, foreigners in a new territory, probably persecuted by the Gentiles for being Jewish and persecuted by the Jews for becoming Christians. They were hurting financially, socially, and politically. They were suffering, and it didn't make sense. If Jesus was the Messiah, why didn't He do something about their suffering? If He is God, if He is all-powerful, all-knowing, and all loving, how could He allow this kind of suffering to come to His own chosen children? This is their problem. It's a problem for the ages. How can a loving, omnipotent God and undeserved suffering coexist? Peter has an answer. It's not the only answer. But it is more definitive and encouraging than most of the literature written on the subject that was supposed to encourage us. In this passage (1 Peter 1:6-9) we have: 1) The Requirement of Suffering, v.6; 2) The Reason for Suffering, vv. 7-8; and 3) The Rewards for Suffering, v. 9.

I. REQUIREMENT OF SUFFERING   6

In this you greatly rejoice, though now for a little while, if need be, you have been grieved by various trials . . .

Peter says his readers' suffering may be for just **"a little while."** He is comparing this life to eternity. He isn't comparing two years to seventy years. He is comparing seventy years to eternity—a little while. Our existence has three stages or phases. In the first stage we are in complete darkness—about nine months. We can't see anything, but God is making eyes; we can't hear anything, but God is making ears; we can't smell anything, but God is developing the olfactory nerves. Why does God spend so much time developing physical senses we cannot use? Well, we all know the answer. These senses are being developed for use in the next stage of our existence. The second stage of our existence lasts seventy or eighty years (Psalm 90:10), if we are blessed.

If we become Christians during the second stage of existence, then this world serves as something of a womb. And during this stage God is building spiritual eyes to see Him, spiritual ears to hear His voice, spiritual taste buds to taste that His word is good, spiritual sensitivity to reach out to touch someone. But why? Right now, we get just little glimpses of the spiritual world. We know the answer. He is developing the spiritual senses we will use full-time in the third stage of our existence. Our time in the womb of this world is absolutely essential for the full development of the spiritual senses if we want to maximize the third stage of our existence where there will be no need for our physical senses.

This, then, brings us to an option in the second stage of existence we don't have in the first. For all practical purposes, a baby does not self-abort. But in the second stage of our existence, we can abort God's work. We can resist the Spirit. We can quench the Spirit. We can grieve the Spirit. We can harden our hearts.

Peter talks to us not about deserved suffering, but undeserved suffering. And it's during this undeserved suffering I get most confused. If I'm one of God's children and He loves his children, what did I do to deserve this? I'm tempted to drop out of the program. And I'm tempted to be disillusioned with God himself. It doesn't make sense that the children He loves should go through this kind of intense suffering.

Peter goes on to say, **". . . if need be."** There're four different ways in the Greek language to propose the condition "if." One of these four means "if and it's really true" (at least for the sake of argument). Some even translate this use as "since." And you guessed it; that is the precise meaning of "if" in this verse. "If need be, and it really does need to be"—a statement of reality. What is he saying here? Just this: trials are not optional in the Christian life; they are inevitable. Suffering for the Christian is not optional; it's part of program.

James also writes to the Jewish Christians of the Diaspora. And he opens his book talking about the inevitability of trials and suffering in the Christian life. He doesn't say, "Count it all joy _if_ you fall into various trials." He says, "Counted all joy <u>when</u> you fall into various trials" (James 1:2). Entering the Christian life is a lot like going to a military academy, like West Point or Annapolis. Everyone gets a free ride; everyone has a full scholarship. Someone else paid the price for an entrant to go to the university. But to graduate from the university this person will take some required courses and some elective courses. We usually like the elective courses; the required courses—not so much. When I went to Rice University in 1963, everyone got a free ride. William Marsh Rice paid the price for all the students to go free of charge. But once

I was in and declared my major as premed, I thought I would just be taking science and math courses that I would enjoy. After all, Rice University used to be Rice Institute of Technology, like MIT or Caltech. But by entering the world of universities the powers that be wanted more well-rounded students. So, I had to take English and history and philosophy and psychology and German–all sorts of things that I didn't particularly like or enjoy.

God's University has a lot of courses we will really enjoy. But it also has some required courses if God is going to develop the full potential of His students. Some of those courses involve intense suffering. It's very important if the One who paid the price for our education is going to be proud of us on graduation day that we not drop out of these required courses. Yes, Peter says suffering is a requirement in this stage of our existence. But he doesn't leave us without some reasons for a suffering.

II. REASONS FOR SUFFERING 7-8

> . . . that the genuineness of your faith, being much more precious than gold that perishes, though it is tested by fire, may be found to praise, honor, and glory at the revelation of Jesus Christ, whom having not seen you love. Though now you do not see Him, yet believing, you rejoice with joy inexpressible and full of glory . . .

Peter speaks of the "**genuineness**" of our faith. The word used here (*dokimos*) was also used of putting a work of pottery into the kiln, bringing it out, and inspecting for cracks. If it had cracks, then they would stamp *adokimos* on that piece of pottery. That meant it was defective. The word was also used of testing a coin by biting it to see if it was genuine. But here the word is not being used to see whether the faith of the believer is real gold or fool's gold, genuine faith or fake face, enough faith or insufficient faith. The assumption is that it is real gold. But real gold isn't necessarily pure gold. Real gold can have impurities in it. So, you heat up the gold in order to get the impurities out. This is the story of Job. The quality of our faith can increase as its impurities are removed, and indeed, the strength of our faith can increase as we pass through the trials of suffering.

It's not that you didn't genuinely believe when you trusted in Christ. But God uses these times of difficulty to make our faith even better. When Christ comes back, what is He looking for? Will He find faith? Without faith it is impossible to please Him (Hebrews 11:6). We make it our goal to please God (2 Corinthians 5:9, a verse that leads up to the Judgment Seat of Christ in v. 10). We do that by faith. The finer the faith, the greater the glory.

But suffering often doesn't make sense. I read about one man who was put into solitary confinement in prison. He had been able to hide something in his mouth the guards did not notice. It was simply a marble. He had no books to read, no one to talk to. All he had was his marble. So, every day he would bounce his marble around the room. He liked to hear it carom off the walls. In the darkness he would search around until he found his marble. Then he was happy and would throw it out into the darkness again.

But one day he threw his marble up, but he heard no sound. His marble seemed to have evaporated into thin air. He searched every corner, every crevice, every nook and cranny of his cell, but he couldn't find his marble. It didn't make sense to him. And then he became so distraught he pulled his hair out, lost the rest of his marbles, and died.

When they found him dead in his cell, with the lights on, while cleaning up his cell, a guard looked up and saw the lost marble caught in a cobweb. He asked, "I wonder what this marble is doing here?" You see, it all made perfect sense—with the light on. But the prisoner was in darkness. Sometimes our trials plunge us unprepared into the darkness. It could be you're holding on something like a marble which helps you keep your sanity. But, then, what happens if you lose your marble? Could your faith be shaken? Without faith we may drop out of the Christian life. Ever wonder why there are so few older people in most of our churches?

But perhaps this still isn't making any sense to you. You see the Requirement for Suffering (v. 6) and the given Reasons for Suffering (vv. 7-8), but you need some motivation. Peter gives it. In 1:9 we read about the Reward for Suffering.

III. REWARD FOR SUFFERING   9

. . . receiving the end of your faith—the salvation of your souls.

One key to unlocking this verse is the word translated **"receiving."** The Greek word behind it has also spawned an English word that will help us. From *komizō* we get the word "commission." The word usually means to receive what has been earned.[21] Of course, we are not excluding grace from the picture. One of the great misunderstandings in Protestantism is to think that grace and works are mutually exclusive. Grace and works done through the energy of the flesh are mutually exclusive. But we were created for good works (Ephesians 2:10). It is grace and work done through the power of the Spirit that are not mutually exclusive. It is God who works in us to give us both the desire and the power to do His good pleasure (Philippians 2:13). So, it is with grace and rewards.

At the Judgment Seat of Christ, we will receive back for the works we have done. Our works are judged. But those done with the wrong motive through the wrong power source are burned up (1 Corinthians 13:3). Those done with the right motive and through the power of the Holy Spirit come through the judgment as gold, silver, and precious stones. But, however we shake it out, this word "receiving" is a reference to our commission given for the work we have done.

The next word we need to take a look at is the word **"end."** It comes from the Greek word we use for telephone, teleprompter, and

---

[21] See Moulton and Milligan, *The Vocabulary of the Greek New Testament* (Grand Rapids, Michigan, 1930), 354.

telegram. It is the word *telos*, and it usually means "the goal, the result, the end." It is very important that we understand what the goal of our faith is. Ever since the days of Augustine (died AD 430) the church has taught that the goal of our faith is to get into heaven when we die. Of course, we all want that. But may I submit to you that this is not the ultimate goal. It is a biblical starting block. But Peter isn't talking about the starting blocks here. He is talking about the goal line. How silly to put the emphasis on the starting blocks.

It would be like watching the Olympics on TV. You want to watch the 400m race. You're sitting in Texas, and the race is being run in Athens or Beijing. Everyone is loose, every runner is ready. They lineup; they get in their starting blocks. The gun goes off, and the race has begun. But the cameraman keeps a camera on the starting blocks. He never does aim his camera at the race. You want to see who wins the race, who breaks the tape, who reaches the goal line first. But alas, the crazy cameraman has the emphasis on the wrong place. His entire focus is on the starting blocks. He forgot about the race.

Western Christianity has done the same thing for the most part. We have turned the starting blocks into the goal line. That's why there's so little discipleship going on in most churches. "Getting saved" for most people means getting to go to heaven when they die. Don't misunderstand me. There's nothing wrong with the starting blocks. If you don't get into the starting blocks, you don't get into the race. But the biblical emphasis, even in the great commission (Matthew 28:19-20), is on the race, not the starting blocks. And where is the focus of the people running the race? On the starting blocks? I don't think so. It's on the goal line.

The goal of the Christian life, the goal of our faith, is the salvation of our *psychē*. Unfortunately, the way that word is translated has fed into the idea that getting to heaven is the goal of Christianity. However, when we realize Peter is using the word the same way Jesus used it in Matthew 16:24-27, it all starts to make sense. This word *psychē* means "our time on earth"—our life. We find out how much of our life has been saved to bring glory to our Savior for all eternity at the Judgment Seat of Christ.[22] The first shall be last, and the last shall be first.[23]

CONCLUSION

When I was growing up my mother used to take us kids to musicals like *South Pacific, West Side Story, Oklahoma, Brigadoon,* and others. One of them was about a storyteller in Holland named Hans Christian Andersen. One of his stories was called "The Ugly Duckling." Perhaps you remember it. One of the little ducks is bigger than his brothers and sisters, rather awkward, and certainly ugly. The other ducks were always poking fun. In the movie version Danny Kaye played Hans, and he turned the story into a song:

There once was an ugly duckling,
With feathers all shabby and brown,
And all the other birds, in so many words,
Said, "Scat, get out of town. Scat, get out,
Scat, get out, scat, get out of town.

---

[22] This concept of the saving of the life-soul in terms of living a life that is to be rewarded at the Bema seat (Judgement Seat; 2 Corinthians 5:9, Romans 14:10) has a long history. See Robert Govett, *Reward According to Works* (Miami Springs, FL: Schoettle Publishing Co.,1989), 11 and *Kingdom Studies* (Miami Springs, Florida, 1989), 6. Also see Watchmen Nee, *Salvation of the Soul* (1932), G.H. Lang, *First Born Sons: Rights and Risks* (Schoettle Publishing Co., 1997), Eric Sauer, *The King of the Earth* (Great Britain: The Paternoster Press, 1962), 186, Randolph Yaeger, *The Renaissance New Testament: Matthew* (Firebird Press, 1998), Zane Hodges, *The Hungry Inherit* (Chicago, IL: The Moody Press,1972), 66, *The Gospel Under Siege: Faith and Works in Tension* (Dallas, TX: Rendencion Viva, 1981), *Grace in Eclipse* (Dallas, TX: Rendencion Viva, 1985), 33, and *First Peter: The Salvation of the Soul* (Denton, TX: Grace Evangelical Society, 2017).

[23] See Matthew 19:30 and 20:16 for a similar use of the phrase.

SAVING THE SAVED

Well, of course over the wintertime the ugly duckling turns out to be a swan, most beautiful bird on the pond.

When I was a youth pastor, we had an ugly duckling in our group. He had cystic fibrosis, a bad case of acne, weighed barely ninety pounds, walked with a limp, and sometimes had a bit of drool—something of an embarrassment to the other kids. After church on the first Sunday of the month we went to Love Field, a local airport in Dallas, Texas, to share our faith. Craig, our ugly duckling, never missed. We were never obnoxious or pushy. If we saw someone sitting alone waiting for their plane, we would ask them if they were willing to take a religious survey. Most of them were happy to have someone to talk to as they passed the time. At the end of the survey, if they indicated that they would like to have a more personal relationship with God, we would offer to show them how to do that. If they invited us to share, we did so.

We had Sunday evening church in those days, and the pastor always let the kids come up front to share what God had done that afternoon at Love Field. Anyone could come up. Most were pretty shy about sharing in front of a large crowd, but not Craig. He would limp down the center aisle and, in his gravelly voice, tell the crowd what the Holy Spirit had done. It was very humbling to listen to him.

After four years as his youth pastor, I graduated and moved out of Dallas to help start a new church. But Craig and I kept in touch. He would call now and then to tell me what was going on in his life. One night he called and said, "Dave, I can't get a date. I know no one is going to marry me, but I just want someone to talk to." I didn't know what to tell him and can't remember what I said. I'm sure it was inadequate. A few months later, when I hadn't heard from Craig for a while, I called his mother. She said Craig had died.

Yes, Craig died an ugly duckling. But there is no doubt in my mind that when I see him in heaven he will be a swan, one of the most beautiful birds on the heavenly pond.

4

"ALL NIGHT, ALL DAY"
1 Peter 1:10-12

INTRODUCTION

"All night, all day, angels watchin' over me, my Lord," is a line from an old Negro spiritual. The reference is to guardian angels (Matthew 18:10) who are appointed for our protection. Do you believe in guardian angels? According to a Gallup poll, Americans have a widespread belief in angels. About half the adults and three fourths of our teenagers believe in these heavenly beings. "People are recognizing their own sense of powerlessness," said Eileen Freeman, editor of the *AngelWatch* newsletter.

In the opening chapter of *Celebration of Angels*, Walt Shepard, a minister in Louisiana, shares what led him into full-time Christian service. It was 1971 and Shepard was so miserable he decided to commit suicide by driving his sports car into an automobile parked along Interstate 10. The collision threw Shepard through the windshield onto the engine. As the two cars exploded, the hood, hinged at the front, popped open, trapping the unconscious man in the flames.

At this point in the story, Shepard relies on eyewitnesses. The manager of the Holiday Inn across the road called for help. By the time the highway patrol arrived, the fire's searing heat prevented them from freeing the trapped man. Then the troopers and the hotel manager noticed two strangers, though it was 3:40 AM and the highway was otherwise deserted. Although the intense heat kept everyone else at least 50 feet back, the two figures calmly walked to Shepard's car, pulled him out, and helped the attendant put him into the ambulance. The strangers simply disappeared. Though a number of people saw what they did, no one could describe them. It was Shepard's father, a Presbyterian minister, who first suggested to his son that angels had saved his life. During the months of painful recovery that followed his accident, Shepard reflected often on his Christian upbringing. One day while still enveloped in a full body cast, he rolled over in bed and surrendered his life to Christ.

Apparently, guardian angels are interested in "saving lives" physically. But there are some other angels, perhaps the same angels for all I know, that are interested in saving lives spiritually. These are the angels mentioned in 1 Peter 1:12. What can we call these angels? Watchers, Inspectors, Curious? It seems that they're very much interested in this mysterious plan God has for "saving the saved."

We are finishing up the introduction to this letter from Peter on "saving the saved." What we mean by this is that Jesus introduced a concept of salvation in Matthew 16:24-27 different from anything Peter had ever considered. This plan of salvation was not one to get him into the kingdom or into heaven. That was a free gift coming through Christ and his work on the cross (Ephesians 2:8-9). No, this plan of salvation was for the people who already had received the free gift of eternal life. This was a plan to save their temporal lives not physically, but spiritually. It was a plan to make their time on earth count for eternity. It was how to save the temporal significance of their lives forever.

But what the angels found so mysterious was God's process for doing the spiritual life-saving. It involved suffering before glory. And there are aspects of this plan that pique the curiosity of the angels. One is the concept of saving time. You see, though the angels are not eternal, once created they will be around forever. Time is almost as meaningless to their existence as it is to God's. So, the idea of saving a few measly years on planet Earth and all the trouble God has gone to enable men to do this is quite mystifying to them.

The second thing that had the angels watching with great curiosity was the fact that the angels don't suffer. The good angels have never experienced the effects of sin first-hand in their lives. They, of course, observe humans sinning, and they are aware of the evil angels, but they themselves only know suffering and evil intuitively, not experientially. So, a plan of salvation that includes the two elements combined that are foreign to their experience, time and suffering, was more than an idle curiosity for them. In fact, I might suggest that the entire human scenario is more amazing to them than the original creation of entire universe. But let's jump into 1 Peter and learn more.

1 PETER

"Saving the Saved"

I. RESEARCH ON THE PLAN OF OUR SALVATION 10

Of this salvation the prophets have inquired and searched carefully, who prophesied of the grace that would come to you,

There are many subthemes (*leit motifs*) in these verses: the work of the Trinity, Inspiration, Dispensationalism, Progressive Revelation, Progressive Illumination, and so forth. But our focus is on the main theme of these verses, and that is the great paradox of a plan of salvation which prescribes suffering before glory for God's children.

Remember, the subject here is "saving the saved." In other words, these people were already "born again" (1:3, 23 and even 1:2). The question here is how can born again people *save their lives* for eternity rather than lose them. How can they discover their unique purpose in life and live it out? We need to remember the message of Matthew 16:24-27. One who would save his life for his own selfish desires will lose it (its significance for eternity), and One who will (in the eyes of the world) lose his life, will find it (save its temporal significance for all eternity). In other words, in this plan of salvation there's a plan to make one's life on earth count for eternity. That's why the we call this a book about "saving the saved."

Verse 10 tells us these prophets do not understand what they were prophesying about (see Daniel 12). **"Searched diligently"** implies a careful study of their own writings (see John 5:39 and 7:52). The paradox that had them dumbfounded was the Messiah that suffered before His glorification. They had no concept of this Suffering Messiah. They clearly did not understand Isaiah 53.

II. REVEALER OF THE PLAN OF OUR SALVATION 11

searching what, or what manner of time, the Spirit of Christ who was in them was indicating when He testified beforehand the sufferings of Christ and the glories that would follow.

Of course, these prophets were curious not only about a plan of salvation in which suffering preceded glory, but they also wanted to know when the Messiah would come and what sort of time or era it would be. Notice these prophets were very much aware that the Spirit of Christ (the Holy Spirit) was speaking through them (see 2 Peter 1:19-21; 3:15-16).

The same Holy Spirit who prophesied about our sufferings is here to *parakaleō* (to comfort, guide, and counsel) us through our sufferings.

III. RECIPIENTS OF THE PLAN OF OUR SALVATION 12

> To them it was revealed that, not to themselves, but to us they were ministering the things which now have been reported to you through those who have preached the gospel to you by the Holy Spirit sent from heaven—things which angels desire to look into.

Notice that the Old Testament prophets also realized that they would not be alive during the "fulness of times" (Galatians 4), that is, when the Messiah would come and the Good News (Gospel) about Him would spread throughout the world. They knew they would not be the recipients of the Promise, but they still persevered in the face of suffering (Hebrews 11). How much more should we be willing to persevere having known Christ and seen His example of suffering before glory (1 Peter 2:21ff)?

CONCLUSION

We want to move into a survey of the body of this letter. It falls into three sections. In these three sections, we see God's strategy to save the saved. We are talking about "saving" the meaning and significance of our lives forever. These are not the only ways, but these are the three primary ways Peter wants to emphasize: Personal Sanctification (1:13-2:12), Personal Submission (2:13-25), and Personal Suffering

(3:8-4:19). The emphasis in each section, respectively, is on our Character in the face of temptation, our Conduct in a world of rebels, and our Courage in the face of suffering.

1. Our Character (Personal Sanctification)

We live in a land where people are in pursuit of happiness. And there's nothing wrong with this pursuit. After all, it's one of our inalienable rights. But when the pursuit of happiness displaces the pursuit of holiness, it is a vain pursuit. A. W. Tozer puts it this way: "No man should desire to be happy . . . who is not at the same time holy. Go to God and have an understanding. Tell Him that it is your desire to be holy at any cost and then ask Him never to give you more happiness than holiness . . . in the end you will be as happy as you are holy."

You see, holiness involves many character traits, but at the root of them all is personal integrity. As Pat Morley says in his book *Man in the Mirror*,[24] "Frankly, dishonesty is so prevalent that we have accepted it as the norm—and it is." Watch the news or read the headlines:

"Pentagon probe aims at payoffs."
"Mr. _____ denies charge of influence peddling."
"The Ethics Committee of the House issues censure."
"20 percent of GDP goes unreported to Uncle Sam."
"College cheating ring uncovered."

Could it be that a daily dose in the news of our own political and athletic heroes being investigated for scandals of one sort or another has numbed our national consciousness to the point that we have lost touch with our personal conscience. Diogenes, the Greek philosopher, lighted a candle in the daytime and went around looking

---

[24] Patrick M. Morley, *The Man in the Mirror* (Nashville: Thomas Nelson Publishers, 1992), 250-55.

for an honest man. Blasé Pascal said he didn't expect to meet three honest men in a century. The Institute of Behavior Motivation has found that ninety-seven of a hundred people tell lies—and they do it about a thousand times a year.

George Burns, an early television personality, said, "The most important thing in acting is honesty. If you can fake that, you've got it made." I wonder how many of us would win the Christian Academy Awards if they were held in our church. Do you remember why God was pleased with Job? We find out in Job 2:3: "Have you considered my servant Job? There is no one on earth like him: he is blameless and upright, a man who fears God and shuns evil. *And he still maintains his integrity,* though you incited me against him to ruin him without any reason."

And note, it is in the midst of suffering, especially unjust suffering, that the man of integrity is most tempted to compromise, to no longer maintain his integrity. That's why the first great section of 1 Peter is on being holy, on Personal Sanctification, on Character, on integrity. If we can maintain our integrity in the midst of trials, we have one step up on saving our lives for eternity. So, the first section of the Body of 1 Peter addresses our Character; the second section challenges our Conduct. The first "life-saving" quality was primarily internal and observable by God; the second is primarily external and observable by God and men.

2. Our Conduct (Personal Submission)

Now it should be axiomatic that our conduct flows directly out of our character. What we do is directly linked to who we are. Again, as Tozer puts it:

The supreme purpose of the Christian religion is to make men like God in order that they may act like God. In Christ the verbs *to be* and *to do* follow each other in that order. In other words, there should be no divorce between who we are and what we do, or what we believe and what we do. Rightly understood faith is not a substitute for moral conduct but a means toward it. The tree does not serve in lieu of fruit but as an agent by which fruit is secured. Fruit, not the tree, is the end God has in mind in yonder orchard; so Christlike conduct is the end of Christian faith. To oppose faith to works is to make the fruit the enemy to the tree.[25]

Specifically, Peter says it is our conduct that the world is watching. They, like the angels, do more watching than listening. They don't care so much about what we say if they observe that what we say contradicts how we live. That's why conduct is the key to 2:11-12 and 3:1-6 where good conduct lays the foundation for credibility and authenticity. The unbelievers are first won by our lives and then by our lips. They're interested in listening to our philosophy of living only after they have observed living that is consistent with our verbal profession of faith.

3. Our Courage (Personal Suffering)

If we are going to be people of outstanding character and people of outstanding conduct, we must also be the people of outstanding courage. It takes courage to have the right character and the right conduct in this world. We have to swim upstream; we have to be willing to stand alone, even when it might cost us our job or an engagement or some friends.

Whatever else happened at Pentecost, we know this band of men changed from men of cowardice to men of courage. They became courageous to the point of complete abandon. Dante, on his imaginary journey through hell, came to a group of lost souls who sighed and moaned continually as they whirled about aimlessly in the dusky air. Virgil, his guide, explained that these were the "wretched people," the "nearly soulless," who, while they lived on earth did

---

[25] *Tozer on the Holy Spirit: A 365-Day Devotional,* compiled by Marilynne E. Foster (Chicago: Moody Press, 2000), 27.

not have moral energy enough to be either for or against God. They had earned neither praise nor blame. And with them and sharing in their punishment were those angels that take sides neither with God nor Satan. The doom of all the weak and irresolute crew was to be suspended forever between the hell that despised them and a heaven that would not receive their defiled presence. Not even their names were to be mentioned again in heaven or earth or hell. "Look," said the guide, "and pass on."

Is that what Jesus was talking about when he said to the church at Laodicea that He would prefer people to be either hot or cold rather than just lukewarm? I get the impression sometimes with Bible Belt Christianity that we would prefer to fit in rather than stick out. Ray Stedman, a California pastor who went to seminary in Texas, was asked by some of his Texas friends how he could risk raising his kids in California where there were so many radicals. He turned the tables on them by saying he would prefer to raise his children in California where spiritual interest is either black or white. He said in Texas, as he experienced it, there was a lot of gray. He would prefer his children to have to declare themselves one way or another, rather than simply melting into the color of their surroundings. Once again, from the pen of Tozer:

> Yes, if evangelical Christianity is to stay alive, she must have men again, the right kind of men. She must repudiate the weaklings who dare not speak out, and she must seek in prayer and much humility the coming again of men of the stuff prophets and martyrs are made of. God will hear the cries of his people as he heard the cries of Israel in Egypt. And He will send deliverance by sending deliverers . . . And when the deliverers come . . . they will be men of God and men of courage.[26]

---

[26] *The Best of A. W. Tozer*, compiled by Warren W. Wiersbe (Camp Hill, PN: Christian Publications Inc., 1980).

Angel was just such a person, only she was not a man. I met her in Jordan while teaching for Jordan Evangelical Theological Seminary in Amman. She was one of five hundred thousand Iraqi refugees living in Amman after fleeing the oppressive regime of Saddam Hussein. She got her nickname, Angel, because of some of the courageous things she had done to share her faith. She told me a couple of stories I'll never forget. The one I will share occurs in 1996 in Bagdad. Uday Hussein, one of the two sons of Saddam Hussein, was in the hospital after an assassination attempt. The people of Iraq hated Saddam's sons. They had a reputation for having their henchmen pick young girls off the streets of Bagdad, take them to the sons for their sexual gratification, and then tossing them off multistoried buildings to their death (which they thought was more merciful than putting them back on the street where their family might be bound to enact an honor killing). The assassination attempt on Uday was probably orchestrated by some vengeful fathers.

Angel was just sixteen. She lived about forty miles from the hospital where Uday was in recovery. His vehicle had been ambushed and riddled with bullets (think Bonnie and Clyde), but he survived. Angel believed the Lord was leading her to go to the hospital to bear witness to Uday. You have to remember that Uday is a Muslim, and sixteen-year-old girls are a red flag to a sexual predator like Uday. Her mother begged her not to go. She could not refuse the leading God had given her. So, her mother insisted that she go along to protect her daughter.

The two women caught a bus into Bagdad and went to the hospital. It was a military hospital with a guard room several hundred yards in front of the hospital. When they arrived, a guard asked what they were doing there. Angel replied, "I have a message from the Lord Jesus Christ for Uday Hussein." The guard just laughed and told them to get lost. Angel said, "I have a message from the Lord Jesus Christ for Uday Hussein. I will sit here in front of this guard house until I see him or you arrest me." To her mother's surprise, the guard picked up a phone and called Uday's room. He said, "There is a young girl here at the gate who says she has a message from the Lord Jesus Christ for Uday."

Next thing you know Angel and her mother are escorted to the hospital. With fear and trepidation, they enter Uday's room. He beckons her forward. Her mother falls to her knees and begins to pray. Angel opens her mouth and says, "The Lord Jesus Christ, Creator of the universe and all mankind, has spared your life so you can be kind to the Christians living here in Iraq and to tell you to stop raping the daughters of Iraq." Then she gave him a Bible and left. We don't know if Uday ever believed in Jesus, but this much is true. There was no more record of raping, and he went on national TV to call for an end of the persecution of Christians. He even gave $2,000,000 for the restoration of churches destroyed because of persecution.

Angel was a woman of courage.

CONCLUSION

Yes, all night and all day the angels are watching over us. But it is not just for the sake of *protecting* us; it is also for the sake of *inspecting* us, or rather inspecting God's plan for saving the saved, a plan which includes suffering before glory. But to get a better understanding of this plan, let's back up to the beginning in order to grasp God's purpose for the human race. Let's get the Big Picture. It all starts in the beginning of the Bible.

Genesis 1:26-28. Though most Bible scholars would probably offer the Abrahamic Covenant of Genesis 12:1-3 as the most important covenant in the Bible, it may well be that the original "pact" with man made by God with Adam is the foundation for all the others. Here in Genesis 1:26-28 we read:

> 26 Then God said, "Let Us make man in Our image, according to Our likeness; let them have <u>dominion</u> over the fish of the sea, over the birds of the air, and over the cattle, <u>over all the earth</u> and over every creeping thing that creeps on the earth." 27 So God created man in His *own* image; in the image of God He created him; male and female He created them. 28 Then God blessed them, and God said to them, "Be fruitful and

multiply; <u>fill the earth and subdue it; have dominion</u> over the fish of the sea, over the birds of the air, and over every living thing that moves on the earth" (emphasis mine).

We must notice that the emphasized words point toward world dominion, that is, a kingdom over all the earth. This was God's first and foremost intention for man. It is directly connected to His creation of man. But why, we must ask. What is so important about dominion over the earth and subduing it? In order to answer this question, we must slip behind the curtains of creation to that which existed before the earth was created. The drama begins to unfold for us in Job 38:1-7:

Job 38:1-7

1 Then the Lord answered Job out of the whirlwind, and said:
2 "Who *is* this who darkens counsel
      By words without knowledge?
3 Now prepare yourself like a man;
      I will question you, and you shall answer Me.
4 "Where were you when I laid the foundations of the earth?
      Tell *Me,* if you have understanding.
5 Who determined its measurements?
      Surely you know!
      Or who stretched the line upon it?
6 To what were its foundations fastened?
      Or who laid its cornerstone,
7 <u>When the morning stars sang together,</u>
      <u>And all the sons of God shouted for joy?</u>

Clearly the Lord speaks to Job out of the whirlwind concerning the original creation of the earth. But even if the universe was created *ex nihilo* (out of nothing) as most theologians suppose, this passage in Job affirms that something existed before the creation of the earth besides God. It is the angels. The "morning stars" and the "sons of God" were the angels. Surely there is no reference here to men for they did not exist before the creation of the earth. These are the angels, the good and holy angels.

This passage helps us understand the purpose for the creation of the universe. Apparently, it was a display of the glory of God. The "glory" of anything refers to an "open, public display of the nature or character qualities thereof." Since we are speaking of the "glory of God," we mean an open, public display of the character qualities (attributes) of God. The creation of the universe did not display all of His attributes, but most certainly some of them—His omnipotence, His omnipresence, and His omniscience, for starters. And when the angels saw this incredible creation (the Big Bang, perhaps) and subsequent formation of the earth, they sang and shouted for joy. Imagine the wonder we have on July 4th over a phenomenal fireworks display. If you are in a big crowd, you can hear the oohs and aahs when a particularly spectacular rocket explodes. Compare that to what the angels saw, and we get a little hint at their rejoicing.

Genesis 1:2. We are suggesting that this entire event described in Job 38 occurred before we ever get to Genesis 1. One of the main reasons for thinking this is the description of the earth in Genesis 1:2. There we are told that the earth was "formless and void." In the Hebrew language in which the OT was written, it says the earth was *tohu wabohu,* and in our language this Hebrew phrase has the ring of "topsy turvy." However, the phrase has a negative connotation. The only other use of this term in the OT is in connection with judgment. In Jeremiah 4:23 the Lord parallels the judgment to come upon unfaithful Jerusalem with the state of the earth in Genesis 1:2. It is a warning to them. If they do not repent, He will turn them upside down. He will make them formless and void. We are left with a picture of judgment on the earth in Genesis 1:2. Not only was the earth *tohu wabohu,* it was also covered with darkness and saltwater. These too are used repeatedly in the OT as symbols of God's judgment (Amos 5:20—Is not the day of the Lord darkness and not light; is it not very dark with no brightness in it?).

But what would cause the earth to be found in such a state of judgment when we open the Book of Genesis? How could something created to proclaim the glory of God (Job 38:1-7) to the angels not be described as under some form of judgment? Perhaps the history of the angels will again help us get the Big Picture.

Isaiah 14 and Ezekiel 28. We are told in Isaiah 14 and Ezekiel 28 that Lucifer was the most gifted, most beautiful, most intelligent of all the angels. Because he had a corruptible nature different from God's incorruptible nature, he was capable, as were all the angels, of sin. And sin he did. He challenged God's right to rule the universe, both spiritual and physical. In challenging God, he persuaded a third of the host of heaven to stand behind him. Because God cannot dwell with evil and the boastful cannot stand in His sight (Psalm 5:4-5), Lucifer and Company had to go. They were cast down to Planet Earth. Somehow they turned what could have been a garden into a garbage heap. However, only spiritual beings could live on the earth at that time. God decided to put the earth into a state of judgment. And this is how we find the earth as the curtain of clouds is pulled back in Gen 1:1.

Genesis 1:1 and Psalm 8. Actually, Genesis 1:1 might best be understood as an introductory statement just like any topic sentence we would find at the beginning of a paragraph. He basically says, "I want to tell you how God refashioned the atmosphere and earth" so that a being a little bit lower than the angels could live here. Genesis 2:1 is a summary statement looking back on the refashioning of the atmosphere and the earth.[27] The Bible speaks of three heavens: our atmosphere, the interstellar spaces, and God's home, so to speak. When "the heavens and the earth" are mentioned in conjunction, it is a reference to our planet and our atmosphere.

Some might suggest that the word for "create" in Genesis 1:1 means *ex nihilo*. However, we know this is not true because of its use in Psalm 51:10 where David pleads with God to "create" a clean heart within him after his sins surrounding Bathsheba. In both Genesis 1:1

---

[27] See Bruce K. Waltke *Creation and Chaos* (Portland, Oregon: Western Conservative Baptist Seminary Memorial Lecture Foundation, 1974).

and Psalm 51:10 we have the same word for create (*bārā'*). David did not lack a heart. But it was a dirty heart. It needed refashioning, cleaning up. So did the earth. Genesis 1:2 serves as a parenthetical statement to describe the state of the earth when the recycling began. Genesis 1:1-3 might be translated:

> When God began to refashion the heavens and the earth, (and the earth was formless and void and there was darkness over the face of the deep and the Spirit of the Lord hovered over the face of the waters), God said, "Let there be light," and there was light.

So, God refashioned the atmosphere and the earth so a being more limited than the angels (Psalm 8 and Hebrews 2) could live here—more limited in intelligence, power, mobility (physical instead of spiritual), and revelation of God. Why? To answer the two great questions of the universe raised by the rebellion of Lucifer: 1) Is God sovereign; and 2) Is God love?

The Two Big Questions. Does God have the right to rule the universe, and is God worthy of being loved? God could not allow this challenge to go unanswered. Thus, by creating a being more limited than the angels God felt He could settle these two questions. He laid His eternal reputation on the line when He made mankind. It is His intention to prove to the angelic world that He does have the right to rule the universe (He is sovereign), and He is worthy of being loved (He is love).

Lucifer, who became Satan, opened to question these character qualities of God. Therefore, he wants to prove that he can rule the universe as well or better than God. Thus, the angelic conflict of the ages will be settled on the battlefield of planet earth. Will men follow God or Satan? The answer to that question will also determine the answers to the other two concerning God's sovereignty and God's love.

So, God refashioned the atmosphere and the earth for physical beings. He made man and challenged him to take dominion over the earth. There was much to do and only one "do not." Do not eat of the tree of the knowledge of good and evil. Unfortunately, Adam and Eve did eat of this tree. Their failure and its consequences affected all their offspring, that is, the entire human race. Men, animals, fish, birds, even the earth itself would feel the effects of the Fall of Adam and Eve. And the rest of the Bible is the story of God's salvation plan, His plan to restore to mankind what was lost through Adam and Eve.

Revelation 21-22. The best way to get a feel for the flow of Scripture and God's restoration plan is to look at the beginning of the Bible and the end. We have already looked at the beginning. Now let's look at the end. Here in Revelation 21 we see the New Jerusalem coming down out of the third heaven to a new heaven and a new earth. When we realize that everyone living in this New Jerusalem will have a glorified body such as Jesus had after His resurrection, we realize that once again only spiritual beings will be living on the earth. The earth itself will once again be "perfect," just as it was when created in Job 38. What we mean by "perfect" is that there will be no sin on the earth and no effects of the same. There will be no fallen angels on the earth, and every man and woman has been "perfected" in the sense that their sin nature inherited through Adam has been completely removed when they received their glorified body. From the perspective of the earth, things have come full circle.

Five Stages for the Earth. We might actually visualize the earth in five stages: 1) The original creation of Job 38 where only spiritual beings could live on the earth; 2) The state of the earth in which physical beings could live as long as a thousand years like Methuselah; 3) The state of the earth today after the flood of Noah when all creation groans and labors, waiting for the day of redemption (Romans 8:20-23) when it will be delivered from the bondage of corruption; 4) The state of the earth during the one thousand year reign of Christ where men can once again live to be a thousand; 5) The state in which only spiritual beings can live here once again as revealed in Revelation 21-22. And so, we see symmetry: Original State → 1,000 Year Life Span State → Present State of Groaning → 1,000 Year Life Span State → Original State—full circle. It is God's plan of restoration.

However, as we see God's plan to restore the earth to its original state, we must not lose sight of the fact that He also intends to restore man to his original purpose in taking dominion over the earth. This is the Kingdom Concept. Dominion = Kingdom. The reign that man was to have in the beginning will be realized in the end. The second Adam (Jesus Christ) will realize what the first Adam lost dominion over the earth.[28] And in setting up His kingdom on earth, the second Adam will be joined by those faithful to Him to reign right alongside with Him. In other words, they will be reigning with Him in His kingdom just as the offspring of Adam were supposed to reign with him over planet earth.[29] And it is in the achievement of the kingdom reign over the earth that God answers these questions about His character. Through man's reign God answers the question about his own reign.

In John 14:21 Jesus says, "He who has My commandments and keeps them, it is he who loves Me. And he who loves Me will be loved by My Father, and I will love him and manifest Myself to him." Whenever I obey one of God's commandments, I am helping to answer the two key questions. I am saying, "Yes, Lord, you are sovereign and have the right to rule the universe, and yes, Lord, you are worthy of being loved." To obey His commandments is to be submissive to His Lordship, and to obey His commandments is to tell Him we love Him.

On the other hand, whenever I rebel against His commandments, I am casting my vote for Satan as the rightful ruler of the universe, and I am telling God I do not love him enough to obey Him. This is Satan's will for my life—to get me to assert my own independence against God and His reign over my life. That is what the Bible calls pride, the very essence of Lucifer's original sin.

Summary. So, before the earth was created habitable for man, God and the Lamb reigned over the universe. In Revelation 22:1-5

---

[28] See Sauer, *King of the Earth.*

[29] See Revelation 2:26-27 for the future realization of this mandate.

once again God and the Lamb are reigning, forever and ever. But this reign was opened to question by Lucifer. So, man was created to solve this dilemma concerning the sovereignty of God. In Genesis 1-2 man was created to reign, not over the universe, but over planet earth. He failed, but in Revelation 20:4, 6 we find redeemed man reigning over planet earth for 1,000 years. John Milton wrote the well-known *Paradise Lost* and *Paradise Regained*, both based on the biblical narrative of the Fall and the Restoration. He might have titled it *Kingdom Lost* and *Kingdom Regained*, for that is the biblical story of how the kingdom that man was supposed to have in the beginning of human history was lost, but one day that kingdom reign will be realized as the God/man Jesus Christ leads many sons to glory and they reign with Him in His kingdom. That is why when Jesus made His ministerial entrance, the good news (gospel) He announced was the good news about the kingdom. What did this mean? It meant He was the King ready to set up the kingdom promised to these people in the OT. This would be the kingdom where those who believed and followed Him would reign for 1,000 years. Perfect justice would be meted out through the King and those servant-kings who would reign with Him. Remember when Peter asked Jesus in Matthew 19 what they would get out of giving up everything to follow Him, Jesus replied, "To you it is granted to sit on the twelve thrones reigning over the twelve tribes of Israel in the regeneration." Of course, these disciples did not know what He meant by "the regeneration," but they knew if they were faithful to Him, they would reign with Him.

This is the Big Picture, and the angels watch its unfolding with intense interest.

5

"TAKE TIME TO BE HOLY"

1 Peter 1:13-17

INTRODUCTION

In many ways life on earth is like climbing a mountain of sorts. It is arduous, difficult, but rewarding. And with steady, persistent effort we get to a point where we can see the top. We can almost smell the victory. We sense the flush of success. And then it happens. Completely out of the blue–the unexpected knocks us down just before we reach the top.

That's what happened to Jay Rathman.[30] He was hunting deer in the Thehema Wildlife Reserve near Red Bluff in northern California. He had climbed to a ledge on the slope of a rocky gorge. As he raised his head to look over the ledge above, he sensed movement to the right of his face. A coiled rattler struck with lightning speed, just missing Rathman's right ear. The four-foot snake's fangs got snagged in the neck of Rathman's wool turtleneck sweater, and the force of

---

[30] Charles R. Swindoll, *The Quest for Character* (Grand Rapids: Zondervan Publishing House, 1982), 17.

the strike caused it to land on his left shoulder. It then coiled around his neck.

Rathman grabbed the snake behind the head with his left-hand and could feel the warm venom running down the skin of his neck, the rattles making a furious racket. He fell backward and slid headfirst down the steep slope through brush and lava rocks, his rifle and binoculars bouncing beside him. "As luck would have it," he said in describing the incident to a Department of Fish and Game official, "I ended up wedged between some rocks with my feet caught uphill from my head. I could barely move."

Rathman got his right hand on his rifle and used it to disengage the fangs from his sweater, but the snake had enough leverage to strike again. It made about eight attempts and managed to hit Rathman with its nose just below his eye about four times. He kept his face turned so it couldn't get a good angle with its fangs, but it was very close. Rathman and the snake were eyeball to eyeball, and the hunter found out that snakes don't blink. It had fangs like darning needles . . . Rathman choked the snake to death. It was the only way out.

When he tried to toss the dead snake aside, Rathman couldn't let it go—he had to pry his fingers one by one from its neck. Rathman, who works for the Defense Department in San Jose, guesses his encounter with the snake lasted twenty minutes.

How much like life, Rathman's encounter with this snake. At the most unsuspecting moment, life pounces. With treacherous strength its snakelike assaults have a way of knocking us off-balance as they wrap themselves around us. Exposed and vulnerable, we can easily succumb to the attacks. They come in the form of physical pain, emotional trauma, marital conflicts, carnal temptations, financial setbacks, demonic assaults, . . . whap, whap, whap, *whap*, WHAP!

And we struggle, all the while knowing that if the poison of these attacks reaches our heart, we are spiritually doomed. We can go into a spiritual death that leaves us looking like spiritual zombies. At the very least, a spiritual stupor coming as an aftershock from these bites can render us ineffective for the Lord. It can keep us from redeeming the time for his kingdom. This spiritual stupor can even cause us to lose the significance of our lives forever. But let's be clear. We are not talking about losing our justification. We are talking about the spiritual death of defeat in our Christian walk, despair over having any hope for victory over our private vice, discouragement to the point of walking out on even trying to live a life that would glorify our Savior. Such a life is "lost" in the sense of finding meaning and purpose for living. Peter was written to avoid such a tragedy. Peter wants to "save the saved," to make their lives have an impact on eternity.

Ironically, we have seen in the introduction to this letter that the very trials of life that would rob us of our spiritual vitality can make us more spiritually alive if we react properly to them. The Body of this letter tells us how to make our lives count for eternity in three ways, specifically when we are suffering undeservedly: through our Character, our Conduct, and our Courage. The first section deals with our Personal Sanctification (our Character): "be holy, because I am holy."

"SAVING THE SAVED"
1 Peter

Salutation		1:1-2
Introduction		1:12
Body	"Our Plan of Salvation"	
I. Through Personal Sanctification--Our Character		1:13-2:10
A. Mandate for Holiness		1:13-17
1. Looking to the Future		13
2. Leaving the Past		14
3. Living in the Present		15-17
B. Motive for Holiness		1:18-21
C. Means to Holiness		1:22-2:10

I. OUR SANCTIFICATION: LOOKING TO THE FUTURE   13

> Therefore gird up the loins of your mind, be sober, and rest
> your hope fully upon the grace that is to be brought to you at
> the revelation of Jesus Christ;

When things aren't going our way, we tend to let our mental skirts hang down. We wallow around and are not much use to anybody. In light of the introduction (1 Peter 1:3-12) we need to be ready for action, for service, for battle. That's what it means to **"gird up the loins of your mind."** And **"be sober"** (*nēphontes*) spoke of balance, like a sober man being able to walk a straight line. So, don't let your suffering leave you in a metal stupor with a spiritual hangover. Be balanced, self-controlled, no mental or spiritual drunkenness.

Sometimes when things get bad enough in this world, all we have to hang onto is the next. At times it's best not to rest our hope on a change in our circumstances but rather to sink the anchor of our hope into the calm, bay waters of His glorious return. G. Campbell Morgan wrote: "The future is the perpetual light burning which makes the present endurable." We are to be absorbed by the prophetic consummation of our experience. Does your basic objective in life lie within the bounds of time—or on the border of eternity?

Grace School of Theology is blessed to have a couple who moved from Washington, D.C., to Houston just to help our ministry. Bob and Carmen Pate have been instrumental in helping many ministries through the years. Carmen used to be President of "Concerned Women for America." She also used to run the radio ministry for D. James Kennedy. Later she worked with Kirby Anderson and his radio outreach through Probe Ministries. But not long after joining our team, Carmen contracted leukemia. She spent months in the medical center undergoing chemo and a bone marrow transplant. The results of the transplant were not what they were expecting. So now after a respite of six months she finds herself back in the medical center undergoing chemo five times a day. On the second day of her new month-long tenure at the hospital she sent this text:

Prayer warrior update—Day 2: I wish I could explain how I "feel" your prayers! God is hearing and He is at work on my behalf. The first three chemo doses were given through the night. This is aggressive chemo, but today I have had no side effects. In fact, I have an appetite; I have walked and felt strong enough to encourage others! One of the nurses, whom I knew from my previous stay on this wing, came by and we spent time catching up. I had the privilege of praying with this sweet sister, for the Lord to meet her needs. As I was walking later, I saw a patient in her room weeping. We are not allowed to go in other patients' rooms, so I stood at the door. We had a nice talk as this sister in the Lord shared how she experienced one setback after another. I could certainly empathize, and I told her that I weep too. Cancer is a terrible disease. But I told her how I am learning to focus on my identity in Christ and all the benefits to believers. It is truly a win-win for us. And when I do that, it helps to take the focus off my circumstances. She said she wanted to do that, and we prayed that she would be able! I will get to check on her regularly. So tonight, through the night, I receive my second series of three chemo treatments. The doctor told me that I will be in the hospital at least a month. Please pray particularly against bad side effects that can happen beginning the third week. And by then, I will lose my hair again! The adventure continues, and I praise Him for the peace and joy He is giving me through it all. Thank you for joining me in what has turned out to be a very long journey!

When I read a first-hand account like this one from Carmen, it is difficult for me to describe what is going on inside of me. For one thing, it makes all the physical ailments I wrestle with seem pretty small and petty. Secondly, it is very humbling to be taken into the very personal life struggle of one of those whose life is totally set apart for the Master's use. And thirdly, I am left with a sense of wonder and awe as I get a peek into the hope of someone who finds her entire rest in Him and His return. And rather than wallow in self-pity she walks the halls looking for opportunities to share with others the reason for the hope within her.

And talk about **"grace."** The inheritance laid up for us (v. 4) and the salvation of our lives (the amount of which will be revealed when Christ returns at His Judgment Seat—2 Corinthians 5:9-10) is still properly seen as a product of His grace. Though we are rewarded for our faithfulness to Him, if He were not first faithful to us, there would be no reward at all. From the beginning to the end of our faith we are but the objects of His grace. Carmen knows that—which is why she moved to Houston and volunteered to help us with our podcasts and other media outlet opportunities for free. Telling others about God's marvelous grace not just to open the doors of heaven but to bring a taste of heaven to earth is the driving motivation of her life.[31]

But proper sanctification is more than just looking to the future. It also involves leaving the past.

II. OUR SANCTIFICATION: LEAVING THE PAST   14

as obedient children, not conforming yourselves to the former lusts, as in your ignorance;

"Conforming" (a present participle that can point to an on-going process more than a particular point in time) is the same word used in Romans 12:2 where Paul speaks of the prerequisites for being used by God to the fullest: 1) Dedication; and 2) Transformation. Our dedication can come at a point in time, but our transformation will take place over a period of time. Both Romans 12:2 and 1 Peter 1:14 use the same word for conformity: *syschēmatizō*, which means

---

[31] Since this chapter was written (the summer of 2018) Carmen's leukemia has gone into total remission and she has turned her hospital journal into a book you can get through Amazon: *In Our Weakness, God is Strong* by Carmen Pate, a must read for anyone looking for light in the midst of the fog.

to be formed or molded according to something. There is the idea of an external pressure squeezing us into a form or mold. In Romans it is the world pressuring us; in 1 Peter it is various lusts from our past.

Depending on our age when we came to Christ, a number of different lusts may have had their tentacles around us. There could be habit patterns reinforced by years of repetition. There could also be strongholds of the flesh caused by breaking moral laws of the universe during our teenage years. There could also be unconscious forces as a result of childhood abuse driving us to act out in ways of which we are ashamed. Or, as more than one promiscuous person has told me, "I just didn't think it was wrong."

Peter says we can no longer claim ignorance. Whether our past lusts that controlled us were money, sex, material things, recognition of the world, or whatever, we are called to make a clean break with these lusts. Ephesians 4:22-24 says to take off the old man and to put on the new. Let the liar lie no more; let the thief steal no more; let the angry person not let the sun go down on his wrath. As 1 Peter 2:11 says, these lusts will battle against the significance our lives on earth. They can destroy our lives and cause us to lose their eternal significance. How many, many parents grieve over gifted, children of promise, who fell into the drainage ditch of drugs, completely wasting the years of their youth. They've lost their motivation to work, lost any motivation to study, and frankly lost their motivation to do anything productive with their lives.

I remember one such man I met in the psychiatric ward at Ben Taub hospital in Houston. Mark came from a fun family and had high performing siblings. But Mark was a nonconformist. His parents asked if I would pay him a visit. That usually doesn't work— it's hard to help people who don't want help. When I walked into his room, he practically sneered at me with his glaring eyes and his anti-establishment hairdo.

"Who are you, another preacher sent by my parents? Are you going to lay hands on me and try to get me to speak in tongues like the last guy? I told him to get lost." I started to turn around and walk away, but it had taken me an hour to get there, so I just let him vent for a while. He said, "I don't need your help. There's nothing wrong with me. I'm completely free. I just came back from Austin. I skipped from this hospital and took the TV with me. I just walked right out with the TV. Tomorrow I may go to Dallas, so don't bother me with the Jesus stuff, OK? That's for losers."

I said, "No I won't bother you with that. In fact, I'm going to leave. You obviously don't think you need any help. But before I go, I just wanted you to know you are one of the biggest slaves I've met for a while." "How's that?" "Well, just look at your hair. Whose idea was it that you wear that long ponytail? That come from the people you hang out with? Do they wear their hair like that? And look at your clothes. Do the same people dress like that? You're just another conformist, but you conform to a different crowd. And I'll bet you are a slave to your sexual urges, not to speak of your drugs. What a slave. So, I'm going to go now, but please don't talk to me about how free you are."

"Wait a minute. Come back here. No one's ever talked to me like that before. Just who are you?" By God's grace Mark found true freedom in Christ. First of all, he received the free gift of eternal life by believing in Christ as his Savior. But then he made a complete break from his past. We have to look to the future and leave the past, if we want to be holy. But we also have to live in the present.

III. OUR SANCTIFICATION: LIVING IN THE PRESENT 15-17

> but as He who called you is holy, you also be holy in all your conduct, because it is written, "Be holy, for I am holy." And if you call on the Father, who without partiality judges according to each one's work, conduct yourselves throughout the time of your stay here in fear;

This passage directly ties our holy living today to our judgment tomorrow. And notice the word **"all."** No closets. A little leaven leavens the whole lump. Even though Jesus spoke those words with direct reference to the sin of hypocrisy, they can be applied to known sin in general. If I have a private closet of sin where I believe I can indulge with impunity, I am self-deceived. The power of Satan is in darkness. That dark closet is his wedge into my life. Even though my wife or husband may not know, my boss or friends may not know, other church members or small group members may not know, there are three who definitely know: God, the devil, and I. That's all it takes to rob my Christian life of its spark, its power, and its intimacy (fellowship) with God.

There are two OT passages where **"be holy as I am holy"** jump out at us: 1) Leviticus 20:7-8, which says "Consecrate yourselves therefore, and be holy, for I *am* the Lord your God. [8] And you shall keep My statutes, and perform them: I *am* the Lord who sanctifies you"; and 2) Leviticus 19:2ff, which says, "You shall be holy, for I the Lord your God *am* holy.[3] Every one of you shall revere his mother and his father, and keep My Sabbaths: I *am* the Lord your God." Both passages list a number of important commandments. The message is clear: there is a connection between keeping God's commandments and holiness. This is progressive sanctification.

And observe once again Peter's appeal to rewards, just as Jesus taught him in Matthew 16:27. It is surprising, or perhaps not, the number of English translations that lop Matthew 16:27 off from the preceding three verses, even though the first word in the verse ("for") clearly connects v. 27 with vss. 24-26. Why? It is because the word "save" confuses them into thinking vss. 24-26 must be about how to go to heaven, whereas v. 27 is obviously about rewards since Jesus uses the word "reward." But the salvation, how many times shall we repeat it, in Matthew 16:24-27 is not about going to heaven. If it is, you get there by self-sacrifice (v. 24). No, it is about saving your life (your time on earth) for eternity.

In light of that, the last part of 1 Peter 1:17 should make perfect sense: **"conduct yourselves throughout the time of your stay *here* in fear."** Do you see the phrase **"time of your stay"**? What else could that be referring to other than our life, our time on earth. His appeal to holy **"conduct"** is that this time on earth will be judged by God and rewarded. It can be saved or lost.

One of the most encouraging aspects of this passage is the equal opportunity system. God will judge without partiality. That means everyone plays on a level field. No one has an advantage. The preacher has no advantage over the waiter, the CEO over the janitor, the man over the woman, the career woman over the housewife—all have an equal opportunity to make their time on earth count forever.

Someone will ask about those whose lives were cut short by disease, war, or even persecution. The answer to that is no mystery. When we look at the martyrs from the Tribulation Period in Revelation 6:10-11, 7:14-17, and 14:12-13, we see a special reward for those who had their lives cut short because of their faithfulness to Christ. And the parable of the vineyard looks at those who had different amounts of time to work in the vineyard, but all got the same wage. This would indicate two things: 1) All God expects is that we be faithful to the time we have been given; 2) Even rewards are by grace; we can never show up and the Judgment Seat of Christ and say, "God, you owe me."

Now, we should not leave this passage without mentioning the word "fear" (*phobos*—reverence or respect according to *BDAG*). Fear can be crippling and can keep us from performing at our top level. In fact, one of the wonderful blessings of having assurance of our salvation is that we don't have to fear hell if we don't perform up to snuff. Nevertheless, fear can have a positive effect as well, or Peter wouldn't mention it. We are in a family. God is our Father. A good father motivates his children positively and negatively. To motivate his child to do well, the father might offer certain rewards, even if it is just the reward of praise and approval. On the other hand, it helps the child to know there will be negative consequences should he or she choose to misbehave. Heb 12:5-11 tells us chastening from our heavenly Father for our misbehavior is a sign that He loves us: "For whom the Lord loves he chastens . . . But if you are without chastening, of which all have become partakers, then you are illegitimate and not sons."

I can never forget when my older son was about twelve. He had been outside playing with friends. He came in all out of breath, came up to me and said, "Dad, you won't believe this, but Bobby's dad doesn't love him." "Really. How do you know?" "Because Bobby told me his father has never spanked him." Somehow, we had gotten the message across that we wouldn't spank Jimmy if we didn't love him and want the best for him. And we wanted him to have a healthy respect for the negative consequences that could be meted out should he choose to misbehave. We are calling this healthy respect "fear." So, there is a balance. God will reward us and praise us if we have been faithful, but there will be negative consequences as well for the unfaithful. The nature or duration of these consequences we really don't understand. We do know that in the New Jerusalem there will be no more tears. That tells us that whatever the negative consequences might be, they are temporary, and they are designed to motivate us to holiness.

How, then, can we summarize the meaning of holiness?

CONCLUSION: HOLINESS IS:

1. Separation—from the world system.

In order to separate from the world system, one must become sensitized to how the world system causes us to be "conformed." The Greek word here (*syschēmatizomenoi*—think schematic) is in a form that means either we do it to ourselves or we allow it to be done to us. I prefer the latter. We actually allow the world to squeeze us into its mold. Why do we allow it?

Can you remember where you were on the morning of March 16, 1968? I can't either. But there is a group of men who will never forget. They had a tough assignment . . . a search and destroy mission, a combat deployment of Task Force Barker, assigned to move into a small group of hamlets known collectively as MyLai (Me-Lie) in South Vietnam.

When "Charlie" Company moved nervously into the MyLai region that morning, they discovered not a single combatant. Nobody was armed. No one fired on them. There were only unarmed women, children, and old men. The things that occurred are somewhat unclear. No one can reproduce the exact order of events, but neither can anyone deny the tragic results: between five and six hundred Vietnamese were killed in various ways. In some cases, troops stood at the door of the village hut and sprayed into it with automatic and semi-automatic rifle fire, killing everyone inside. Others were shot as they attempted to run away, some with babies in their arms. The most large-scale killings occurred in the particular hamlet of MyLai4 where the first platoon of "Charlie" Company, under the command of a young lieutenant named William L. Cally, Jr., herded villagers into groups of twenty to forty or more, then finished them off with rifle fire, machine guns, and/or grenades.

The killing took a long time, like a whole morning. The number of soldiers involved can only be estimated. Perhaps as few as fifty actually pulled triggers and yanked grenade pins, but it is fairly accurate to assume that about two hundred directly witnessed the slaughter. We might suppose that within a week at least five hundred men in Task Force Barker knew that war crimes had been committed. Eventually, you may remember charges were to be considered against twenty-five, of whom only six were brought to trial. Finally, only one was convicted, Lt. Cally . . . though, if we got specific about it, many were guilty. Failure to report a crime is itself a crime. In the year that followed, guess how many in Task Force Barker attempted to report the killings. Not one.

So much for March 16, 1968. It happened. It's over. It occurs as a documented, classic illustration of what one professional calls "psychic numbing," which often occurs within a group . . . sort of an emotional self-anesthesia. In situations in which our emotional feelings are overwhelmingly painful or unpleasant, the group aids in the capacity to anesthetize one another. It is greatly encouraged by being in the midst of others doing the same thing.

As M. Scott Peck describes it so vividly in his book *People of the Lie*, "It is a simple sort of thing . . . The horrible becomes normal and we lose our sense of horror. We simply tune it out."[32] That explains why peer pressure is so powerful, so potentially dangerous. And it explains how the world puts the squeeze on us. The smirks or shouts of the majority have a way of intimidating integrity. And if it can happen to soldiers in Vietnam, it can just as surely happen to folks like you and me.

"Don't be misled," warns the apostle that stood alone, "bad company corrupts good character" (1 Corinthians 15:33). Psychic numbing. You question that? Then consider Jonestown, or Watergate, or the Holocaust, or the group that screamed, "Crucify Him."

In order to separate from the world, we must be willing to resist the cries of the crowd.

2. Reservation—for God's use.

Romans 12:1 tells us to present our bodies a living sacrifice. Lest you think this is too severe, let me share with you an excerpt from an actual letter written by a young communist to his fiancée, breaking off their engagement. The girl's pastor sent the letter to Billy Graham, who published it a number of years ago. The communist student wrote:

> We communists have a high casualty rate. We are the ones who get shot and hung and ridiculed and fired from our jobs and in every other way made as uncomfortable as possible. A certain percentage of us get killed or imprisoned. We live in virtual poverty. We return back to the party every penny we make above what is absolutely necessary to keep us alive. We communists do not have the time or the money for many

---

[32] M. Scott Peck, *People of the Lie* (New York: Simon & Schuster, 1983), 69.

movies, concerts, or T-bone steaks, or decent homes, or new cars. We have been described as fanatics. We are fanatics. Our lives are dominated by one great overshadowing factor: the struggle for world communism. We communists have a philosophy of life which no amount of money can buy. We have a cause to fight for, a definite purpose in life. We subordinate our petty personal selves into a great movement of humanity and if our personal lives seem hard or our egos appear to suffer through subordination to the party, then we are adequately compensated by the thought that each of us in his small way is contributing to something new and true and better for mankind.

There is one thing in which I am in dead earnest about, and that is the communist cause. It is my life, my business, my religion, my hobby, my sweetheart, my wife, my mistress, and my bread and meat. I work at it in the daytime and dream of it at night. Its hold on me grows, not lessens, as time goes on; therefore, I cannot carry on a friendship, a love affair, or even a conversation without relating to this force which both drives and guides my life. I evaluate people, looks, ideas and actions according to how they affect the communist cause, and by their attitude toward it. I've already been in jail because of my ideals, and if necessary, am ready to go before the firing squad.[33]

Wow. Find twelve men with that kind of commitment and I'm just guessing you could change the world. Could a better statement of all-out discipleship to Christ ever be written? Total conformity to the cause of Christ, whose end-goal (on earth at least) is the same as the communists: world dominion. No wonder Douglas Hyde, former head of the Communist Party in London observed,

---

[33] https://www.crosswalk.com/devotionals/insights-from-bill-bright/a-communist-youth-march-1.html, accessed May 14, 2019.

communism got most of its philosophy on making disciples from the Bible.[34]

Herein lies one of the great keys to holiness: all-out commitment to Christ. Unfortunately, most of us in Western culture are more committed to the world than we are to Christ. If so, why does it surprise us to find ourselves being squeezed by the world's values and lusts? In a classic description of discipleship Paul compares the disciple of Christ to a good soldier: "You therefore must endure hardship as a good soldier of Jesus Christ. No one engaged in warfare entangles himself with the affairs of *this* life, that he may please him who enlisted him as a soldier" (2 Timothy 2:3-4). When a soldier gets in shape for battle, he does not concern himself with the pleasures of this world, but rather, he trims the fat by disciplining himself for the fight ahead. He wants to be alert, in shape, sensitive to a sneak attack by the enemy. No time for over-indulgence.

3. Purification—within and without.

It is interesting when we look at the Old Testament quotations in this passage to see how many of them are attached to obedience-obedience to the commands of God. Obedience is often left in the shadows by those who stress grace, but it should be like a neon sign in our front yards. Our obedience is not to be hidden in the closet but displayed in the foyer; not under the counter, but on the shelf. Obedience is the key that unlocks the door to holiness.

But you know the real test of obedience? It's when we think no one who knows us is watching. Pat Morley tells about a man sitting next to him on a plane who ordered a drink—a bourbon and Coke. The busy flight attendant said she would come back for his money, which he left lying on his tray. She passed up and down the aisle several times. It became obvious the flight attendant had forgotten

---

[34] Douglas Hyde, *Dedication and Leadership* (Notre Dame: University of Notre Dame Press, 1977).

his money. After she made a half-dozen trips, the man reached over, picked up his money, and slipped it back into his coat pocket. The price for his integrity? Sold—for a two-dollar drink. Without integrity in the little things, we won't have integrity in the big things. "Whoever can be trusted with very little can also be trusted with much, and whoever is dishonest with very little will also be dishonest with much."

The great heroes of the Bible came from many diverse backgrounds. Some were kings; others, like Gideon, came from the worst families. Samson was a powerful figure, while Timothy was timid. Jonah doubted, while David was courageous. What common trait or characteristic did these men possess besides their faith in God? What attracted God to these men of such diversity? The answer will be painful to some of our ears: God knew He could trust these men when they were alone. Some of these men willingly obeyed God and were faithful, but others were like pouty children, scoffing and kicking and protesting all the way. But each had integrity. They obeyed God when they were alone. This characteristic, more than any other, distinguished the lives of these Bible heroes.

That's what holiness is all about. As the Puritans put it: Holiness is practicing the presence of God. Certain illustrations stick with you. Tony Evans gave one I'll never forget. He said he was driving down the freeway in Dallas going his usual speed (5-10 mph over the speed limit). He noticed a police car coming on to the freeway just behind him. He immediately slowed down to the speed limit and kept his eye on the police car. Then the police car pulled up right beside Tony and stayed there for a couple of minutes. Tony's eyes kept checking his speedometer to make sure he wasn't over the speed limit. After about a mile the police car pulled off the freeway. Tony gave a sigh of relief and immediately increased his speed to what it was before he noticed the police car (now don't get all self-righteous and be hard on Tony; what driver among us hasn't done the same thing?). Then he said, "I wonder what it would be like to drive as though I always had a police car behind me. Would it affect how I drive? I think it would," he concluded. Then he asked,

"I wonder how it would affect my Christian walk if I thought God was following right behind me, or, better yet, right beside me?"[35] Practicing the presence of God. As the hymn writer put it: "Take time to be holy." The time we spend in the hall of holiness will never be lost, but time spent in the courtyard of the unholy is like throwing coins into the sewer: it's gone forever. Take time to be holy . . . because that's redeeming the time.

---

[35] Tony Evans, message given at First Baptist Conroe, March 4, 2011.

6

"LOVE'S LABOR'S NOT LOST"

1 Peter 1:18-21

INTRODUCTION

B rian Styer loved to surf.[36] On a warm summer day in 1973 he was wading in shallow Pacific waters, bound for another session of surfing north of Scripps Pier in La Jolla. Suddenly he saw a shadow moving toward him beneath the waves. It was a stingray—with the wingspan later estimated at seventeen feet. With a lightning quick flip of the tail this venomous sea creature fired its sharp barb through the surfer's left kneecap and out the back of his leg.

For ten days Styer, then eighteen, lay partially paralyzed, wondering if he would ever walk again. He did, after doctors removed a portion of the barb, declared him fit, and released him from the hospital. But a sliver of the stingray's weaponry escaped detection by x-rays and remained lodged in Styer's knee for more than a year,

---

[36] http://articles.latimes.com/1985-09-25/local/me-19849_1_surfing/2, accessed May 14, 2019.

causing fierce infection that gradually invaded the surfer's entire leg, eroding muscle and bone surrounding the knee joint. He nearly lost his limb.

Twelve years and fourteen operations later, Styer was back on his board—dancing across the tops of waves with the help of a custom-made alloy brace that supports and strengthens his virtually useless knee. And in 1985, after countless hours of practice, Styer realized his lifelong dream and qualified for a professional surfing contest—the world-famous Stubbies Pro International Surfing Tournament at Oceanside. His goal: catch the eye of a sponsor and become the first disabled competitor on the pro surfing circuit.

Joining the pro tour would be no small accomplishment. For one thing, the condition of Styer's knee and the pain it causes will restrict his maneuvers and limit the length of time he can remain in the water. In addition, surfing sponsors are few, and those few may be reluctant to bet their bucks on a competitor who is twenty-nine—considered over the hill in the grueling water sport–and whose physical condition isn't a hundred percent.

There is another problem. The massive doses of drugs used years ago to battle the infection creeping through Styer's body so weakened his immunity that the surfer has a sixty percent chance of contracting bacterial cancer in his leg. He is also highly susceptible to new infections, which flare up and require hospital care once every two months. A serious infection could resist treatment and force doctors to amputate.

The damage inflicted by the festering wound caused another obstacle to Styer's dreams of surfing prowess—pain. For almost ten years the surfer relied on heavy doses of Percodan, Demerol, and other potent drugs to help him live with the pain, which is constant and is aggravated by walking, climbing stairs, and other movements. Finally, feeling like a vegetable and convinced the narcotics would kill him, Styer attended a workshop on living with pain and successfully weaned himself from the drugs. He now conducts similar pain courses at area hospitals. These days he relies on a wide array of measures to minimize the pain, including icing the knee, biofeedback, ultrasound, and physical therapy. And while he sleeps each night, he wears a neurostimulator that essentially blocks electrical impulses that inform the brain of pain in his knee.

Why, we might ask, does Styer keep coming back in spite of all this pain? Obvious. He loves surfing. He loves surfing more than anything on earth. How can a Christian endure pain time after time and year after year and keep coming back for more? Obvious. Because he loves Jesus Christ more than anything on earth. And that's our focus in this lesson: a passion for God, a love relationship with Jesus Christ that overwhelms anything else this earth has to offer that no matter what the cost, no matter what the pain, suffering, or trial, we keep coming back. Why? Because we're masochistic or have a martyr complex? No. It is because living without His love is not living at all.

Emily Brontë died of tuberculosis when she was only thirty. Before she left the planet she wrote a novel about one of most tortured souls in all English literature, a man named Heathcliff, portrayed on film by the great Sir Lawrence Olivier in perhaps his greatest role. The love of Heathcliff's life was Catherine, and when she died in the bloom of life, he cried out:

"May she wake in torment!" he cried with frightful vehemence, stamping his foot and groaning in a sudden paroxysm of ungovernable passion . . . "I pray one prayer—I repeat until my tongue stiffens—Catherine Earnshaw, may you not rest as long as I am living! . . . Be with me always—take any form—driving me mad! Please do not leave me in this abyss, where I cannot find you! Oh, God! It is unutterable! I *cannot* live without my life! I *cannot* live without my soul!" For Heathcliff, living without love was not living at all.

I would change that just slightly but significantly: living without the love of God is not living at all. It's a comparison thing. Do unbelievers live fulfilling lives? Some of them do. Do unbelievers discover cures for diseases that save millions of lives? Yes. But when a believer that has walked closely with Jesus compares his life with Jesus to his life before Jesus, it is as though he had never lived at all. And it is that deep relationship with Him that moves us to be holy.

Titus 2:11-12 says it well: "For the grace of God that brings salvation has appeared to all men, ¹² teaching us that, denying ungodliness and worldly lusts, we should live soberly, righteously, and godly in the present age." God's grace, which forgives our sins and shortcomings, actually teaches us to be more godly. How? Because God's grace is an expression of His love for us, and when He gives us an undeserved favor (grace) after we sin, we hate that sin and long to be more holy. And becoming holy is one way to save (preserve) our time on earth (our life) for eternity. Let's see how as we look at the Motive for Holiness in 1:18-21.

"SAVING THE SAVED"
1 Peter

Salutation		1:1-2
Introduction		1:12
Body	"Our Plan of Salvation"	
I. Through Personal Sanctification--Our Character		1:13-2:10
A. Mandate for Holiness		1:13-17
B. Motive for Holiness		1:18-21
1. God's Love: Its Measure 18-19		
2. God's Love: Its Manifestation 20		
3. God's Love: Its Mission		21
C. Means to Holiness		1:22-2:10

I. GOD'S LOVE: ITS MEASURE   18-19

knowing that you were not redeemed with corruptible things, like silver or gold, from your aimless conduct received by tradition from your fathers, but with the precious blood of Christ, as of a lamb without blemish and without spot.

We want to say a word about motive. Why should we want to be holy? Though Peter could probably list a number of reasons, it is significant what he doesn't mention: fear. Though there is a place for fear (2 Corinthians 5:9-11), the motive Peter emphasizes is love. How different from the dark, somber sword of Damocles held over the heads of parishioners for centuries. Fear of hell is a real fear, but that is not something Peter mentions. Why? Could it be because people that are already born again and eternally secure don't have to worry about hell? That's why the Council of Trent (1545-63) was so against the gospel of the Reformation—because it claimed our future sins are already forgiven at the cross when we trust Christ as Savior. The Roman Catholic cried, "Foul. If you take the fear of hell away, people will live like hell." But in reality, the love motive is much stronger than the fear motive. "We love him because he first loved us" (1 John 4:19). When you love somebody, you want to please them. In fact, you're always looking for little ways to please them. And the by-product of doing things to please them is joy. By contrast, obedience out of fear alone may produce the same conduct as obedience out of love, but there won't be the joy.

And how do we know God loves us? The price He paid. Sometimes rich kids complain that they had everything they could want in life except their father's love. The father might protest by pointing out that he had provided everything his children could ever wish for. Their comeback might be, "Yeah, you provided everything money could buy, but it was money you will never miss; what you didn't provide was yourself. You never spent time with us."

Well, our heavenly Father did not buy us out of the slave market ("redeem"—*lutroō*, to buy a slave at auction) with money He would never miss. Rather He paid for us with the life of His Son. Leviticus 17:11 said, "For the life of the flesh is in the blood, and I have given it to you upon the altar to make atonement for your soul; it is the blood which makes atonement for the soul." And 1 John 4:16: "By this we know love, because He laid down His life for us." To give money is one thing; to give your life is another. There is no greater love. So much for the measure of His love. What is the manifestation?

II. GOD'S LOVE: ITS MANIFESTATION   20

He indeed was foreordained before the foundation of the
world, but was manifest in these last times for you . . .

Here is another statement reflecting God's omniscience and
sovereignty. The suffering Christ endured did not catch the Godhead
off guard. The decision to make a provision for man's sin was made
before the foundation of the world. They knew there would be
suffering before glory. Only now in the fullness of times did God
choose to make His plan of suffering before glory visible (manifest).
Imagine that. All the millennia of human existence were but a
prelude to the greatest event of human history, the sacrifice of the
unblemished Lamb for us.

Around the turn-of-the-century I spent some time in India.
Things were tense on the Christian front because persecution of
Christians was on the rise. Graham Steins and his two sons had just
been burned to death in their station wagon by a radical political
party. Steins was an Australian who came to India as a missionary
to the lepers. At that time the government of India did not even
officially acknowledge that there were lepers in India. Even I knew
there were because I visited a school for nine hundred of their
children. The children of leprous parents could not stay with their
parents for obvious reasons. Can you imagine the love Steins must
have had for these lepers in order for him to leave his own country
to bring them a measure of health and a boat load of hope? But can
you imagine how much more love it must've taken for him to bring
his two sons with him (ages nine and seven)? Our Father in heaven
had only one Son, but He sent Him to bring a foreign people healing
and hope.

The cross is both the measure and the manifestation of God's love
for us. What about its mission?

III. GOD'S LOVE: ITS MISSION   21

... for you who through Him believe in God, who raised Him from the dead and gave Him glory, so that your faith and hope are in God.

"You who . . . believe"–God did this for us. We are the mission. If you had an only child, would you send him or her to die for us? My wife and I have been married over fifty years. During those years I've spent a lot of time watching sports and old movies on TV. Betty doesn't want to waste her time watching TV, especially since she has no appetite for sports. But during the last six months there is a program she has me record so she won't miss it. You'll never guess. *Forensic Files.*

Forensic Files? You've got to be kidding. It's full of gruesome, sordid, psycho crimes and how law-enforcement uses scientific evidence (quite often DNA) to catch the criminals. I find it a depressing show. It's a steady diet of cesspool humanity. I asked my wife why she likes to watch this show. She says it's because she has been naïve all her life about how women get attacked. She said she's getting an education on mistakes not to make. I tell her she is getting an education on how to knock me off for the insurance without getting caught. Just kidding. At our age we have no life insurance. But I must say the show has given me a whole new appreciation for what it meant for God to send His only begotten Son to save fallen mankind from our sins. I couldn't have done it. I'd say, "Bring on the flood." Good thing I'm not running the universe.

CONCLUSION

Why did God go to all this effort? Why such a complex, complicated plan? Isn't it evidence of God's incredible desire to be loved? He longs for a people that have no greater passion than Him. Moses put this desire into words:

For I, the Lord your God, *am* a jealous God, visiting the iniquity of the fathers upon the children to the third and fourth *generations* of those who **hate** Me, but showing mercy to thousands, to those who **love** Me and keep My commandments (Deuteronomy 5:9-10).

Did you see those words "jealous" and "hate" and "love"? Wow. What a passionate God. Well, how can we develop the kind of passion for God that would cause me to choose His commandments before my own pleasure? The same way you would develop any love relationship:

1. Spend time together just having fun.

Despite the curse with its sweat and toil, life was intended to be more than drudgery. God created us with the capacity for laughter. And, indeed, laughter is one of the keys to any love relationship. When asked why she loves a certain man, more than one woman has said, "Because he makes me laugh." In the book *His Needs, Her Needs*, the second greatest need Harley lists for a man is the need to have a recreational companion.[37] He suggests a flourishing relationship requires ten to fifteen hours a week of quality time, which does not include time watching television. We love to be around people that help us have fun. Life is serious as it is, let alone when unexpected suffering invites herself into our home as an unwelcome guest. We need to laugh.

If we are going to be in love with Jesus, we need to do things that are fun. How many Christians have a concept of holiness that frowns on laughter itself? A couple of summers ago I spent a month writing near Guadalajara, Mexico. I stayed in a compound owned by a successful but retired Afrikaner. He was raised Dutch Reformed in South Africa. His grandparents fought against the British in the Boer Wars. He said at his church smiling was not allowed inside the

---

[37] Willard F. Harley, Jr., *His Needs, Her Needs* (Grand Rapids: Fleming H. Ravel, 1994), 80-92.

building. If a parishioner had the urge to smile, it was understood that he would go outside.

Chuck Swindoll has an interesting statement about this in his book *Laugh Again*:

My vocation is among the most serious of all professions. As a minister of the gospel and as the senior pastor of a church, the concerns I deal with are eternal in dimension. A week doesn't pass without my hearing of or dealing with life in the raw . . . The most natural thing for me to do would be to allow all that to rob me of joy and change me from a person who has always found humor in life—as well as laughed loudly and often—into a stoic, frowning clergyman. No thanks.

Matter of fact, that was my number one fear many years ago. Thinking that I must look somber and be ultra-serious twenty-four hours a day resulted in my resisting a call into the ministry for several years. Most of the men of the cloth I have seen look like they hold a night job at the local mortuary. I distinctly remember wrestling with the Lord over all this before He put me to mat and whispered a promise in my ear that forced me to surrender: "You can faithfully serve Me, but you can still be yourself. Being my servant doesn't require you to stop laughing." That did it. That one statement won me over. I finally decided I could be one of God's spokesmen and still enjoy life.[38]

And later on, Swindoll wrote:

This long-faced, heavy-hearted attitude has now invaded the ranks of Christianity. Visit most congregations today in search for signs of happiness and sounds of laughter and you often come away disappointed. Joy, "the gigantic secret of the Christian," is conspicuous by its absence. I find that

---

[38] Charles R. Swindoll, *Laugh Again* (Dallas: Word Publishing, 1992), 13.

inexcusable. One place on earth where life's burdens should be lighter, where faces should reflect genuine enthusiasms, and were attitudes should be uplifting and positive is the place this is least likely to be true.[39]

2. Learn to communicate on a deeper level.

If a love relationship between a man and woman is ever going to get off the ground, the couple needs to learn to talk about more than the local football team. Most communications specialists tell us there are five levels of communication. Only on the third level do we begin to share our feelings. And we men are not very good at that. But I assure you, if at some point along the way a man doesn't say, "I love you," she's not going to say yes when he asks for her hand. And after marriage if a man doesn't continue to verbally affirm his affection for his wife, the love embers will lose their glow, and the fire that fueled their relationship in its early development will grow cold.

It's no different with Jesus. The interesting thing about our emotions is that God made them. They're not bad. And when they're cooped up, denied, or downplayed, they don't like it. They huddle up in our souls and start talking to each other. "How long has he kept you locked up in here?" "Twenty years? Oh, my gosh." Sometimes they gang up and revolt. The fall-out is usually not very pretty.

One of the biggest hoaxes of evangelical Christianity is that *agapē* love came into the world naked of emotions. "Any emotional display on the part of a Christian borders on fanaticism," we have been told. But if we listen to the greatest of all commandments, it says to love the Lord our God with all our heart, with all our soul, all our mind, and all our strength. That's *agapē* love. Does it sound to you like there is no emotion here?

The late Haddon Robinson once told me that another hoax is the Love Totem Pole. He said most of us in evangelical Christianity have been taught the highest form of love is *agapē* because it is a

---

[39] Ibid., 20.

spiritual love; the lowest is *eros* because it is a physical love; and *phílē*, emotional love, is in the middle. But he claimed this approach caused suppression. *Eros* was suppressed during the Victorian Era, and *phílē* during the current era. But God created all these forms of love and they are all good. At different times and in different situations there is need for one over the other two or maybe a combination thereof, but they are all good. Of course, *eros* and *phílē* could be perverted by the devil, but as God created them they were good and needed. When something God has made is suppressed, suggested Robinson, it may pop up in society in an unhealthy way. Suppression of *eros* led to the Hugh Hefner revolution and the unhealthy preoccupation with sex in today's society. So also, a suppression of the emotions helped lead to the outbreak of the charismatic movement.

In 1746 Jonathan Edwards published a book, *The Religious Affections*, in which he argued that:

> True religion must consist very much in the "affections." . . . one of the chief works of Satan was to propagate and establish a persuasion that all affections and sensible emotions of mind, in things of religion, are nothing at all to be regarded, but are rather to be avoided and carefully guarded against, as things of a pernicious tendency. This is the way to bring all religion to a mere lifeless formality, and effectually shut out the power of godliness, and everything which is spiritual and to have all true Christianity turned out of doors . . . As there is no true religion where there is nothing else but affection, so there is no true religion where there is no religious affection. . . .[40]

But a love relationship means sharing all sorts of intimate feelings, thoughts, goals, and not just love. This kind of sharing brings closeness and intimacy. The greatest intimacy between Christ

---

[40] Jonathan Edwards, *The Religious Affections*, I.2., http://www.covenant ofgrace.com/religious_affections_part1_2.htm, accessed May 14, 2019.

and His disciples expressed on the pages of Scripture comes from the stylus of John, who, quoting Jesus, wrote: "You in Me and I in you" (John 14:20). The intimacy is so great that you and the Savior are one. This is what M. Scot Peck calls *cathexis*, where the ego boundaries open up and a merging of the souls takes place.[41] Sometimes lovers will describe their partner as their "soul mate." There are no secrets. There's total honesty.

The beauty of this kind of intimacy is that it can continue to grow deeper over time. In fact, couples have been described in the later years of their marriages as so close they can finish each other's sentences. That same intimacy with God can grow deeper over time as well. In fact, I would suggest that one of the rewards given to the faithful believer when Christ returns is a greater intimacy (Revelation 2:17 and the term of endearment).

But this brings us to the third ingredient of a love relationship.

3. Learn how to resolve conflicts.

In premarital counseling I usually ask the prospective couple when they had their last fight. I know a marriage counselor that actually tries to get a fight between the couple while they are in front of him. Why does he do it? He said it was because he needed to see how they responded to conflict. According to Norm Wright, there are five fighting styles: withdrawal, yield, compromise, win, and resolution.[42] Many couples never learn how to handle conflict, so they live their entire marriages in an unspoken cold war half the time and an open war zone the other half. But couples that learn to resolve conflict can actually find themselves closer than ever after the conflict.

My older daughter and her husband did a lot of fighting during their first year of marriage, she confided in me. I was astounded.

---

[41] M. Scott Peck, *The Road Less Traveled* (New York: Simon & Schuster, 1978), 91-97.

[42] H. Norman Wright and Wes Roberts, *Before You Say "I Do,"* (Eugene, OR: Harvest House Publishers, 1977), 65-72.

Christie did not seem like a fighter. She said, "Well, dad, I never saw you and mom fight. Consequently, I didn't know how to fight, productively speaking. I did not know how to resolve conflicts." Wow. I was partly responsible for a combustible first year of marriage in the case of my older daughter. It was true, my wife and I rarely fought, but when we did so, it was never in front of the kids. I thought that was a positive thing. Turns out it was negative in that my daughter never saw that committed, loving life partners can work through their conflicts and have a stronger marriage than if they simply buried their conflicts and never addressed the issues.

You see, there is security, safety, and love in a relationship where conflicts are resolved. Each person in the relationship knows from past experience that he or she is committed to the relationship, that they both do love each other, and that they will work this out. And a key element of resolving conflict is to search oneself for his or her part in said conflict.

The unique aspect of our love relationship with Christ is that the source of conflict is always within us. As James says (James 4:1), "Where do fights and wars come from? Is it not from your lusts which wage war within you?" It's our sinful nature that causes the conflict between us and God. And He has told us in His Word how to resolve these conflicts. We must come to Him in openness and honesty, admitting where we went wrong, and seeking His forgiveness.

I've heard some married people remark of their partner, "He/She just doesn't know how to say he/she's sorry." Or, "I've never heard Sue admit she was wrong." That's sad. Those couples can't resolve conflicts. Deep intimacy is not possible. Just so, we must come to the Lord in open, honest confession where we have gone wrong and seek His forgiveness if we want to restore intimacy (fellowship). Oddly enough, we are capable of being closer to God after the resolution of a conflict than we were before the problem ever came up. When He takes us back into His loving arms and says, "I forgive you . . . and I've missed you . . . I've been waiting right here for you . . . Welcome home." That kind of unconditional love is reassuring of love relationship that will never die.

This is a book about "saving the saved," or "redeeming the time," or about preserving the significance of your time on earth (your life) forever, about saving your life instead of losing it (Matthew 16:24-27). One way to do that is through personal holiness, progressive sanctification. Why should we want to be holy? Because we were not purchased by pieces of silver or gold, but by the very lifeblood of the One who scaled every barrier we could erect to prove His love for us. As the Countess said to Maria in "The Sound of Music," "No man can resist a woman who truly loves him," the Savior's unconditional love overwhelms us. We love Him because He first loved us. And a love like this moves us toward doing the things that please the One we love, that is, keeping His commandments. And as we do them, we become more holy. This holiness results more from desire than from discipline. It is the result of our passion for God. We don't have to force ourselves to obey or will ourselves to obey; it's what we want to do, what we desire to do. We echo the psalmist when he wrote (Psalm 42:1-2):

> As the deer pants for streams of water,
>   so my soul pants for you, O God.
> My soul thirsts for God, for the living God.
>   When can I go and meet with God?

Or (Psalm 63:1):

> O God, you are my God,
>   earnestly I seek you;
> My soul thirsts for you,
>   my body longs for you,
> In a dry and weary land
>   where there is no water.

That's how love works. Shakespeare wrote a play call *Love's Labour's Lost*, in which the king of Navarre and three of his lords have sworn for three years to keep from the sight of women and to live studying and fasting. But the arrival of the princess of France on an embassy with her attendant ladies causes them to disregard their vows "of mere necessity." The king is soon in love with the princess and his lords with her ladies. Courting begins in earnest. But alas, news of the death of the princess's father interrupts the wooing, and the ladies leave to go back to France. The play ends with the beautiful owl and cuckoo song, "When icicles hang by the wall." And so, it is with love between human beings. Sometimes all of love's labors are lost and, alas, the lovers left forlorn and lonely. Heathcliff is left on his knees beside Catherine's bed wailing for that which will never be requited in this life. Scarlet is left at the front door grasping after Rhett as he disappears into the mist.

But not so with love's labor for God. Hebrews 6:10 says God is not unjust to forget your labor of love but will one day reward you for it. What I'm saying is that a deep passion for God, a love so great it can be described as one with all your heart, and all your soul, and all your mind, and all your strength—love like that will labor for God and live for God—and a life like that will never be lost. When the love of your life is Jesus, Love's Labor's *Not* Lost.

7

"LOVE LETTERS"
1 Peter 1:22-25

INTRODUCTION

Nothing in our culture seems to last very long. Especially material things. Clothes wear out. Car models change. And computer equipment? Wow. I actually read an ad for a computer costing several thousand dollars, and in the ad it said this computer would serve you well for the next couple of years. Think of that. Only a couple of years. But we expect that of material things. What about values? I was amused recently when I read a list of duties for nurses in a hospital in 1897. Each nurse was responsible to care for fifty patients. But in addition:

1. Daily sweep and mop the floors of your ward, dust the patient's furniture and windowsills.

2. Maintain an even temperature in your ward by bringing in a scuttle of coal for the day's business.

3. Light is important to observe the patient's condition. Therefore, each day fill the kerosene lamps, clean

chimneys, and trim wicks. Wash the windows once a week.

4. The nurse's notes are important in aiding the physician's work. Make your pens carefully; you may whittle nibs to your individual taste.

5. Each nurse on day duty will report every day at 7 AM and leave at 8 PM, except on the Sabbath, on which day you will be off from 12 noon to 2 PM.

6. Graduate nurses in good standing with the director of nurses will be given an evening off each week for courting purposes or two evenings a week if you go regularly to church.

7. Each nurse should lay aside from each payday a goodly some of her earnings for her benefits during her declining years so that she would not become a burden. For example, if you earn $30 dollars a month, you should set aside $15.

8. And a nurse who smokes, uses liquor in any form, gets her hair done at a beauty shop, or frequents dance halls will give the director of nurses good reason to suspect her worth, intentions, and integrity.

9. The nurse who performs her labors and serves her patients and doctors faithfully and without fault for five years will be given an increase by the hospital administration of five cents a day, providing there are no hospital debts that are outstanding.[43]

No doubt women were lined up to become nurses. I suppose we can rejoice that some of those things have changed, but is there anything that lasts anymore? The Bible says, "Now abide faith, hope, and love—these three." Love is supposed to last. But it would seem that love is

---

[43] Swindoll, *The Quest*, 159.

the hardest of all virtues to capture for any length of time. Trying to maintain a love relationship seems as hard as nailing Jell-O to a tree. We picture the nervous lover sitting under a tree picking away at a dandelion: "She loves me, she loves me not; she loves me, she loves me not; she loves me, she loves me not."

A man on the street was researching for an article on romantic love. He asked one woman what she thought about falling in love. She said, "Oh, that sounds wonderful. But I really don't want to. It seems to mess up all my friends. And it's so painful, because it never seems to last." M. Scott Peck would agree with that. In his book *The Road Less Traveled* he claims that a hundred percent of all couples that fall in love also fall out of love. He describes falling in love as a psychological state known as *cathexis*, where the ego boundaries open up and the two become one; they merge, so to speak.[44] On average this state lasts for two years. Then the couple demerges–*decathexis*. The *cathexis* state has been described by some as like being on a drug—cloud nine, the elixir of life, heavenly. This drug is so powerful some people drift from one relationship to another in their search for another high from *cathexis*. They may find it, but alas, it doesn't last. The only things that seem left over from these busted relationships are the scars and the love letters. Yes, the love letters. Letters that promised a love that would last forever, until the end of time, until the waves stop rushing to the shore, until the stars stop their shining. All too often the stars in their eyes turn to sand.

Yet no matter how painful the sting of a busted romance, much of America in the Western world still clings to the idea of a love that lasts. Half the songs and romance novels seemed to be based on finding it, and the other half about losing it. And apparently over five million women waited around for decades to see if Scarlett got Rhett back, attested to by the number that gobbled up the sequel to *Gone with the Wind*.

Well, I've got good news. There is a love that lasts. And for those

---

[44] Peck, *The Road*, 94.

who find it, they can become lasting lovers. The problem seems to be that we are looking for love . . . in all the wrong places. It's found right here in 1 Peter 1. We have said that 1 Peter is about making things last. Like time. It's about making your time on earth, your life, last forever in the sense of counting for eternity. One way that is done is by developing the right character, specifically, holiness. In the first major section of the body of this letter we are challenged to be holy. The emphasis in this section is on our vertical relationship with God. It is described as a father/child relationship. Then in verse 22 the context switches to horizontal relationships. This is brother to brother. When you get to 2:11 Peter switches again to our relationship with the world, but here in 1:22-25 it is in the church. And just as we learned last week that God proved His great love for us by sending His Son to die for us that we should love Him, so now we learn that we have a basis to love each other. That's what all these verses are about: love. God to man, man to God, and now brother to brother. But here we learn how to have a love that can last, and why we can reach out and love after we have been hurt.

In the section on personal sanctification we have seen the Mandate to Holiness (1:13-17), the Motive for Holiness (1:18-21), and now the Means to Holiness (1:22-2:10) through the Word of God (1:22-2:3) and the Son of God (2:4-10). This lesson focuses on God's Word: Purification through the Word of God (22) and Permanence of the Word of God (23-25).

I. PURIFICATION THROUGH THE WORD OF GOD 22

Since you have purified your souls in obeying the truth through the Spirit in sincere love of the brethren, love one another fervently with a pure heart;

This verse says we have been purified for a purpose. The word "purified" is written in the perfect tense in Greek, which means this purification took place the moment we trusted Christ as our Savior.

It was complete in the past with results up to the present. Of the four types of sanctification (prospective, positional, progressive, and perfective) this would fit in with our positional sanctification. It is who we are "in Christ" in "heavenly places" (Ephesians 1:3).

When Peter mentions "obeying the truth" he is speaking of our response to the gospel the same way Paul did in Romans 1:5 when he mentions "obedience to the faith." The word "obey" in its verb form (*hypakouō*) also means "to hear." The idea of hearing that shades over into obedience is similar to the argument of James when he urges his listeners to be more than just "hearers" of the Word; he wants them to be "harkeners." In other words, hear and obey.

The way "in sincere love of the brethren" reads can also be confusing. It might sound like they were purified because they loved the brethren sincerely. No, the little word "in" (*eis*) usually means "with a view to." In other words, we were purified for a purpose. The purpose mentioned here is not to go to heaven when we die; no, it is to have a sincere love for our brethren. The word for "sincere" (*anypocritos*) means "not hypocritical." "Sincere" is a positive way of saying "without hypocrisy" or "not hypocritical." Too many churches are peppered with people that smile at each other and shake hands, all the while thinking or saying evil things about the same people behind their backs.

Rather than being hypocritical in our love we are to love each other fervently. This word "fervently" (*ektenōs*) is used consistently in the LXX (the Greek translation of the OT, which was originally written in Hebrew) in reference to prayer. *BDAG* suggests "eagerly, fervently, constantly." And the love spoken of here is from *philē* + *adelphia* (*philadelphia*). It is not *agapē*. But, interestingly, Paul runs these two words for love together when he says, "But concerning brotherly love [*philadelphia*] you have no need that I should write to you, for you yourselves are taught by God to love [*agape*] one another" (1 Thessalonians 4:9). It's a beautiful thing. We don't have to conjure up love for each other. It isn't forced. Love is a fruit of the Spirit (Galatians 5:22). Paul says he doesn't need to write a bunch of books on how to love the brethren. God does it for us as He teaches us how to love. If we simply walk by the Spirit, we will enjoy His fruit, one of which is love.

Anyone that has been on a mission trip knows whereof I speak. It doesn't matter the race or the social standing, there is a supernatural love Christians have for each other. Are some of us obnoxious and less likeable than others? Sure, but Paul says, "Endure one another's petty faults" (Galatians 6:2), my translation. When we do that, he says we "completely fulfill the law of Christ," which was to love each other. Loving the lovely fulfills His commandment but loving the unlovely **completely** (the idea is to fill until overflowing) fulfills His law. Fulfill is *plēroō*, but this word is *ana + plēroō*, which means "to fill up all the way, to completely fulfill." Of course, this is a supernatural standard, which requires supernatural enablement. That's why we can only do this without hypocrisy when empowered by the Holy Spirit. But this very love will be noticed by the world as something unusual, something more than human. This is how Jesus said the world would recognize His disciples (John 13:35).

There is something that can gum up the works and keep us from loving as God wants us to love. It is an impure conscience. In reference to his command to avoid divisive doctrine Paul tells Timothy, "Now the purpose of the commandment is love from a pure heart, from a good conscience, and from sincere [*anypokritos*, the same word as in our passage] faith." This is not a mystery. When we knowingly sin, we quench the flow of the Holy Spirit. Thus, we cut off His fruit, the first of which is love.

Again, the Christian life is more of a trust than a try, more of a rest than a work, more of a following than a fighting, more of an abiding than agonizing. I know there are Scriptures that tell us to fight the good fight, that we were created for good works, and that we are to strive to keep the unity—but we must always be careful not to slip over into the energy of our flesh to live out the Christian life as opposed to our dependence on the Holy Spirit. The former leads to inner turmoil and disgust; the latter leads to life and peace. I try and I fail; I trust, and He succeeds.

II. PERMANENCE OF THE WORD OF GOD   23-25

> . . . having been born again, not of corruptible seed but
> incorruptible, through the word of God which lives and abides
> forever, because, "All flesh is as grass, and all the glory of man
> as the flower of the grass. The grass withers, and its flower
> falls away, but the word of the Lord endures forever." Now this
> is the word which by the gospel was preached to you.

This is the second time we have run into this concept of being "born again." In verse 3 the NKJ said "begotten . . . again." It is the same word in Greek (*anagennaō*), but the first usage (v. 3) uses the aorist tense, which is befitting to convey a point in time occurrence like a birthing. The second use, which is right here, is in the perfect tense, which indicates a completed work and results extending to the present. In a way, both tenses tell us that the new birth is not a process taking place over a long period of time. The English word used by theologians for this birthing term is regeneration. Since AD 100 the early church seemed to think regeneration took place at water baptism. Somewhere after AD 200 the church began baptizing babies (paedobaptism), and it was thought that babies were regenerated at that time. By the time we get to Augustine (d. 430) he was teaching a regenerated, "born again," baby still might not go to heaven if he or she was not elect. In fact, in his system, over ninety percent of all babies who die before the age of two go to hell. This shouldn't be surprising since he thought ninety percent or more of all humans would be tortured by God forever in hell no matter when they died.

What we can say from this text is that the readers of 1 Peter were "born again." It happened at a point in time for each individual and the event was complete. Just the metaphor (birth) should suggest irreversibility. Some things are irreversible. Once water and cement are mixed, the concrete result is irreversible. Once a child is born, it cannot be unborn. Once we are in God's family, we are there forever, even if we, God forbid, bring shame on the family name.

"Incorruptible" is a word used before in this chapter as well (v. 4). It is used only 8x in the NT, and three of them are in this short letter (see 3:4 in reference to the incorruptible beauty of a gentle and quiet spirit). Peter's readers lived in a world of decay. Everything material decays: houses, chariots, and all things flesh. Finding something permanent would be a treasure indeed. Peter makes that claim for our inheritance held for us in heaven. But he also makes it for the seed God used to regenerate us, His Word. He has used procreation terms: "born" and "seed." But he is letting us know that this new birth and the steadfast love it engenders is permanent, not passing away, not subject to decay or corruptible.

In 1993 I was visiting a missionary in Kenya at the exact time the rebellion broke out in Somalia ("Black Hawk Down"). One day the missionary asked me, "Do you hear the bells?" I allowed that I did. He went on, "They ring about every hour. It means someone else has died of AIDS. It is not spread here by homosexuality. It is spread by female circumcision with a common knife. When I was in the States I used to speak of sin in terms of 'nobody is perfect, are they?' in order to get people to admit that we are all sinners. Here I don't have to do that. All I have to do is ask them about the bells. They know what the bells are saying. Then I just go into the wages of sin . . . death. We are surrounded by death and decay."

It reminded me of Hemingway's book, *For Whom the Bell Tolls*, where practically every character in the book, including Pilar and Jordan, stares death in the face. As John Donne wrote, the common denominator of all members of the human race is death and decay: "No man is an island, entire of itself; every man is a piece of the continent, a part of the main. If a cod be washed away by the sea, Europe is the less, . . . any man's death diminishes me, because I am involved in mankind, and therefore never send to know for whom the bell tolls; it tolls for thee."[45]

---

[45] John Donne, *Devotions Upon Emergent Occasions, Meditation XVII*, https://www.phrases.org.uk/meanings/for-whom-the-bell-tolls.html, accessed May 17, 2019.

But for Peter's readers there is a way out. There is something that does not die or decay.

There is no *cathexis* and *decathexis*. With Him there is no variableness or shadow of turning (rotation). He is immutable (unchanging), as is His love for us. There was a time Israel questioned that love. As many as two million had been deported in three waves by the Babylonians (603-586 BC). During this captivity many if not all of the Jews wondered about the Abrahamic Covenant. Are God's promises to our Father Abraham still valid? What about the land? What about the Messiah?

Peter dips his stylus into what may be the most comforting news the OT Jews ever heard. It's Isaiah 40:6. But the preceding five verses begin the great prophecies to the Jews that their time of suffering was over. They had paid for their sins double, and now the Lord was going to deliver them from the Babylonians. He had not forgotten His promises. The passage is so significant in the Judeo-Christian tradition that Handel began his *Messiah* with 40:1-5:

> "Comfort, yes, comfort My people!" says your God. "Speak comfort to Jerusalem, and cry out to her, that her warfare is ended, that her iniquity is pardoned; for she has received from the Lord's hand double for all her sins."

> The voice of one crying in the wilderness: "Prepare the way of the Lord; make straight in the desert a highway for our God. Every valley shall be exalted, and every mountain and hill brought low; the crooked places shall be made straight and the rough places smooth; the glory of the Lord shall be revealed, and all flesh shall see it together; for the mouth of the Lord has spoken."

> The voice said, "Cry out!" And he said, "What shall I cry?"

> "All flesh is grass, and all its loveliness is like the flower of the field. The grass withers, the flower fades, because the breath of the Lord blows upon it; surely the people are grass.

The grass withers, the flower fades, but the word of our God stands forever."

No matter how bad the Jews of the Diaspora thought they had it, their situation paled in comparison to those carried captive by Nebuchadnezzar. Isaiah reminded those people that God's Word is good forever. "Indeed, let God be true but every man a liar" (Romans 3:4). We know at some point Peter's readers wrestled with whether God's promises were valid, for mockers had or would come that asked, "Where is the promise of His coming?" (2 Peter 3:4). He encourages his readers with the same beautiful words Isaiah had used for the same purpose centuries before.

CONCLUSION

1. God's Word is supernatural.

The text says the Word of God is alive. It's living. When I was just a church goer who thought he was a Christian, the Bible was just a history book to me full of some old stories. But when I met the author that lives on its pages, I realized this book was different. It was alive. As Hebrews 4:12 claims, it was capable of cutting to the quick.

The book is supernatural. Just imagine that forty different authors wrote it over a sixteen-hundred-year period, yet anywhere you slice into the Bible, it bleeds. It's His story, all right, the story of Christ. And it bleeds because from Genesis and the blood sacrifice of Abel right on down to the end of the Revelation, we read about the precious blood of Christ shed for us. In Revelation 19:13, the final vision John has of Jesus, it says, "He was clothed with a robe dipped in blood, and His name is called the Word of God." Surely, we don't think these forty human authors collaborated over their sixteen-hundred-year span. No, the book has a common theme, and all the books of the Bible come together to offer a central message because in actual fact there is a divine Author behind the human authors. God wrote the book (2 Peter 1:20). It presents His perspective on human history. It tells us where man came from and where he is going.

It is a book of one fulfilled prophecy after another, each representing one of God's footprints telling us that a supernatural person communicated this book. And because the Bible came from a supernatural Author, it has a supernatural message. When we read it, we change. As the late Howard Hendricks used to say, "When you back into 400,000 volts of electricity, you don't just stand there, you move."

And that is why we openly declare that we stand on the inerrancy of God's Word. In its first copy given to the human authors, it was without error with regard to history, science, geography, theology, and any other area of truth. We're not claiming it was a science book, but we do not think it conflicts with science. The contradictions proposed by some atheists concerning science and the Bible all have good, plausible scientific explanations.

2. God's Word is a means of continual purification.

The living, timeless message of the Scriptures acts as a cleansing agent. That's what verse 22 said about the gospel message itself. And that's what we read in John 17:17—"Sanctify them through truth; your word is truth." Or Psalm 119:9—"How shall a young man cleanse his way? By taking heed unto your word." Or Ephesians 5:26 speaks of a husband's responsibility to love his wife as Christ loved the Church and gave Himself for her that He might sanctify and cleanse her with the washing of water by the word."

One of my favorite illustrations of this principle revolves around a young preacher in England during the 19th century. Since he was new to preaching, he often wondered how he was doing and wanted some feedback. There was one old lady in the church who never missed. So the young preacher decided to pay her a visit. No one answered the front door, so he walked around to the back of the house. He saw the old woman washing clothes using one of those old hand crank washing machines.

After some words of appreciation for her faithful church attendance the young preacher asked the old woman if she enjoyed his preaching. She responded with an enthusiastic yes. So, the preacher asked her what the main point of last Sunday's message was. The old woman apologized and said she couldn't remember. So, the preacher asked her if she remembered the passage from which the message came. Somewhat embarrassed, the old woman said she couldn't even remember the passage. Now the preacher thought he was talking to a hypocrite. He said, "You must be mocking me. You say you like my preaching, but you can't remember a thing about it." "Oh, no," replied the old woman. "You see this sieve I'm washing the clothes with? As I crank clothes through the sieve, the water flows over them and takes the dirt away. Pastor, it's the same with your sermons. They may go in one ear and out the other, but when they do, they take the dirt away. I'm sorry I can't remember the content of your sermons, but I know they make me a better person. They take the dirt away." Just so with God's Word.

3. God's Word is a basis for abiding love.

In many ways the Bible is this series of love letters from God to men. Some would say that the central message of the Bible is wrapped up in John 3:16, which speaks of God's love for the whole world as seen by His providing His Son for our salvation. This is a love that lasts. Jesus gave his costly blood just for us as an outpouring of God's unending love for us. That's great news in a world where everything seems to be passing away.

Teddy Stallard wasn't one of the kids you pick as most likely to succeed. Disinterested in school, he was one of those kids with the deadpan face and an expressionless, sort of glassy, unfocused stare. He wore musty, wrinkled clothes. His hair was never combed. When Miss Thompson spoke to Teddy, he always answered in monosyllables. Unattractive and distant, he was just plain hard to like even though his teacher said she loves all her class the same. Down inside she wasn't being completely truthful.

Whenever she marked Teddy's papers, she got a certain perverse pleasure out of putting X's next to the wrong answers and when she put F's at the top of his papers, she always did it with flair. She should have known better; she had Teddy's records and she knew more about him than she wanted to admit. The records read:

- First grade: Teddy shows promise with his work and attitude but has a poor home situation.

- Second grade: Teddy could do better. His mother is seriously ill. He receives little help at home.

- Third grade: Teddy is a good boy but too serious. He is a slow learner. His mother died this year.

- Fourth grade: Teddy is very slow, but well-behaved. His father shows no interest.

Christmas came, and the boys and girls in Miss Thompson's class brought her Christmas presents. They piled the presents on her desk and crowded around to watch her open them. Among the presents there was one from Teddy Stallard. She was surprised that he had brought her a gift, but he had. Teddy's gift was wrapped in brown paper and was held together with scotch tape. On the paper were written the simple words, "For Miss Thompson from Teddy." When she opened Teddy's present, out fell a gaudy rhinestone bracelet, with half the stones missing and a bottle of cheap perfume.

The other boys and girls began to giggle and smirk over Teddy's gifts, but Miss Thompson at least had enough sense to silence them by immediately putting on the bracelet and putting some of the perfume on her wrist. Holding her wrist up for the other children to smell, she said, "Doesn't it smell lovely?" And the children, taking their cue from the teacher, readily agreed with oohs and ahhs.

At the end of the day, when school was over and the other children had left, Teddy lingered behind. He slowly came over to her desk, and said softly, "Miss Thompson . . . Miss Thompson, you smell just like my mother . . . and her bracelet looks real pretty on you, too. I'm glad you liked my presents." When Teddy left, Miss Thompson got down on her knees and asked God to forgive her.

The next day when the children came to school, they were welcomed by a new teacher. Miss Thompson had become a different person. She was no longer just a teacher; she had become an agent of God. She was now a person committed to loving her children and doing things for them that would live on after her. She helped all the children, but especially the slow ones, and especially Teddy Stallard. By the end of that school year, Teddy showed dramatic improvement. He had caught up with most of the students and was even ahead of some.

She didn't hear from Teddy for a long time. Then one day, she received a note that read:

Dear Miss Thompson:
I wanted you to be the first to know.
I will be graduating second in my class.
Love,
Teddy Stallard

Four years later, another note came:

Dear Miss Thompson:
They just told me I will be graduating first in my class. I wanted you to be the first to know. The university has not been easy, but I like it.
Love,
Teddy Stallard

And four years later:

Dear Miss Thompson:
As of today, I am Theodore Stallard, M.D. How about that? I wanted you to be the first to know. I am getting married next month, the 27th to be exact. I wanted you to come and sit where my mother would sit if she were alive. You are the only family I have now; Dad died last year.
Love,
Teddy Stallard

Miss Thompson went to that wedding and sat where Teddy's mother would have sat. She deserved to sit there; she had done something for Teddy that he could never forget.[46] If one gift of love from a bedraggled, rejected little boy can transform the life of a schoolteacher like Miss Thompson, think what the greatest gift of love the world has ever seen from another bedraggled Man, rejected and forsaken by men, can mean to you. It's the kind of love that lasts forever. And it's the kind of love you want to pass on to those around you. It's a love that lasts.

---

[46] Swindoll, *Quest*, 177-78.

8

"TIME TO GROW UP"

1 Peter 2:1-3

INTRODUCTION

Clearly one of Walt Disney's all-time classics is *Snow White and the Seven Dwarfs*. Of course, we get all caught up in the beauty of Snow White, the ugliness of the wicked witch, and the plot with the poison apple. But the most endearing part of the story probably involves the little people we call the seven dwarfs. These folks lived in their own little world, perfectly content to go their merry way, oblivious to the world around them. Of course, they all had names: Grumpy, Dopey, Bashful, Doc, Happy, Sleepy, and Sneezy. It's easy to see ourselves in these dwarfs, so much so that we forget they're dwarfs at all. Just what are dwarfs, anyway?

Well, apparently there're three types of dwarfs and three causes of dwarfism. The pituitary dwarf is one that looks perfectly normal as far as proportion and features are concerned, but they're small. It's caused by a malfunction in the pituitary gland, for which these dwarfs are named. Cretinism is another form of dwarfism caused by a malfunction in the thyroid gland. And finally, there is achondroplasia, a type of dwarfism in which the legs are short, the head is large, but the trunk of the body and arms are normal. And this is caused by a malfunction in one of the endocrine glands. In any case, science knows no remedy to make these people grow to the normal height for most human beings.

But that's not true of Christian dwarfs. We know exactly why certain Christians never grow up. We know the cause and we know the remedy. It's all written down for us in 1 Peter 2:1-3. The first great section of the letter is about making our lives count for eternity through personal sanctification. We're to be holy as God is holy. That's the Mandate for Holiness. Now we're looking at the Means to Holiness: God's Word. We've seen that purification comes through the Word of God, but we are also going to see that this kind of purification does not come instantaneously. It is a growth process.

We just want to look at three verses in this lesson: Barriers to Spiritual Growth (v. 1), Food for Spiritual Growth (v. 2), and the Goal of Spiritual Growth (v. 3). Let's start with Barriers to Spiritual Growth.

I. BARRIERS TO SPIRITUAL GROWTH   2:1

Therefore, laying aside all malice, all deceit, hypocrisy, envy, and all evil speaking, . .

Too many weeds can keep the soil from growing well. They can choke the seed. The soil needs cultivation; the weeds need pulling. Here are the weeds that can be barriers to spiritual growth:

- **"Malice"**—*kakia*—ill will toward a brother or sister; an attitude not becoming members God's royal family. We have certain expectations for the conduct of a royal family. Will the world ever look the same at the royal family of England since the tawdry affair of Prince Charles and the death of Princess Di? Pulling the curtain back to see the sordid world of royalty made us want to turn away and say it isn't true. But what about God's royal family? Shouldn't there be a certain degree of the decorum and mutual respect among its members? Ill will toward one another does not promote or create an atmosphere for growth.

- **"Guile"**—*dolos*—a devious approach to people which covers a hidden agenda

- **"Hypocrisy"**—*hypokriseis*—living a lie; professing one thing, his life doesn't harmonize with his lips; he wears a mask.

- **"Envy"**—*phthanos*—an evil eye towards someone who has some position, power, or possession you wish you had; envy is the running buddy of self-promotion.

- **"Evil Speaking"**—*katalalias*—putting others down; the verbal action which reduces others to a common denominator lower than myself; it is the vomit coming out of the mouth of one with the internal stomach problems just mentioned.

Any one or a combination of these weeds will be a barrier to growth. It must be removed for the seed to grow properly.

To change the analogy for moment, if you see a little kid playing in the dirt, you don't give it a second thought because kids play in the dirt. They scrub themselves in dirt. Dirt is a toy to a kid. But if you see a 21-year-old man playing in the dirt, rubbing himself with it and trying to eat it, you would be justified in thinking said guy had some serious issues. But the only difference between the child and the man is time. By the age of twenty-one, a person ought to know that dirt is not a toy.

Unfortunately, we have too many Christians who have been saved too long still playing in the dirt and having fun with it. We could understand if they were brand-new baby Christians, who didn't yet know that dirt is something you don't play with. But Christians can't be exposed to the truth of God's Word week after week and month after month without knowing mud when they see it. And God isn't just trying to keep us out of the dirt pile. He wants to show us something so much better that we would never want to play in the dirt again. Friends, these attitudes are like dirt. To have been a Christian a long time and to display these is like watching an adult play in the dirt. It's like watching the little kid who opens his mouth and sits there with a dumb look on his face while the dirt comes out. But he's an adult, and this dirt will keep him from growing. He may be an adult, but he's a spiritual dwarf.

II. FOOD FOR SPIRITUAL GROWTH 2:2

as newborn babes, desire the pure milk of the word, that you may grow thereby, . . .

"**. . . as newborn babes**"—notice it does not say they are newborn babies. They were to act as though they were newborn babies and their insatiable desire for milk. In the word for "**desire**"–*epipotheō*— the preposition *epi* intensifies the meaning of the main verb, which is *potheō*, meaning "to long for or desire." We might think of a "burning desire" or "eagerly desire."

And what is this milk we are to eagerly desire? It is described as *logoikon*, the root being *logos* (word). God's Word. What is the basis for consistent growth in the Christian life? Some would say it is the baptism of the Holy Spirit. Until then, we are like Peter before Pentecost: up-and-down. Others would say the key to consistent growth is plenty of praise and worship. Unless we stoke the emotional fires of our spiritual temperatures, we will always be blowing hot and cold. Still others will tell us the key to consistent growth is to have plenty of Christian friends. Everyone knows one log burning alone soon dies, but several logs burning together make a bright light. But what does 1 Peter say? God's Word. It is the only means presented in the Scriptures themselves that can bring one to maturity (Hebrews 5:12-14), stability (Ephesians 4:11ff), equipping for service (2 Timothy 3:16-17), and holiness (John 17:17).

Fellowship, prayer, witnessing, praise and worship, spiritual gifts—all these help provide an atmosphere for growth, but the life is in the seed; growth comes from the seed; everything else softens or prepares the soil for growth of the seed. After hanging around Christian circles for over fifty years I have observed that mature Christians have one thing in common other than the indwelling Godhead–an abiding knowledge of God's Word. I know some who would argue with this, but unless we want to contradict Ephesians 4:11ff, the statement is true. Why? Because Ephesians 4 defines immaturity as a Christian that can be blown about by every wind of doctrine. Does this mean someone needs to go to seminary to become a mature believer? Of course not. But they need exposure to God's Word somewhere–sermons, Bible studies, radio, TV, podcasts, personal study.

Someone will surely say, "But I don't have a burning desire or an eager desire for God's Word. Is there something I can do to get it?" There is, actually. It reminds me of after I got engaged to my wife of fifty-two years. I had always been a skinny basketball player (6'4" and 185 lbs). I had never weighed over two hundred pounds. I wanted to impress my new bride on our wedding night with bulging muscles. We planned to marry on my graduation day from Rice University, nine months away. So, I put together a diet plan to gain weight but not fat. To do that I had to stimulate my appetite.

At first, I had to force it. I started with breakfast in the morning at Baker College, one of the men's colleges at Rice, where for $.50 I could eat all I wanted. But I couldn't just eat sweet rolls. Instead I put ten soft-boiled eggs in a glass, stirred it up, and drank it. To that I added some bacon, a sweet roll, orange juice and milk. Next was lunch. A block from our campus was Foot's Cafeteria where I could get one meat and one dessert, but all the salads and vegetables I wanted for $1.04 (1966-67). So, in addition to my meat and dessert I had five salads and thirteen vegetables. I repeated this regimen for dinner. I soon discovered that my digestive system was shooting so much acid into my stomach to handle all this food that at midnight it was burning me up inside, so I cooked a pound of round steak and drank a can of Nutriment. In addition to all this food I also began to lift weights. After nine months of this I had gained fifty pounds, but my waist stayed the same. I couldn't wait to impress my new bride. So, on our wedding night, as I began to disrobe and flex my muscles, all I heard her say was, "Could you turn out the lights, please?" But, but, but, but. . . .

I know, I know–pretty pathetic. Oh, what we men will do to impress a woman. But lest all this effort be wasted, the Lord did have a lesson in it or me. Just as we can stimulate physical hunger, it occurs to me that we can stimulate spiritual hunger. How? Not that complicated, really. Just two things: 1) Exercise more than normal; and 2) Eat more than normal. When I first got to seminary, I didn't know Genesis from Revolution, but I knew I needed to learn the Bible. So, I studied. But it was drudgery and discipline–had to make myself do it, like eating health food and taking supplements. But as time went on a hunger was growing within me. It took a couple of years but feasting on God's Word became like eating Homemade Blue Bell Vanilla ice cream. For those of you who don't know what that is, the Bible calls it manna. I couldn't get enough. I had trouble putting it down. That hunger has never left, but it is something that had to be developed. You don't start out with meat and potatoes. As Peter says, you start off with milk, like any newborn baby.

You know, sucking is one of the main pastimes of babies. Have you noticed that? You say, no, it's crying. Well, it's been a long time since I helped raise one of those little suckers, but that's why they call them little suckers. They suck. Do you remember what a binky is? It's how you fake them out when you want them to be quiet. Why are they crying? Because they usually want some milk. So, you pop all those fake plastic things in their mouths. Put a little honey on it, and it lasts longer. But they suck. They suck for years. If it's not a bottle, it's a binky; and if not a binky, it's their thumb.

Want your spiritual life to grow? Want to avoid spiritual dwarfism? Then be a sucker. I don't mean a sucker in business, but a sucker in the Christian life. But don't be a sucker for binkies. Don't be faked out by sucking up something just because there's a little honey on it. Go for the milk of God's Word. That's the only way to grow.

But why, we might ask? Why should I grow? What is the goal?

III. GOAL OF SPIRITUAL GROWTH   2:2c-3

> . . . with respect to salvation . . . if indeed you have tasted that the Lord is gracious.

Why should you grow? Because that is one way to save your life for eternity. Specifically, this portion of the book of 1 Peter (1:13-2:11) is about growing in holiness. As we allow the Word of God to purify our lives, we are growing, and we, by power of the Holy Spirit, are saving our lives and their significance forever. The words **"with respect to salvation"** are not in the NKJ but are found in the Majority Text for those of you with some background in textual criticism.

The **"salvation"** is the same **"salvation"** Peter has talked about in 1:5, 9, and 10. It can't mean getting into heaven or that issue would be based on the amount of our spiritual growth. No, it refers to how much of our lives on earth will be saved for eternity, that is, will count forever. James 1:21 uses "salvation" or the word "save" in exactly the same way. There James says we should receive the engrafted Word which is able to "save our lives," expressing the concept almost exactly the way Peter did in 1:9.

Is kingdom living a top priority in your life, or are you saving your life for this world? Tony Evans says:

> God's kingdom is lived from the perspective of heaven, not earth. That's why Jesus said, "Seek first His kingdom and His righteousness, and all these things will be added to you" (Matthew 6:33). The pagans may run after the physical, visible things in life (see v. 32), but we are called to prioritize God's kingdom . . . If you lose sight of the kingdom, God's perspective gets lost and you start focusing on the physical and temporal things in life. When that happens, your judgment begins to be skewed and your decisions become

short-sighted. Rather than fulfilling your God-ordained destiny and purpose, you end up with wasted time, effort, energy, and emotions.[47]

One way to answer the question about whose kingdom I am living for is to see whether I give God the first fruits or the leftovers. It is like the farmer who had two prize-winning calves. He was so excited that he told his wife, "Honey, I'm going to let the Lord know that I recognize these calves are gifts from Him. We are going to give one calf to the Lord and keep the other." A few weeks later he came in dejected. His wife asked, "What's wrong?" "Honey, the Lord's calf just died." Well, it's always the Lord's calf that dies, isn't it? When we have to make choices, the Lord loses unless we prioritize His kingdom and His glory. As we grow in Christ, His priorities become our priorities, and we are saving our lives for His kingdom.

One final word as we finish this lesson. **". . . if indeed we have tasted that the Lord is gracious."** The word translated "gracious" is "*chrēstos,*" which usually means "kind, or tender-hearted," although the word is only used 4x in the epistles. Again, context is king, and this is a context of eating (taste) and drinking (milk). It doesn't make a lot of sense to say we have tasted that the Lord is kind or gracious in a context of eating and drinking. However, I like the suggestion of a dictionary of primarily extra-biblical Greek (Liddell and Scott), which says it means "satisfying." Ahh. Perfect.

When we spend our lives going for the gold in this world, we may well find life very unsatisfying. Jeremiah tells the people of Israel they have been trying to slake their thirst in broken cisterns: "For My people have committed two evils: they have forsaken Me, the fountain of living waters, and hewn themselves cisterns—broken cisterns that can hold no water" (Jer 2:13). The water they are drinking can never satisfy, and the water they are drinking will never be enough because the cisterns from which they are drinking are broken. But Jesus tells

---

[47] Tony Evans, *The Kingdom Agenda* (Chicago: Moody Press, 2013), 33.

the woman at the well that if she drinks of the water He offers her, she will never thirst again. His water satisfies.

I can't tell you how many men I have talked to that have grabbed for the brass ring and reached it, many before the age of fifty, only to find themselves unsatisfied. "Is this it?" they ask. "Is this all there is?" Again, Jesus says, "Blessed are those who hunger and thirst after righteousness, for they shall be filled." The word "filled" (*chortazō*) means "to eat one's fill, to be satisfied" (*BDAG*). I think it would be fair to say that certain secular endeavors can be rewarding, but I question whether they can fully satisfy the craving of the human heart for an intersection with eternity. Nothing else satisfies like the manna from on high.

When one tastes that the Lord satisfies in a way this world never can, he or she wants to live for nothing else. That doesn't mean they want to retreat from this world and live in the desert like the desert mystics in early church history. Quite the opposite. When one has been cured of cancer, he wants nothing more than for others to enjoy this same healing. They charge into the world to spread the good news. Only the Lord satisfies. Want a taste? Put His kingdom before your own and the sawdust in your mouth will turn to manna.

CONCLUSION

You know, the seven dwarfs could probably have kept on going just fine if Snow White hadn't stumbled onto them. She changed their lives forever. They had to get their eyes off their own immature attitudes for which some of them were named and risk a little something to help someone else.

Spiritual dwarfs can go on remaining spiritual dwarfs all their Christian lives. And grumpy attitudes like the ones listed here can guarantee dwarfism. Spiritual dwarfs can go right on doing their work, feeding themselves, and let the world go right by without ever reaching out to make a difference. During the week they can get up in the morning singing, "Hi ho, hi ho, it's off to work we go." Or on Sunday morning they can get up and sing, "Hi ho, hi ho, it's off to church we go," completely oblivious to Father Time ticking away the days of their lives. The problem is their lives can pass right by without ever having an impact that will count in the life to come. It took Snow White to tell them there's another world out there. And Jesus Christ, pure as the driven snow, tells us there is another world out there. He says, we don't have to stay dwarfs forever. We can spit the mud right out of our mouths, become suckers for the milk of the Word, and grow with the goal of saving our lives by having an impact in the other world. Jesus even might say:

It's time to grow up!
So, take time to grow up.
And that's redeeming the time.

9

"LIVING STONES"

1 Peter 2:4-10

INTRODUCTION

The prophet Jeremiah once asked, "Can the Ethiopian change his skin, or the leopard his spots? Then may you also do good, who are accustomed to do evil" (Jeremiah 13:23). In other words, can a person change his or her basic nature? Can the cruel become kind, the vulgar become refined, the coward become courageous?

It is an important question. Few of us are all we want to be. Is there any hope for us? Albert Einstein once said it is easier to denature plutonium than it is to denature the evil spirit of man. And Will Rogers once said, "You can't say that civilization doesn't advance . . . For in every war they kill you in a new way." In 1961, Bruce Catton, editor of *American Heritage* and an authority on the Civil War, spoke on the theme, "What 1861 has to say to 1961." In his address he emphasized that although weaponry has changed over the past century, man's most explosive problem has not—that is, man's own nature. The chief problem in the world in 1786 was the same as the chief problem in 2019–it is man himself. Just listen to the saber rattling of the United States, North Korea, Russia, China, Iran, Syria, and Israel in 2019 to realize the basic nature of man hasn't changed.

Is there no hope for humanity? Is there no hope for us as individuals? The late Samuel Heffenstein said, "Wherever I go, I go too, and spoil everything." And there is early television personality Jack Paar's classic line: "Looking back, my life seems like one long obstacle race, with me as its chief obstacle." Many of us can identify with those assessments. Is it possible for us to change?

The answer is yes and no. No, our fallen, sinful nature is not going to change. But yes, with the Holy Spirit living inside of us and with the new nature born from the incorruptible seed of God (1 John 3:9; 5:18), a person as a whole can change. Consider for a moment the apostle Paul. By his own admission he persecuted the early Christian church. He was a zealous advocate of the Jewish faith. He was fanatically attached to his brand of orthodox Judaism such that he could not tolerate conflicting points of view. The important thing, however, is that Paul did change. And he wrote about change when he exhorted his followers to be transformed by the renewing of their minds (Romans 12:2), to take off the old man and put on the new (Ephesians 4:22ff), and the sanctifying work of the Holy Spirit to transform one from self-centeredness to Christ-likeness (2 Corinthians 3:18).

But that is Paul. What does Peter have to say about the transformation process. How does the Father form and shape us to become like His Son? That is our lesson in 1 Peter 2:4-10 as we become Priests like Him (4-5), Precious like Him (6-8), and Peculiar like Him (9-10).

I. PRIESTS LIKE HIM   4-5

Coming to Him as to a living stone, rejected indeed by men, but chosen by God and precious, you also, as living stones, are being built up a spiritual house, a holy priesthood, to offer up spiritual sacrifices acceptable to God through Jesus Christ.

"Coming to Him" may well indicate just how this transformation process is going to take place. I call this "edification by association." We usually become like the people we hang around. In time we talk the same way, dress the same way, and often act the same way. It is no different when we come to Jesus. The word translated "coming" (*proserchesthai*) may well point to a practice or a custom (customary present or even gnomic present)[48], which would then be translated, "To whom, whenever you come, you are built up." It's the idea of drawing near with the intention both to stay and to enjoy personal fellowship.

The great thing about coming to hang out with Jesus is the **"built up."** He is never there to put us down. That is the devil's forte. Jesus wants to give us rest (Matthew 11:28-30) and to build us up. He is well aware that we have been called to a supernatural standard. The face of our walk will always be pock-marked by failure. But Jesus is not standing by to point a finger every time we fail and to mock us and make fun of us because of our weakness. No, He's there to shout and cheer when we get it right.

My younger daughter and her husband adopted biracial twins. As I write they are about three. The whole world is an adventure, and they are learning new things daily. With her iPhone my daughter is able to send us pictures of their new escapades at least every week. The newest was little James singing "Happy Birthday." But James is singing it to himself: "Happy birthday to me . . . Happy birthday to me . . . Happy birthday, dear James . . . Happy birthday to me." Text me and I'll send you pictures of my grandchildren.

Now one of the interesting things about these little snippets is the background cheering. The pictures are of the kids, of course. But in the background, you can hear mom and dad cheering. My son-in-law (Adam) definitely has the gift of encouragement. He grew up playing a lot of sports and went to college on a football scholarship.

---

[48] Daniel Wallace, *Greek Grammar Beyond the Basics* (Grand Rapids: Zondervan Publishing House, 1996), 519-25.

So, he has been exposed to a lot of coaches. Some of them motivate by yelling at their players and making fun of them; others by cheering them on when they get it right. Adam is the latter. So is Jesus. Little kids need lots of encouragement. They actually learn by making mistakes. You might say they learn to walk by falling. They won't progress very fast if a harsh father is there to laugh at them when they fall.

Now the imagery of a stone and a building is important here, especially with Matthew 16 as a background for this letter. We remember Matthew 16:18 where Jesus speaks of Peter's confession that He is the Christ, the Son of the living God as a rock on which He would build His church. Most likely that is in Peter's mind as he refers to Christ in this passage as a "stone," especially since he is about to call Him the "cornerstone" (v. 6). And everything in this passage is carefully designed to show us how we become like our Great Leader, our Lord, our Savior. He is a "living stone"; we become "living stones"; He is "precious"; we become "precious"; He is "elect"; we are "elect"; He was a priest; we become priests; He is holy; we become "holy."

We become like Jesus as we spend time with Jesus. While I was going to seminary in the late sixties, there was one professor that stood out as a disciple maker. His greatest impact might have been the disciples he made through the years. It was pretty easy to spot a Howard Hendricks disciple because of the way they walked and talked. How was that? They walked and talked like Hendricks. Not exactly, of course. But they picked up some of his mannerisms, his gestures, his aphorisms. And just how did they do that. Do you think they sat in class while he was lecturing and disciplined themselves to copy his delivery? No. They just spent time with him. They picked up his ways subconsciously. Of course, it helped that they admired him and his gifts.

We have read Peter's claim that we become Priests like Him; he also says we become Precious like Him (6-8).

II. PRECIOUS LIKE HIM   6-8

> Therefore, it is also contained in the Scripture, "Behold, I lay in
> Zion a chief cornerstone, elect, precious, and he who believes
> on Him will by no means be put to shame." Therefore, to you
> who believe, He is precious; but to those who are disobedient,
> "The stone which the builders rejected Has become the
> chief cornerstone," and "a stone of stumbling and a rock of
> offense." They stumble, being disobedient to the word, to
> which they also were also appointed.

"Therefore." All of 6-10 is designed to support how when we
come to Him, we become like Him. In v. 4 it says He is chosen and
precious; so, in 6-8 we see how we become precious, and in 9 and
10 how we are chosen. Chiasm is a popular literary device to make
things easier to memorize: ab:b'a'—chosen (a) precious (b): precious
(b') chosen (a').

The quote from Isaiah 28:16 gives OT support to the claim of
v. 4 that Christ was a *stone, elect,* and *precious.* The **"cornerstone"**
(*acrogōniaios*) was the primary foundation stone at the angle of the
structure by which the architect would fix a standard for bearing the
walls and cross-walls throughout. Christ is God's great Cornerstone
for the Church. By Him God measures all things and fixes the ultimate
standard for all who come to Him.

"*He is* precious"—the words in italics are not in any Greek text.
The NIV and KJV and NKJV have wrongly turned a noun into an
adjective here. J. Ramsey Michaels correctly translates, "The honor
[or preciousness, or value] belongs to you who believe"[49] (brackets
mine). See also the NASB. The point is that we become precious like
Him when we come to Him. The value attached to The Living Stone
is attached to those who are attached to Him. I would translate it:
"Therefore, this value is ***attached*** to you who believe."

---

[49] J. Ramsey Michaels, *Word Biblical Commentary, 1 Peter* 49 (Waco, TX:
Word Books, 1988), n.a.

I caught a glimpse of what this means years ago when the late Continental Airlines was making its inaugural flight of its 777 to Tel Aviv. The president of the airlines, Greg Brenneman, asked me if I would lead a group of his executives and their families on a tour of the Holy Land. He didn't have to beg us, so off we went. Now I had never ridden first class before. Greg just told me and Betty to stick close to him and his wife Rhonda. As such, we were treated like royalty. Whatever drinks we wanted, hot fudge sundaes, cashews, filets—we ate like kings and queens. Why? We had no more intrinsic value than before we got on the plane. Why? You know why. It was because we were connected to the president of the airlines. The crew and flight attendants treated him and his wife like royalty, and in turn they treated anyone closely connected to them as royalty as well.

Need I point out that Jesus is royalty? So is anyone connected to Him.

III. PECULIAR LIKE HIM   9-10

> But you are a chosen generation, a royal priesthood, a holy nation, His own special people, that you may proclaim the praises of Him who called you out of darkness into His marvelous light; who once were not a people but are now the people of God, who had not obtained mercy but now have obtained mercy.

Christ was chosen (elect) and precious (vv. 4 and 6). It is crucial to see this, for it is essential to prove that as we come to Him we become like Him. Remember, this entire section of the book (1 Peter 1:13-2:10) was designed to show us how we can "save our lives" through progressive sanctification, or holy character. Vss. 9 and 10 bring this concept of "holiness" (set apart for a special purpose) into sharp focus: "a chosen generation, a royal priesthood, a holy nation, His own special people, . . . the people of God."

Betty and I have four new grandchildren. After battling infertility for years, my daughter and her husband decided to adopt. They were chosen out of fifteen families to adopt biracial twins from Florida. They are now three years old and hungry for stories, any story. So, they jump in my lap whenever they can and ask for a story. I have begun a series of children's stories. They all have the same plot. Poor Ellie the Elephant was born without a trunk. All her siblings laughed and poked fun at her strange and peculiar appearance—an elephant without a trunk, of all things! After embellishing the situation a bit, I mention that some of her siblings began to disappear. Turns out that a giant crocodile waited very quietly in the water beside the watering hole for the elephants. It would jump up out of the water and grab one of the baby elephants by the trunk and pull it into the water for the death spiral.

But one day the big croc made a fatal mistake. It jumped out of the water to grab Ellie, but missed because Ellie didn't have a trunk. She immediately pounced on the killer croc and crushed it by sitting on its back. She became the heroine of the tribe—all because her Creator made her without a trunk. You get the picture? Well, on one visit it was time for bed after several of these stories about Ricky the Rabbit, Freddie the Fox, Daphne the Duck, etc. James had his jammies on and was being led up the stairs, when he turned back and said, "I want to hear about the mouse who had no tail . . . and just one eye." Well, I hadn't told a story about a one-eyed mouse with no tail. But it didn't take long for little James to warm up to the idea that a person could be handicapped but at the same time be very special to his or her Creator with a very special purpose in life. We are His own special people even if we do have some flaws here and there. We are here for a reason; there is purpose.

What can we conclude from all this?

CONCLUSION

1. We become what we think about, all day long.

This truth is illustrated in Nathaniel Hawthorne's story, "The Great Stone Face." In a beautiful Appalachian Valley there was a strange legend about a wise and beneficent man who would someday come to the valley and do much good for all who learned from his wisdom. They would recognize him by his strong resemblance to a configuration known as the "Great Stone Face" high in the hills above the valley. A little boy named Ernest was determined to be the first one to spot the wise man that would look like the Great Stone Face, so he would walk the valley on the way home after school and sit below the Great Stone Face to study every feature in detail.

The first man to come to the valley was a wealthy shopkeeper named Gathergold. But his face lacked the beneficence of the Great Stone Face, and he was miserly. The next candidate was a great general dubbed Old Blood-and-Thunder. This man had a strong will and a hard face, but not the wisdom and love of the Great Stone Face. Another man had left the valley to run for president and came back to campaign. They called him Old Stoney Phiz. Ernest had high hopes for Old Stoney Phiz, but he had a "weary gloom in the deep caverns of his eyes" like a child who had grown weary of his toys. He was a man of no lofty ideas or purpose in life.

Finally, years later a well-known poet came to the valley to meet Ernest, who was now old but known far and wide for his wisdom and sagacity. On meeting the poet and admiring his poems, Ernest studied his features, only to find that his likeness did not match the Great Stone Face; but at least he had a new friend. One evening they walked to the foot of the Great Stone Face, where Ernest often enjoyed sharing his wisdom with many admirers who gathered to listen.

> Ernest began to speak, giving to the people of what was in his heart and mind. His words had power, because they accorded with his thoughts; and his thoughts had reality and depth, because they harmonized with his life which he had always lived. It was not mere breath that this preacher uttered; they were the words of life, because a life of good deeds and holy love was melted into them. Pearls, pure and rich, had been dissolved into this precious draught. The poet, as he listened, felt that the being and character of Ernest were a nobler

strain of poetry than he had ever written. His eyes glistening with tears, he gazed reverentially at the venerable man, and said within himself that never was there an aspect so worthy of a prophet and a sage as that mild, sweet, thoughtful countenance, with the glory of white hair diffused about it. At a distance, but distinctly to be seen, high up in the golden light of the setting sun, appeared the Great Stone Face, with hoary mists around it, like the white hairs around the brow of Ernest. Its look of grand beneficence seemed to embrace the world.

At that moment, in sympathy with a thought which he was about to utter, the face of Ernest assumed a grandeur of expression, so imbued with benevolence, that the poet, by an irresistible impulse, threw his arms aloft, and shouted, "Behold! Behold! Ernest is himself the likeness of the Great Stone Face!"

Then all the people looked and saw that what the deep-sighted poet said was true. The prophecy was fulfilled. But Ernest, having finished what he had to say, took the poet's arm, and walked slowly homeward, still hoping that some wiser and better man than himself would by and by appear, bearing a greater resemblance to the GREAT STONE FACE.[50]

As we behold the Lord, we become like the Lord (2 Corinthians 3:18).[51] We become what we think about, all day long.

---

[50] Nathaniel Hawthorne, *The Great Stone Face and other Tales from the White Mountains* (San Diego, CA: ICON Group International, 2000), 23-24. This illustration was used by this author in *Portraits of Righteousness* (Lynchburg, VA: Liberty University Press, 2013), 52-53.

[51] We are *not* promoting the power of positive thinking. Merely *thinking about* Jesus could not transform us without the supernatural power of the Holy Spirit (2 Corinthians 3:18).

2. When we draw near to Him, He draws near to us.

That is a promise from James 4:7. I think I began to understand this verse years ago when my first child was about five.[52] We were living in a four-bedroom house with the master bedroom set off from the other three. My son was in one of those bedrooms and my daughter (about three) in another. We used the fourth for reading and TV.

On Saturday nights I always like to save a couple of hours before bed to meditate on the ministry of the next day and to pray. It was something of a ritual for me. So, the kids were asleep, and I had my back to the wall, leaning back on a couch. While meditating with my eyes open, I noticed the door handle slowing turning. The door pushed open a bit, and a little hand started crawling around the edge of the door as it was pushed open slightly.

Now you have to understand that I did not like being disturbed during my Saturday evening ritual. Finally, the door was open, and Jimmy stepped in. He was a cute kid with big blue eyes, and they were wide open. He wrestled some with nightmares, and I could tell he was scared, but I didn't want to be disturbed. I was being spiritual, you understand. So, I asked, "Jimmy, what do you want? You are supposed to be in bed." He looked at me with those big eyes and said, "Daddy, I don't want anything; I just want to be close to you."

Ahhh, man, what are ya gonna do? "Jimmy, what do you want—a pony, a Cadillac? Come over here." I held out my arms to him, he ran over and jumped up against my chest, and I drew him close with my arms around him. That's when I began to understand this verse. "Yes, Lord, I know you are busy. But things are a little tough in my life right now, and I am scared. I'm not even asking for anything at the moment. I just want to be close to you." That is nearly irresistible. He will wrap his loving arms around you and pull you close. And when

---

[52] This illustration is taken from David R. Anderson, *Triumph through Trials* (The Woodlands, TX: Grace Theology Press, 2013), 173-74.

I am that close, I cannot help but to see more of his infinite holiness and my pathetic sinfulness.

A college girl from years ago sent me a letter from school. It included a poem that really hits the nail on the head concerning the attitude of humility I am talking about:

To have been the cup His lips touched and bless;
To have been the bread that He broke;
To have been the cloth that He held as He served;
Or the water He poured as He spoke.
To have been the road He walked on His way,
To have been His print in the sand;
To have been the door that opened His tomb;
But I was the nail in His hand.

10

"WAR OF THE WORLDS"
1 Peter 2:11-12

INTRODUCTION

There seems to be a new fascination with the concept of life on other planets, and especially intelligent life that invades planet earth. Ever since Orson Welles' spoof about Martians invading the earth that literally fooled so many radio listeners back in 1932 and caused a temporary panic, people have been fascinated with the prospect of contact with intelligent life forms from other parts of the universe. The original classic film called *War of the Worlds* was remade this century with Tom Cruise as its star. Academy Award winner Jodie Foster played the central role in a movie called *Contact*, which utilizes SETI, the mega million-dollar project searching the skies 24/7 for an intelligent message from outer space. SETI stands for Search for Extra Terrestrial Intelligence.

Sound pretty far-fetched? Well, even the rather levelheaded astronomers are getting hyped up about life on other planets. Rarely does a year go by that another planet has not been discovered, some of which these astronomers think could support intelligent life. Three of these planets were discovered by Geoffrey Marcy and Paul Butler of San Francisco State University.[53] Both of these planets are a mere 200 trillion miles away (34 light years). But these astronomers are convinced these planets could have liquid water, a prerequisite for life as we know it. Man, in a search to understand himself and his origins, is on a desperate mission to prove there is life on and from other planets.

But why spend all this money to do it? The Scriptures tell us there is life from other planets. The Bible says this planet was invaded by aliens long before mankind was even created. But not only in the ancient past, but the earth is also being visited in the present by these alien beings. Who are they? Where they come from? The Scriptures tell us they are angels, real people of superior intelligence to human beings, who can materialize and dematerialize, and beings with the mode of travel we as yet do not understand. In fact, a classmate of mine from Rice University wrote a book called *UFOs: What on Earth is Happening?* in which he posits fallen angels as the very best explanation for the varied characteristics of UFOs as reported by witnesses. Whether he is right about his UFO interpretation or not, I couldn't say, but I can say on the authority of God's Word that there are alien beings in this world, and these beings are out to take over the earth from mankind in an effort to prevent the Son of Man from returning in the sky to set up His promised kingdom on earth and reign for a thousand years. Yes, we might call this "The War of the Worlds." Satan, the god of this world, is on a collision course with Jesus Christ, who will bring us a new atmosphere and a new earth, a whole new world.

When we leave 1 Peter 2:10, God is ready to send us on a mission into this world. He pictures a war with us as soldiers ready, willing (Psalm 110:4-5), and able to fight against the soldiers of Satan, the original fallen angel cast down to this earth. Sound far-fetched? Don't

---

[53] https://www.berkeley.edu/news/media/releases/2000/08/07_planets.html, accessed 6/25/2019.

be fooled, my friend. Remember, one of Satan's greatest tactics is to make us believe he doesn't exist. "Only one life, 'twill soon be past; only what's done for Christ will last." Our enemy, the devil, knows this. Therefore, he is doing his best to destroy our lives. How does the devil go about trying to destroy our lives? What can we do to stop him? These are the questions we want to answer in this lesson.

"SAVING THE SAVED"
1 Peter

Salutation	1:1-2
Introduction	1:3-12

Body "Our Plan of Salvation"

I. Through Personal Sanctification—Our Character	1:13-2:10
A. Mandate for Holiness	1:13-17
B. Motive for Holiness	1:18-21
C. Means to Holiness	1:22-2:10
II. Through Personal Submission—Our Conduct	2:11-3:7
A. Our Conduct in the World	2:11-17
B. Our Conduct in our Jobs	2:18-25
C. Our Conduct in the Home	3:1-7

Transition: the verses on which we focus in this lesson are transitional. They're taking us away from the idea of saving our lives through *personal sanctification* to saving our lives through *personal submission*. Whereas in the first section of the body the focus was on our character, now Peter turns to our conduct. These verses actually introduce this section about our conduct much like a topic sentence at the beginning of a paragraph. The two verses really are one sentence; verse 11 tells us what not to do, while verse 12 tells us what we should do. So, we have the "Avoidance of Bad Conduct" in verse 11 and "Adhering to Good Conduct" in verse 12.

I. AVOIDANCE OF BAD CONDUCT 2:11

Beloved, I beg you as sojourners and pilgrims, abstain from
fleshly lusts which war against the soul, . . .

Peter has been talking about our holy character within ourselves
and the church. Now he turns to our conduct and its effect on
unbelievers. He calls his readers **"sojourners"** or "aliens," *paroikous,*
in the original. The world has been invaded by aliens, only we
Christians are the aliens. Our trusty Greek dictionary (*BDAG*) says
this term for aliens "speaks of the Christian's earthy life far from his
heavenly home."

Here Peter pictures us as those that have been transferred from
death into life, as those that no longer belong to this world, as aliens
in this world, people whose home is far away. It is as though we had
made a trip to Mars, but our real home was on earth. Perhaps there
are things on Mars that would awaken a whole set of unhealthy
lusts in our lives, lusts which could expose us to deadly germs that
might destroy our lives. Our captain might warn us and remind us
that we are but aliens on the foreign planet of Mars. He would tell
us not to get too attached, that sooner than we might think we will
be going home to the world where we really belong. That's the way
Peter views the Christian in this world. He says we must be careful
about getting too attached to this world. He even suggests that lusting
after this world and some of its pleasures can be harmful to our
spiritual health.

Peter tells us to abstain from these earthly lusts. **"Abstain"**—
apechō—means (*BDAG*) to be distant from (far from a house, a
city, the land). It is the idea of just staying a healthy distance away
from fleshly lusts. With Joseph in mind, perhaps, Paul says to "flee
fornication" (1 Corinthians 6:18). The Corinthians had labor unions
or guilds. Part of being a member was to go with other members
down to the local temple for some R&R. However, part of that
program was to engage in temple prostitution. The Christians knew
that was wrong but felt pressure to be with the group at the temple.
Somehow, they had it in their minds they could sit in the corner

and play chess while others close by were engaging in fornication. Paul says you're nuts. Let the one who thinks he stands take heed lest he fall (1 Corinthians 10:12). Get too close to the fire and you will get burned. The safest policy is to stay completely away from the fire. We pray for God not to lead us into temptation, but then we tempt/test God ourselves by flirting with the temptation or getting too close.

Every home is different. I used to commute from Houston to Dallas once a week to work on my dissertation. I stayed at the home of some very strange people. What is so strange about them? They actually stock Blue Bell Homemade Vanilla ice cream. That's right. I said stock. That's an impossibility in my house. My children have inherited my genes. And I'm convinced that a certain strain of the genetic code could be labeled, "Blue Bell Bytes." That's Bytes, no fun intended. This is binomial language in the genetic code for a Blue Bell eater. It's programmed into us by God. We can't help it, really. Here's how it works. One Wednesday night I was in Dallas. I'd been there two days. When I got back from the library around 9:30 PM, my hostess told me she had been to the store and got my three favorite types of Bluebell: Homemade Vanilla, Cookies and Cream, and Pralines and Cream. I said, "But, Jimmie, I'm leaving in the morning . . . I can never eat all that tonight." She said, "Oh well, it will be there for you when you get back later in the summer." So, I went to my room with great intentions. But a person programmed with Blue Bell Bytes (not bits) can only resist so long. I believe the record (which I hold, of course) is forty-eight minutes. So, at midnight, I ate the Homemade Vanilla. At one o'clock the Cookies and Cream. Do I need to explain what happened at two in the morning?

At our house we have discovered the only way to overcome the Blue Bell lust: just not have any in the house. If it's in the house, it will be eaten. That's the way it is with lots of lusts. "Abstain" means to get away, keep a safe distance, don't go near it. What are these lusts? The text calls them **"fleshly"** lusts. The word for fleshly (*sarkikōn*) is used not just of the body, but also our sinful nature. Galatians 5:16ff speaks of the lust of "the flesh," which includes things like anger and jealousy, sins of the psyche, not sins of the body. To be controlled by our lusts is to experience death even though we live, like the young widow who chooses to live for pleasure instead of remarrying (1 Timothy 5:6). This is the death of Romans 7:24 and 8:6—the depression that comes from the agony of defeat, the discouragement of being a slave to our sinful nature: an addict.

Now Peter mentions **"war"** (*strateuontai*). It's the picture of two opposing armies. Our lusts are portrayed as a detachment of soldiers set out to destroy us. The word translated **"soul"** (*psychēs*) is the same one that is used in 1:9 and Matthew 16:25-26. This is not a reference to that which goes to heaven or hell when we die, but rather it refers to our lives, our time on earth (see 1:17 in reference to the "time" of our "sojourning" on this earth). Fleshly lusts can destroy our lives, cause them to be lost forever, to not count for eternity, to miss the very purpose for which we were created. You say, "How can this happen?" It usually comes from the development of a stronghold, or what we might call an addiction. There are lots of addictions that can destroy our lives. But how do they develop? A little at a time.

Bob had a hip replacement two years ago. It had totally collapsed to the point he could not walk. From a fall on the ski slopes or in the shower? No. He had osteonecrosis in his hip from drinking. Bob grew up in a Christian home but strayed from his faith in college. He married a girl that did not believe in any form of religion. Over time Bob began drinking to cope with the pain in his marriage. It only got worse when his older daughter chose a homosexual lifestyle. Because of his hip problem and the warning from the doctors that the same thing would happen to his other hip if he didn't stop his drinking, he abstained for a couple of years and lost a bunch of weight on a keto diet. But when his daughter announced her engagement to a lesbian and set a wedding date, Bob went back to drinking. If you ask him why, he will say because of the pain over his daughter. Now drinking has a firm stronghold in his life that actually has the potential to rob him of much of his life (his time on earth) either in actuality or quality. But it just began a little at a time.

Joe was a committed Christian and married a committed Christian. When interviewing for a job after college, he looked for one where he would not have to travel. He'd had a problem with pornography during high school and the old demons returned in earnest when he was alone, so he didn't want to travel. All went well for about ten years. Then as his responsibility with his company increased, they needed for him to travel. It all began in China. He went to a massage parlor. Once . . . twice . . . three times. Then they asked him if he would like the full treatment. You can imagine what that was. A couple of years later the stronghold in his life developed to the point that he would find girls in every city he traveled to through the internet. He didn't have to go to them. They came to him and were not prostitutes. One of them decided to be his travel companion. She actually went with him on business trips. Of course, she expected him to eventually leave his wife and children and marry her.

Finally, Joe's wife caught on. He repented, but when he tried to break the stronghold, he felt a demonic power pulling him back in. Truly it was a war for control of his life. Everything he had dreamed for his family and career was about to go up in smoke. One night his wife called me and asked me to come over to their home. Why? "Because someone or something is trying to kill Joe." I rushed over to their house even though they were not in my church. I heard him screaming on the second floor. I went up and found him writhing around on the floor. But his head was stationary as though someone was standing on his neck. Sensing he was demonically oppressed or possessed, I resisted the demonic forces in the name of Jesus, and they left during one blood-curdling scream from Joe. Then he passed out.

I went back the next day to check on Joe. I asked if he remembered anything from the night before. He said, "Yes, when you drove up, I heard them say, 'The preacher's coming.' Then I remember them yell as they left. And that's all I remember." That was ten years ago. I have tracked the family since, and Joe has remained victorious, primarily through support groups. He knows his enemy, and he knows how a stronghold develops: a little at a time.

Both these cases illustrate something the late M. Scott Peck called "ego boundaries."[54] He explains that we come into the world feeling pretty much at one with the universe. We have no sense of an ego boundary. With this oneness with the universe goes a sense of omnipotence. My three-year-old grandson asked me the other day (as he pranced around with in his Superman outfit) if I wanted to see his home. Of course, I did. He said, "It's Krypton, and it's very cold." He didn't come out of character for five minutes. As far as he was concerned, he was Superman.

However, as we approach the teen-age years our ego boundary begins to close. When it has fully formed, we have a sense of uniqueness—there never has been or ever will be someone exactly like us. That's good. We need this to become a mature adult. But with the awareness of our uniqueness comes a profound sense of loneliness. We long for the days when we felt one with the universe and less impotent. Peck says when we find someone we'd like to share our life with, our respective ego boundaries open up and we merge— something he calls *cathexis*. We call it falling in love. And with this merging of the ego boundaries comes a sense of omnipotence. It doesn't matter that I'm 75 and you're 25. Our love can overcome all obstacles; it can bust all barriers. Peck says the merging lasts about two years, on average. Then we *decathect*. He says that is a good thing because if we stayed in the *cathexis* state no one would pay the bills. *Cathexis* is cloud nine, the elixir of life, a most sought after drug. In Robin Norwood's book *Women Who Love Too Much*,[55] she says many people are just in love with love, meaning they are in love with the state of *cathexis*. When that wears off, they start searching for another partner with whom they can cathect and recapture that cloud nine feeling. It is very much like a drug, which brings me around to why I am discussing all this.

---

[54] Peck, *The Road*, 84-97.

[55] Robin Norwood, *Women Who Love Too Much* (New York: Pocket Books, 1985).

There are other things besides love that can open up our ego boundaries. Like drugs. When people drink, they often say their inhibitions are down. That is another way of saying their ego boundary has opened up. They will say things and do things they would never do in a sober state. Other types of drugs can do the same thing. Sexual orgasm can do it. Unfortunately, with our ego boundaries opened or down, we are open also to all sorts of influences that can build strongholds in our lives. That's what Joe ran into in China. During the "full treatment" his ego boundary opened up and demonic forces came in. We don't know all the spiritual damage that can happen with our ego boundaries opened. Paul speaks of the danger of becoming one with a harlot (1 Corinthians 6:15-20), arguing from the base that sexual intercourse is more than just a physical act. It can affect our spirits. In Malachi 2:14-16 the author warns about the danger of divorcing the wife of one's youth to marry the daughter of a foreign god. Twice he says, "Take heed to your spirit." The merging of the flesh can have a spiritual impact.

Well, we have gone from the relatively harmless (Blue Bell ice cream) to the utterly destructive (demonic oppression or possession) to illustrate the need to avoid bad conduct. But that's just half the story in these verses. We also need to adhere to good conduct.

II. ADHERE TO GOOD CONDUCT   2:12

> . . . having your conduct honorable among the Gentiles, that when they speak against you as evildoers, they may, by your good works which they observe, glorify God in the day of visitation.

This first word, "**having**," is from *echō*, which is the same as the word "abstain" in the Greek except "abstain" has a little preposition on the front: *apo* + *echō*. It is like the difference between *disassemble* and *assemble*. So, if "abstain" means to "keep your distance," then this word means the opposite: "get close." Other pictures are of *holding* something in your hand, *wearing* clothing, or to *possess* something as your own.

Peter describes the kind of conduct he wants us to have as **"honorable."** The word is *kalēn*, which usually means "good" in the observable sense: attractive (*BDAG*). This is what we are to wear, to hold, to possess: good (attractive, becoming) conduct. I saw an example of this word some years ago. A friend invited me to play in a fund-raising golf tournament for a good cause. Said he would pick me up and showed up in a beautiful Corvette. I had never ridden in a Corvette. When we got out on the road, he felt obliged to put this fine-tuned machine through some of its paces, weaving in and out of traffic as we cruised down the freeway.

So, when our round was over, and we approached his road machine, I calmly asked, "Mind if I drive? You owe me a couple of favors." "Are you kidding me?" he moaned. "With your track record?" (I had had a number of dirt bike and motorcycle wrecks with the broken bones to prove it, but never a car wreck). "Oh, OK, but be careful, and now we are even." I fired it up and went out on the road. Now, what I didn't realize was the power of the Corvette as a babe magnet. Although I was over sixty and driving about sixty in the right-hand lane of the freeway, these two young chicks pull up next to us in a truck. We are in a convertible. The young thing in the passenger's seat kisses me through the window. Of course, I play it cool, acknowledge her gesture with a nod, and speed off down the road.

Now that was an example of *kalēn*, in case you didn't get it. You see, in that car, *I looked good.* The word means externally attractive. (Don't worry; I knew it was the car that looked good, not me.) But God is saying this of our outwardly, observable conduct. It is supposed to be attractive, something that will draw bugs to the light. What about you? Does your conduct attract or repel?

Some of these Gentiles may have been detractors. Christianity was something new, and people are skeptical and love to criticize things that are new. But Peter says with good behavior it will be hard for would-be detractors to be critical. In fact, he is suggesting that the right kind of behavior may turn detractors into believers. Then they would become defenders of the faith and would bring glory to God when He comes back for judgment. In other words, he claims that our lives may have as big an impact as our lips.

My worship leader for almost twenty years was an unusual man whose pastoral heart was as big or bigger than his command of music and instruments and vocal arrangements. His musical team was his flock, and he was their pastor. He loved the Lord, as it should be, and he also loved people. Tray always had a winsome smile and a positive word of encouragement. One day a man that had been visiting our church for a while called me to invite me to play golf with him. He'd never done that before, so I assumed there was something on his mind. Both his teenage sons had recently trusted in Christ on our youth ski trip. They came back and told their parents about it, but it's not easy for parents to receive enlightenment from their own teenage boys. But they did start visiting our church.

After about six months of this I got the phone call from the father with the golf invitation. We got on about the third tee when Will began talking about our worship leader, Tray. Said he'd never met anyone quite like Tray. After a few more complimentary observations he said, "I want some of that." "Some of what?" I asked. He said, "Whatever he has. I want it." Will trusted Christ as his Savior right there on the golf course. That was over twenty years ago. He and his wife have served faithfully all these years, and one of his two sons went on to seminary and joined our church staff for a time.

What was it that moved Will and Linda to trust Christ? Was it one of my scintillating sermons? Was it *A Case for Christ* by Lee Strobel or *Evidence That Demands a Verdict* by Josh McDowell? None of the above. It was what they saw in Tray Morgan, a man who loved his Lord and genuinely cared about other people. That's what attracted Will to Christ.

I shared not long ago about Carmen Pate who suffers from Leukemia in the medical center here in Houston. She is another one who acts like a light in a dark place. She shares her journey with us daily via text. Here is one of her text daily texts, after being warned that she was wearing herself out with her daily exercise routine of walking the floors:

"Stay in your room and they will come!" Because of my high fever last night, and being in a neutropenic state, I was isolated to my room today. But what a glorious day it was! Starting with the morning PCA, who asked if I would pray for her regarding her continuing education. She wants to be an RN, because her dad was one. He had been her cheerleader to pursue her dream, and then he passed. She said she lost her drive and motivation after that, yet deep inside she knows that is her calling. We had a wonderful talk about purpose and calling and how your greatest joy comes when your passions and gifts fall in line with what you do! We prayed for her to have the courage to move forward, the wisdom to learn and retain, the motivation to study hard and let God deliver the results! Pray for "Jeanne."

My day nurse is the one that cared for me well during 2016. She became one of my "adopted spiritual daughters," and we have stayed in touch. It was such a blessing to pour into her life today and to hear of her own journey this past year. I believe God is working in her life and in her boyfriend's life, and I pray they will be sensitive to his leading. Pray for "Cathy."

I was pleasantly surprised to have a visit from a male nurse on the bone marrow transplant side of the wing, who took such good care of me there during my months in that unit. I called him my "silent angel" as he was not only quiet spoken, but a man of very few words. I would ask, "How can I pray for you today?" He would grin and say, "That my daughter would marry." He came into the room today and said, "My daughter is married." So now we are praying for grandchildren.

As evening approaches my fever is beginning to spike, and I am lying here packed in ice. I'm also dealing with infection today, so I am connected to IV antibiotics. But I'm peacefully resting in the fruit that God allowed me to bear today. I know I will rest well. Bless you for your continued prayers.

Does it surprise you to know that people find all sorts of reasons to drop by Carmen's room? And what great work is she doing for God? Just loving people and giving them a reason for hope—that's all.

This is talking about our lives matching our lips, walking the walk, no divorce between what we believe and how we behave. We can only be the light to the world if we shine brightly in contrast to the darkness around us. When our morality is just one step above the world's standard, they don't see much difference. We ponder about Lot and his daughters in Sodom and Gomorrah. They were virgins. They're his daughters. But rather than turn over his angelic visitors to the homosexuals, Lot offered them his daughters. We cry out, "Lot, say it isn't so. How could you possibly do that?" Answer? He pitched his tent near Sodom, so it says in Genesis 13:12. Every day when he walked out of the front of his tent, he looked down at the city of Sodom. As he kept his gaze on Sodom, it was only a matter of time until he gave up his nomadic life and moved into Sodom. He knew it was a wicked city, but he was attracted to its comforts and amenities. In time he illustrated a moral principle: the bar of self-righteousness is usually just one rung above our neighbors.

As the decades go by, most conservative Christians would agree that the standard of morality in western culture has declined in general. But so has that of the Christian culture. It seems to be like Lot, just one rung above the world. As the morality of the unbelieving world declines, so does the morality of the believing world. We justify our behavior through comparison: "At least we don't do what they do." With almost half of young people today living together or co-habiting outside of marriage, church people would seem legalistic, stuffy, and self-righteous if they were to suggest that the old-fashioned way might be better. One churchgoing mother, whose father was a preacher, after equipping her daughter with birth control while she was high school said to me, "Isn't it great that kids have so many more options today than we did when we were teenagers?" Would parents even think that way forty years ago?

So, if we are going to be lights to the world, there must be some way to distinguish our behavior from that of the world. But here is a word of caution. It is better to be a soft bulb than a searchlight. If someone is coming out of darkness, a light that is too bright will only turn them away. A soft answer turns away wrath, and advice is like snow: the softer it falls, the longer it stays. That's how it is with a soft bulb as well.

We can only be the salt of the earth when our lives and lips make people thirsty for Christ. There is a subtle hint in the "Beatitudes" as to what might make people thirsty for Christ. It's locked into the word *makarios*, which is translated "blessed" in Matthew 5:3-11, but just as easily could have been translated "happy." In fact, one preacher called the "Beatitudes" the Be-happy-tudes. Jesus' Sermon on the Mount is as attractive to unbelievers today as it was in His day. In fact, Mahatma Gandhi said this sermon alone was nearly enough to convert him to Christianity. It wasn't until he got to know Christians that he rejected Christianity. But he never rejected the Sermon on the Mount. It became the basis for his peaceful, nonaggression approach to fighting the Pakistanis. In the movie *Gandhi*, starring Ben Kingsley, I thought the climax of his Academy Award winning performance was when the Hindu man came to him and said that a Pakistani had killed his son. The Hindu man was seething with vengeance oozing from his mouth. He wanted Gandhi's advice. Gandhi said, "Go find a Pakistani boy whose father has been killed and adopt him. Raise him as your own son and raise him to be a Muslim." The man walked away in shock. Well, where did Gandhi get that kind teaching? It was from Jesus (aside from the religious part), of course, who, as far as I know, the first religious leader or philosopher to teach people to love their enemies and to do good to those who persecute them. In fact, in persecution Jesus said you can find your greatest joy (Matthew 5:12). Talk about a lightbulb. When the world looks at that, believe me, they are attracted.

When the world sees kindness for hurt, love in place of hatred, goodness for evil, they're looking at the supernatural. They will come, and they will follow. Martin Luther King, Jr. did the same thing. Others wanted violence. Who wouldn't? If White Supremacists had blown up my little girl while she was at church, I'd want violence too. But he insisted on peaceful protests. Now practically every city in America of any size has a street named after Martin Luther King. Why? Because King did the supernatural. He was a light in a dark place and his light was attractive. Everyone wants to be happy. If you told people you didn't want to be happy, they might suggest you check into the local nut house. So, when we can find happiness in the midst of poverty, joy in the midst of persecution and injustice, and contentment when surrounded by depravation—watch out; here they come.

CONCLUSION

Yes, we are caught in a war between two worlds, a war between the god of this world (the devil) and the God of the universe. Much of the conflict revolves around control for the lives of men. If the devil can wedge his way into our minds, emotions, and will (our psyche), then he can control our lives and keep them from counting for God's kingdom. They lose their significance. Don't let him win.

Now I want to say a word to those of you who have "messed up." Somewhere along the way you have done something you think disqualifies you from running the race. There are many passages that portray the Christian life as a race. Perhaps none is better than Hebrews 12:1—"Therefore we also, since we are surrounded by so great a cloud of witnesses, let us lay aside every weight, and the sin which so easily ensnares *us,* and let us run with endurance the race that is set before us." Philippians 3:12-16 also uses racetrack imagery: a goal line, a lane marker (*kanos*), and a prize.

Anyone who has run track knows if you fall in the middle of race, the race is over, at least for you. Some of us can remember the famous incident in 1984 between Zola Budd and Mary Decker. Each of them was a favorite to win a medal, but because Zola inadvertently tripped

Mary in the middle race neither one won a medal. All the more inspiring, then, to watch *Chariots of Fire* a film featuring a rivalry between Harold Abrahams, a Jew, and Eric Liddell, a Christian who died for his faith in a Japanese POW camp in 1945. Both won medals in the 1924 Olympics. When Abrahams first saw Eric Liddell run in person, it was a 400m race, once around the track. But at the quarter turn Liddell fell. Anyone else would've walked off the track, but Liddell got up and began running after the pack. He ran so fast he caught them. Then he lifted his eyes to the sky on the homestretch, and with his famous finishing arm pump he won the race. Reflecting on this with his trainer at a later date, Abrahams said of Liddell, "I've never seen such heart."

So, let me ask you, my friend. Which is harder: to run a race without falling, or to finish the race after you fallen? It's almost a rhetorical question isn't it? Obviously, it's harder to run after you fallen. But if you don't get up and get back in the race, guess who wins? Guess who tripped you? If you just lie there feeling sorry for yourself or withdraw completely from running, the only person who wins is our enemy, the devil.

Hebrews 12 is drawing an inference from what has preceded, and what has preceded is a long list of spiritual heroes, some of whom became martyrs for their faith. They all faced hardship of one sort or another, but none of them quit. So, the writer to the Hebrews calls upon them as our witnesses to urge us to run with endurance the race set before us. Yes, if we quit the race after we fallen, the only one who wins is the devil himself. Don't let him win.

11

"SUBMISSION IMPOSSIBLE?"
PART 1

1 Peter 2:13-17

INTRODUCTION

Never before in American history has there been more disrespect for human government. Corruption on the political front seems to be an assumption; sexual immorality of government leaders, an irrelevant issue. Presidents are the brunt of derisive, acerbic jokes on the lighter side and violent protests on the serious side. Washington is so infested by political insects that the skeptical public refers to our democratic system as a swamp.

Even our protectors like the FBI have been used as an excuse to bomb Federal buildings (Oklahoma City following the Waco disaster). Now (2019) with the exposure of James Comey and his sidekicks it looks like even those at the very top of the FBI ladder cannot be trusted.

What should be the response of a believer to a corrupt government, an overbearing or even unscrupulous employer, or a non-Christian husband? Answers to all these questions come in 1 Peter 2:13-3:6.

"SAVING THE SAVED"
1 Peter

I. EXHORTATION TO SUBMISSION   2:13-14

Therefore submit yourselves to every ordinance of man for the Lord's sake, whether to the king as supreme, 14 or to governors, as to those who are sent by him for the punishment of evildoers and for the praise of those who do good.

Since "**submission**" is the primary subject of this section of 1 Peter, it might be a good idea to understand the meaning of the word. I think we all have a pretty good idea: yield. Yes, but I think we can break the word down into its component parts without committing the root fallacy.[56] The word is made of two words: *hypo* + *tassō* =

---

[56] The root fallacy assumes that the root of a word, which might be five hundred years old, has the same meaning as the root originally did at the time of its use in whatever body of literature you might be studying. In other words, the meaning of words often change over time. See D. A. Carson, *Exegetical Fallacies* (Grand Rapids: Baker Books, 1996), 28-33. However, often breaking a compound word into its component parts helps us understand the word better without committing the root fallacy. I think that is the case with the word "submit."

under + to place = to place under. There is one more important element to the verb. It is a middle voice, which means the subject of the sentence is acting upon itself. In other words, "Place *yourselves* under." This is important to bring out the voluntary nature of the act or attitude.

Peter tells us to submit to "**every**" ordinance of man. Notice it does not say every other ordinance; it says every ordinance. We don't get to pick and choose. That gets difficult because we wonder sometimes if anyone was home when some of these ordinances get established. The word translated "**ordinance**" (*ktisei*) usually refers to *divine creation*; the implication may be that these human institutions have divine backing of some sort. "**For the Lord's sake**" suggests that the Lordship of Christ is directly linked in some way to these human institutions of authority.

Of course, when I see a word like "every," my mind starts looking for exceptions. Are there exceptions? Sure:

1. Life-taking. If the government orders me to kill deformed children or people over ninety, I should refuse. Why? After all, this is an ordinance from God's ordained authority, the government. God makes this issue clear with the case of the Egyptian mid-wives. The government ordered these mid-wives to kill newborn Jewish babies. They disobeyed the government and saved the lives of the children. We are told God blessed them for saving these lives.

2. Idolatry. Daniel's three friends, Shadrach, Meshach, and Abed-Nego were supposed to pay homage to the statue of Nebuchadnezzar. To them such homage would be an act of idolatry. They refused to obey the "government," and God protected them in the fiery furnace.

3. Religious Suppression. In Acts 4 Peter and John were ordered by the Sanhedrin (the government) to stop talking about Jesus. They responded, "Whether it is right

in the sight of God to listen to you more than to God, you judge. For we cannot but speak the things which we have seen and heard."

In a perfect world untainted by sin, principles like obeying the government and saving lives would never conflict. In a fallen world, at times they do.[57] The believer is under no obligation to sin in order to fulfill a governmental ordinance. In fact, the entire subject of submission to authority falls under what I call the "Triangle of Submission." It looks like this.

Triangle of Submission

THE LORD

Officers — Soldiers
Teachers — Students
Government — Citizens
Employer — Employees
Husband — Wife
Parents — Children

What this chart is trying to convey is that the ultimate authority is the Lord Himself. The solid black line means that any directive from a person of authority first goes up to the Lord and then comes down to the one that is to submit. The dotted lines show the person in authority and those over whom they have authority. But the line between the two is dotted to indicate that the directive does not go out immediately or directly to the one that is to submit. It goes to the

---

57 See Norman Geisler, *Christian Ethics* (Grand Rapids, MI: Baker Academic 1989), 113.

Lord first. The Lord acts as a filter. If the directive from an authority figure goes contrary to the clearly revealed desire of God (lifesaving, for example), then it is as though that directive never gets to the person who is supposed to obey. The Lord catches it in His filter, and the one under authority is exempt from any sin in the matter. We would say the Egyptian midwives did not sin when they saved the Jewish babies. They picked the highest of three absolutes (saving innocent lives over truth telling and obedience to the government) to obey and were exempt from sin by not telling the truth to the government or obeying the government.

All this comes back to our witness in the world, doesn't it? Does the world look at us like a bunch of rioting, rabble rousers? Doing good in the community is far more attractive to a skeptical world than some rebel group running around with sawed-off shotguns. Florence Nightingale has probably had a wider and more lasting impact on the world than most of the anarchists. She did it by peacefully going about establishing hospitals to help the physical suffering of men, women, and children across the globe. The text goes even further when it claims these kings and governors (would that point to federal and state law in our democracy?) are "**sent by him**"? These kings and governors are sent to praise some and punish others, to praise the good and punish the evil.

Just as capital punishment was instituted by God in Genesis 9 to restrain evil on the earth, so it is His primary human tool to restrain evil today, at least in some places. Although scholars argue the case for and against capital punishment as a deterrent for crime, most studies I read find a direct correlation between the use of capital punishment and crime. For example, a 2000 ban on executions that was placed into effect in Illinois is believed to have increased the homicide rates by at least 150 per year.[58] Conversely, the second safest country in the

---

[58] https://brandongaille.com/17-notable-capital-punishment-deterrence-statistics, accessed July 16, 2019.

world is Jordan (Greenland is the safest). They use capital punishment there, but they do it swiftly compared to America.

Well, if we have the Exhortation to Submission in vv. 13-14, then Peter gives us a brief Explanation of Submission in v. 15.

II. EXPLANATION OF SUBMISSION   2:15

For this is the will of God, that by doing good you may put to silence the ignorance of foolish men . . .

One of the accusations against this relatively new religion was that their followers were revolutionaries that wanted to overthrow the government. They did not want to call Nero "Lord." So, Peter tells them to disarm their attackers by doing the opposite of a takeover. Instead of trying to overthrow the government, Christians should set an example of model citizenship. That should look for opportunities to do good in their communities.

I admire one of the primary supporters of Grace School of Theology for his involvement in his community. He gives a lot of money to his alma mater, to his church, to our school, to other charities, but also to the local hospital and other community endeavors. He told me once that he thought Christians that have been blessed in a community should give back to that community. As such, he has a stellar reputation throughout the community. They can see he's not living a self-centered life, but an other-centered life.

When we "do good" in this way we "**put to silence**" the ignorance of foolish men. "Put to silence" is from *phimoun*, which means "to muzzle." When a cowboy muzzles his horse, he is putting something over its mouth to keep it from eating or causing a big fuss. Doing good shuts the mouths of critics. It can even be disarming. I remember as a boy I wanted to drive from Nashville where we lived up to Cincinnati to visit my grandmother. I left at about 11 that night, thinking the roads would be pretty empty and it would be a good time to drive. This is 1961 before they had freeways going through Kentucky from

Nashville to Cincinnati. So there was a series of small towns as I drove through the night in Kentucky. Small towns in the south all look pretty much the same. They all have a town square with the courthouse in the center. Around the perimeter of the town square are small shops. Sometimes the traffic around the square is in one direction.

Well, I came to one of these small towns at about three in the morning. I thought I was awake, but apparently, I wasn't. When I got to the town square, I turned the wrong direction. A policeman quickly stopped me. Being as it was three in the morning and I was just sixteen years old, he was pretty curious about what I was up to. I tried to explain that I was driving from Nashville to Cincinnati to see my grandmother. What's wrong with that? Well, he was still skeptical, but after verifying my license and that I wasn't driving a stolen car, he said, "OK, son, I want you to run around the town square going this direction (and he motioned with hand signals the preferred direction) and go out the other side." Showing the utmost respect and not wanting to spend the night in jail, I took off. I ran just as fast as I could around the town square. I don't know if I set a new state record for running around a town square in Kentucky or not, but this policeman was duly impressed. He was leaning on the hood of his cruiser laughing as hard as he could. I thought I had done pretty well, so I didn't have a clue as to what he was laughing about. He said, "Son, I meant for you to **drive** your car around the town square and go out the other side on your way to Cincinnati, not **run** around the town square on foot." Wow. And here I thought he was letting me off easy by having me take a little run instead of giving me a ticket. I bet he is still telling his grandchildren about that one. All I know is that my respectful behavior turned him from a hostile skeptic to a compassionate constable.

The Exhortation; the Explanation; what about the Execution?

III. EXECUTION OF SUBMISSION 2:16-17

. . . as free, yet not using liberty as a cloak for vice, but as bondservants of God. Honor all people. Love the brotherhood. Fear God. Honor the king.

We can always tell when the message of grace is being properly taught. How? Because there will be accusations of license. The obvious question is, "Are we are free in Christ to behave as we wish?" Why not go wild (Romans 5:21-6:1)? Paul wrote Romans 6 to answer this very question. Here Peter urges us to use our freedom as an opportunity to be *douloi*, slaves or servants of God. Again, Paul makes a similar argument in Galatians 5:13—don't use your freedom as an opportunity for the flesh, but to serve one another in love. In other words, with privilege goes responsibility.

Of course, here we have the key to all submission. We are not directly obeying the human institutions. No, we are directly obeying God, who in turn tells us to obey human institutions (see chart above). But submission involves more than just the right **actions**; it also involves the right **attitudes**. Notice how the submission of 2:18 and 3:1-2 both involve the right conduct with the right attitude (*phobō*—reverential respect).

The word **"honor"** is *timē*. The verb form of this noun is used here, the same word we had in 2:4-10 when it kept telling us that those stones that get near the Cornerstone become valuable and precious just like Him. *Timaō*, the verb, means "to honor, to esteem highly, to cherish." In our American culture that would mean to honor and esteem highly our President. I was born about the time Truman took over and didn't pay much attention to Presidents until John F. Kennedy. I suppose there were jokes about the President in those days because there is always political satire by TV comedians, but I really don't remember a lot of jokes about the Presidents from Kennedy through George Herbert Bush. But from Bill Clinton on, it seems our national respect for the Presidents has gotten lower and lower. Now with Trump in office it is downright hostile, and the press seems to treat everything he does as a joke or a serious threat to our national security. I wonder what Peter would say to America if he were given a TV slot. There is no question that the Roman emperors during his life were on average much more flawed and immoral than our leaders today. Yet, Peter tells these Christians to honor the king. Do you think he would say less to us about our elected leaders? This is a bipartisan comment. I've heard about as much disrespect for Clinton and Obama as I have heard for Bush and Trump. How do you interpret this directive: honor the king?

CONCLUSION

Since I have usually been the head of whatever organization I am working for (church or seminary), there haven't been a lot of opportunities to demonstrate submission to an authority figure (an individual as distinguished from a board; I have always had boards to submit to). So, one way my wife and I do this is in our relationship with policemen. We live in a time when they appear to be under siege and suffer a lot of disrespect. Sometimes when we see them at our local cafeteria, my wife will go up to them and thank them for their service to or community. And I have found that when I show them respect, they reciprocate.

How can I ever forget one Saturday morning when I was up at my office and a new disciple called to see if I could meet with him to answer a few questions. He was at work about fifteen miles away. I agreed to meet him them in an hour. Since I was the only one at the office, I had worn gym shorts and was riding my motorcycle. I didn't have any pockets in these shorts, so when it came time to leave, I just stuck my study Bible down the front of my shorts, got on my motorcycle and took off.

About halfway along the route a policeman stopped me. "You're going 45 in a 35 zone." Actually, he was wrong. I was in a 35 zone that had changed to 45, but this wasn't the time to point out his error. "Can I see your driver's license and proof of insurance." I couldn't provide them since I had left my wallet in my car back home. "It looks like the registration on your license plate has expired along with your inspection sticker." Guilty. "Do you have any way to prove who you are?" I said I was a local pastor and tried to prove it by pulling out my Bible with my name on it. That wasn't satisfactory. So, I said, "If you'll let me use your phone, I call my wife."

So, I called Betty. I said, "Could you please go out to the car and get my license and insurance info from my wallet." Why? "It doesn't matter. Please just get them." Why? "OK, this nice policeman has stopped me for speeding and needs this info." Oh, OK. So, she got the info. I said, "Officer, I want to thank you for stopping me. I haven't had a ticket in years, and this will be a good reminder." He looked up my info and said, "You really haven't had a ticket in years, have you?" "No, sir, but I want to thank you for doing your job. This will be a great reminder."

All this time the policeman had his head down as he was writing. "So, you think this will be a good reminder?" Oh, yes, sir. "Well," he said, "Here are five good reminders for you: speeding, no license, no proof of insurance, expired license plate, and expired inspection sticker." I gulped, but he said, "The reminders are all warnings; no tickets." "Wow," I said, "what an example of grace. I am going to include this in my sermon tomorrow morning as a great example of God's grace, an undeserved favor. I deserve five tickets, but you gave me five warnings." He said, "Are you really a pastor?" I told him it was true and invited him to church the next day to hear how I was going to use this gracious event in my life to illustrate God and his grace toward men.

I thanked him again and went to my motorcycle. Unfortunately, I had left the key on, and the engine wouldn't turn over for lack of juice. So, I went back to him, told him the problem, and asked where he was going. I wanted to hitch a ride to my appointment. He said, "I can't let you ride in here. Have you ever push-started that bike?" No. "Well, let's try." Now this guy was a well-built black man who looked like he was a running back in the NFL. He actually pulled his patrol car across a busy street, got behind my bike with me on it, and began pushing with all he had. When he let go, the engine just sputtered. I looked down and saw that after turning the key off, now I had forgotten to turn it on as he was pushing. I looked at him huffing and puffing and said, "Almost." I didn't have the heart to tell him I had forgotten to turn the key on. He looked at me and said, "OK, one more time, but that's it." This time the engine kicked off, I waved my thanks and went down the road.

What a guy. But I am convinced if I had argued with him about the speed zone and even proved I was right, he would have just said I could protest in court, but here are five tickets. Though this may be a rather bizarre example, I really believe the Lord blesses us when we show respect to those in authority over us and rewards us accordingly, if not in this life then in the next.

12

"SUBMISSION IMPOSSIBLE?"
PART 2

1 Peter 2:18-25

INTRODUCTION

It was a pivotal point in my life, although I didn't know it at the time. I was going to graduate school in Dallas with a wife and two children. I supported our family by working as a doorman at the Fairmont Hotel in Dallas, which, at the time, was the nicest hotel in Texas. By working just four nights a week I earned within $3000 of the same salary Roger Staubach earned that year in 1971: $24,000. You can do the math. That means Roger only made $27,000 that year, the same year they won the Super Bowl over the Miami Dolphins. Can we say that salaries of star athletes have changed somewhat over the years? Anyway, my biggest night of the year was New Year's Eve. I usually got three times as much in tips on New Year's Eve compared to other nights. The wealthy elite would come to the hotel and wanted me to hold their fancy cars for them up front. Of course, I was well rewarded for doing so.

But as I walked in the lobby with my tales and top hat on, the concierge informed me that I wouldn't be working out front this New Year's Eve. Of course, I wanted to know where I would be working. He said I would work in the parking garage just opening doors, earning $2/hr instead of getting $400 in tips out front. I wanted to know who was going to work out front. He said we only had three doormen, and I was only one who was white. He thought it would look funny to have a white doorman and a black doorman working at same time. So, he wanted the two black doormen working out front while I worked down below. Of course, I knew down below I wouldn't get any tips. So, it was going to be a big blow to our income that week. I also thought it was discrimination. Here was an opportunity that was rightfully mine since my shift was the night shift, but because of the color my skin I got bumped.

My shift began at 4 PM. I was down below in the parking garage with nothing for me to do since the parties didn't begin until eight o'clock or so. So, I just sat around and stewed over this unfair situation. The place where I was standing was only about twenty steps from the hotel manager's office. He liked me, and I knew if I went in and complained, he would override the concierge and reinstate me back up front. I prayed about what to do. If I went to the hotel manager, I would be going around the concierge, my direct boss. What to do? I was strongly tempted to see the hotel manager. He was a new Christian and specifically hired me as a seminary student knowing I would not run prostitutes through the hotel during the night shift. The former doorman who had my shift was also a pimp for six girls he ran through the hotel.   And then it hit me. I had been memorizing the very passage we are going to start covering in this lesson: 1 Peter 2:18-25. Specifically, it's about submitting to the authority above you when you're not being treated fairly. And it gives you motivation to do so. As I reflected on that, all of a sudden it transformed my entire attitude toward what was going to happen that night. How so? Let's take a look.

We're in a section on Personal Submission. Peter is giving us three primary ways we can make our lives count for eternity. The first primary way is through Personal Sanctification or our Character;

the second way is going to be through Personal Submission or our Conduct. We saw our Conduct in the World in 2:13-17; now we want to look at our Conduct in our Jobs in 2:18-25. I say our jobs, but in reality, this message is addressed to slaves about their submission to their masters. It's important for us to remember that historians estimate that fifty percent of Rome was made up of slaves, while the other fifty percent were citizens. So, slavery is not an American invention. It's been around a long, long time. Of course, antiquity of practice does not make the practice right. And wherever there is slavery, there's bound to be abuse, cruelty, and unfairness. So, Peter is trying to tell these household slaves how they can actually make their lives count for eternity by having the right actions and also the right attitudes in their submission to their masters. We don't have slavery in the Western world anymore, praise God. But the same principles can be applied to anyone that is an authority over us.

By way of interpretation, this passage is talking about household slaves and their masters. But by way of application, we will use it to describe the proper relationship between employers and employees. In Bible study we like to say there's one interpretation and many applications. In other words, there's only one thing the Holy Spirit had in mind when He gave us a portion of Scripture, but once we understand that correct interpretation, we may have many different applications for the principle(s) that are valid. We will apply the principles of this passage primarily to the relationship between employers and employees. In this passage there's an Exhortation to Submit (18), an Explanation of Submission (19-20) and an Example of Submission (21-25).

"SAVING THE SAVED"
1 Peter

Let's start off by looking at the Exhortation to Submission in 2:18. In this exhortation we want to look at the Attitude of Submission (18a) and the Extent of Submission (18b-c).

I. EXHORTATION TO SUBMISSION   18

A. Attitude of Submission   18a

Servants, be submissive to your masters with all fear . . .

We mentioned that as much as fifty percent of Rome was made up of slaves, but Peter is writing to believers in Turkey. Well, Turkey was still part of the Roman Empire, and slavery was part and parcel of that empire. We don't have any estimates on the percentage of people living in Turkey that were slaves, but it must've been a prevalent practice or Peter would not have addressed this segment of society.

This text makes it clear that our attitude coupled with our action gives the correct picture of biblical submission. The little girl that told her parents she was sitting down on the outside but standing up on the inside exemplifies the right action with the wrong attitude. This text says we are to be submissive **"with all fear."** That word **"fear"** (*phobos*), when used of our attitude toward God, is usually explained as "reverential respect," not cowering fear. Of course, that would be man to God. Here we are talking about human to human, so the reverential part would not apply. Perhaps "compliant respect" gets the idea across. In any case, we are talking about an internal attitude. Again, we can be compliant on the outside and defiant on the inside. Obedience with defiance does not qualify as true, biblical submission.

But, again, we have to ask ourselves what's the big deal? In light of the metanarrative we described earlier, it should be apparent that when we submit to God-ordained authorities, we are submitting to God Himself. In so doing, we are answering one of the great questions of the universe: who has the right to rule? Is it God or Satan? My first-born son, Jimmy, was always a good kid. He was a pretty good football player, but his football buddies influenced him to become somewhat rebellious at age 15. This went on for about a year—nothing on a behavioral level, but definitely on an attitude level.

I had been discipling Jimmy and his younger sister for several years. During their junior high years, I took them through the Navigator series "Design for Discipleship." Then we got into some inductive Bible study. But during his sophomore year I noticed this somewhat defiant attitude in Jimmy. So, I decided to use these inductive skills to study the question of authority and submission in the Bible. I can remember the day Jimmy got it. His eyes got as big as saucers as he realized his life could be saved or lost based on his attitude toward those in authority around him—teachers, coaches, the police, yay verily, even parents. Suddenly, when I asked him to take out the trash, he would jump up and say, "Yes, sir!" Then he would run to the trashcan and take out the trash. He was never the same. He got it. Have you?

Of course, I've tried to practice what I preach, and some of my best opportunities have come with policemen. I remember driving back from the lake one evening after a day of boating with the kids. A policeman stopped me for going 65 in a 55 mile an hour zone. As I handed him my license and insurance, I said, "Officer, I want to thank you for stopping me. I haven't had a ticket for many years, and this is a good reminder for me. I appreciate you guys and the job you're doing to keep us safe." He went back to his cruiser to check out my license and car registration. When he came back, he said, "Well, you really haven't had a ticket for a long time, have you?" No sir. "Well, my dispensing of tickets is attitude dependent, and you have such a good attitude I'm just going to give you a warning. Let's slow it down. A lot of people come back from a weekend at the lake with a belly full of beer, so be careful." Apparently, our policemen are not always greeted with a respectful attitude.

But this leads to an obvious question or objection. In 2019 more than at any time in my life there is a backlash against police. Just up the road from us four policemen were killed in Dallas in retaliation for the perceived abuses of black people by the police. So, what if I believe the authority over me is abusive? Do I have to play doormat to an abusive husband, boss, coach, policeman? Let's try to answer this question with the rest of 1 Peter 2:18.

B. EXTENT OF SUBMISSION   18bc

. . . not only to the good and gentle, but also to the harsh.

This verse goes directly to the question of unfair situations. We are supposed to submit to the **"good"** (*agathos*) person. The word good here refers to their intrinsic character. It's what we mean when we say, "He's *good* people." The next word translated **"gentle"** (*epiēikes*) refers to someone who doesn't press his rights. It is used of God in the Old Testament where He was within His rights to wipe out Israel because they had broken the law, but at times He would choose not to press His rights. The Septuagint (the Greek translation of the Hebrew OT) uses this word to describe God in that situation. So, this kind of employer is in a position of authority, but he is kind and chooses not to throw his weight around.

The passage assumes there is no problem with submitting to this kind of person. The problem comes with the next guy, the man who is **"harsh."** This word is the translation of *skolios,* the word from which we get "scoliosis," or curvature of the spine. "Harsh" or "unkind" would be a benign way to translate this word; "crooked" might be more in keeping with a literal understanding of the word. You might even go so far has to say "unscrupulous." Now that puts a whole new wrinkle on things. It's one thing to submit to an authority figure that is unfair or treats people harshly. It's a whole different thing to be expected to submit to someone who is unscrupulous. *BDAG* suggests: "crooked, unscrupulous, dishonest, harsh, or unjust."

So, what about it, do we have to submit to a corrupt government official or employer? Perhaps this chart can help:

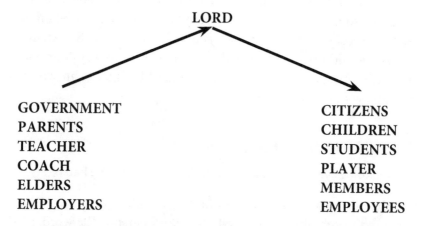

LORD

GOVERNMENT	CITIZENS
PARENTS	CHILDREN
TEACHER	STUDENTS
COACH	PLAYER
ELDERS	MEMBERS
EMPLOYERS	EMPLOYEES

Principle: whenever the one in authority asks you to go against God's clearly revealed will, don't do it.

There are some clear Biblical examples we mentioned earlier (see p. 149): idolatry and murder of innocent children. If we know that it is clearly God's revealed will that an authority figure is violating, then the Lord Himself acts like a filter to keep the commandment from ever reaching us. In other words, every directive from an authority figure goes up to heaven first and then down to us. It doesn't go directly from the authority figure to the person under submission. God acts as a filter. If He has revealed something that contradicts the directive from the authority figure, then that directive is cast out.

However, if we refuse to do something an authority figure commands, we better be very sure that we have something clearly revealed from God that goes against what we are being asked to do. So, if my employer asks me to do something dishonest in business, I simply refuse. Of course, that would probably cost me my job. But that is where faith kicks in. Though I may not see where the next job is coming from, I still don't compromise my integrity just to keep my job. So, if I'm asked to lie, to steal, to falsify records (bear false witness), to take clients out to strip joints or worse, I am under no obligation to be submissive. But this passage would tell us to be respectful and submissive in situations where we are treated, at least in our eyes, unfairly:

- Janice is newer on-the-job than I am, and she got a raise; I didn't. That's unfair. I'm starting to resent my boss.

- My husband goes out to play golf every Saturday morning with his buddies while I'm stuck here at home with three kids and the weekend chores. I work outside home five days a week just like he does. It's not fair to leave me alone with all this. And then guess what he wants to do on Saturday night, and he wonders why I'm not submissive?

- I had tickets to the Masters. It is the only time in my life I've actually gotten tickets to the Masters. I planned the trip with three buddies months in advance. But then I got a new boss who clearly doesn't like me. He knew what my plans were for the Masters. So, he decides to send me on an out-of-town trip for the company to California during Masters week. I asked him twice if we could rearrange the business trip. The answer was no. I think I hate the guy. I really think he is trying to get me to quit.

In looking at the Exhortation to Submission we have seen both the correct attitude in submission and just how far we have to go, meaning, do we have to submit to authority figures that are asking us to do something directly contradictory to God's clearly revealed will? Now we want to turn to an explanation for this kind of submission. What's the motivation and is there some clarification?

II. EXPLANATION OF SUBMISSION 19-20

A. The Motivation 19

> For this is commendable, if because of conscience toward God one endures grief, suffering wrongfully.

Notice the daisy-chain of logic signified by three uses of the word **"for"** (*gar*) beginning v. 19, v. 20, and v. 21. This helps us trace the author's chain of thought. Each verse beginning with "for" is giving us a reason or an explanation for what he said in the previous verse. So, "why" should we respectfully submit to an authority figure over us even if he is *skolios* (harsh or even unscrupulous)? Why? Because (*gar*) of what Peter says in. v. 19. Peter says this kind of submission is **"commendable."**

It might surprise you to realize that this word translated "commendable" is the word *charis*, which is usually translated "grace," an undeserved favor. But that doesn't make sense in this context, so some translate it "commendable" (NKJ, NIV); others translate it "favor" (NASB–find favor). Here it is being used as Jesus does in Luke 6:31-36. It means "reward" (see *BDAG* 877:2b). Many think this is the meaning of *charis* in 1:13 as well, where we wait for the *charis* being brought to us at the revelation of Jesus Christ, an obvious reference to everything he referred to in his introduction (1:3-12) regarding the future inheritance to be revealed at the Judgment Seat of Christ, a reward that will measure how much of our life will count forever (be saved).

But there are two qualifications for getting this reward:

1. ***Awareness of God's presence.*** The NKJV and the NASB make this sound like our "conscience" is motivating us. Here the NIV has it right: it is because we are "conscious of God." It's like the angels in 1:12—they're watching the human conflict, and obviously, so is God. But, again, our understanding of God here is important. I remember reading the parenting book years ago that encouraged us to outnumber our criticisms of our children by compliments on a 10 to 1 ratio. In order to do that, the author suggested switching our focus from catching them doing something wrong to catching them doing something right. Every time we caught them doing something right we would verbally compliment them or even set up a system of rewards, depending on the particular behavior we were trying to develop.

   Well, our heavenly father is like that. He is a good parent. He's a loving parent. He isn't just looking over our shoulder all the time trying to catch us doing something wrong so He can scold us or beat us. Quite the opposite, He may be looking over our shoulder, but He's looking for something we're doing right so He can encourage us and reward us. I once had a teacher in sixth grade who was a negative motivator. She was always walking around room trying to catch someone doing something wrong. We did what she asked us to do, usually, but it was always out of fear. If we didn't behave, we were sent to the principal's office. The next year was quite the opposite.

   My seventh-grade teacher, Mr. Allen, also had a part-time job as an official timer at the local university's track meets. He liked to reward his students by allowing them to be backups for him when he timed races. This is in the day before electronic timers. So, if I got 100 on the test, he would let me come to the track as a backup for his timing of races. One of my young thrills was timing the great Glenn Davis of Ohio State University when he set the world record the 440-yard dash, a record that held up for over 30 years. Needless to say, I loved to perform for Mr. Allen, and I didn't do it out of fear. I did it because I wanted him to be proud of me and to enjoy my feeling like I had an important role to play at an official collegiate track meet.

2. **Undeserved suffering.** The NASB and the NIV have "unjust suffering." The Greek word is *adikōs*—unfair. That's it, folks. The situation is *unfair*; it's not right. The next verse clarifies what he means by "unfair."

B. The Clarification   20

For what credit is it if, when you are beaten for your faults, you take it patiently? But when you do good and suffer, if you take it patiently, this is commendable before God.

"**For**" explains what he means by unjust suffering. The word "*kleos*" is really key. It occurs only once in the NT—right here. In 1 Clement (our earliest non-canonical Christian document written from the church at Rome to the church at Corinth around AD 97) it is used in connection with the verb for "possession" (*peripoieō*), a word used in the LXX interchangeably with the word for "inherit." The Jews were to "possess" the land; it was their inheritance. Thus, inheritance, as we saw in 1:4 is our reward (see Colossians 3:24), how much of our life we have possessed (see Hebrews 10:39 for the word "possession" in connection with our "life"). And so, "**credit**" is not a bad translation here for *kleos*. We get the picture of an account in heaven. When we are respectfully submissive in an unfair situation, we get a "credit" in our heavenly account (see Philippians 4:17 where the word *logos* is used for our account in heaven).

In his clarification Peter wants us to understand when we do not get a credit and when we do. We do not get a credit when we suffer because of our sins. The NASB has it right here: "when you sin." The NIV ("doing wrong") and the NKJV ("for your faults") just don't get it because they are not strong enough. This isn't talking about our petty faults or peccadillos. It is talking about our sins. The NASB has it exactly right because the word *hamartanontes* speaks very definitely of sin, for it comes from the verb "to sin."

We speak of suffering in two categories as we pointed out in the beginning of this work: deserved and undeserved. Our deserved suffering is because of our sins or our foolishness. When an inexperienced motorcycle rider tries to take a turn with an inverse camber and a decreasing radius too fast, he will probably fall. We would call that foolishness, not sin. But when someone robs a bank and gets caught and sent to prison, we don't call that foolishness; we call that sin. There is suffering in both examples, but one is the result of foolishness while the other is the result of sin.

Now we don't have any problem with suffering for sin; it is deserved. Our problem is, of course, just as in this passage, suffering when we have not sinned or been foolish. In other words, undeserved suffering. That's when Peter says we get a credit in our heavenly account. "**Take it patiently**" comes from *hypo* (under) + *meneite* (remain) = "to remain under" the circumstances that are unfair (don't worry, we are not going to condone abuse, which we will discuss later). When we respectfully obey an unfair boss, we get a credit in our heavenly account. The word for "commendable" is the same as in v. 19 and 1:13—*charis*, the word we normally translate "grace." The word actually lends a nuance to the idea of rewards in that even they are grace-based. We can't turn rewards into another form of legalism. The essence of legalism is to put God in our debt. It would be to tell Him He owes us because of our good behavior. That's legalism. The parable of the vineyard (Matthew 20) teaches that even rewards are matter of God's marvelous grace.

Do you see how Peter begs for us to turn our focus into the unseen realm? When we do that, we have an awareness of the angels watching us and God watching us. As in Moses' case (Hebrews 11:27) the unseen realm can become more vivid and real than our thinking in the realm of the physical world of four dimensions. In this very passage it is our awareness of God and the spiritual dimension that shapes our behavior in the very world we can see and touch. With this in mind, we become willing to forfeit something in this seen world in order to leave an imprint on the unseen world. When we suffer undeservedly at the hands of unjust men, the world may scream for rebellion or retribution or disrespect. No, says Peter. Our concern is not to be rewarded by men, but to be rewarded by God. Peter says when we do good and suffer for it, it is commendable with God, commendable in the unseen realm.

With this passage in mind my unjust, unfair situation on New Year's Eve at the Fairmont Hotel in 1971 flipped upside down. All of a sudden, I could visualize the $400 I might make that night being spent for rent, electricity, and groceries within a month. But this was a life-changing opportunity. If I responded with the correct attitude in this unfair situation, there would be a credit in heaven that might show up some day at the Judgment Seat of Christ as a small jewel in one of the crowns I would cast at Jesus' feet. The sparkle from my little jewel might bring glory to Him forever ever and ever and ever. Do you get the point? Who in his right mind would trade time for eternity? Can we compare temporal loss with eternal gain?

The guests started piling in around eight o'clock. There was nothing for me to do but to stand there and look fancy with my tails and top hat and open the passenger doors. I purposed to have a cheerful attitude and wish everyone a Happy New Year with a smile. I worked steadily from eight o'clock until one in the morning and didn't receive a single tip–except in heaven, I trust. It was one of the greatest nights of my life.

Thus, Peter exhorts us to make our lives count through Personal Submission; then he explains why; finally, he gives us an example.

III. EXAMPLE OF SUBMISSION   21-25

For to this you were called, because Christ also suffered for us, leaving us an example, that you should follow His steps:

22"Who committed no sin,
    Nor was deceit found in His mouth";

23 who, when He was reviled, did not revile in return; when He suffered, He did not threaten, but committed Himself to Him who judges righteously; 24 who Himself bore our sins in His own body on the tree, that we, having died to sins, might live for righteousness—by whose stripes you were healed. 25 For you were like sheep going astray, but have now returned to the Shepherd and Overseer of your souls.

We will look at these verses in greater detail in our next lesson but let us begin by noticing the **"for"** (*gar*) that kickstarts the example. This tells us that Peter is using this example as one more reason or motivation for us to submit in the face of unfair circumstances. Why? **"For to this you were called."**

I can never forget the middle-aged executive describing what it was like to be married to an alcoholic. "When I married, she was a respectable, attractive, demure Christian lady, but twenty years later alcohol has turned her into a shrew." He described business gatherings where she would get drunk and begin cussing at him loudly in front of a speechless group of witnesses. He would have to take her home, forcibly. And then some nights he would come home and find her passed out on the kitchen floor, besotted with her favorite brand of bourbon. She hid bottles all around the house. She made sure that she always had access to her drug of choice.

"Pastor, I do have the biblical right to divorce her, don't I?" I had Bob turn to this very passage. "Can we agree that you have not yet died on cross?" I asked. "I certainly don't want to minimize your suffering in anyway. But still, it is not a crucifixion." But that is the unjust situation God choses to use as His example. And the text actually says we have been "called" to some of these unjust situations. That's pretty hard to swallow. It helps to keep three things in mind:

CONCLUSION

1. The Judgment Seat of Christ (1 Corinthians 3, 2 Corinthians 5, Romans 14) is the great equalizer.

Does it make sense to you that a loving God would call His children to undeserved suffering and not have somewhere to equalize the injustices of this world? Though human works or merit can never win our acceptance into heaven, it is very clear that the good works of a child can bring glory to our Father in heaven. I'm not talking about good works done by human strength or works done to put God in our debt. I'm talking about the righteous, holy life lived by one who wants to glorify the Father because of his love for Him. For such children as these to be placed in and even called to unfair life situations implies that God will do something somewhere to recognize that faithful service for Him, even though it involved undeserved suffering. That place is the Judgment Seat of Christ.

In fact, if we understand Romans 8:18-19 correctly, the Judgment Seat of Christ is not even an equalizer; it's an un-equalizer. It says the sufferings of this world are **not worthy to be compared** to the glory that will be revealed in the sons of God. No, the glory will not equal the suffering. The glory in that future age for those who suffer unjustly will be greater by a factor of X, and we don't know what X is. We just know that when we see it, we will declare God's name to our brethren and will praise Him in the assembly (Psalm 22:22).

I remember another couple struggling with an incredibly unfair situation. I asked them to humor me for a moment as we went through this passage. Then I said, "Suppose Bill Gates offered to give you $1 billion if you patiently endure your situation for one more year. Would you do it?" The couple agreed that not only could they do it, but they could become almost giddy doing so. That's what God offers at the Judgment Seat of Christ, only it's better than a billion dollars.

2. God paints a picture about undeserved suffering as a great privilege in the Bible.

In Philippians 1:29 we find the word for "grace" turned into a verb: "For to you it **has been granted** on behalf of Christ, not only to believe in Him, but also to suffer for His sake." Do you see what that is saying? If we understand grace to be an unmerited favor from God, then this is telling us that God has granted us the favor of not only believing in Christ for eternal life but also the privilege of suffering for Him. You know, the only way to lock into that promise is from a heavenly perspective. Philippians is one of those prison epistles written in the 60s when Nero was persecuting and crucifying Christians. Paul himself was sitting in jail. And he found joy in jail. The only way he could do that was to believe that undeserved suffering is more than just a calling; it is also privilege.

If you've seen Steven Spielberg's movie *Jurassic Park*, you might remember the scene when the park project manager, Hammond, asks one of his park employees, Muldoon, to go fetch his grandchildren, who are stuck in the park where a power failure has exposed them to some of the dinosaurs, like TRex. You can see Muldoon wasn't too happy about the request. You see, both Hammond and Muldoon were mercenaries. What they were doing was for money. Neither wanted to risk his life for the success of the project.

What a contrast was Spartacus, the Roman gladiator and slave that led an army of slaves in a rebellion against Roman in 71 BC. Twice they bested Rome but were finally conquered by Marcus Crassus after a long siege and battle. There were a thousand slave/soldiers left. Crassus called out: "You have been slaves. You will be slaves again. But you will be spared your rightful punishment of crucifixion by the mercy of the Roman legions. All you need to do is turn over to me the slave Spartacus, because we do not know him by sight."

Nobody stirred. Then Spartacus stood up and said, "I am

Spartacus." But immediately the man to his left stood and said, "No, I am Spartacus." Then the next man: "I am Spartacus." Within seconds everyone in the rebel army stood and claimed to be Spartacus. According to Peter Singe,[59] it does not matter if this story is apocryphal or not. It illustrates the principle of a shared vision. By standing up, each of these men chose death. Their loyalty was not to the man Spartacus; no, it was to their shared vision of freedom that Spartacus inspired in them. It was so compelling they would rather die than go back to their lives of slavery.

Jesus inspired a shared vision of spiritual freedom. His army of former slaves to the flesh have volunteered to fight for that freedom in His army. They saw it as a privilege to fight for this cause and vision.

3. It takes faith for this approach to life to work, and one of the keys to a strong faith is a vivid imagination.

Years ago, John Lennon wrote a song which became one of his most popular. It's lyrics go like this:

Imagine there's no heaven
It's easy if you try
No hell below us
Above us only sky

Imagine all the people
Living for today

Imagine there's no countries
It isn't hard to do
No greed or hunger
And no religion too

---

[59] Peter M. Singe, *The Fifth Discipline* (New York: Doubleday, 1990), 205-06.

Imagine all the people
Living life in peace

You may say I'm a dreamer
But I'm not the only one
I hope someday you'll join us
And the world will live as one.

Imagine no possessions
I wonder if you can
Nothing to kill or die for
A brotherhood of man

Imagine all the people
Sharing all the world

You may say I'm a dreamer
But I'm not the only one
I hope someday you'll join us
And all the world will live as one.

Though I appreciate the sentiment behind the desire for a brotherhood of man and a world of peace, I can't agree with the theology the late Beatle thought would get us there. So, I'm taking the liberty of rewriting this song to better reflect the kind of theology that can achieve that brotherhood of man.

IMAGINE

Imagine you're in heaven
It's easy if you try
There is a hell below us
The very day you die

Imagine all God's people
Loving every day

SAVING THE SAVED

Imagine no more countries
It isn't hard to do
No greed or hunger
And no more crying too

Imagine all God's people
Living life in peace

You may say I'm a dreamer
But I'm not the only one
I hope someday you'll join us
When believers will all be one.

Imagine no possessions
I wonder if you can
Nothing to kill or die for
A brotherhood of man

Imagine all God's people
Sharing all the world

You may say I'm a dreamer
But I'm not the only one
I hope someday you'll join us
When believers will all be one.
Just imagine.

13

"ERRORS OF SUBMISSION"
1 Peter 3:1-6

INTRODUCTION

An attractive woman of about forty came in my office with a friend to talk about some marriage difficulties. I noticed as she came in, she was shaking slightly. When I asked if she was okay, she said she was afraid of men and that's why she was shaking and needed to bring a friend with her. I must confess it was a bit discomforting to find out someone was so afraid of men. She was shaking when she came to visit her own pastor. But she was there, so we got into it. "What's the problem?"

"Well," she began, "I resent my husband so much, I don't think I can be a Proverbs 31 wife. I know that's what I'm supposed to be, but I just can't do it." Well, tell me a little more. "You see, I'm afraid of my husband." Does he beat you? "No, but he spits beer on me." Excuse me? "When we go out to dinner, he spits beer on me." He spits beer on you? "Yes." How long has it been going on? "Eighteen years. It really began in our first year of marriage." Why do you let him do that? "Well, what am I supposed to do? It says in 1 Peter 3 I'm to win my ungodly husband without a word. So, when he starts spitting,

I just clam up. But, after 18 years of this, he hasn't changed. It's causing me to doubt God's Word, and I'm afraid to let my husband touch me."

This dear lady is conflicted by what I would call an "error of submission." There are a number of them floating around the Christian world, all of which discredit the biblical meaning of submission. We want to expose some of them in this study. Here is just a partial list of some of the things I hear from good, well-meaning Christian women:

1. My husband cheats on our income tax. But every year he shoves that return under my nose and tells me to sign it. Like Sarah of old I am submitting to my husband and trusting in God to protect me supernaturally even though I know I'm breaking the law.

2. My husband dislikes himself so much that he tears all the rest of us down. He constantly berates me in front of the kids. When he's really mad, he has a cussing fit and calls me every name the book. I just want to scream and run away, but 1 Peter 3 tells me to silently submit, doesn't it?

3. I'm so sick of hearing you male chauvinists bark about submission. You use it like a club. I know I'm supposed to submit. But not to a tyrant. Ephesians 5:21 says my husband is supposed to submit to me, doesn't it? Doesn't the Bible teach mutual submission?

4. I realize I am supposed to submit to my husband. But he is supposed to love me like Christ loved the church. If he doesn't love me like Christ loved the church, then I'm off the hook. I don't have to submit to him.

5. Pastor, you have to realize that I'm the talker in the family. I love to talk; my husband loves to listen. I think we make a great team. For me to be meek and quiet goes against my nature.

6. Pastor, what about temperaments? I'm a choleric-sanguine temperament, you know, the outgoing, take

charge type. My husband it is melancholic-phlegmatic. He was born tired and had a relapse. If I don't do it, nothing will get done.

7. Pastor, you just don't understand. You see, I'm a natural born leader. My husband is a great follower. I need to lead, and he needs follow. That's just the way it is. I can't be a 1 Peter 3 wife.

We find ourselves right in the middle of the body of 1 Peter. In the body of this letter Peter is telling us three ways we can save our time on earth (our life) for eternity. Jesus taught Peter that our time on earth can be saved or lost (Matthew 16:24-27). Peter does not want the significance of his life to be lost. Nor does he want the significance of our lives to be lost. So, he passes on to us three ways we can make our lives count for eternity: Personal Sanctification (1 Peter 1:13-2:10), Personal Submission (1 Peter 2:11-3:7), and Personal Suffering (1 Peter 3:8-4:19). We are in the middle of the section on submission. We have seen submission in the world and submission in the workplace. Now we are looking at submission in the home, specifically submission of the wife to her husband. We will look at the Exhortation to Submission (1-2), the Explanation of Submission (2-4), and an Example of Submission (5-6). Let's jump into the Exhortation to Submission (1-2).

I. EXHORTATION TO SUBMISSION (HER BEHAVIOR) 1-2

A. Act of Submission   1

Wives, likewise, be submissive to your own husbands, that even if some do not obey the word, they, without a word, may be won by the conduct of their wives,

We need to start off with the word "**likewise**." Like what? Only one option. Go back. Peter just explained how servants were to submit to their masters. Now he draws a parallel in the Christian home. Just as servants were to be submissive to their masters, so "likewise" wives are to be submissive to their husbands. This will be important for understanding the "without a word" phrase.

A word needs to be said about "**your own**" husbands. Many Christian wives are married to men that are either unbelievers or they just don't care about being involved in church or spiritual things. Some of these men are quite accomplished in their own careers, and that is part of the problem. Since they are leader types but expend all their energy succeeding in the marketplace, they have little energy left to be a spiritual leader. Since they can't "compete," many of them just opt out. Meanwhile, their wives begin to fantasize about Elder Bob or Pastor John. "Bob is such a godly man and knows the Word so well. I wish my husband could be like Bob." Then in family discussions the wife can't hide her admiration for Bob when she keeps flaunting him in front of her husband: "Well, Elder Bob said. . . ." It quickly becomes apparent that the wife admires Elder Bob more than her husband. That only drives him further from spiritual things. After all, how can he compete with Elder Bob?

Perhaps that is one reason 1 Corinthians 14 encourages wives to ask spiritual questions of their husbands at home rather than during the church service. Even though her husband may not be as versed in Scripture or spiritual experience as Elder Bob, it lets her husband know that she is looking to him for spiritual guidance and encourages him to be her spiritual leader. The text acknowledges that some of these husbands may "**not obey the word**." The "**word**" refers to the Word of God. That would then identify this husband as either an unbeliever or a disobedient believer. In either case, his life is not in sync with God's Word. The text further assumes that the wife in this case is obedient to God's Word and would like her husband to be obedient. Is there something she can do to help move him along spiritually?

Absolutely, says Peter. They can win their husbands to a life in accordance with God's Word. But, ironically, they are to win him to God's Word without "**a word**." In other words, she is to win him without preaching to him. She can influence more spiritually by her life than by her lips, her conduct as opposed to her carping. Men have a deep need to feel competent. When his wife is always telling him what to do or pointing to the example of another as to how he should be, he runs. Why? Because with each word she is telling him how incompetent he is.

Enter the strange woman of Proverbs 6:24 who seduces with a "flattering tongue," or the adulteress of Proverbs 7: "With her enticing speech she caused him to yield, with her flattering lips she seduced him." She doesn't seduce him with her body; it is with her lips. It is what she is saying to him. What is she saying to him? We don't know exactly, but you can bet she is saying things that build up his ego, make him feel competent and admired—just the opposite of what his wife is doing. Proverbs 5:3 says, ". . . the lips of an immoral woman drip honey, and her mouth is smoother than oil." One fallen pastor told me the woman in the church that seduced him said he was a cross between Superman, Billy Graham, and Robert Redford . . . and he thought she had discernment.

So much for the Act of Submission; what about the Attitude?

B. Attitude of Submission   2

> . . . when they observe your chaste conduct accompanied by fear.

"**Observe**" (*epopteuō*) is a word used only here and in 2:12 in the entire NT. That makes it a word unique to Peter. *Opteuō* means "to see." When you put the little preposition *epi-* on the front of *opteuō*, it means "to see carefully" or "to look carefully." The idea is that the world is watching (2:12) and our skeptical spouses are watching as well. How many children have used the inconsistency of their parents as their excuse for opting out of Christianity: "My parents were one way at church, but at home they fought like cats and dogs." No one gets a closer view of us than our families, especially our spouses.

A woman's husband may be like the employer in 2:18ff. He's just unfair or harsh. But he is watching her carefully. It is her actions + her attitude that has the greatest possibility of winning him over. The passage offers no guarantees, but it does suggest a winning formula. "Fear," as explained before, does not speak of cowering but rather respect. A person in authority can usually tell if his subordinates are obedient with an attitude, meaning an attitude of disrespect. But the right conduct with the right attitude has the best chance of leaving a favorable impact.

In this passage the husband observes the "chaste" behavior of his wife. The word for "chaste" (*agnēn*) points to sexual purity. Not much different from today, the men in Paul's day had a double standard. It was all right for men to be married and engage in temple prostitution, but such promiscuity was not tolerated on the wife's side. Does this double standard seem unfair? Of course. But again, the parallel is drawn between the employee and his unfair boss and the wife and her unfair husband. There is no condoning of wife-abuse here, but there is the urging to combine the right conduct with the right attitude to win the husband over to biblical values. Why is the act + the attitude such a powerful combination? It probably gets back to our basic needs. Though Maslow as an unbelieving psychologist may not have the right answers, I think he does have the right analysis when it comes to understanding the needs of the human being. He pictures our needs as a hierarchy with one need not being a primary drive until the need below it is met.

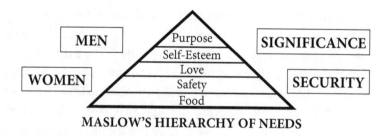

MASLOW'S HIERARCHY OF NEEDS

According to this hierarchy, all humans have two basic drives: security and significance. We tend not to worry about our significance until we feel secure. Security is pretty well bound up in getting our needs for food, safety, and love met. Significance comes from our sense of self-esteem and the discovery our purpose in life and living it out (what Maslow calls "self-actualization"). Although all humans have all of these needs, men tend to be tilted toward significance as the stronger need, and for women it is security. Assuming the need for food and safety are met, we can simplify all this by saying women primarily want to be loved, while men primarily want to be admired.

When a wife begins preaching to her husband, not only is she saying that she knows better than he about such and such, she is also telling him he is incompetent. Not exactly dripping with admiration. Quite the opposite. A man will run from that kind of woman, if not physically then psychologically. He retreats into his Man Cave and tunes her out.

So, we have looked at the Exhortation to Submission, the Act and the Attitude. But what about some sort of Explanation? That's next (vv. 3-4), but before we go there let's make a few observations about what we have covered so far:

1. The Scriptures do not teach wife abuse.

Unfortunately, Christian marriages can easily take advantage of the Scriptures to develop a sick codependency. Power hungry husbands can use passages like 1 Peter 3 to beat their wives into submission, even excusing their own ungodly behavior from this same passage because it says the wife should submit to a husband that is disobedient to the Word. On the other hand, some Christian wives become enablers who use biblical submission as their excuse to stay in sick, abusive relationships. Dr. Laura gives an example in her book *Ten Stupid Things Women Do to Mess Up Their Lives*:

> A woman whose husband is accused of poisoning her and killing two others with cyanide tainted capsules says she considers their relationship normal even though she once dialed 911 seeking help during a fight.
>
> Joseph Meling is charged with six counts of product

tampering, two counts of perjury, and three counts of insurance fraud. He is accused of putting a cyanide capsule into a Sudafed package in February 1991 to kill his wife for $700,000 of life insurance. He also was accused of tampering with five Sudafed packages in stores to make it appear a random killer was at work.

Kathleen Daneker, 40, of Tacoma and Stan McWhorter, 44, of Lacey died of cyanide poisoning from Sudafed purchased around Tacoma and Olympia. Three other cyanide filled capsules were found in Sudafed packages during a recall of the product.

Mrs. Meling nearly died but eventually recovered. She filed divorce papers after the cyanide incident, but later went back to her husband and is testifying in his defense.

Mrs. Meling said she felt the conflict in her marriage was normal. At times in tears, Mrs. Meling said she still loves Meling, and believes he is innocent . . .

Go figure![60]

Don't misunderstand. I am not counseling divorce here. Though I do believe Jesus allowed divorce for two biblical reasons, it is never the ideal. Healing, restoration, and reconciliation is the ideal. However, sometimes reconciliation requires loving confrontation and even separation. When a husband starts beating his wife, she better get some help quick, and temporary separation maybe the only road to healing.

2. The Scriptures do not teach mutual submission in home.

I don't know how many Christian books teach this. It comes from a misinterpretation of Ephesians 5:21. For a detailed discussion see

---

[60] Laura Schlessinger, *Ten Stupid Things Women Do to Mess Up Their Lives* (New York: Villard Books, 1994), 68-69.

my book *Position and Condition*.[61] The first word for "submitting" in that passage is the last of five participles (words ending in "-ing" in the NKJ) attached to the command "be filled" in Ephesians 5:18. It does not begin a new section on submission in the home. It's the last instruction on how to conduct a Spirit-filled worship service. Think of 1 Corinthians 14 and you'll get the picture. Those that wanted to speak should be mutually submissive to others that wanted to speak, so the body would be alive and vibrant instead of falling asleep while one person filibustered.

Telling husbands and wives to be mutually submissive would be like telling parents and children they should be mutually submissive, which, by the way, is exactly what one popular Bible teacher tells his readers (he has to in order to stay consistent with his interpretation on mutual submission in 5:22) Though the authority position can certainly be abused by insecure husbands (controllers are always insecure), that possibility doesn't negate the responsibility of submission any more than a harsh boss negates the responsibility of his employees' submission to him.

3. Without the respect of his wife, a husband cannot be a leader in his home.

What Scripture does teach is mutual respect in the home (see v. 2 and v. 7). This mutual respect is the key to a loving marriage. Why? Because it affirms the value and worth of each person. The opinion and point of view of each partner deserves to be heard. Glenn Zaephel, in his book *He Wins, She Wins*, makes this observation:

> The philosopher Rodney Dangerfield correctly hit upon one of the real killers of relationships with his immortal words, "I don't get no respect." Supreme levels of respect and dignity originated in the working of the Godhead. Christian

---

[61] Dave Anderson, *Position and Condition: An Exposition of the Book of Ephesians* (Grace Theology Press, 2017).

relationships don't have a chance to survive and grow without these core ingredients. Christian couples are to esteem, value, and prize each other and to actively communicate these things rather than assume the other person fully recognizes them. Our behavior toward each other is to be loving, honorable, and noble. Mutual worth and value are acknowledged and appreciated. We are to esteem the other person more highly than ourselves (Philippians 2:3).[62]

It is interesting in Scripture that the wife is never commanded to love her husband. She is to learn from older women how to have romantic love (*philē*) for her husband (Titus 2:4), but she is never commanded to have *agape* love for her husband as he is exhorted to have such love for his wife (Ephesians 5:24ff). She is told to respect him (Ephesians 5:33).[63] That is a choice. Only when she respects him and his position in the home can he fulfill that position. And only when he is respected for that position can he defer to her. 1 Peter 3:7 says he is to defer honor to his wife as the weaker vessel. One can only defer when he is in the position not to differ. If the authority in the home has been usurped by his wife, a man is not in a position to defer honor.

The biblical wife can help the controller to heal by calling his bluff. Behind the illusion of intimidation is an insecure little boy that desperately desires to be loved. Most of these men were never close to their mothers. By letting such men know that their abuse will not be tolerated, but that you do love them and are committed to a biblical resolution to conflict, the illusion can go up in smoke. A loving relationship built on mutual respect can begin.

---

[62] Glenn P. Zaephel, *He Wins, She Wins* (Nashville: Thomas Nelson, 1994), 142-43.

[63] See how understanding the balance between the husband's love and the wife's respect changed the ministry of Emerson Eggerichs, *Love and Respect* (Nashville: Thomas Nelson, 2004).

II. EXPLANATION OF SUBMISSION (HER BEAUTY) 3-4

A. External Beauty   3

> Do not let your adornment be merely outward—arranging the
> hair, wearing gold, or putting on fine apparel . . .

We live in a culture obsessed with external beauty. Males now
spend over ten billion annually to improve their looks. Dr. Paul Striker
of New York says his plastic surgery is forty percent male. Women
pay even more at the Church of Our Lady of Perpetual Beauty. But no
matter how beautiful the woman, her beauty fades.

Hedy Lamarr was one of the most beautiful faces to grace the
silver screen during the middle of the 20th Century. She was discovered
by Louis B. Mayer on an ocean-going trip across the Atlantic. She
was from Austria but was determined to make it in Hollywood. She
did, striking it big with the role of Delilah opposite Samson (Victor
Mature). But what most people never knew about Hedy was that
she was also a mechanical genius with numerous inventions. Most
notable was her suggestion on how to beat the U-Boats of Germany
during WWII.

When she suggested a remote-controlled torpedo, the idea failed
under scrutiny because the Germans could jam the radio signals to
the torpedo. So, she came up with the idea of shifting signals (spread
spectrum and frequency hopping). Every half second the frequency
would shift or hop so there was not time to jam the signal. She
patented her idea, but it wasn't picked up until the end of the war.
After the war the idea sat idle for about twenty years, long enough
for the patent rights to run out. When the military did use her patent,
they did not pay her for it as they legally should have because they
had briefly used it at the end of the war. Ultimately her son received
an award from the scientific community posthumously. Her idea
is at the basis of GPS, WiFi, etc., and its commercial value today is
estimated at twenty-four billion dollars.

I tell that story to demonstrate her genius. Now let's apply that to
beauty. She was the first to show how plastic surgery could be used

to prolong beauty. She showed the doctors where to cut behind the ear, under the chin, and various other techniques that started a run on plastics, so to speak. It worked . . . to a limited degree. Toward the end of her life she had had so many plastic surgeries to try to maintain her beauty that she looked freakish. She refused to be seen in public. Despite man's best attempts, or woman's, physical beauty fades. So, then what?

Well, dress it up: fancy hairdos, expensive jewelry, and gorgeous clothes. And let's not forget cosmetics. Kylie Kardashian is soon to become the youngest billionaire in American history (age 20), primarily from her cosmetic company. I wonder how many billions are spent every year in beauty salons, jewelry stores, and the fashion industry.

It is important to note that Peter does not condemn external beauty. The Bible tells us of Sarah's beauty and David's good looks. Joseph must have been attractive. That's the way God made them, and what He has made is good. Peter only tells us not to be obsessed with external beauty. It's a losing effort.

B. Internal Beauty   4

> . . . rather let it be the hidden person of the heart, with the incorruptible beauty of a gentle and quiet spirit, which is very precious in the sight of God.

When Peter mentions **"the hidden person of the heart,"** he is obviously turning the focus upon inner beauty. Since this kind of beauty is not physical, it cannot be corrupted. Time has no negative effect on it. It can never fade away, wrinkle, or wear out. But what inner beauty is Peter talking about? You might think he is referring to the fruit of the Spirit. Certainly, the person full of love, joy, peace, kindness, et cetera, is an attractive person. True, and we would not want to exclude these qualities from inner beauty, but Peter has something else in mind—a gentle and quiet spirit.

The word for **"gentle"** is *praus*, the same word mentioned in one of the beatitudes but translated "meek." The word is used of a horse that has been broken. The strength of the horse is still there, but the horse is under control. Its will has been broken, but not its spirit. God is not asking married women to be namby-pamby, mealy-mouthed, spineless weaklings. Not at all. Most men would not respect women they can walk all over and never have anything unique to offer the relationship. But their spirit is not to be that of a wild, unbroken horse that is always contradicting their husband and telling him how wrong he is.

Another word used to describe the inner spirit of the attractive wife is **"quiet."** The Greek word is *hēsuchias*. Synonyms are tranquil, calm, peaceful, and soothing. For the opposite see Proverbs 19:13, 25:24, and 27:15. Each speaks of a contentious and quarrelsome wife. Better to live on the roof than to share a house with such a woman. She is compared to a continual dripping. Living with her is like being nibbled to death by a duck.

Notice that Peter does not refer to the tongue or the voice of the wife. His focus is on her **"spirit."** Not every woman can have a meek and quiet personality, but every woman can cultivate a meek and quiet spirit. This doesn't mean to change one's personality, temperament, or gifts. It is not a question of personality, temperament, or talkativeness. One can be a leader, have a take charge temperament, and even be the talker in the family if one has the right spirit. A meek and quiet spirit is encouraged as we develop the fruits of the Spirit, one of which is self-control. Since James says no man can control the tongue (James 3:8), and I assume that includes women, then the control of the Holy Spirit is our only hope.

In fact, this should be very encouraging for every wife. Not every wife can be a beauty queen, but with a meek and quiet spirit every wife can be a magnet at home. A meek and quiet spirit draws a man like honey draws bears. It is irresistible. On the contrary, the loud, domineering, obstreperous woman has spawned the man-cave industry. Men will retreat into their caves to find some peace and quiet. And woe to the wife that enters the man-cave uninvited.

But the most powerful magnet of all combines the meek and quiet spirit of a wife with a sincere admiration for her husband. In a culture that has emasculated men on its road to empower women, many men would push over the Great Wall of China to find a woman that combines these two qualities. I often think of Nancy Reagan in this regard. I have no idea what she was like to live with, but in public I was struck by her admiring gaze at her husband whenever he was at the microphone. She left no doubt in his mind that she felt he was a man competent for the season as President of the United States. As Willard Harley advises in his book *His Needs, Her Needs*, "Behind *every* man should be an admiring wife."[64]

So, we have looked at Peter's Exhortation to Submission (1-2) and his Explanation of Submission (3-4); what about some Examples of Submission (5-6)? Peter gives both General Examples and a Specific Example.

III. EXAMPLES OF SUBMISSION   3:5-6

A. General Examples   5

> For in this manner, in former times, the holy women who trusted in God also adorned themselves, being submissive to their own husbands . . .

Many Bible studies teach that Abraham is a parallel to the husband who is "disobedient" to the word in 3:1 when he told Sarah to tell Pharaoh (Genesis 12) and Abimelech (Genesis 20) that she was his sister. According to these studies, Sarah submissively obeyed her husband's request and God blessed her for it by protecting her from these pagan kings. Thus, it is taught that a wife should submit to her husband's requests to falsify the truth (or commit other sins). God will protect the wife and judge the husband. After all, isn't this what Rahab and the Egyptian midwives did? They lied in order to save

---

[64] Willard Harley, *His Needs, Her Needs* (Grand Rapids: Flemming H. Revell, 2001), 153.

lives, and God blessed them for it. Is this passage teaching Christian wives to do the same? I don't think so.

"For this manner" probably looks back to all of 3:1-4, the Behavior of Wives (1-2) and the Beauty of Wives (3-4) since this verse refers both to their Beauty (adornment) and Behavior (submission). **"Holy women"** probably refers to the wives (Sarah, Rebecca, Leah, and Rachel) of the patriarchs (Abraham, Isaac, and Jacob). They **"trusted in God,"** and it was this trust that enabled them to submit to their husbands. She or he who puts her or his trust in humans will be disappointed.

The word for **"adorned"** (*ekosmoun*) is in a tense in Greek (imperfect) that refers in this context to their custom of life. It wasn't occasional, but customary. Their cosmetics were a meek and quiet spirit. They put this on every morning by choice, like lipstick and mascara. This refers back to verses 3 and 4. The word **"submissive"** looks back to verses 1 and 2. It is important that the wife be submissive to her own husband despite what Elder Bob down at the church has to say (unless, of course, her husband is asking her to do things that are immoral). But this leads us into the example of Sarah. Didn't Abraham ask her to do something immoral, and didn't she submit to him? Is this our example to follow? Many Bible studies say yes; I would say an emphatic no.

B. Specific Example   6

> . . . as Sarah obeyed Abraham, calling him lord, whose daughters you are if you do good and are not afraid with any terror.

Sarah **"obeyed"** (*hypēkousen*) Abraham. The tense of this verb is aorist, which in this context most likely refers to a particular occasion (a point in time) when Sarah obeyed Abraham. We might think of the scenario with Pharaoh (Genesis 12) or Abimelech (Genesis 20). But **"calling him lord"** helps us identify the occasion. We have no record of her calling Abraham "lord" in either Genesis 12 or 20. The only time we have on record when she called him lord was in Genesis

18:12 when the promise of Isaac was given. She initially doubted the promise of their Divine Visitor when He said she would bear a child. She laughed. However, we know she submitted to the divine imperative for her life by joining with Abraham with the anticipation of pregnancy.

The mention of daughters can be problematic. It looks like you can become daughters of Abraham by doing good and not being intimidated. But Scripture (Galatians 4:23-28 and Isaiah 51:2) teaches us that all believers in Christ are the spiritual children of Abraham. The qualification is belief in Christ, not doing good. So, what is this all about? Nowhere else in this epistle or in the New Testament is doing good a condition for becoming a child of God. Furthermore, the *"if"* is in italics because it's not literally found in the Greek text. The translators put it there because they thought it made the best sense of the text according to their theology. Despite the translations of NKJ, NASB, and NIV, a period should probably come after **"whose daughters you are."** Then we have two concluding commands: **"Do good and don't let any intimidation frighten you."** So, rather than teaching that a wife should do evil if her husband tells her to or tries to intimidate her into it, this teaches just the opposite: "Do what is good and don't let your husbands intimidate you into doing evil." [65]

CONCLUSION

1. God never directs his people to sin; He always provides a way out–1 Corinthians 10:13.

A wife should never use her husband as an excuse to sin. Sarah was absolutely wrong in what she did. In fact, it looks as though Sarah has developed a habit of lying that stretched over many years. She lied in Genesis 12 to Pharaoh, in Genesis 18 to the Lord, and in Genesis 20 to Abimelech. Of course, those may have been isolated instances,

---

[65] J. Ramsey Michaels, *Word Biblical Commentary* (Dallas: Word Books, 1988), 166-67.

but maybe not. That history covers twenty-five years. Like Abraham, her faith lagged at points. Many of the plagues that hit Egypt while Sarah was in Pharaoh's harem were because she listened to the advice of her husband. Moral? Never listen to the advice of one's spouse? Nonsense. But don't listen to it if he goes against the clearly revealed will of God.

A wife might say, "I had no choice; he made me do it." No. 1 Corinthians 10:13 promises us God will never put us in a position where we have to sin. There is always a way of escape. But what about Rahab and the Egyptian midwives? Didn't they lie to save lives? Yes, they did. But no lives are being threatened here. In both cases, with Pharaoh and Abimelech, they made it clear that they would not have taken Sarah if they had known she was Abraham's wife. It was Abraham's fear and a lack of faith that caused him to sin. And it was his feeling of indispensability to God's plan that caused him to become a manipulator to help accomplish His divine plan. If Abraham had remained faithful, God would most likely have protected him from his enemies just as He protected Sarah in spite of their sin (obviously there are exceptions—like martyrs who are faithful but still die for their cause).

2. God blessed Sarah's obedience, not Abraham and Sarah's sin of equivocation (a half-truth). See Genesis 18:12-15 and 20:9-13.

The sins of Abraham and Sarah did not simplify God's plan or help accomplish His plan. Their sins caused a lot of trouble. God had to do some miracles in order to get them out of the messes they created. And they left a bad witness. Abimelech, especially, seemed to know who the Lord was when confronted by Him in a dream. But we have no record that he ever trusted in Yahweh, even though Abraham continued to live in his region for some time.

Another problem caused by these sins was that of a generational curse. The sins of the parents are passed down to the third and fourth generation. Genesis 26 tells us that Isaac picked up the same sister act with his wife Rebecca to save himself from the son of Abimelech a hundred years later.

Abraham's sin was an equivocation, a half-truth. Abraham told the truth, but not the whole truth. Sarah was his half-sister. But she also became his wife. He justified his actions by telling a half-truth. But God clearly revealed that this was a terrible sin. No, Sarah was not called a holy woman of old and held up as an example because her sin, but because of her obedience. She submitted to her husband regarding the promise of a seed. She no longer supplied handmaidens. She trusted in God that she would be used to help produce the child that could be the Savior.

3. A married man reaches his highest potential when supported by a submissive wife adorned with a meek and tranquil spirit.

In discussing this need of a man Harley says:

While criticism causes men to become defensive, admiration energizes and motivates them. A man expects and needs his wife to be his most enthusiastic fan. He draws confidence from her support and can usually achieve far more with her encouragement. . . You've heard the saying, "Behind every great man is a great woman." I'd like to amend it to make Harley's Sixth Corollary: Behind every married man should be an admiring wife. Biographies of great men prove it, and lives of all men show it: a man simply thrives on a woman's admiration. To a great extent men owe gratitude to their wives for this kind of emotional support, for without it, their confidence—the major source of their success—erodes and eventually crumbles.[66]

Steve Morris became a popular entertainer in his time. In an interview with Paul Harvey, he told about the turning point in his life. It was the recognition and admiration of a woman. It wasn't his wife or his mother, but a teacher in Detroit. You see, a mouse had

---

[66] Harley, 157-58.

been lost in the classroom, and Steve's teacher asked him to help her find it. Even though Steve had been born blind, God compensated by giving him a remarkable pair of listeners on the side of his head. He had an incredible sense of hearing. But this is really the first time Steve had been shown appreciation and admiration for those talented ears. That encouragement meant so much to him that it was the beginning of a new life. You see, Steve Morris is none another then Stevie Wonder, one of the most popular pop singers and songwriters of our time, not to mention a versatile musician.

Ah, . . . the power of a woman.

14

"OMISSION IMPOSSIBLE"
PART 1

1 Peter 3:7a

INTRODUCTION

Some years ago, there was a TV series called "Mission Impossible." It would begin with a secret agent named Jim listening to a short tape of instructions from an anonymous authority figure concerning a mission Jim was to undertake if he so chose. Then the tape would self-destruct. Tom Cruise reprised the role in a series of action movies with the same title. For a moment, let's imagine God as the authority figure sending Jim on a mission to love his wife as Christ loved the church. The short tape might go something like this:

"Jim, this is the Lord speaking. I am thrilled that you have decided to give your life to working for my kingdom instead of your own. And I have an amazing purpose for your life. But before I can reveal that to you, we have some prerequisites or test cases to see if you are ready for the big one. In fact, we are going to start in your home, since you are a married man. Paul, you might remember from the Book of Ephesians, instructed husbands to love their wives as Christ loved the church. Wow. A daunting task—in fact, an impossible task, a mission impossible—without Christ Himself loving her through us. But Paul just lays out the general responsibility without really giving us any tips on how to do it. That's where Peter comes in. He gives us three tips on how to love our wives. In fact, omitting these tips makes loving our wives impossible. We want to look at them one by one to make sure we are not guilty of omitting them from our relationship with our wives. Your mission in this lesson is to learn how to love your wife, should you choose to accept it. Omit this and your marriage is doomed to coexisting behind walls at best. Or your whole marriage could self-destruct at worst."

Way back in 1986 the number of middle-class runaway wives exceeded the number of runaway husbands for the first time in America. Obviously, these wives were unhappy. But what is happiness in a marriage for a woman? Is it to have a lovely home? Happy and healthy children? A successful husband? Time for talents? No money problems? Is it a successful homemaker? Is it to be admired by her associates? All these things are important and some essential, but there is one need which is fundamental: **the need to be loved and cherished by her husband.** Peter gets into the nuts and bolts of how to do this better than any other NT author even though the word "love" never occurs in 1 Peter 3:7.

MASLOW'S HIERARCHY OF NEEDS

"SAVING THE SAVED"
1 Peter

I. THE INTERPRETATION—"WHAT DOES IT MEAN?"

> Husbands, likewise, dwell with them with understanding,
> giving honor to the wife, as to the weaker vessel, and as being
> heirs together of the grace of life, that your prayers may not
> be hindered.

What does **"likewise"** mean? It is the same Greek word as the
"likewise" in 3:1 (*homoiōs*). But there the "likewise" referred to wives
submitting to their husbands just as bond slaves were to submit to
their owners. It's not teaching the husbands to submit to their wives.
Also, in 3:1-6 the wives are married either to unbelieving husbands
or husbands that are not walking by the Spirit in obedience to God's
Word. This verse is not referring to a Christian husband married
to an unbelieving wife because Peter's use of "co-heirs of the gift of

life" indicates Christian wives. Therefore, we suggest this translation: "Husbands, *as for your part, ...*"

So, what is the husband's part? If the wife is to submit with a good attitude and a meek and quiet spirit, what is the husband supposed to do? First of all, he must **"dwell."** Well, duh. Of course, he is supposed to live with his wife. That is so obvious many interpreters take the word (*synoike*) to mean total intimacy—body, soul, and spirit. OK. But he is supposed to do this **"according to knowledge."** The concept (*kata gnōsin*) is so cryptic, we have a number of suggestions from different translations: "be considerate" (NIV); "in an understanding way" (NASB); "with understanding" (NKJ); *according* (*BDAG*, 4071I5B) *to knowledge* ("know how"—Michaels[67]). But if we go with Michaels' suggestion, what does it mean to dwell with our wives according to "know how"?

In my quest to understand this phrase I went to the bookstore and bought twenty-one books on marriage. And while performing a wedding I challenged the groom to buy those twenty-one books and read one a month. Everyone to my surprise started laughing. I asked my wife after the ceremony what was so funny. I was dead serious. She just said, "Oh, Dave, you Rice (my alma mater) people are the only ones in the world who would go to the bookstore and buy twenty-one books on how to love your wife. Sometimes you're just not real."

Well, I'm not going to pretend to have the definitive answer here but consider the following tips after fifty plus years of marriage and over forty of pastoring churches and TWENTY-ONE BOOKS ON HOW TO LOVE YOUR WIFE.

---

[67] Michaels, op. cit., 168.

II. THE APPLICATION—"HOW DO WE DO IT?"

A. Understand Her Needs[68]

1. Her Need for Affection. If the most common complaint I hear for married men is they do not get to enjoy they're conjugal rights often enough, the most common complaint I hear from women it is they don't get enough affection. Neither side seems to understand the strong need of the other. And the number one need of a woman is for affection. Unfortunately, men don't seem to understand what affection does for a woman. It tells her she is loved, cared for, protected, and cherished. Her participation in conjugal bliss is more of a choice. A mental thing. She can choose yes or no. But she finds affection irresistible.

Ironically, if she thinks your affection is goal oriented in terms of conjugal rights, then this kind of affection can cause her to doubt her husband's love. She suspects it is a manipulation to get her to reciprocate in kind to meet his needs. The most meaningful kind of affection for a wife is completely disconnected from conjugal bliss. Not to say there is no affection in the midst of conjugal bliss, but that is not the affection she is longing for. She wants her hand held, her back rubbed, her lips kissed, her shoulders squeezed, and especially hugs. Other forms of affection that are not physical include phone calls, letters, flowers, cards, and on it goes.

But some men have never seen affection modeled by their own fathers, or they're macho men that cannot make a display of affection anywhere but with the lights turned off. These men are just not the affectionate type. Well, gentlemen, if you aren't the affectionate type, you may find that your wife is not the sexual type. Affection sets the mood in the marriage, the atmosphere in the home.

My wife and I have a rule: if one of us comes home and knows the other's there as well, the one just arriving must hunt the other down wherever he or she might be in the house and give him or

---

[68] These are straight out of Harley's book *His Need, Her Needs,* op. cit.

her a big kiss. Let me tell you, I know of no other investment in a man's marriage that will create greater dividends than learning to be affectionate apart from anything sexual. Betty had to train me over the years. Forgive me if you have read this in another of my books, but it's important to tell you about a turning point regarding affection in our marriage.

We had been married for eleven years and were watching the Muppet movie together. Somewhere in the middle of the movie Betty grabbed my arm, pointed to the screen, and said, "That's me." "Who's you?" I asked. "She is," Betty claimed emphatically, pointing directly at Miss Piggy. "No, Betty, you are not Miss Piggy" (Betty is a very beautiful, feminine lady). "Oh, yes I am," she reaffirmed.

Well, I didn't think any more about it. Then a couple weeks after seeing the movie we were lying in bed about to go to sleep. Completely dark; no sound; a foot apart on our backs in a king-sized bed. Then I heard a squeaky little voice say, "Kermie, whisper sweet nothings in my ear." Now a man knows when he's being manipulated, so I just laid there silent and unresponsive, completely oblivious to the fact that Miss Piggy has several voices. The next thing I hear is: "NOW" in a deep guttural voice. Well, this has become a power struggle, so while still lying on my back I began to snore, completely oblivious to the fact that Miss Piggy knows karate. The next thing I hear is, "Haaayaaah!" as she delivers a sharp karate chop to my stomach.

Believe it or not, that's the night I learned the importance of sweet nothings, that is, nonsexual affection. By the way, forty years have passed since that night, and Betty still thinks her alter ego is Miss Piggy. Of course, that makes me Kermie, and I'm here to tell you, it's not easy being green. Sometimes when we're driving along in the car and I get too talkative, Betty will just say, "Quiet, frog." But remember, the husband without affection is a man without understanding (at least when it comes to his wife).

2. *Her need for conversation.* Like many couples, years after they have married, Betty and I were reminiscing about what drew us

together. I asked her why she was attracted to me? In my mind I'm going over my Rolodex of virtues she might mention. But it was none of the above. She said, "I wanted to keep dating you because you were the first guy who would listen to me. All the other guys I've dated just wanted to talk about themselves." Ladies love to talk, but if we do all the talking in an effort to impress them with how great we are, we might find ourselves talking to the wall.

Many people in my last church I pastored for almost twenty years have told me what a wonderful conversationalist my wife is on the phone. But women don't want to talk to just a bump on a log. They want response and interaction. Sometimes it seems that my mind is wandering while Betty is talking, and I don't interact sufficiently to let her know I am really listening. So, she has trained me to say, "Ugh," to let her know I am following her.

Women need to talk. It's how they relate. That is how they build relationships. It makes sense, doesn't it, that if two people never talk, there is no relationship. In general, men are not good at relationships, simply because most of us are cave dwellers. We go off into our caves to solve our problems. When we call someone on the phone, it's usually a very businesslike: "Golf this Saturday at ten? Sure. What course? . . . OK. See you there." Click. Women aren't like that. Have you ever wondered what they're saying when they go on-and-on on the phone? Sometimes I listen and wonder. "What was that all about?" I asked one time. Betty responded, "About? What was it about? Who knows? It doesn't have to be about anything. We were relating. That's the problem with you men. You don't know how to relate."

But listen, guys, if you want your wife to relate to you, then you better start talking. Remember all the talking you did before marriage? That went a long way toward winning your wife's hand in marriage. If you stop talking after marriage, she will find someone to talk to, and you might not be too happy about the person she chooses. You see, for a woman to be responsive in the conjugal area, she needs to feel bonded, feel united, to feel one with her husband.

Did you notice how many times I just use the word feel? Here's a conversational tip for men. Ask her how she feels about this, thus, and so. While you may want to tell her what you **think**, she is dying to tell you how she *feels*. Women need to reveal their feelings. Give them a chance by encouraging them with a question like, "How did you feel about . . . ?" I really have it easy. Because my wife is a political activist, all I have to do is ask, "How did you feel about the debates (or almost anything else going on in the political world)?" She gets animated quickly.

Now this can sound pretty manipulative. However, since I really do love my wife, I want to try to help meet her needs. She has a need to talk. If I can help with that by listening even to subjects I am not interested in, I try to do it.

3. Her need for honesty and openness. Trust is the foundation for a good marriage. If she can't trust you, she can't respect you. If she can't respect you, she can't love you. If she can't love you, she's not happy. And if mama ain't happy, ain't nobody happy. When you stop trusting someone, everything they do and say becomes suspect and can be viewed suspiciously through jaundiced eyes. She desperately needs to trust you. Help her by calling when you're away or going to be late. Let her know where you are.

4. Her Need for Financial Support. Financial tension is the number one cause of divorce in America. You'll notice on Maslow's hierarchy of needs financial security is a basic need that must be attended to before we can move up to more intangible needs like belonging, love, and self-esteem.

5. Her Need for Family Commitment. If you put money making before your commitment to the family, she will begin to resent your career. This makes it hard for her to respect you, admire you, and support you as you try to move ahead. Passive-aggressive behavior will undermine your best efforts. Soon you will find the two of you working at cross purposes, and your home will turn into a war zone instead of a refuge center.

B. Understand Her Nature

1. Her Temperament. Usually opposites attract. That includes opposite temperaments. If you are a melancholic temperament, you will likely be attracted to a sanguine temperament. That means the moody, diffident man will quite likely be attracted to a bubbly, vivacious woman. Well and good. You can be stronger together because of your combined strengths

Maybe she's a choleric and you're a phlegmatic. A mosquito bite turns her into the Terminator but getting you to fight it is like getting an elephant to react to the bite of a red ant. She flares up faster than a thunderstorm in Houston, but they named Lake Placid after you. Understanding how to cope with these temperament differences helps immensely in trying to achieve a peaceful life at home.

2. Her Personality Profile. Many think the Myers-Briggs personality profile is an even better way to predict or define problem areas in a marriage. Many businesses use this with their employees as a matter of course even to help place them in the company according to their personality traits: (E=Extroverts/I=Introverts, S=Sensor/N=Intuitive, J=Judge/P=Perceivers, F=Feelers/T=Thinkers). You can pick up a book called *Type Talk*, which will help you spot your own personality profile as well as that of your wife. The authors note that although opposites attract, the attraction is only initial. Later on, when the fuzz has worn off, the very thing which attracted you may become a major source of irritation. They observed the people that are alike have much more long-term success in marriage than those that are opposites.

Of course, they leave out the Holy Spirit. That's why I prefer a book like Tim La Haye's *Transformed Temperaments* because he teaches us how the Holy Spirit can enhance our strengths and control our weaknesses.

3. Her Biological Profile. Betty and I married right after my graduation from college. We had no premarital counseling. No one told me about hormones and how they can affect a pregnant woman. We had been married about a year when Betty got pregnant. Her personality changed a bit, and I wasn't ready for it. Then after Baby Bear was born, there were even more changes. One day I came home from school and stuck out my cup for some love, and Betty turned on me with claws out and went, "Grrrrrrr." That's when I learned that Papa Bear wasn't the number one priority for quite some time. There was something about Baby Bear and his needs that took precedence over Papa Bear and his needs. Little did I know how hormones affect Mama Bear. It is good for a husband to learn something about his wife's biological profile.

C. Understand Her Love Language

According to Gary Chapman in his book *The Five Love Languages*, husbands and wives usually don't speak the same love language. Because of this difference they often think their spouse doesn't love them when they really do; they just don't speak the same language. If a German man tells a French woman, "*Ich liebe dich*," and she tells him, "*Je t'aime*," they may never get to first base in their relationship. They need to speak the same language.

Chapman says there are five different categories of words and activities that fill the love banks or tanks of most people. Each category is like a love language, and most people have a primary language. They may speak all five of these languages, but one is their primary language, their main source of love that fills their tank.

The five categories are: affirming words, quality time together, physical touch, special gifts, and acts of service like helping with the dishes, laundry, et cetera. He suggests that each person finds out the primary language of his or her mate and learns to speak that language. Then he suggests a game couples can use to learn how to keep their tanks full. When the husband comes home from work, he's to say to his wife, "Tank check." She replies on a scale of 0 to 10 how full her love tank is. If she says "seven," then he replies by saying, "What can I do or say to help fill your tank?" And she is supposed to do this in return. He suggests three times a week for three weeks. By then, says Chapman, the game is a lot of fun and rather addicting.

Occasionally, Chapman finds men who don't like the game. One husband said to him, "I don't like that love tank game. I played it with my wife. I came home and said to her. 'On a scale from 0 to 10, how is your love tank tonight?' She said, 'About seven.' I asked, 'What could I do to help fill your tank?' She said, 'The greatest thing you could do for me tonight is to do the laundry.' I said, 'Love and laundry? I don't get it.'"

Chapman said, "That's the problem. Perhaps you don't understand your wife's love language. What's your primary love language?" Without hesitation he said, "Physical touch, and especially the conjugal part." "Listen to me carefully," said Chapman. "The love you feel when your wife expresses love by physical touch is the same love your wife feels when you do the laundry."

"Bring on the laundry," he shouted. "I'll wash the clothes every night if it makes her feel that good."

When you play this game with your wife, keep track of her answers. She may make requests from all five categories. But most of them will cluster around her primary love language. Learn that language well, and your wife will be assured of your love for her.[69]

CONCLUSION

Our degree of intimacy with our wives is directly proportionate to the degree that we understand (know) our wives and act accordingly. But remember, before we can act according to our knowledge, we must get the knowledge. "That's right, Jim: knowledge. This is your mission should you choose to accept it. And it is a choice. The omission of this will make maximum marriage impossible for you, Jim. I hope you listened well. Tapes of this message may self-destruct in five minutes. But we don't want your marriage to self-destruct for lack of knowledge. Good luck, Jim."

---

[69] Gary Chapman, *The 5 Love Languages* (Chicago: Northfield Publishing, 2015).

15

"OMISSION IMPOSSIBLE"
PART 2

1 Peter 3:7b

INTRODUCTION

"**G**ood morning, Jim. How did it go last week? Are you getting to know your wife's primary language of love? Did you buy any of the books I recommended: *His Needs, Her Needs; Transformed Temperaments;* and *The Five Languages of Love?* A small investment for a potentially great return."

"You see, Jim, what I'm trying to get across to is the importance of these three strategies in 1 Peter 3:7 for loving your wife. The omission of any one or more of these elements could lead to a marriage which will self-destruct. You may dwell under the same roof, but you won't be dwelling according to knowledge with your wife. And if you don't know your wife's needs, it's unlikely you will be meeting them. Momma won't be happy, and you know what we say about mama. But knowing your wife was the last lesson. Your mission this week, Jim, is to respect your wife, another of the key qualities of a loving husband. What's the issue here?"

According to James Dobson in his book *Straight Talk to Men and their Wives*, wives find their greatest satisfaction in marriage during the first two years.[70] Then a downward trend begins that keeps ebbing lower until shortly after the last child leaves home. Why is this the norm? And why is it that so many Christian wives feel like doormats? Is the flight of the woman into the marketplace just economically driven? And what is it that turns a kind, tender, giving woman into a cold, bickering shrew? Could it be they "don't get no respect" in the home? What does Peter mean when he says that husband should "give honor to the wife"? That's what we want to find out in this lesson.

"SAVING THE SAVED"
1 Peter

Salutation		1:1-2
Introduction		1:3-12
Body	"Our Plan of Salvation"	
I. Through Personal Sanctification—our Character		1:13-2:10
II. Through Personal Submission—our Conduct		2:11-3:7
A. Our Conduct in the World		2:11-17
B. Our Conduct in our Jobs		2:18-25
C. Our Conduct in our Homes		3:1-7
1. Conduct of the Wife		1-6
2. Conduct of the Husband		7
a. Knowledge of His Wife		7a
b. Respect for His Wife		7b
c. Bonded to His Wife		7c

. . . giving honor to the wife, as to the weaker vessel, and as being heirs together of the grace of life . . .

---

[70] James Dobson, *Straight Talk to Men and Their Wives* (Waco, TX: Word Books, 1980), 99.

I. THE INTERPRETATION

The word **"giving"** (*aponemō*) means "to render what is due" and it occurs just once in the New Testament. It is used for paying the rent or paying taxes. So, to respect their wives is only rendering to them that which is rightfully due. When you pay your mortgage, they don't send you a thank you note. It is simply that which is due.

The word **"honor"** means "value, highly esteem, respect." This word or a variation of it is found in 1 Peter 1:7, 19; 2:7, 17; and here. It is often connected with the value of money (see 1:19 and 1 Corinthians 6:20, and 1 Timothy 5:17). And children are told to "honor your father and mother" (Ephesians 6:2). So, our wives are like precious jewels, more valuable than gold, and deserving of the highest respect. A Rolex watch, the Presidents version is kept in a special place, protected, cherished, and valued. This is how we should treat our wives.

Now, what should we do with the words **"weaker vessel"**? First of all, I think these words are to be connected with 7b as the KJV, NKJV, and the NIV do rather than with 7a as does the NASB. It certainly does not mean weaker spiritually because on average women seem to be more spiritual than men, probably because they don't have that streak of independence and male pride found in most men. So, I would suggest weaker physically, usually, and possibly psychologically in that they are usually more sensitive, fragile, and more easily wounded. Bottom line: the husband can bully his way around, become overbearing, dominate and intimidate his wife just because she is the "weaker vessel."

It reminds me of the story of the men who died and went to heaven. These men were separated into two lines, the first line for all the men who had been henpecked by their wives while on earth, and the second line for all the men who had not been henpecked by their wives while on earth. The first line stretched way out beyond the pearly gates, but there was only one guy standing in the second line. St. Peter went to this guy and asked him what he was doing in that line. The guy said, "I don't know. This is where my wife told me to stand." We can smile at that because in reality this is usually not the case. Far more men tell their wives what to do, and often they are not so nice about it.

Peter says that wives are "heirs together" with their husbands. In 1 Peter 1:4 and passages like Colossians 3:24 we see that the concept of inheritance usually involves rewards for faithful service. And this is very exciting. God is an *Equal Opportunity Employer*. A wife's contribution to the family package is just as valuable to God as the husband's. If that is not obvious to their husbands now, it will be once rewards are handed out at the Judgment Seat of Christ (2 Corinthians 5:10; Romans 14:10-12). **"Heirs together"** (*snyklēronomos*) occurs four times in the New Testament (see Romans 8:17 where joint-heirs = coheirs = equal heirs = men and women are exactly equal in value before God). And remember, ladies, even if your husband doesn't esteem you highly as he should, there's One who does. Believe me, this is one verse you're not going to find in the Koran or in either the Upanishads or the Gita (both sacred texts of the Hindus).

We are told that wives are coheirs of **"the grace of life."** The word life is not the word used for physical life (*bios*) from which we get "biology," but *zōē*, which in 110x out of 125 occurrences in the NT refers to "spiritual life" and usually in conjunction with "eternal." This helps us see that heirship here is not referring to physical life on earth but rather the inheritance to be revealed when Christ returns (1:4 and 9). So much for the interpretation of this part of verse 7. What about the application?

II. THE APPLICATION

In many unhealthy marriages the husband becomes the *power* partner and the woman becomes the *passive* partner. The power partner is a control addict. Because of his own sense of insecurity and insignificance, he must control everyone and everything around him. Everything has a place. There is order. If he loses control of his environment, he becomes frustrated and anxiety ridden—unglued. Here are ten characteristics of the power partner:[71]

1. Controlling and dominating

2. Blaming, unable to admit he is wrong, to ask for forgiveness, to say he is sorry

3. Intimidating—he makes those around him feel inadequate or inferior—uses his intelligence and arguing ability to belittle others

4. Stubborn–unable to be reasoned with, close-minded, obstinate, inflexible

5. Authoritative—he is the final expert on the matter and always right in his opinion

6. Uncompromising–everything is black-and-white

7. Rigid and legalistic–goes by the rules

8. Inconsiderate of the feelings and opinions of others

9. Defensive–easily threatened

10. Demanding and impatient

Unfortunately, many Christian husbands gravitate toward being power partners. The rules of Scripture feed their neurosis. They see the submission passages for wives as divine sanction to browbeat their wives into submission, quoting Scripture to them all the way. They turn their wives into doormats. These guys are mice, not men. They use their family as steppingstones to fortify their own sick egos. And their denial systems are so strong they will rarely admit having a control problem. If their wives weren't passive partners when they met, they will often turn into passive partners after a few years of marriage. What are the characteristics of the passive partner?

---

[71] Glenn Zaepfel, *He Wins, She Wins*, 32.

1. Passive–waits for things to happen; has problems being direct; is fearful of taking a leadership role; avoids conflict

2. Others-oriented–a pleaser who seeks approval; taken advantage of by others; unable to say no; nonassertive; accepts blame when she shouldn't; tolerates emotional abuse

3. Insecure–has low self-esteem; lacks self-confidence

4. Dependent–indecisive, unsure, undemanding, subordinates her own needs to those of others; an intense fear of loneliness or abandonment.

Unfortunately, misuse of Scripture again traps the passive partner into her unhealthy behavior. We're told to be sacrificial in our love for others, to put the needs of others before our own, to avoid conflict, and to deny self. But the pathologically passive partner reads so much self-denial into all these passages that they allow their power partners to treat them like dirt, like nobodies. Because of their low self-esteem, they do not command or even demand respect. And when they see disrespect in their mate's eyes and behavior, their self-esteem gets even lower.

These women need to look their abusive husbands in the eye and say, "George, I love you, but I also love myself. You're treating me like I don't exist, like I'm a donut hole or a ghost. George, I'm a real person, just as valuable to God as you, and completely equal to you as a person. It's not healthy for either of us to let you treat me this way. I must insist that you stop this disrespectful behavior toward me right now." If they don't respond, walk away.

You see, the Bible does not teach mutual submission, but it does teach mutual respect. Without respect, I'm not sure there can be love. We just don't love people we don't respect. Why? Because a large component of healthy love is admiration. Invariably you admire the person you love. But you don't admire people you don't respect.

Why do so many couples find that they don't love each other after seven years of marriage? It's because they have been focusing on the faults of the other person discovered since the marriage and staring at these faults long enough has caused them to lose respect for their mate. Respect must be restored for the marriage to mature and for love to blossom again. Here are some suggestions to help you display an attitude of respect for each other, but remember, I am primarily addressing this to husbands:

1. **Respect your wife's feelings**. You don't have to understand or agree with your wife's feelings, but, brother, you better esteem and honor them as valid. Draw her feelings out. Wives are more emotional than husbands, who tend to be more cognitive. Learn to ask her what she feels instead of what she thinks. And then don't make the mistake of trying to correct her or telling her she shouldn't feel that way. That invalidates her feelings. Rather say something like, "Wow, honey. If that happened to me I would probably feel the same way." Of course, whatever you say must be genuine. She can see right through insincerity.

2. **Respect your wife's opinions**. At the base of disrespect is the attitude that the other person doesn't really count. Hence, their opinions don't count. The power partner is always right in his own mind, so he shows his disrespect for his wife's opinions by cutting her off, smiling, or laughing at her while she tries to express herself, which reflects an attitude of: "I'm superior to you. Your opinions rank somewhere between those have a hippopotamus and an amoeba. Why don't you stop wasting our time and let me tell you how it's going to be and why?" A respectful mate doesn't have to agree with his mate, but he must honor his mate's ability to think and reason. Don't view these different opinions as threats to yours, but as enhancing and complementing yours.

3. **Respect your wife's interests and desires**. Maybe you like sports, but she doesn't. Don't laugh at her or make fun of her for her lack of sports knowledge. Perhaps she likes gardening and you don't. Show respect for her individual interests by having her teach you something about gardening. Ask her to tell you why she likes it so much. And when you're going out together, why don't you alternate between doing something you like and something she likes? That says, "You count, and I count," rather than, "I count, but you don't count."

4. **Respect your wife in front of your children and your friends**. If you don't respect your wife, guess why your male children have trouble respecting women. They will probably treat their own wives the same way you treat yours. Why? Because you have modeled disrespect for women to your sons.

5. **Respect your wife by helping to relieve her stress around the house**. You like to have some relief after a stressful week, so you want to go play tennis with the boys and not have your wife complain about it. Show her the same respect. Help arrange some time away while you watch the kids.

6. **Respect your wife's needs by becoming a minister rather than a manipulator**. Larry Crabb claims most marriages are like a tick on a dog. Ticks do their best to suck blood out of the host. The only purpose for the host is to meet the needs of the tick. Most people come to the altar looking for the other person to meet their own needs. Without audibly expressing it, the groom is standing there looking at his bride and saying, "Sweetheart, you admire me more than any woman I've ever known. You make me feel like superman. And now I'm about to give you the opportunity to make me feel that way for the rest

of my life." Now when she stops making him feel that way, he will begin to manipulate. And it's the same on the other side. We call this a marriage of manipulation instead of ministry. In a marriage ministry each partner is looking for ways to minister to the needs of the other person.

I want to finish up by contrasting two men. One is found in an old song and is the perfect picture of the self-absorbed Power partner:

Put another log on the fire
Cook me up some bacon and some beans
And go out to the car and change the tire
Wash my socks and so my old blue jeans.

Come on, Baby.

You can fill my pipe and then go fetch my slippers
And boil me up another pot of tea
Then put another log on the fire, Babe
And come tell me why you're leavin' me.

Now, don't I let you wash the car around Sunday?
Don't I warn you when you're getting fat?
Ain't I gonna take you fishing someday?
Well, a man can't love a woman more than that.

Ain't I always nice to your kid sister?
Don't I take her driving every night?
So, sit here at my feet
'Cause I like you when you're sweet
And you know it ain't feminine to fight.

Come on, Baby.

You can fill my pipe
And then go fetch my slippers
And boil me up another pot of tea
Then put another log on the fire, Babe
And come and tell me why you're leaving me.

Yeah, I wonder, don't you? There is nothing so ugly as a husband who bitterly attacks and demeans his wife. But there's nothing so beautiful as a loving relationship that conforms to God's magnificent design. Listen to these words from Dr. Richard Selzer in his book *Mortal Lessons: Notes in the Art of Surgery*. He writes as the surgeon observing one of his patients.

I stand by the bed where a young woman lies, her face post-operative, her mouth twisted in palsy, clownish. A tiny twig of the facial nerve, the one to the muscles of her mouth, has been severed. She will be thus from now on. The surgeon had followed with religious fervor the curve of her flesh; I promise you that. Nevertheless, to remove the tumor in her cheek, I had to cut the little nerve.

Her young husband is in the room. He stands on the opposite side of the bed, and together they seem to dwell in the evening lamplight, isolated from me, private. Who are they, I ask myself, he and this wry mouth I have made, who gaze at and touch each other so generously, greedily? The woman speaks.

"Will my mouth always be like this?" she asks.

"Yes," I say, "it will. It is because the nerve was cut."

She nods and is silent. But the young man's smiles.

"I like it," he says. "It's kind of cute."

All at once I know who he is. I understand, and I lower my gaze. One is not bold in an encounter with a god. Unmindful, he bends to kiss her crooked mouth, and I am so close I can see how he twists his own lips to accommodate to hers, to show her that their kiss still works. I remember that the gods appeared in ancient Greece as mortals, and I hold my breath and let the wonder in.[72]

"Jim, your mission this week, should you decide to accept it, is to respect your wife as the weaker vessel, but as one esteemed by God to have value equal to you. If you omit this ingredient from your marriage, it will be impossible to love your wife as Christ loved the church. Good luck, Jim."

---

[72] Richard Selzer, *Mortal Lessons: Notes in the Art of Surgery* (New York: A Harvest Book, 1974).

16

"OMISSION IMPOSSIBLE" PART 3

1 Peter 3:7c

INTRODUCTION

"**G**ood morning, Jim. Since you're still listening to these tapes that must mean you have accepted the mission to love your wife as Christ loved the church. Congratulations! As we have said, there're three essentials which cannot be omitted if you want to successfully complete your mission: 1) Get to know her (needs, nature, love language); 2) Value and respect her as a co-heir of eternal life; and, finally, your mission this week, should you choose to accept it: 3) Understand, protect, and strengthen the spiritual bond between you and your wife."

"Spiritual bond?" you ask. "What's so important about that? Besides, I leave spiritual things to my wife. She has delegated authority in that area. She picks the church, she reads stuff to the kids, and she teaches Sunday School. I don't have time for all that, especially with all these other missions you sent me on. Sometimes I'm gone for weeks at a time. What do you want out of me? I can't do everything."

"I understand, Jim. But I am only asking for the essentials here. Three things. Omit one or more of these and it will be impossible to maximize your marriage. And, guess what. If you're married and can't maximize your marriage, you can't maximize your life. I didn't put you on planet Earth to grow up, make some money, have some kids, and die. Just like Adam, I created you and placed you at a strategic place on this planet so you could have a global mission, a global outreach, and to continue this vision through the legacy of your children. And, guess what, Jim. If you're married, you cannot fulfill this vision without spiritual harmony with your wife. You are one now. You move as one. And to find and fulfill your purpose in life, you must be spiritually one with your wife. Your vision must be her vision. And without a vision people lose their zest and enthusiasm for life because they never figure out what it's all about."

Helen Keller was once asked, "Is there anything worse than being blind?" She said, "Yes, the most pathetic person in the whole world is a person who has sight but no vision." What is vision, after all? Vision is possessing a sense of purpose in life.[73] One with vision leaves a mark on the present by visualizing the future. Jonathan Swift (1699) said, "Vision is the art of seeing the invisible." "Jim, having vision is to sense and believe that I am a God of order and design and intelligence. Your lives are not the product of chance, but design. I have a design and purpose just for you and your wife. Your excitement and fulfillment in life will increase if you look for, pray for, and discover, one step at a time, that purpose."

"OK, OK. But what does this have to do with my wife?" "A lot, Jim. You see lots of men go off on their own to discover their destiny and leave their wives by the wayside as if their lives don't have equal value. The wife is just there to have the kids, clean the clothes, fix the meals, and a few other things, you know. Some fine Christian men

---

[73] Dennis Rainey, *Building Your Mate's Self-Esteem* (Nashville, TN: Thomas Nelson Publishers, 1995), 220.

even think the 'help-meet' passages teach that the woman is just there at the man's side to help him fulfill his destiny. She is simply a tool for him to use to fulfill his potential. This approach demeans the woman and completely overlooks the spiritual oneness between the husband and wife. 1 Peter 3:7c talks about the spiritual results of not treating your wife with respect as a coequal. Take a look at it."

"SAVING THE SAVED"
1 Peter

Salutation   1:1-2

Introduction   1:3-12

Body   "Our Plan of Salvation"

  I. Through Personal Sanctification—our Character   1:13-2:10

  II. Through Personal Submission—our Conduct   2:11-3:7

    A. Our Conduct in the World   2:11-17

    B. Our Conduct in our Jobs   2:18-25

    C. Our Conduct in our Homes   3:1-7

      1. Conduct of the Wife   1-6

      2. Conduct of the Husband   7

        a. Knowledge of His Wife   7a

        b. Respect for His Wife   7b

        c. Bonded to His Wife   7c

I. THE INTERPRETATION

A. Our Passage—1 Peter 3:7

. . . that your prayers may not be hindered.

"That" (*eis to* + the infinitive) introduces a purpose or result clause, probably a result clause in this case. That is, if a husband does not give his wife the respect and honor she is due, then the *result* will be an ineffectual prayer life (see v. 12). **"Your"** is plural, leading many scholars to believe that this refers to the prayer life of both the husband and his wife. The home is seen as a mini church. Thus, when the husband treats his wife disrespectfully, the spiritual bond between them is threatened. Their spiritual relationship is not affected, but their spiritual fellowship is broken, thus hindering their spiritual effectiveness and thus also their spiritual mission.

B. Other Passages

1. Genesis 2:24—Therefore a man shall leave his father and mother and be joined to his wife, and they shall become one flesh.

"One flesh" = complete bonding: body, soul (mind, emotions, will), and spirit. When this bonding is broken, there is a scarring of the soul and a tearing of the spirit.

2. 1 Corinthians 6:13b-20—Now the body *is* not for sexual immorality but for the Lord, and the Lord for the body. [14] And God both raised up the Lord and will also raise us up by His power. [15] Do you not know that your bodies are members of Christ? Shall I then take the members of Christ and make *them* members of a harlot? Certainly not! [16] Or do you not know that he who is joined to a harlot is one body *with her*? For *"the two,"* He says, *"shall become one flesh."* [17] But he who is joined to the Lord is one spirit *with Him*. [18] Flee sexual immorality. Every sin that a man does is outside the body, but he who commits sexual immorality sins against his own body. [19] Or do you not know that your body is the temple of the Holy Spirit *who is* in you, whom you have from God, and you are not your own? [20] For you were bought at a price; therefore glorify God in your body and in your spirit, which are God's.

Fusion of the bodies leads to fusion of the spirits; fusion of the spirits also leads to fusion of the bodies. One of the greatest forms of spiritual intimacy is praying together.

3. Malachi 2:14-16—Because the Lord has been witness
Between you and the wife of your youth,
With whom you have dealt treacherously;
Yet she is your companion
And your wife by covenant.
¹⁵But did He not make *them* one,
Having a remnant of the Spirit?
And why one?
He seeks godly offspring.
"Therefore take heed to your spirit,
And let none deal treacherously with the wife of his youth.
¹⁶"For the Lord God of Israel says
That He hates divorce,
For it covers one's garment with violence,"
Says the Lord of hosts.
Therefore take heed to your spirit,
That you do not deal treacherously."

Because of the way these men were treating their first wives, God would not accept their worship (2:13). **"Treacherously"** = *bgd* = to be deceitful or faithless, or to deal deceitfully or faithlessly regarding a promise or covenant. When these women were young, their husbands took vows to be faithful until death. Now they wanted to trade them in for younger models.

Here is what I think is going on with this verse: "But did He not make *them* [not in original text] one (*woman for Adam*), although He had plenty of the spirit of life left over (*to make more wives if He wanted to*) (Italics mine)?" In other words, if God intended Adam to have more than one wife, He would have made more than one wife for him.

"Take heed (*shmr* = guard, watch over) your own (*Niphil stem in the Hebrew is reflexive*) spirit (*ruah* = spirit; not *nephesh* = soul)"—to be deceitful or faithless to one's wife is to stop guarding one's spirit (see also vs. 16).

II. THE APPLICATION

A. The Husband is the Spiritual Guardian of his Home.

1. For Himself—Malachi 2:15-16: **We've seen that he is to guard or watch over his own spirit.**

2. For His Wife—Ephesians 5:25-26: **Husbands, love your wives, just as Christ also loved the church and gave Himself for her, [26] that He might sanctify and cleanse her with the washing of water by the word, . . .**

The husband is the protective shield of his wife to make sure she isn't subjected to false doctrine and to make sure Satan doesn't deceive her through feelings and emotions. The lives of both Solomon and Samson ended in tragedy because each let his feelings for his wives or wife lead them into false doctrine. Will you note the emphasis here in Ephesians on the washing of the water of the Word? Whether it's in church or in our homes, without a prominent place for the Word of God, there will be no sanctification. Jesus prayed for his disciples: "Cleanse them through truth; your Word is truth" (John 17:17).

3. For His Children—Ephesians 6:4: **"Fathers, provoke not your children to wrath, but bring them up in the training and admonition of the Lord."**

Note that "mothers" are conspicuous by their absence in this command to the fathers. It's not that mothers are nowhere in the background because they were included in the "parents" of 6:1. So the Holy Spirit very purposefully left the mothers out when assigning spiritual responsibility to the fathers for his children's rearing.

B. When a husband "acts treacherously" towards his wife, he wounds her spirit, his spirit, and the Spirit.

1. The Spirit—Ephesians 4:40: **"Do not grieve the Holy Spirit of God by whom you are sealed for the day of redemption."**

Will you look at the context here? It is one of derogatory words, anger, bitterness, unforgiveness. Although the interpretation here includes all Christians, it certainly doesn't exclude husbands and wives. When Christian husbands make up for their bruised egos by belittling their wives, who may have been home all day working away to make them happy, it grieves the Holy Spirit. It wounds Him.

Much of our disrespect is expressed in our words, which are like seeds planted into the spirit which can grow and sprout plants of pain and agony. Here is how one godly woman handled her husband's ugly words: "Bob, it's obvious you are really upset with me. In your shoes I might be upset too. But I know when your anger subsides, you will be sorry for what you've said to me. Therefore, I'm choosing not to receive these ugly words in my spirit. We'll talk again when your anger subsides and you can speak respectfully to me."

But since these lessons are primarily directed toward husbands so that we can better love our wives as Christ loved the church, let's remember the children's song about "Ants'hillvania."[74] It is about a prodigal ant, Ant-ony, who becomes an "independ-ant." Through his newly found independence, young Ant-ony left the ant hill and went off to do his own thing. He was going to be greater than all the great ants before him: Alex-anter the Great, Michel-ant-gelo, and Napole-ant. Ant-ony's friends tried to warn him with this little song about reaping what you sow:

First you pull the weeds then you rake and hoe,
Then you plant some seeds, that's the way you sow;
Just you wait and see, everyone will know
What you planted there when they start to grow.

Every plant has little seeds
That make others of its kind;
Apple seeds make apple trees,
And will do it every time.

---

[74] Ibid., 110.

Seeds make flowers and shrubs and trees,
Seeds make ferns and vines and weeds . . .
What do you plant is what you grow,
So be careful what you sow.

If we sow derogatory words in our marriage, words that tear down our wives, these insults, sarcasms, cynicisms, and criticisms will spawn their own seeds until our wives picture us as pits of pain. Proverbs 12:25 says, "Anxiety in the heart of a man weighs it down, but a good word makes it glad." If our wives associate us with verbal pain, their stomach will be in knots when they hear our car roll into the driveway. Your wife loves a good word; it brings gladness to her heart. As Mark Twain said, "I can live for two months on a good compliment." Praise is defined as "to give value, to lift up, to extol, to magnify, to commend, to applaud." Is that not what we have said "honor" means?

2. His Spirit—Malachi 2.

"Take heed to your spirit," the Lord says to the husbands that were dealing treacherously with their first wives. The husband who does this has his guard rail down; he exposes his spirit to all kinds of darts from the devil as well as self-inflicted damage. Remember, the human being is likened to a tabernacle in its make-up. His body is the outer court, his soul (mind, emotions, will) is the holy place, and his spirit is likened to the holy of holies.

In the holy of holies is the ark of the covenant. First of all, this ark contains the law of God that instructs the Israelites on what they should do. God thereby reveals himself and his will through the law. In like manner God makes himself and his will known to the believer's intuition that he may walk accordingly. Secondly, upon the ark we find the mercy seat sprinkled with blood. Here, God manifests his glory and receives man's worship. Similarly, every person redeemed by the blood has his spirit quickened; through this quickened spirit he worships and communes with God. As God formerly communed with Israel on the mercy seat, so he communes today with a believer in his blood-cleansed spirit. Thirdly, the ark is called the ark of testimony because it contains the Ten Commandments. Just as the two tablets of the law silently excused or accused the acts of Israel, so the believer's conscience, on which God's Spirit has written the law of God, bears witness for her against the conduct of the believer. "My conscience also bearing me witness in the Holy Spirit" (Romans 9:1).

Keil wants to say we lose our spirit when we deal treacherously with our wives.[75] That would contradict my understanding of the New Testament. But may I suggest when we deal treacherously with our wives, we allow Satan to influence our spirits to damage or darken our sense of intuition so that we make career and family decisions that are clouded and only according to human reason. Our communion with God is blocked so He doesn't listen to our prayers for our businesses or families, and our consciences become scarred over until we cannot feel the pricking of the Holy Spirit.

3. Her Spirit.

The major source of depression for a married woman is a wounded spirit. And the primary source of a wounded spirit for wives is the disregard and disrespect of their husbands. They just don't feel loved and appreciated by their husbands. How does this situation develop? Most of us marry people we love. And if we love them, certainly we respect them. How then does our respect degenerate into disrespect?

Harley has a good explanation in his book *Give and Take*.[76] He distinguishes between romantic love and caring love. Romantic love is something we experience when someone else meets our needs. Caring love is what someone else experiences when we try to meet their needs. Before marriage, engaged couples experience both types

---

[75] Carl Friedrich Keil, *The Twelve Minor Prophets*, vol. 2 (Grand Rapids: Wm. B. Eerdmans Publishing Company, 1967), 453.

[76] Willard F. Harley, Jr., *Give and Take* (Grand Rapids: Fleming H. Revell, 1996), 19ff.

of love. In fact, one leads to the other. When we care for someone we are dating, that is, making every effort to meet their needs without focusing on our own, they begin to feel romantic love for us, because romantic love is what we experience when someone else of the opposite sex meets our needs. They are making deposits into our love bank. When the account reaches a certain level, romantic love begins to blossom. Of course, these feelings of romantic love also cause us to care for the other person, and we want to meet their needs without regard to our own. Then when their love bank is at a certain level, they begin to experience romantic love, and the spiral goes up and off the charts in the form of a helix.

On the other hand, after marriage, what went up can easily come down. It works like this. Sue and John were deeply, romantically in love. They married and headed for a week of bliss in Cancun. John was looking forward to touring the nearby Mayan ruins, and Sue was expecting to relax on the beach between shopping excursions. Before they got married, Sue would have insisted on seeing the ruins just to make John happy, and John would have expressed enthusiasm about sunning and shopping. But on this day a change took place that would alter the course of their marriage.

John felt it was time for him to exert his leadership by directing Sue toward activities that would be educational and edifying instead of frivolous. "Honey," he said, "Today we will be going to Tulum!" If he had asked, she would have been willing to join him, but he made it sound as if she had no choice in the matter. On the defensive, she replied, "If that's how you want to spend your day, go right ahead, but you'll be going alone."

In the past, John would have apologized immediately, sensing her hurt feelings. But this time he thought she was being stubborn and foolish. "Open your eyes and take in the world around you," he pontificated. "You'll miss the best life has to offer." She shot right back: "My eyes are open, wide open–and I don't like what I'm seeing."

"Honey," John responded, pushing even harder, "if you don't broaden your horizons, you'll become an ignorant housewife, just like your mother." Oops. In a flash, there're more ruins in Mexico.

In a moment, everything changed. John wanted to go to the ruins so badly that he sacrificed Sue's happiness. When he tried to justify his own itinerary by mocking her plans for the day and her mother, she was doubly offended. What happened to Sue and John?

Instead of an upward spiral into the heavens, they experienced a downward tornado of feelings which led to a loss of romantic love. It's what some call "the negative feedback loop." In short, they stopped caring for each other. During their courtship, both made the decision to care for the other, based on their first impressions. That decision was a decisive moment because, once it was made, romantic love was almost inevitable. The effectiveness of their mutual care drove their love banks through the threshold of romantic love, and then they had both kinds of love–the decision to care and the feeling of irresistible attraction.

The concepts of caring love and romantic love usually come together in marriage. We care for our spouses when we try to make them happy and avoid making them unhappy. That, in turn, causes our spouses to feel romantic love for us. Our spouses' care for us causes us to feel romantic love in return. You see, romantic love is a litmus test of our ability to care. If we are effective in our caring, romantic love is the outcome, because we are depositing love units and avoiding their withdrawal. When our spouses no longer feel in love with us, we are failing to care for them effectively. Romantic love is simply the result of effective caring.

Before marriage, Sue and John followed the rule of caring love: Do whatever you can to make the other person happy and avoid anything that would make the other person unhappy. But after marriage, John started a new rule, the rule of not caring: Do whatever you can to make yourself happy and avoid anything that makes you unhappy. It wasn't long before Sue was following the same new rule. 1 Peter 3:7 is about caring love, *agape* love. When this is practiced, romantic love is almost inevitable. When it is not practiced, the wife senses her husband doesn't care. Her spirit is wounded. In time, she also ceases to care.

"Jim, to put all this together, what I'm trying to do is to expand your concept of your mission in life to include your wife. The two of you are one flesh. And the strongest bond between you is the one you can't even see–it's spiritual in nature. By moving in union with mutual respect for the talents and gifts, the feelings and opinions, and the needs of each other, you can discover the very purpose for which I created you. And when you have discovered and lived it out, you in turn can pass this down as a legacy to your children and grandchildren. This is maximized marriage because it is maximized love."

In her book, *Gift from the Sea*, Anne Lindbergh says, "Love does not consist in gazing at each other, but in looking outward together in the same direction. In other words, love doesn't turn us inward toward one another; love in its highest form so unites two so that they become one, and in their oneness their shared love faces outward to have an impact on the society around them."[77] "Love—inside/out; this, Jim, is your ultimate mission, a global mission, a world vision. For your sake, I hope you decide to accept it."

CONCLUSION

Our God is a God of restoration, but repentance precedes restoration. Perhaps you have dealt treacherously with the wife of your youth. You have put your needs before hers, have not honored and respected her as an equal, wounded her spirit, maybe even traded her in for a new model.

Remember Ant-ony from an Ants'illvania? Ant-ony finally concluded that he had been sowing the wrong seeds in his independence. The parable ends as he becomes a "repent-ant" and decides to come home. You too can enter the blessing of God again in your marriage, but before restoration comes repentance. Like Ant-ony, you must become a repent-ant. You must come home. So, what are you waiting for? Come home.

---

[77] Anne Morrow Lindbergh, *Gift from the Sea* (New York: Pantheon Books, 2005), n.a.

17

"THE GOOD LIFE"
PART 1

1 Peter 3:8-9

INTRODUCTION

You've seen the headlines blazing that our schools are in crisis; you've heard our educators bemoan the fact that Johnny can't read, can't spell, and can't do his math. But one headline you won't see, because people don't recognize the problem: Johnny can't *feel!*

Johnny Carlton was taught early in life to keep his needs and feelings to himself. "Keep a stiff upper lip," was his father's favorite phrase. His mother echoed that sentiment with a stern admonition, "Big boys don't cry." When Johnny fell down and cut his knee, he knew better than to run home blubbering. If he held the tears back and assured his mother it didn't hurt when she applied the stinging red iodine, she would reward him with an approving smile. Is it any wonder, when Johnny married Marla, she accused him of being distant, unapproachable, and unfeeling? The vulnerable little boy was locked deep inside a fortress of self-preservation-built stone by stone by parents who thought they were doing the right thing.

We are all programmed from an early age to focus on achievement, not on emotional development. Young children are praised for learning to tie their shoes, but who helps them identify times when they're sad, angry, or happy? School-age children begin the treadmill of activities–Scouts, dance, sports, piano–but when do they learn to deal with the rejections and disappointments that inevitably accompany these activities? And what happens when we grow up? Most of us enter marriage without an adequate "feelings vocabulary," or much experience in emotional sharing. Is it any wonder our marriages lack closeness?

Think about it. You probably married with hopes of developing a deep emotional closeness only to find that neither you nor your partner knew exactly how to achieve such a relationship. Frustrated by the lack of intimacy, one or both of you (perhaps unconsciously) began seeking a way to escape. At some point, you woke up one morning to find that you and your partner had drifted apart into very separate worlds. One or both of you may be absorbed by the demands of the office or workplace; you may have escaped into the role of "super parent"; or you may be consumed by an endless onslaught of activities. Busy work. Anything to keep you from feeling the pain of your relationship.

What kind of life is that? In 1 Peter 3:8-12 we want to look at what we will call the "Good Life." When I say, "Good Life," what pops into your mind? I'll just bet most of us have lived long enough to realize the "Good Life" does not consist of the things we possess. Rather, may I suggest the quality of your life can be measured by the quality of your relationships. But therein lies the problem. What are we supposed to do about those who hurt us? That is a relational monkey wrench most of us don't know how to solve.

In John 10 Christ said He came that we might have life and have it abundantly. That refers to life in the here and now, not in the hereafter. But earlier in the verse it said that the thief comes to steal and to rob. The thief is Satan, who comes to keep us from having the quality of life, the "Good Life," the abundant life Christ wants us to have. And I would suggest that the main strategy used by the devil is to ruin our horizontal relationships. He wants to keep us from getting close to anyone. And the tools he uses to do that are the hurts we inflict upon each other as we bull-rush through life. These hurts are real feelings that must be dealt with if we are ever going to have the quality of life our Savior offers. But how do we do it?

"SAVING THE SAVED"
1 Peter

Salutation	1:1-2
Introduction	1:3-12

Body   "Our Plan of Salvation"

I. Through Personal Sanctification—our Character	1:13-2:10
II. Through Personal Submission—our Conduct	2:11-3:7
III. Through Personal Suffering—Our Courage	3:8-4:19
A. Suffering without Fear	3:8-22
1. A Proper Attitude	8-15a
2. A Prepared Answer	15b-17
3. A Perfect Appeal	18-22
B. Suffering in the Flesh	4:1-11
C. Suffering for the Faith	4:12-19

In dealing with this problem of horizontal crashes and clashes we want to look at our proper response when others are hurt (8); then we will look at the right response when we are hurt (9).

I. OUR RESPONSE WHEN OTHERS ARE HURT   8

Finally, all of you be of one mind, having compassion for one another; love as brothers, be tenderhearted, be courteous . . .

This whole section parallels Romans 12:9ff to extent that commentators wonder if Peter is using Paul as he writes this. Romans

12:9ff is a section on loving relationships, as is this. It is difficult to decide if 1 Peter 3:8-12 goes with the preceding section on household relationships or with what follows. Perhaps it is best to see it applying to both. It serves as a transition as we move to the third main portion of the body of this letter. The first section of the letter focused on our character, our sanctification; the second part of the body looked at our conduct, our submission to authority; this final section turns our eyes toward our courage in the midst of personal suffering. In any case, the big idea is this: **the quality of our life depends on the quality of our relationships.**

In verse 8 we have five adjectives in a row (in the Greek). All deal with our feelings except the first one: "one mind" = *homo* + *phrones* = same + attitude = the same attitude. We are all to have the same attitude. What attitude is that? The following four adjectives describe it for us:

1. **"Having compassion for one another"** = *sympathies* = be sympathetic = **feel** for the other person. Much of compassion involves not just seeing the situation or hurt from the wounded person's point of view, although that's a good place to start, but it is to actually feel what they feel to some extent. Obviously, if we have not experienced their hurt, we cannot feel exactly as they do, but if we can imagine being in the same situation, we can usually feel some of their pain.

2. **"Love as brothers"** = *philē* + *adelphoi* = have emotional love for your brothers = feel affection for your brothers.

3. **"Be tenderhearted"** = *eu* + *splanchnoi* = good + deep feelings. We find this same word used by Paul in a section on good horizontal relationships. He uses it in Ephesians 4:32 in connection with forgiveness: "Be kind to one another, tenderhearted, forgiving one another, even as God in Christ forgave you." This is all counterintuitive. When someone has hurt us, our natural feelings are

anger, bitterness, perhaps even hatred. Forgiveness and tender feelings are the furthest things from our mind. Once again, it's an example how God has called us to a supernatural standard of living. Of course, this is impossible to do with our natural abilities. It requires supernatural power; it requires the power of the Holy Spirit. But it's also one of the most beautiful experiences in the Christian life. When we are able to forgive and feel compassion for the people who have hurt us, we know that God is alive and well within us. We didn't do it; He did.

4. **"Be courteous"** = *philē* + *phroneō* = have an attitude of affection, warm feelings. Some translations follow a different Greek text tradition and have the word *tapeino* here instead of *philē*. The first word speaks of "humility" while the second we have already seen speaks of emotional love. Either way the right attitude is the key to harmonious horizontal relationships.

We would conclude the thrust of this verse as: **We are to validate each other's feelings.** But what does it mean to validate someone's feelings? Simple, but difficult. To validate in this context simply means to acknowledge the reality of your friend, mate, or child's feelings. If they're crying, the opposite of validating their feelings would be to tell them to stop crying. Or, to tell them there's no reason for crying. Or, to fill them in on the facts in order to get them to stop crying. Maybe crying is just what the doctor ordered. "Blessed are they who mourn, for they shall be comforted." Maybe they can't be comforted until they mourn. And Romans 12:15 says you are to mourn with them: "Rejoice with those who rejoice and weep with those who weep."

When I saw Betty crying at a wedding recently, I made the mistake of asking, "Why are you crying? This is the beginning of the wedding." She simply responded by saying she was a woman and didn't have to have a good reason to cry. On the other hand, if she comes in on cloud nine, bubbling over and giddy over who knows what, the last thing she needs from me is some statement like, "What are you so happy about? Don't you know the sky is falling?" I am to rejoice with her. You see, we can never really be close until we are able to validate each other's feelings. If I can't tell someone how I feel, then I will be **alone with my feelings**. That only increases my loneliness. And that is why relationships are so important.

People will say, "Well, I just take my feelings to the Lord. He's all I need." Okay, then you are an abnormal Christian. I don't mean to offend you. God can certainly comfort us. But Adam had God in the garden before sin and before Eve, and God said it wasn't good for Adam to be alone. So, God has three institutions to offset our loneliness: marriage, family, and the church (which is a family of brothers and sisters in Christ).

But for all this to work, we must break the negative feedback loop. That means, when you hurt me, I'll hurt you. If you show me you don't care for me, then I'll show you I don't care for you. If I want to spend time alone with you, but you never give it a second thought, I feel hurt. Instead of speaking the truth to you in love, I decide to hurt you in return by not doing something you want me to do, like being the spiritual leader in the home, or fixing the leaky faucet, or carving time out for family activities. I'm suddenly awfully busy at the office. These are the common ways people deal with each other.

Our next verse anticipates this unhealthy way of dealing with pain.

II. OUR RESPONSE WHEN WE ARE HURT   9

> . . . not returning evil for evil or reviling for reviling, but on the contrary blessing, knowing that you were called to this, that you may inherit a blessing.

There is a healthy way to deal with our own hurts, and there is an unhealthy way. The latter is to hurt those who have hurt us (to return evil for evil and insult for insult). The most natural response to an attack is to attack back. If you hurt me, I'll hurt you. So, we are told not to return evil for evil or insult for insult. On the contrary, we are to do just the opposite. Rather than verbally attacking, we are to speak a "blessing."

"Blessing" = *eu* + *logeō* = good + to speak = to eulogize = to say something good. In Ephesians 4:29 we read, "Let no corrupt word proceed out of your mouth, but what is good for necessary edification, that it may impart grace to the hearers." The word "corrupt" (*sapros*) is not talking about cussing. It is used of that which is rotten or spoiled like fish or fruit. It is the opposite of that which edifying or builds up; it depreciates or tears down. Our flesh loves to tear down those who have hurt us. Others may not know what a rotten person they really are, so we feel compelled to enlighten them. Even if there is a moral lapse or glitch in their lives twenty years prior, we feel others must know about it. Paul tells us to stop this kind of tearing each other down. We are on the same team. The devil is our enemy, not other brothers and sisters in Christ. People make mistakes. Let's purpose to show them some grace. Isn't that what the end of the verses challenges us to do ("impart grace")? We hear a lot about racism in America these days. At Grace School of Theology we like to call each other **gracists**. We purpose to impart grace whenever we get a chance.

Peter echoes Paul's thinking but adds a new dimension to motivate us. He says if we bless others, we will be blessed. And by coupling the word "blessing" to the word "inherit," the implication is that this blessing may be at the Judgment Seat of Christ where our ultimate inheritance is revealed (1:4 and 3:7). Speaking well of those who have hurt us may not yield any positive feedback here on earth, but it will someday: "Well done, good and faithful servant." Now that's a blessing!

But doesn't this mean I must stuff my hurts? No.

1. Ephesians 4:15 tells us to "speak the truth in love." This is done in the context of family members (in this case, it's members of the family—the Body of Christ). To not do this is to keep us from "growing up" (Ephesians 4:15). So,

if a family member hurts me, I need to tell him or her in love.

2. Romans 12:15 tells us to rejoice with those who rejoice and weep with those who weep. (Note that both Romans 12 and Ephesians 4 begin with teaching about the Body of Christ–family truth.) I am to validate my brother's feelings. But he is also to validate mine. Perhaps that is why 1 Peter 3:8 begins with an adjective telling us to have "the same mind (attitude or mindset)." We must mutually agree to bear one another's burdens so as to completely fulfill the law of Christ (Galatians 6:2).

3. Putting Ephesians 4:15 and Romans 12:15 together with 1 Peter 3:8-9:

    a. Hurt by a family member—I should tell them in love (don't clam up or blow up), and they should validate my pain and seek forgiveness for causing the pain (assuming they did).

    b. Hurt by a non-family member—since they probably are not committed to these principles, it will only hurt more to expose your pain to them. That is what family members are for. So, I should go to a family member committed to the same principles. That's what three of God's divine institutions are for (marriage, physical family, and spiritual family): to take away our loneliness. If I bury my pain, I extend and increase my own loneliness.

CONCLUSION

How can I ever forget Rene Morrison. After about twenty years of marriage his wife became a believer and invited Rene to our church. No way. But he saw such a change in her that he said, "OK, I'll go, but if just one man tries to put his arms around me, I'll never go back." Rene stood at the back—never sat down during the service and ran like a scared rabbit when the service was over. But he kept coming. He was a tough guy; football scholarship to college; running back; worked out five days a week to maintain his college weight and physique. Feelings were for women and little children, but not men, especially tough guys.

One day he came to me and asked when the next trip to Israel was coming. He said he wanted to be baptized in the Jordan River to declare his new faith in Christ. We did it. When we got back to Houston, I asked him to share his story with the congregation (not thinking he would accept; O, me of little faith). He did. He told them how he had grown up in a convent-like atmosphere where the nuns were constantly trying to scare the hell out of him. Didn't work. He wanted nothing to do with that kind of God. But when he heard about a love you couldn't earn and couldn't lose, Rene was all over it. He trusted Christ as his Savior. He invited anyone that wrestled with fear to come to him. He knew the answer.

Suddenly Rene started losing weight—thirty pounds in one month. He was diagnosed with esophageal cancer. The next month he lost another thirty pounds and died. But before he died his final request was for Paul Barrett, a beloved veterinarian and Sunday School teacher in our church who was dying of ALS, be brought to his home so he could spend some time with him in Rene's bedroom before either of them died. Now get this. At that point, neither of them could talk. But when they wheeled Dr. Barrett into Rene's room on a gurney, you could sense the supernatural in the room. I have no idea what passed between those two before they died, but I know if Rene could have made one more request, it would have been to get a great big hug from Paul Barrett.

Rene had gone from a walled-up macho man to an open-hearted warrior healed from the pain and wounds from his past. How was he healed? By learning to share his own pain and bear the pain of his brothers.

18

"THE GOOD LIFE"
PART 2

1 Peter 3:10-11

INTRODUCTION

Sometime ago there was a *Peanuts* cartoon in which Lucy is in the outfield playing a baseball game. Of course, Charlie Brown is on the mound pitching. Lucy calls out to him, "Hey, manager! Ask your catcher if he still loves me!" Charlie Brown interrupts his pitching and says to the catcher, "She wants to know if you still love her." Then, in the next frame, he turns to Lucy and yells to Lucy, "He says, 'No!'" Then Lucy wants to know why not. He relays the information to Lucy again: "He says there are so many reasons he can't remember them all." This upsets Lucy, and she responds, "Really? That's very depressing." Finally, Charlie Brown, exasperated, cries out, "Do you mind if we get on with the game?" Lucy's response is, "Game? What game?" "The baseball game!" shouts Charlie Brown, to which Lucy responds, "Oh, that's right. I was wondering why I was standing out here."

Lucy's dilemma was not at all uncommon. People can be totally preoccupied with the game of life until they discover their relationships are falling apart and they don't know why. All of a sudden Lucy's main man does not love her, and she couldn't figure out what had gone wrong. And he was too busy playing the game to tell her. Suddenly, she couldn't remember what the game was all about.

Men and women today are busy playing a game I call "The Good Life." The game can be all-consuming. But when relationships start to fall apart, we sit in a stupefied position wondering what the game is all about. Pat Morley in his book *The Man in the Mirror* says,

> In pursuit of the good life, most men leave a trail of broken relationships . . . When we strike the right balance between task and relationship, we have peace. But when our relationships are out of balance, our insides ache.
>
> Most men start chasing the good life with clear thinking and pure motives. Our goal? To improve the standard of living for our family. The task is a means to an end. But we get so involved with the task–and it can be exciting–that we lose sight of why we are working so hard. We become confused, and what originally was a means to an end becomes the end in itself.
>
> The culture we live in values possessions and accomplishments more than people and relationships.[78]

What I am trying to suggest in these lessons on "The Good Life" is that good relationships are the good life. In other words, **the quality of our life is directly proportionate to the quality of our relationships.**

In our last lesson on good relationships we learned the principle of validating feelings. We learned that the Bible itself stresses the

---

[78] Pat Morley, *The Man in the Mirror* (Nashville: Thomas Nelson Publishers, 1992), 84-85.

importance of rejoicing with those who rejoice and weeping with those who weep. Learning to empathize and sympathize with the feelings of others is an important step in developing biblical love on the horizontal plane. And then we learned that we must avoid the negative feedback loop when someone hurts us or shares with us how we hurt them. Instead of attacking them and insulting them and turning our relationship into a war zone, we are to say something good, to give a blessing. If we do this, we shall inherit a blessing. And this brings us to our second lesson. The negative feedback loop or the positive feedback loop is just another way of describing an old biblical principle: as a man sows, so shall he also reap. Why is it that some people seem to attract a life of happiness, while others attract a life of misery? Is this just the hand of fate, or are we part of the cause?

"SAVING THE SAVED"
1 Peter

Salutation		1:1-2
Introduction		1:3-12
Body	"Our Plan of Salvation"	
I. Through Personal Sanctification—our Character		1:13-2:10
II. Through Personal Submission—our Conduct		2:11-3:7
III. Through Personal Suffering—Our Courage		3:8-4:19
A. Suffering without Fear		3:8-22
1. A Proper Attitude		8-15a
2. A Prepared Answer		15b-17
3. A Perfect Appeal		18-22
B. Suffering in the Flesh		4:1-11
C. Suffering for the Faith		4:12-19

THE LAW OF SOWING AND REAPING: WHATSOEVER A MAN SOWS, THAT SHALL HE ALSO REAP.

In verse 9 we were introduced to this law: give a blessing and you will inherit a blessing. Verses 10 and 11 illustrate this law of sowing and reaping.

I. TO SEE GOOD DAYS, SAY GOOD THINGS   10

For, "He who would love life and see good days, let him refrain his tongue from evil, and his lips from speaking deceit. . . ."

The word for **"good"** here is *agathos*, which is a word pointing to an intrinsic good, a good that is not necessarily observable externally. We find the same word in Romans 8:28 where we are promised that all things can work together for good for those who love God and are called according to His purpose. Usually it takes a lengthy period of time before we can see the good that comes out of even tragedies in our lives. I can imagine Elisabeth Elliot was in a great deal of shock when she learned that her husband and his friends had been killed by the Auca Indians in Ecuador. They were just peaceful missionaries trying to share the good news of Jesus. But decades later, after seeing the thousands of young people inspired to the mission field because of the sacrifice of her husband and his four friends, she could see the good coming from their sacrifice.

James tells us, "See how great a forest a little fire kindles! And the tongue *is* a fire, a world of iniquity. The tongue is so set among our members that it defiles the whole body, and sets on fire the course of nature; and it is set on fire by hell" (James 3:5b-6). Here we see the negative potential of the tongue. The story comes from a small Hungarian village. The little boy was playing with matches and accidentally started a fire that went on to destroy every house in the village–over two hundred homes. Just a little match.

Jesus said, "But those things which proceed out of the mouth come from the heart, and they defile a man" (Matthew 15:18). The spoken word itself can defile a person. When we say dirty things, we become dirty and we feel dirty. Or what about an argument? Ever "win" an argument and have a bad after-taste in your mouth? And what about manipulation? We use our tongues to manipulate a situation to meet our own needs. That's why manipulators rarely reflect joy. There is no joy from serving self. Joy comes from serving others (John 13:17).

Want to see good days? Say good things. One of the best things we can do with our tongues is to show genuine admiration for others. After World War I the German Kaiser was extremely disliked and despised by the people of Europe. Even his own nation turned against him, and he had to flee into Holland to save his life. The hatred against him was so intense that millions of people would've loved to tear him from limb to limb or burn him at the stake. In the midst of all this hatred, one little boy wrote to the Kaiser a simple, sincere letter glowing with kindness and admiration. This little boy said no matter what the others thought, he would always love Wilhelm as his emperor. The Kaiser was deeply touched by this letter and invited the little boy to come to see him. The boy came, and so did his mother. The Kaiser wound up marrying the mother of this little boy. Wow. What one word of admiration can do.

But the sowing principle involves more than just words.

II. TO SEE GOOD DAYS, DO GOOD THINGS   11a

Let him turn away from evil and do good . . .

Once again, the word for **"good"** is *agathos*, the word for an intrinsic good not necessarily observable from the outside. As James said, in the midst of trials if you're feeling depressed, find someone else who is worse off than you and help them. He says, "You'll be happy in your doing" (James 1:25). Jesus was teaching the same truth when He told His disciples in the upper room that the greatest among them would be their servant. Essentially, He's saying as we serve others we find fulfillment and joy. But He also says it's not enough just to know that fulfillment comes through serving others. You have to do something about what you know: "If you know these things, happy are you if you do them" (John 13:17).

Martin Ginsberg, a student of Dale Carnegie in Long Island,

New York, reported on how a nurse once did something that affected his life forever. He said it was Thanksgiving Day. He was ten years old and he was in a welfare ward of a city hospital and scheduled to undergo major orthopedic surgery the next day. He knew that he could only look forward to months of confinement, convalescence and pain. His father was dead. His mother and he lived alone in a small apartment and were on welfare. His mother was unable to visit him the day before his surgery.

As the day went on, Ginsberg became overwhelmed with feelings of loneliness, despair and fear. He knew his mother was home alone worrying about him, not having anyone to be with, not having anyone to eat with and not even having enough money for a Thanksgiving Day dinner. Tears welled up in his eyes, and he stuck his head under his pillow, pulled the covers over it, and cried silently, but also bitterly, so much that his body was racked with pain.

A young student nurse heard his sobbing and came over to him. She took the covers off his face and started wiping his tears. She told him how lonely she was, having to work that day and not being able to be with her family. She asked whether he would have dinner with her. She brought two trays of food: sliced turkey, mashed potatoes, cranberry sauce and ice cream for dessert. She talked to him and tried to calm his fears. Even though she was scheduled to go off duty at 4 PM, she stayed on her own time until almost 11 PM. She played games with him, talked to him and stayed with him until he finally fell asleep.

Many Thanksgivings have come and gone since Ginsberg was ten, but one never passes without his remembering that particular one and his feelings of frustration, fear, loneliness and the warmth and tenderness of the stranger that somehow made it all bearable.[79] Ginsberg learned a life lesson that Thanksgiving: **TO SEE GOOD DAYS, DO GOOD THINGS.**

---

[79] Dale Carnegie, *How to Win Friends and Influence People* (New York: Gallery Books, 1998), 64.

However, there is a qualifier, isn't there? Before we can do good things, we must "turn away from evil." The word for **"turn away"** (*ekklinaō*) means "to change one's course of travel." As the story goes a wealthy Englishman came to a point of despair in his life and decided to end it. He went out to the Thames River with the intent of jumping off and killing himself. As he approached the bridge, he felt in his pocket a bag of gold coins that he always carried with him. He thought to himself, "Well, these gold coins won't do anyone any good at the bottom of the river, so before I jump, I'll find some needy soul and give them to him." Before long he saw some hungry urchins on the street and followed them to their home. He asked politely if he could come in. Their mother was lying sick on her couch surrounded by squalor. The children were wearing rags and it looked like they hadn't bathed for a month. He pulled out the bag of coins and gave them the whole bag. They were so shocked they were speechless. The Englishmen turned and left, but as he walked down the street he was so happy that is depression lifted. He thought, "If that small act of kindness brings me so much joy, I think I'll dedicate my life to philanthropy." That's exactly what he did. By turning away from the act of suicide and finding someone else to help the course of his life changed. **TO SEE GOOD DAYS, DO GOOD THINGS.**

Sowing principle number one: To see good days, say good things; number two: To see good days, do good things; and number three: To see good days, pursue peace.

III. TO SEE GOOD DAYS: PURSUE PEACE   11b

Let him seek peace and pursue it.

Peter says we must **"seek"** peace and **"pursue"** it. Peace is trying to run from us. She is elusive. Peace must be sought and chased after. Jesus said, "Blessed are the peacemakers, for they shall be called the sons of God" (Matthew 5:9). Paul wrote: "If it is possible, as much as depends on you, live peaceably with all men" (Romans 12:18). The writer to the Hebrews offers this: "Pursue peace with all men . . . lest any root of bitterness springing up cause trouble, and by this many become defiled" (Hebrews 12:14-15). And James echoes the above when he observes: "Now the fruit of righteousness is sown in peace by those who make peace" (James 3:18).

The bottom line: if we don't learn how to resolve conflicts, we will not love life or see good days.

So, what are the biblical steps toward conflict resolution? Here are four taken from Philippians 4:4-9. The situation was a conflict between two key women in the local church: Euodia and Syntyche. Paul urges one of the local members, who remains anonymous, to help these two pillars of the church reestablish a peaceful relationship. How?

1. **Start on a positive note** (Philippians 4:4): "Rejoice in the Lord always. Again, I will say, rejoice!" If everything else seems awry between two believers, at least they have Jesus in common. He is their Savior. And here Paul appeals to him as their Lord. That's one positive thing these two sisters have to rejoice over.

2. **Look at the situation from her perspective**: "Let your gentleness be known to all men" (Philippians 4:5a). This word translated "gentleness" (*epieikes*) speaks of not pressing one's rights. Some translate it **"yieldedness"** (*BDAG*). In other words, you can be so right you're wrong. The person who always has to be right usually runs into problems in his horizontal relationships. Paul puts a higher value on peace than on being right. "But what if I am right?" someone will ask. "Am I supposed to pretend I'm wrong?" No, just don't press it. This word is used of God in the Greek translation of the OT (LXX). Israel was wrong; God was right. And He had every right to wipe Israel off the face of the earth. But He chose not to press His rights. That's *epieikes*. Just adopt the attitude that the other person *might* be right. In other words, sow

a peaceful attitude (not fighting for one's rights) and reap a peaceful relationship.

3. **Look at it from HIS perspective:** "The Lord is at hand" (Philippians 4:5b). Get the big picture. The NT teaches us that Jesus could come back at any moment. We are to live our lives in light of His imminent return. Now, what if He were to come back right now? How important would it be to prove you are right in whatever matter has come between you and another believer? In other words, adopt an attitude of expectancy. Look at your situation in light of eternity. I'm relatively tall (6'4"). Once a short friend of mine, with whom I was not having any conflict, came up to me out of the blue, looked up, and said, "Ya know, Anderson, I'm going to have to put up with you forever. I might as well start now." We both laughed, but he hit on something there. There won't be any war in heaven. All believers will get along and love each other. Why not start now?

4. **End on a positive note: pray with each other.** "Be anxious for nothing, but in everything by prayer and supplication, with thanksgiving, let your requests be made known to God; ⁷ and the peace of God, which surpasses all understanding, will guard your hearts and minds through Christ Jesus" (Philippians 4:6-7). These verses are so comforting that most Bible memory programs have them memorized out of context. No problem. They can stand on their own. However, they do have a context. They come in the midst of a passage on peace between two church workers. The problem of peace or lack thereof is presented in Philippians 4:1-3; the pathway to peace is in 4:4-7; and the preservation of peace is in 4:8-9. Notice how v. 7 promised peace; so does v. 9: "The peace of God will be with you." Essentially vv. 8-9 tell us to focus on the positive traits of the person with whom we have or

had a problem. Our minds tend to drift back to the hurt, the pain, or the way we were unfairly treated. Soon all we can think about are the negative traits of the offender. Paul tells us to stop that. Switch our minds to the positive. Dwell on those things and the peace of God will be with us.

TO SEE GOOD DAYS, PURSUE PEACE.

CONCLUSION

Whatsoever a man sows, that shall he also reap. To reap a good life I must sow good things (good words, good deeds, and good attitudes). St. Francis of Assisi summed it up this way:

Lord, make me an instrument of your peace!
Where there is hatred, let me sow love;
Where there is injury, pardon;
Where there is doubt, Faith;
Where there is despair, hope;
Where there is darkness, light;
Where there is sadness, Joy.

O Divine Master, granted I may not so much seek
To be consoled as to console;
To be understood has to understand;
To be loved as to love.
For it is in giving that we receive;
It is in pardoning that we are pardoned;
And it is in dying that we *shall love life and see good days* (italics and words, mine).

19

"THE LAMPLIGHTER"
PART 1

1 Peter 3:13-17

INTRODUCTION

The persecution of Christians around the world is growing exponentially. The diabolical exploits of Boca Haram and ISIS are well documented. But such persecution is not isolated to Muslim hatred of Christian infidels. In Pakistan a Christian pastor says that in 2016 over sixty people were killed by a bomb in a church. Four of them were his relatives. He himself was arrested for his faith. After four days in jail he told the authorities to just go ahead and kill him—get it over with. For an unknown reason they let him go. But we don't have to go outside America to find persecution. According to Thomas Horn,

> . . . persecution of Christians is on the increase in the United States. What's happening to bring about this change?
> According to some experts a pattern is emerging reminiscent of Jewish persecution in post war Germany. "Isolation of, and discrimination against Christians is growing

almost geometrically," says Don McAlvany in The Midnight Herald. "This is the way it started in Germany against the Jews. As they became more isolated and marginalized by the Nazi propaganda machine, as popular hatred and prejudice against the Jews increased among the German people, wholesale persecution followed. Could this be where the growing anti-Christian consensus in America is taking us?"

Tolerance of anti-Christian attitudes in the United States is escalating. Recently, a woman in Houston, Texas, was ordered by local police to stop handing out gospel tracts to children who knocked on her door during Halloween. Officers informed her that such activity is illegal (not true), and that she would be arrested if she continued. In Madison, Wisconsin, the Freedom from Religion Foundation distributes anti-Christian pamphlets to public school children entitled, "We Can Be Good Without God." The entertainment industry and syndicated media increasingly vilify Christians as sewer rats, vultures, and simple-minded social ingrates. The FBI and the Clinton White House brand fundamentalist Christian groups as hate mongers and potential terrorists. The Council of Religious Leaders of Metropolitan Chicago warns that plans by Southern Baptists to hold a convention in the Windy City next year might foment "hate crimes" against minorities, causing some Christians to fear that speaking openly about their religious beliefs will soon be considered a crime. All this, while Christianity itself is often a target of hate-crime violence. We remember the students at Columbine, and the United Methodist minister who was fatally beaten and burned in a remote part of Chattanooga, Tennessee, to name a few of the recent examples of interpersonal violence aimed at believers.[80]

---

[80] Thomas Horn, "Persecution of Christians Growing in the Unites States," https://www.worthynews.com/1710-persecution-of-christians-growing-in-the-united-states, accessed August 13, 2018.

And this was written almost twenty years ago. Has the attitude toward Christians Improved in America over these two decades? Hardly. Some say we live in a "Post-Christian America"; others say that America is 40% "evangelical." Whether America can be considered a Christian nation are not, this much is sure: Christians in America can no longer be considered unpersecuted. Now, you may not sense any persecution in your neighborhood or at work, but there's no debate that the cause of Christ is actively persecuted in America. What should our response be? Peter has the answer.

"SAVING THE SAVED"
1 Peter

Salutation		1:1-2
Introduction		1:3-12
Body	"Our Plan of Salvation"	
I. Through Personal Sanctification—our Character		1:13-2:10
II. Through Personal Submission—our Conduct		2:11-3:7
III. Through Personal Suffering—Our Courage		3:8-4:19
A. Suffering without Fear		3:8-22
1. A Proper Attitude		8-15a
2. A Prepared Answer		15b-17
3. A Perfect Appeal		18-22
B. Suffering in the Flesh		4:1-11
C. Suffering for the Faith		4:12-19

In I Peter 3:8-12 we see that sowing a "good life" reaps "The Good Life" from God. But what can we expect from men? 1 Peter 3:13ff says normally sowing a "good life" will reap tranquility from men as well (**"And who *is* he who will harm you if you become followers of what is good?"—I Peter 3:13**), although the possibility of trouble is always on the horizon (1 Peter 3:14ff). So, how do we respond to being hassled by humans because of our righteousness? Three ways: BE HAPPY; BE CALM; and BE FOCUSED.

I. BE HAPPY 14a

> But even if you should suffer for righteousness' sake, you are blessed.

When Peter writes **"should suffer,"** he employs a rare way of saying the verb (he uses a mood [the optative] that only occurs about 50 times in the NT). The optative mood speaks of a remote possibility. In other words, if you sow a "good life," you will normally see "good days." However, there is the remote possibility that you will face persecution (see v. 17 for the same idea, where once again with have the optative used in the phrase "if it is the will of God").

It needs to be noted the blessed suffering is **"for righteousness' sake."** There're different categories of suffering. The two broad categories are deserved and undeserved. In the deserved category, there is suffering because of our sin and suffering because of our foolishness. We understand suffering that is the result of our sinfulness. If I rob a bank and get caught and go to jail, my incarceration is deserved suffering. Or if I put all my savings on one stock and I lose that money, that suffering is the result of financial foolishness. So, we understand deserved suffering. We don't get disillusioned with our faith when we suffer for our sin or our foolishness.

The real problem is when we face undeserved suffering. This suffering also falls into two categories: innocent suffering and suffering for righteousness' sake. Innocent suffering would be like a child born with a disease that takes her life when she's five years old. There's no sin involved here on her part. We might link her disease to Adam's sin, but we can't attach it to any personal sin on her part. She was born with this disease. That's innocent suffering.

But suffering for righteousness' sake is suffering that we endure precisely because we are doing the right thing. In 2017 ISIS took the city of Mosul. They found some Christian missionaries there and decided to induce them to convert to Islam. They said they wouldn't behead the missionaries, but if they didn't convert, they would behead their children, which is exactly what they did. I think we can agree that their children would still be alive if these Americans were not missionaries in Iraq. It was a clear case of suffering because of righteousness.

Now the really hard thing to swallow is that Peter tells us in situations like this we are "blessed." This word **"blessed"** (*makarioi*) is the same one used in the "Beatitudes" by Jesus. Some people call the "Beatitudes" the Be-happy-tudes because this word *makarioi* can also be translated "happy." Now wait a minute. God wants me to be happy when my children have just been killed? What is this, some kind of sadistic joke? No, rather it points us to what I call "The Paradox of Persecution" we find in the Scriptures:

1. **The greater the heat, the greater the reward.** The only way to find happiness in this kind of situation is to propel our minds into another world. This is exactly what Jesus was telling his audience in his Sermon on the Mount: "Blessed are you when they revile and persecute you, and say all kinds of evil against you falsely for My sake. Rejoice and be exceedingly glad, for great *is* your reward in heaven, for so they persecuted the prophets who were before you" (Matthew 5:11-12). His answer to unfair suffering, unjust persecution? "For great is your reward in heaven." He takes them into another world. The interesting thing about these words is that they come at the end of the "Beatitudes." They are, in fact, the climax of the "Beatitudes." They build up to a crescendo when Jesus goes beyond "happy" (v. 11) to "rejoice and be exceedingly glad" (v. 12).

2. **The greater the heat, the greater the expansion.** The early persecution of the church just led to greater boldness on the part of the disciples. The Sanhedrin told Peter and

John to stop talking about Jesus, which they refused to do. When they reported their encounter with the Jewish authorities, it only emboldened the church to spread the good news faster.

3. **The greater the heat, the greater the Christ-likeness.** When sending out His disciples for some on-the-job training, Christ told them about the persecution they would attract. But He told them not to be surprised because, "A disciple is not above his teacher, nor a servant above his master. It is enough for a disciple that he be like his teacher, and a servant like his master." In other words, how can we be like Christ without going through some of the things Christ went through?

"The Paradox of Persecution" gives us three reasons to find happiness in the midst of persecution. But Peter tells us more. We can be happy, and we can also be calm.

II. BE CALM   14b

"And do not be afraid of their threats, nor be troubled."

The word for "troubled" is *tarassō*. It was used literally of the stirring or shaking up of water. Figuratively it meant "to stir up, disturb, unsettle, or throw into confusion" (*BDAG*), specifically to throw into mental or spiritual agitation. It is used in the well-known statement from Jesus as He prepares His disciples for His departure: "Let not your hearts be troubled" (John 14:1). In this particular context, *BDAG* suggests "intimidate": don't be intimidated by the threats of the persecutors.

We have mentioned our man in Pakistan. He is a student of Grace School of Theology via distance learning, but he is also the Billy Graham of Pakistan, having led over a hundred thousand teenagers to Christ in the past few years. He also trains two hundred pastors. As such, he is a marked man. Consequently, wherever he goes he has a police escort to protect him. He has been jailed and his family threatened. The only way he can sleep at night is to have offered his body a living sacrifice to the Lord. Such a sacrifice includes the possibility of death. He says once you make that kind of commitment the intimidation of threats is gone. His heart is not troubled; he lives without fear.

Peter quotes Isaiah 8:12 here. The occasion was the invasion of the Assyrians in the Old Testament. The Israelites were not to fear this foreign power, nor were the Christians to fear the Romans, who had invaded their land over six hundred years after the Assyrians. Why shouldn't we be afraid? Matthew 10 gives us three reasons:

1. **The Holy Spirit will give us the words to say.** "But when they deliver you up, do not worry about how or what you should speak. For it shall be given to you in that hour what you should speak; for it is not you who speak, but the Spirit of your Father who speaks in you" (Matthew 10:19-20). Several years ago, I went on an evangelistic trip to the Philippines with my daughter and Bob Tebow (Tim Tebow's dad). Bob has about a twenty-minute gospel presentation he has everyone memorize. Each morning we would start with large schools in the city. The principal would assemble the students, and we would share the gospel. As the day went on, we would go to smaller schools out in the jungle. Around noon we came to a small school with about a hundred students, but they had all gone home for lunch. Rather than sitting around, I asked our interpreter if we could take a walk. After about a half of a mile I saw a small group of people about hundred yards away. I asked the interpreter if we could go share with that group. I wanted to teach my daughter how to share the gospel in five minutes rather than twenty minutes in case she ever needed to do that. My daughter is a beautiful, tall, model stereotype— much desired by men. When we reached the small group

of people (about twelve), I began sharing through our interpreter. As I did so, I noticed an old woman without any teeth sitting in front of me cleaning a gun. Then I saw the man standing behind her with a bandolier of bullets across his chest and a rifle in his hand. Then I noticed they all had guns. All this while I'm sharing the gospel. Suddenly I realized I was talking to people from the New People's Army, the radical group that kills and kidnaps Westerners, and a stab of fear went through my gut. We were prime targets in the middle of their territory. I don't really remember what I said from that point, but God must've given us the words because when I asked them if they would like to receive Christ, at least six of them raised their hands, and I led them in prayer. It's probably the fastest I've ever shared the gospel. We got out of there as fast as we could, but I can truly say that our Great Shepherd prepared a table for us in the midst of our enemies.

2. **Persecutors can only destroy the body**. God can destroy the body and soul: "Do not fear those who kill the body but not the soul. But rather fear him who is able to destroy both soul and body in hell" (Matthew 10:28). Persecutors can only rob us of that which is temporal; God controls both the temporal and the eternal. We are reminded of the words of Jim Eliot: "He is no fool who gives up what he cannot keep to gain that which he cannot lose." We cannot keep our bodies, but our time on earth can be saved forever (1:9) as revealed by an inheritance at the Judgment Seat of Christ that is incorruptible and undefiled and cannot fade away (1:4). I recently suffered a stroke in my right optic nerve. No cure; no regeneration. It has left me two thirds blind in my right eye. They say I have a 30% chance of the same thing happening in my left eye within three years. That would mean no more reading

or driving *pour moi*. I assure you, the prospect of being blind holds no joy for me. I'm too old to learn Brail. But my joy is in knowing that this body is only temporary. An incorruptible body, tailor-made for me, is on its way.

3. **"His Eye is on the Sparrow."** "Do not fear therefore; you are of more value than many sparrows" (Matthew 10:31). Here He argues from the lessor to the greater. If He watches over the sparrows, He will certainly watch over us, who are of more value than sparrows. Or as Jesus put it, "Look at the birds of the air, for they neither sow, nor reap, nor gather into barns; yet your heavenly Father feeds them. Are you not of more value than they?" (Matthew 6:26). Sometimes the Scriptures argue from the greater to the lessor: "He who did not spare His own Son, but delivered Him up for us all, how shall he not with Him also freely give us all things?" If God did the big thing (what's bigger than offering His only begotten Son), of course He will take care of the little things. Either way, whether arguing from the lessor to the greater or the greater to the lessor, we can trust our heavenly Father to protect us. "Then why are some killed for Christ?" someone will ask. The only answer is what we see in Revelation 7:13-17 regarding the martyrs from the Tribulation Period: "Then one of the elders answered, saying to me, 'Who are these arrayed in white robes and where did they come from?' And I said to him, 'Sir, you know.' So, he said to me, 'These are the ones who come out of the great tribulation, and washed their robes and made them white in the blood of the Lamb. Therefore, they are before the throne of God and serve Him day and night in His temple. And He who sits on the throne will dwell among them. They shall neither hunger anymore nor thirst anymore; the sun shall not strike them, nor any heat; for the Lamb who is in the midst of the throne

will shepherd them and lead them to living fountains of waters. And God will wipe away every tear from their eyes.'"

So, in the midst of persecution we can **BE HAPPY** and **BE CALM**; but we can also **BE FOCUSED.**

III. BE FOCUSED   15a

But sanctify the Lord God in your hearts . . .

The word **"sanctify"** (*hagiazō*) means "to set apart." And here I prefer the NASB and NI over the NKJ, which have "Christ as Lord." There should be a special place in our hearts for Christ as Lord of our lives, that is, on the throne of our lives. That is a place set aside for Him. In the midst of persecution, we need to make sure Christ is reigning supreme in our lives. And with Him on the throne we need to focus on Him.

Fear, like faith, is a matter of focus. When I focus on the problem, in creeps fear. I need to focus on the One who can overcome the problem: Christ my Lord. The Lord of the universe is just that. No problem in the universe is bigger than He. His sovereignty and power can prevail over all circumstances.

I once had the opportunity to jump off a 550ft building. It was all quite safe since a wire was attached to a harness worn by the jumper. It's not a bungee jump since you almost reach terminal velocity (122mph) from that height and if you bounced, you'd probably hit the side of the building. So, the wire is programmed to slow you down for a nice, soft landing at the bottom.

I had already checked skydiving off my bucket list. I think that would be fun if you soloed because you could do tricks in the air, but they don't let you solo without a license–you'd kill yourself. So, I did a tandem, which means I was strapped to a professional. Surprisingly, I never had the sense of falling. Since you're flying parallel to the ground at 150mph and after you jump you accelerate to 122mph going down, the vectors are offsetting and there's no sensation of dropping. So, it was pretty boring until we opened the chute. Then it was fun to fly around.

But when you jump off a bridge or a building, you're just going straight down. There are no offsetting vectors. So, I wanted to see what that would feel like. I learned as a kid on roller coasters that if you blow out on the way down, you don't feel the fall. I wondered if that would be true jumping off the side of the building. So, I signed up.

What I was not prepared for was looking down at the street from over 500 feet. When you jump out of a plane for skydiving, you are at 13,000 feet. Everything there just looks flat, like looking down at the globe. So, the view is pretty immaterial; you don't even think about it. But when you're looking down from 500 feet, you see the street below and the people and the cars and other buildings around you– and your mind freaks out. It is saying, "No, no, no. Don't do this." Plus, as you're preparing to jump, your feet are on the edge of the building and you lean way out as far as you can, held back by only a couple three-foot, aluminum poles, one in each hand. That was pretty painful for my left shoulder, which is weak because it's artificial. I was wondering if I would let go too soon because of the pain. As I looked down, I sensed an element of fear. So, I had an idea: I just won't look down. When I jump, I will look at the horizon and I will blow out. And that did the trick. By blowing out as I jumped, I had no sense of falling. And by looking at horizon instead of down, I had no fear. Over in ten seconds.

It's the same way in the Christian life. When I look down at my circumstances, fear flows into my soul like a tsunami. I'm like Peter when he took his eyes off the Lord by looking down at the water and the waves. But when I look up to the heavens and the Lord of the universe, fear dissipates. It's all a matter of focus. If I focus on my circumstances, I feel fear; if I look up and focus on the Lord (Hebrews 12:1-2), I find the peace that passes understanding.

So, how should we respond in the midst of persecution whether it is our lives at stake in some foreign land or our cause right here in America? Peter says, **BE HAPPY**, **BE CALM**, and **BE FOCUSED**.

CONCLUSION

The potential problem facing these Christians was persecution that could lead to death. That may not be our problem, but if we live "good lives," we will still face problems. These three principles still apply: **BE HAPPY, BE CALM,** and **BE FOCUSED.**

As evening shadows faded and dusk was giving way to darkness, Robert Louis Stevenson, a small boy at the time, had his nose pressed against the window pane of his home. He was fascinated by the old-fashioned lamplighter coming down the street lighting the gas street lamps. "Look," he cried out in excitement to his nanny, "there's a man coming down the street punching holes in the darkness."[81] He went on to say that a good poet is able to see the world and life through the eyes of a child. One of his most famous poems, "The Lamplighter," probably reminded him of his own childhood memories:

> My tea is nearly ready and the sun has left the sky.
> It's time to take the window to see Leerie going by;
> For every night at teatime and before you take your seat,
> With lantern and with ladder he comes posting up the street.
>
> Now Tom would be a driver and Maria go to sea,
> And my papa's a banker and rich as he can be;
> But I, when I am stronger and can choose what I am to do,
> O Leerie, I'll go round at night and light the lamps with you!
>
> For we are very lucky, with a lamp before the door,
> And Leerie stops to light it as he lights so many more;
> And O! before you hurry bye with ladder and with light.
> O Leerie, see a little child and nod to him tonight!

Jesus also compared the faith that carries us heavenward as being like that of a child. He said His children are the light of the world. He sends us into a dark world to punch holes in the darkness. I like that.

---

[81] http://www.actsweb.org/darkness.php, accessed 8/23/2018.

It's an active mission; nothing passive about our Christian calling. And when we can respond to the persecution of this world against Christians and the cause of Christ with happiness, calmness, and a heavenly focus that dispels fear, then we can all be lamplighters, punching holes in the darkness of this world.

20

"THE LAMPLIGHTER"
PART 2

1 Peter 3:15b-17

INTRODUCTION

As we witness the attack on our Christian heritage (the Word of God, family values, and morality in general), what is the best way for us to block the erosion of our Christian roots? There're many good things we can do to help stop the steady drip of assaults on our faith: 1) Become informed on issues; 2) Exercise our privilege and responsibility to vote for our values; 3) Give money and time to protect what means so much to us; 4) Galvanize a campaign against the filth in our society. These are all good, admirable, and honorable endeavors. But none of them is the best thing we can do. That's found in 1 Peter 3:15b-17. The best thing we can do is to "punch holes in the darkness." We looked at that concept in our last lesson; this is the second lesson on "punching holes in the darkness." We do it by Planting the Seed, Preparing the Soil, and Pouring on the Salt. That's what we mean by "A Prepared Answer" in our outline.

"SAVING THE SAVED
1 Peter

I. PLANTING THE SEED   15b

> . . . always be ready to give a defense to everyone who asks you a reason for the hope that is in you, . . .

As a new believer when I went to college I certainly wasn't "ready" to give a defense of my faith. The first time I tried to share it was a total disaster. I was what they call a "walk-on" on the basketball team. Not surprisingly my best friends were on the team, but none of them was a Christian. One night my best friend and I went out to go bowling. On the way to the bowling alley I decided to share my faith. I had no training, and I don't even remember what I said. But I know this: my friend was highly offended, and we never made it to the bowling alley. He insisted I take him back to the campus. Essentially, that was the end of our friendship. It's so spooked me that I didn't share my faith again for two years. I simply wasn't ready.

What does it mean to be "ready"? It means to be prepared, to be trained. By learning just a few simple principles anyone can share his faith without any offense (other than the offense of the cross).

The turning point for me came when I agreed to go with a bunch of other college students to witness on the California beaches. Our trainers were Hal Lindsay, Bill Counts, and Jimmy Williams—sort of the Three Musketeers of Campus Crusade for Christ at the time. They made sure we knew what we were doing before we hit the beach. During that week I shared Christ with thirty-two people, and sixteen of them prayed to receive Christ as their Savior. The training made all the difference. Without it I probably would not be in ministry today. Have you been trained in how to share your faith? Most churches have a program to help you. I strongly urge you to take that training. It may well change your life.

The text says we must be ready to give a defense. The word for defense is *apologia* from which we get the English word apology. Apologetics is the field of study (usually associated with religious studies) whereby one prepares to defend his faith. Can you defend your faith? Why do you believe what you believe? According to Ken Ham's book *Already Gone*, evangelical kids don't leave the church during college. By that time he says they're already gone. What does he mean by that? He says that 39.8% of our churchgoing children have their first doubts about the Bible and its veracity in middle school; 47.3% have their first doubts in high school; only 10.6% had their first doubts in college. Although their bodies might be in the pew during middle school and high school, in their hearts they're already preparing their exit, which usually takes place soon after they leave home.[82]

Here are some of the questions in the mind of a typical middle school student before they hit high school:

- Why is there death and suffering if God is a good God?

- Why can't people of the same sex who love each other get married?

---

[82] Ken Ham and Brett Beemer, *Already Gone* (Green Forest, AR: Master Books, 2009), 20-33.

- Isn't it better to get divorced than to live unhappily?

- How can the earth be only a few thousand years old when it "looks" so old?

- Why is Jesus the "only way"?

- How come dinosaurs have nothing to do with the Bible or church?[83]

By now this young student is experiencing the conflict between her faith, which is not observable, and the observable facts she is learning in school. Over time this dichotomy between scientific facts and religious faith puts Christianity into the realm of the unprovable and the irrelevant (see Nancy Pearcy's book *Total Truth* for a full development).[84] Doubt about the Bible begins to sink in. Ham lists eight of the most common doubt starters:

- There is so much suffering in the world.

- The Bible has errors.

- Science shows the world is old.

- The Bible contradicts itself.

- The Bible was written by men.

- Evolution proves the Bible is wrong.

- Christians don't live by the Bible.

- The Bible was not translated correctly.[85]

Ham and Beemer claim we must go straight to the root cause of the erosion of faith among our youth: doubt. To remove doubt, we must have credible answers. We must be able to give an *apologia*

---

[83] Ibid., 97-98.

[84] Nancy Pearcy, *Total Truth* (Wheaton, IL: Crossway Books, 2004).

[85] Ibid., 107.

for our faith. Fortunately, some of the World View academies[86] do a great job of this, but only a small percentage of our kids attend one of these academies. Where, then, will our kids learn to defend their faith? It has to come from the parents first. But are the parents ready? Church? Well, if the pastor and youth leaders understand the importance of this training, they have a great opportunity to reinforce what the parents should be doing at home. Finally, there are some really great private Christian schools and home school materials that can prepare our kids. But mark it down. If we don't address these issues with our kids before they hit high school, it may be too late.

The word for "reason" is also informative. It's the word "word" or *logos* in Greek. In John 1:1 and 1 John 1:1 we are told that Jesus was the Word. At its root, the word meant "reason" or "logic." Its verb form is *logizomai,* which is an accounting term used for adding a column of figures. The point is that it is not a "feeling" word or a word for "emotions." Though the Christian life includes lot of feel-good times, at its core Christianity is based on reason and logic, not feelings and emotions. In other words, it makes sense. It is not fanaticism, which is faith without reason. Our faith is based on reason. When the facts are laid out and summated, the bottom line says, "Jesus is the answer."

When my sister was going to Baylor Medical School here in Houston, a Jewish guy who had graduated from Johns Hopkins University wanted to date her. He was an ardent evolutionist, so much so that even while attending medical school he would take time to go to seminars on evolution around the country to get the latest scoop in evolutionary research. My sister said she would go out with him if he would come to church with her. He agreed. When they walked in, and I did not know they were coming, I was preaching a message in Romans 11 entitled "Jews for Jesus."

They came over for lunch after church and this young man

---

[86] Just Google "Worldview Academy—Midland, TX."

enthralled me with slides showing microevolution (actually just positive mutations within a species). So, I asked him if he had ever observed a positive mutation going from a lower species to a higher species. He said that he had not (no one has). So, I said, "Well, doesn't the scientific method begin with an observation? It's called the 'theory of evolution,' but you can't have a theory without an observation and a hypothesis that is tested over and over under controlled conditions. This 'theory' is a misnomer and violates the law of reason." Believe it or not, the young man became a believer. He realized that evolutionary theory is not based on the scientific method; it's not reasonable.

For every attack against our faith, we have a reasonable answer. I once had a Jewish man start visiting our church. He was an MIT grad, made millions working for Compaq, retired and started teaching computer science at Rice when he got bored of sitting around. I gave him Josh MacDowell's book *Evidence that Demands a Verdict.* I really didn't expect him to read it, but he did. I was excited. We were going to examine the evidence. One evening we got in his electric boat and went out on Lake Woodlands (motorboats were not allowed on this small lake surrounded by expensive homes). I was all ready. He stopped the boat and said summarily, "Well, I'm not going to become a Christian." I was slack-jawed. Here I was all armed and ready. I didn't say anything. He went on: "I'm sure you have a good intellectual argument to refute any intellectual objection I can come up with. So, my rejection is not intellectual. It's social. I am comfortable in my Jewishness with my Jewish friends and my Jewish synagogue." We remained friends. My wife and I spent many evenings for ten years enjoying chamber music in his home, but we never again discussed Christ. He left me nowhere to go when he chose not to "reason together."

Jacob Neusner, a Jewish professor, is the most prolific writer I know of today. When I first started reading him about twenty years ago he had five hundred titles under his name. The joke was that if you call him and his secretary tells you he is working on a book, just say, "I'll hold." In his book *The Talmud*[87] Neusner says orthodox (religious) Jews believe the highest activity in human experience is "to reason Talmud." They actually believe that Moses and Yahweh are in heaven reasoning Talmud as you read these words. My point is that they believe Judaism is "reasonable." Just as the NT speaks of Jesus as the Word (*logos*), so the Old Testament speaks of Yahweh as the Word (*memre*).

We have every reason to believe we can give a good reason for the hope that is within us. And what hope might that be? Usually the NT hope refers to the blessed hope of Christ's return, but I don't think we can rule out of this context all the hope we have for a world where wrong is made right, where there is no more crying and suffering and disease and crime and so on. But let's not forget our main reason for clinging to this hope: an empty tomb. People like C. S. Lewis came to faith by invalidating the suggested options for the empty tomb (swoon theory, guards fell asleep, disciples stole his body, etc.—this is known as an apagogical proof by showing the absurdity of the other available options) until left with the only sensible solution: Jesus rose from the grave.

But just being prepared with a reasonable answer for our hope is not enough; we must also prepare the soil.

II. PREPARE THE SOIL   15c

... with meekness and fear ...

For a seed to grow it normally needs the right kind of soil, but it also needs the right kind of atmosphere. I can plant a seed that's full of life in some fertile soil in Alabama, and it will no doubt germinate. But I can plant the same seed in Antarctica, and it is very doubtful that it would sprout. Sometimes people don't receive our message because of its content; but sometimes they don't receive it because of the manner in which it is given.

---

[87] Jacob Neusner, *The Talmud* (Minneapolis: Fortress Press, 1994).

Peter tells us to give our answer with "meekness." This word (*prautēs*) means not overbearing or overly forceful. It is used to describe a horse in which the will is broken but not the spirit. It is easy to slip into what I call "in-your-face-grace." We have the greatest message in the world. It's about a love that cannot be earned and cannot be lost. No one else has this wonderful message. But to be haughty or judgmental or harsh when we share this message actually defaces the glorious beauty of the message.

By definition apologetics gives the defense of our Christian faith. But a defense often involves argumentation. Argumentation easily slips into ugly arguing. There are a couple of talk show hosts I avoid–not because they are not smart or articulate, but because they're argumentative. They continually butt in when their interviewee is speaking. They maintain the floor by speaking more loudly than the other person. I've often imagined being on their show and just shutting down when they interrupt. As long as they want to keep interrupting, I wouldn't have anything to say. I doubt that they would invite me back.

Another thing that bothers me about the talk show host that continually interrupts his interviewee and talks over him or her is that the host does not show his guest any respect. Peter wants us to give an answer with meekness and "fear." The word for **"fear"** is *phobos*, which probably means respect in this context. In fact, that's how the ESV and the NIV translate it. I had a classmate from Rice who went onto graduate school to get his masters and his PhD in engineering. He wound up managing a lot of people in a major oil company. As such, I picked up a lot of wisdom from him through the years when he wound up an elder in my church. One of those nuggets involved respect. He said we show respect for someone in two ways: 1) we listen to him; 2) we give weight to what he says. When we come across as know-it-alls in our defense of the gospel, we often don't respectfully listen to what the other person has to say or don't give any weight to what he says.

We are to plant a seed, not a sword; we are to plant a seed, not plough the soil. Much has been documented about the power of pets to lower blood pressure, help anxiety, decrease loneliness, and increase feelings of social support.[88] But there is not as much written on why pets have this salubrious effect on their masters. Here are four suggestions:

1. **Love—unconditional**. Someone remarked that their goal in life was to become the kind of person their dog thinks they are. Someone else asked, "How can you tell if your dog or your wife is your best friend? Answer? Put your wife and your dog in the trunk of your car and come back an hour later. Which of the two do you think will be glad to see you?" I know, I know, that's a terrible joke, but it's trying to say something about the love of a dog–it's unconditional.

2. **Warm**. This all goes back to our attitude toward unbelievers or those who oppose us. We are told that one of the main reasons for millennials dropping out of church is what they perceive to be an attitude of intolerance toward those that believe or behave differently from us. Judgmentalism and condemnation will not win many listening ears. I like to go walking at night when it is cooler. Across the street from us, our neighbors have an outdoor dog, a big black Labrador. He doesn't get much attention, so he waits for me to come out at night. I don't make a lot of noise when I walk, so I don't know how he knows when I'm coming. But if I go by his driveway without stopping to pet him, he moans and howls until I come. Because he is locked inside an iron gate, he can't come to me. But I reach through the gate and pet him and throw his bone three or four times. He's so happy he is shaking; it is the highlight of his day. And it draws

---

[88] https://newsinhealth.nih.gov/2018/02/power-pets, accessed October 4, 2018.

me in like a bowl of Homemade Vanilla Blue Bell ice cream.

3. **Not threatening.** A threatening person is an intimidating person. Someone may choose to listen to an intimidating person, but not because they want to; they are afraid not to. But they can scarcely wait to get away. When shared in a nonthreatening way, the gospel of good news is just that: good news. When I was a young pastor, I used to train people in our church to witness door to door. Most of them were afraid initially. But what we all discovered was that it was harder to get out of someone's house than to get in. Once the topic of spiritual things and our relationship with God was opened, people did not want to stop talking. The key was learning how to share Christ in a nonthreatening way. In other words, be a Labrador retriever instead of a Rottweiler.

4. **Value**–Our pets value us highly. Our pets do not come across as superior to us. But it is clear that we just might be the most important person in the world to them. It all goes back to attitude, doesn't it? If we believe as the Bible claims that every person is created in the image of God and has equal value, then we should value everyone equally, and of course that means every person is of equal value to us. Every person should be valued highly. Romans 12 tries to teach the equal value of each member of the body of Christ, in this case the local church. But as Paul launches into this important section in Romans 12 dealing with our horizontal relationships, he says that no one should value himself more highly than others (Romans 12:3). Each member of the body is of equal value and equal importance. And those who are not members of the body should be viewed as future members and friends.

After telling us to plant the seed and to prepare the soil, Peter tells us to pour on the salt.

III. POUR ON THE SALT   16-17

> . . . having a good conscience, that when they defame you as evildoers, those who revile your good conduct in Christ may be ashamed. 17 For it is better, if it is the will of God, to suffer for doing good than for doing evil.

Those who choose to be lamplighters can expect opposition. We will be **"reviled."** This word (*epēreazō*) means "to abuse, to take advantage of, or to say malicious things' (see Matthew 5:44). People will look for ways to discredit us. They especially look for inconsistencies in what we claim to believe and how we choose to behave. Having a **"good conscience"** helps us to arm for these attacks. In other words, we should live our lives with an awareness that others will be looking for any hook they can find to rip our lives apart and thus discredit our message.

The **"good conduct"** of verse 16 parallels the **"doing good"** of verse 17. The point is that those that are resisting the claims of Christ will try to discredit Him by pointing at us. That's why unbelievers are so good at spotting hypocrites. Our lives are supposed to be like light to attract bugs out of darkness, or like salt to either make people thirsty for Christ or to fertilize the soil. When I say pour on the salt, I'm thinking of fertilizer. This is a use for salt we rarely hear about, but Jesus Himself referenced it in Luke 14:34 when He said salt that has lost its flavor is neither fit for the land nor for the dunghill. Salt was used as a fertilizer to enrich the soil for their crops. They did this by putting the salt on the land and also in their compost piles.

But how can salt lose its flavor? In order to understand, we must realize there were two primary types of salt in use during the time of Christ. One was pure salt, just good old NaCl. It was used for table salt and as a preservative. The other was rock salt. This salt was found near the Dead Sea. It was simply a combination of rock and salt. If a block of this rock salt were left in the rain, the rainwater could wash all the salt out of the rock until the block was tasteless, that is, there was no more salt in the block. Now rock salt was preferred to pure salt as a fertilizer in that pure salt was too strong. Kind of like the grass fertilizers we use today. Put too much on and you simply burn the grass. So, they liked this rock salt. But, of course, when the salt had been washed out of the rock, the rock was worthless. Might as well throw it away.

When Jesus says we are the salt of the earth, he is being very literal. He means earth, not world or people. He says we, as Christians, have a function very similar to the rock salt used to fertilize the earth. Just as the fertilizer enriches the soil to make it more productive, so we are to be like fertilizer to make the seed more productive when it falls onto the soil. But how do we do that? How do we help enrich and prepare the soil to make it productive when the seed falls onto the soil? Jesus explains this after telling us we are the light of the world and should not put our light under a basket. Let it shine before men. Why? "That they may see your good works and glorify your Father in heaven" (Matthew 5:16). When they see our good life, they may be attracted to what is behind that life. When we explain Jesus, they may want to receive Him, and if they do so, their lives will glorify God someday in heaven. But remember, our life prepares the way for our lips: good works before good words.

I could have saved a lot of time if I had known this principle earlier, even though it seems intuitively obvious. I spent six years as a new Christian trying to talk my mother into receiving Christ. No headway. She was smarter than I was, so I couldn't outtalk her or outthink her. I was still in seminary in Dallas, but went home to Nashville once or twice a year to visit. After six years without making a dent, I stopped talking. I started praying for something I could do that would show her I was a different and better person than I used to be before Christ. Well, we lived on a small horse farm on the outskirts of Nashville. Instead of asphalt they had what they called hot-shot driveways. The hot-shot consisted of a small red pebble that got mushed to the side and the center of the driveway after lots of use. Normally, you call in some pros to use their machines to flatten the driveway out again. The driveway was long. It would cost several hundred dollars or more.

One morning mom left pretty early for some meetings and wouldn't be back until dinner time. I said, "Hmmm, our driveway needs flattening. Maybe I can do it by hand and shovel." So, I spent the rest of the morning and all afternoon doing just that. I was still out there when she drove home, passed me, and drove into the garage. I couldn't do anymore since it was getting dark, so I headed to the front door. She met me there and was actually crying. She said, "Nothing you have done since you have become what you call a born-again Christian has touched me until today." She became a believer shortly thereafter. Without the life, the lips can harden the soil instead of softening it or enriching it.

CONCLUSION

THE SEED; THE SOIL; AND THE SALT.

Remember these three essentials as you prepare yourself to give an answer for the hope that lies in you. This is an offensive strategy. God used it not to protect, but to propel; not to defend, but to disseminate; not to separate, but to saturate. Share the good news. It's the very best thing you can do. But perhaps the second-best thing you can do is to have a good reason for the hope that is within you. In other words, apologetics (defending the faith). Our country is blessed with a number great apologists. All of the ones I have observed have one thing in common besides being human and being Christians: they take what they're good at and use it to defend the faith.

If I'm looking for powerful apologists, I only have to look around the corner. A few blocks from our school is the ministry headquarters of Lee Strobel. He was a court reporter by training and profession who decided to use his secular training for spiritual purposes. The result is some of the most successful apologetic books of the last twenty years: *A Case for Christ, A Case for Faith, A Case for Miracles, A Case for Christianity*, and counting.

Then a few more blocks away lives Dinesh D'Souza. Best known for his political commentary and documentaries, most don't realize he spent years debating on the college campus and in other forums on behalf of Christianity. In fact, one of his books is *What's so Special about Christianity?* Again, D'Souza took what he was good at—writing—and decided to use it to defend the faith. An English major at Dartmouth University, he told me personally he began writing stories when he was just a little kid. He loves to write.

On the other side of Houston is one of the best Christian apologetics departments in the world at Houston Baptist University. They have scholars like William Lane Craig, but they also have a whole team of female apologists headed up by none other than Nancy Pearcy. She's another who took what God had given her (a great mind and an ability to write) to defend the faith.

But do you have to be a public speaker or writer or a scholar to stand up for your faith and make people thirsty for Christ? Of course not. My next-door neighbor for years was a professional golfer name Don Massingale. He became a believer about halfway through his years on the tour. While he was out there, he and Kermit Zarley helped start the tour Bible study. Then after he joined our church, he would invite someone from our neighborhood to play golf with us on Saturday afternoon. When he began doing this, we had about five families coming to the church from his neighborhood. Within a couple of years, we had over twenty families coming. Don wasn't a preacher or a scholar or a writer, but he took what he was good at and used it to make people thirsty for Christ. His younger brother, Rick, followed in his footsteps. What are you good at? It could be that God will use that to make people thirsty for Christ.

21

"DO I HAVE TO BE BAPTIZED TO GO TO HEAVEN?"

1 Peter 3:18-22

INTRODUCTION

As a pastor for decades it's been my privilege to baptize hundreds of people. Some of these baptisms have been more memorable than others. Like when we used the lake in my first church because we didn't have our own building. It was my first baptismal service and I quickly learned that I had not properly instructed those who were to be baptized. I thought it only proper to start with the girls. There was a cute 16-year-old high school girl who was first in line. So, I said, "Dawn, you can come in first?" She was wearing some cutoff jeans and a sweatshirt. But with no hesitation at all she pulled down her cutoff jeans and pulled off her sweatshirt. Alas, she was wearing a teensy-weensy yellow polka dot bikini (literally). The older men at the event began snickering among themselves, and I was so embarrassed that I submerged. But I learned; from that time forward, I gave everyone careful instructions on what to wear.

Then there was the time a bunch of college kids were driving thirty miles to come to our church. A bunch of them wanted to get baptized. One of the girls wanted to speak to me privately. She explained that she had always wanted to be baptized since she was a little girl but was afraid of the water. Did she have to be immersed? I said she didn't, but she decided she wanted to be immersed but couldn't stay under the water very long. So, the big day came. There were about twenty people lined up. When this young college girl entered the water, I had forgotten about her fear. Instead of lying backwards to go under the water, she just let her knees buckle. Unfortunately, her buckling wasn't enough to completely get her head under the water. So, I gently pushed on the top of her head. I felt resistance, so I pushed again. Then she began shaking, and I suddenly realized who this was and her fear of water. I quickly pulled her up out of the water and apologized profusely.

Humorous as some of these baptismal experiences have been, baptism itself is a serious subject. It's fair to say that most of those who name the name of Christ believe that water baptism is one of the keys that opens the pearly gates of heaven. Verses like Mark 16:16a seem to support this understanding: "He who has believed and has been baptized will be saved." Acts 2:38 is another popular verse used to support the claim one must be water baptized for eternal life: "Repent and be baptized for the remission of sins and you shall receive the gift of the Holy Spirit . . ."[89] By AD 100 all the early writers concerning Christianity saw water baptism as essential for going to heaven.

A completely heretical, but very influential document in the early church was *The Shepherd of Hermas*. The writer claims to have been a contemporary of Clement, presbyter-bishop of Rome (A.D. 92-101). Hermas is instructed by the "angel of repentance" who is dressed up as a shepherd. The call is for a lackadaisical church

---

[89] For an extended discussion of Acts 2:38 see Anderson, *Free Grace Soteriology*, 144-65. The discussion is obviously too long for an expositional book like this one.

to repent. The writing is thoroughly legalistic and never mentions the gospel of grace. He speaks of the meritorious system of good works and the atonement of sin through martyrdom. There is no mention of justification by faith, but water baptism is indispensable for salvation.[90] And water baptism is the seal of repentance which "makes Christians into Christians. . . . Asceticism and penal suffering are the school of conversion."[91] Faith is the fruit of repentance and baptism seals it.[92]

Justin Martyr followed on the heels of Hermas and also saw water baptism as the work of regeneration. He said: "Those who are convinced of the truth of our doctrine . . . are exhorted to prayer, fasting and repentance for past sins; . . . Then they are led by us to a place where there is water, and in this way they are regenerated, as we also have been regenerated; . . . For Christ says: Except you are born again, you cannot enter into the kingdom of heaven."[93] The importance of water baptism for Justin Martyr is underscored when he says "the laver of repentance . . . is baptism, the only thing which is able to cleanse those who have repented."[94]

Irenaeus (d. 200) also linked water baptism with regeneration because of passages like John 3:5 and Titus 3:5. And Cyril of Jerusalem (d. 386) called water baptism the "chariot to heaven." He believed the only way to get to heaven without water baptism was through martyrdom. By the time of Augustine (d. 430), infant baptism was in full vogue. And at the baptismal font, "We are justified, but righteousness itself grows as we go forward."[95] In the *ordo salutis* (order of salvation) Augustine saw predestination, calling,

---

90 Schaff, *History*, vol. 2. *Ante-Nicene Christianity*, 684-87.

91 Behm, "*metanoeō*," 4:1008.

92 Ibid., 4:1007.

93 J. Martyr, *Apol.I.*, c.61.

94 J. Martyr, *Dial.*, 14.1.

95 Augustine, *Sermon*, 158.5.

justification, and glorification. But justification was the umbrella over everything from regeneration through sanctification;[96] and regeneration began at baptism. He actually called it "the saving laver of regeneration."[97] Here the elect receive the external sign (the water of baptism) and the spiritual reality (regeneration and union with Christ). For Augustine, "the sacrament of baptism is undoubtedly the sacrament of regeneration."[98]

But other credible scholars claim that water baptism is simply symbolic of the spiritual reality of our identification with Christ when we receive Him as our Savior. These biblical interpreters say all we have to do to go to heaven is to believe in Jesus as Acts 16:31 explains: "Believe on the Lord Jesus Christ and you will be saved." They would argue that asking people to believe and be baptized to go to heaven is the same as asking people to believe and be circumcised to go to heaven, since both circumcision and water baptism are physical acts done by physical means and are physically observable in contrast to faith.

Who is right? Our passage in this lesson may be the most difficult passage in 1 Peter to explain, and it too appears to present water baptism as an act that can take us to heaven. This lesson will be more theological then exegetical, but there's so much confusion on the Holy Spirit's role in both justification and sanctification that I hope we can use this passage for some clarification. Warning: this will be more technical than anything else we have or will do in this book. If you find it a bit too much, just skip over this chapter. Bottom line: we will try to show that baptism of the Holy Spirit gives us a new relationship with God, but water baptism gives us increased fellowship with God.

---

96 Demarest, *Cross and Salvation*, 351.

97 Augustine, *Sermon*, 213.8.

98 Idem., *On Forgiveness of Sins, and Baptism*, II.43.

"SAVING THE SAVED"
1 Peter

PRINCIPLE: BAPTISM BY THE HOLY SPIRIT ESTABLISHES OUR RELATIONSHIP WITH CHIRST AND IS ESSENTIAL TO ENTER HEAVEN.

Let's repeat that. We want to establish this principle: Baptism by the Holy Spirit establishes our relationship with Christ and is essential in this dispensation to enter heaven. So, in one sense we are agreeing with those who say baptism is essential to go to heaven. We just don't think it's water baptism that is necessary; rather it is the baptism of the Holy Spirit. Our next verse in 1 Peter claims as much:

I. OUR RELATIONSHIP WITH CHRIST   18-20

A. Our Position in Christ—through baptism by the Holy Spirit 18

> For Christ also suffered once for sins, the just for the unjust, that He might bring us to God, being put to death in the flesh but made alive by the Spirit, . . . (3:18)

Our position in Christ is on Peter's mind (3:16). He remembers what it was like to suffer for evil doing when he denied Christ and was afraid of persecution. But after Pentecost this same Peter is a bold witness, not afraid of persecution. It was the baptism of the Holy Spirit that was the basis for his boldness.

Verse 18 is a cameo of Romans 6:1-10. It summarizes what the Holy Spirit accomplished when we believed, that is, He "put us into" (baptism) Jesus, who then "brought us to God." Now we are "in Him" at the right hand of the Father. Because of our new position in Christ through the baptism of the Holy Spirit, we too can have power for boldness in the midst of unjust suffering. Corrie ten Boom is one famous example of this principle. Obviously, her suffering was undeserved as she protected Jews from the Nazi gas chambers.

But if verse 18 is a picture of our Position in Christ, then verses 19-20 point to our Preaching of Christ.

B. Our Preaching of Christ—through the Filling of the Holy Spirit 19-20

> . . . by whom also He went and preached to the spirits in prison, 20 who formerly were disobedient, when once the Divine longsuffering waited in the days of Noah, while the ark was being prepared, in which a few, that is, eight souls, were saved through water . . .

"**. . . by whom**" refers back to "**the Spirit**" of verse 18 and probably should be "**by Whom.**" Christ Himself preached by the power of the Holy Spirit through Noah before the flood. Remember Christ's prediction in Matthew 10:20 in reference to our witness in a hostile world: "For it is not you who speak, but the Spirit of your Father who speaks in you." When we read "by whom also He went and preached to the spirits in prison," it certainly looks like Christ went to the holding tank for the dead unbelievers and preached to them. Or, some would say He preached to the demons of Genesis 6 that tried to corrupt the line of Abel. But that looks like these unbelievers get a second chance at salvation, unless Christ's message to them was one of condemnation, which is claimed by those that think Christ was preaching to the demons. But that leaves us with the impression that Christ is "rubbing it in." Furthermore, to what purpose. There is plenty of opportunity at the Great White Throne (Revelation 20:10-15) for condemnation of unbelievers and even demons (the devil's final judgment occurs just before the Great White Throne).

However, it isn't necessary to read this in a way that sends Christ to prison to preach to the inmates. It could also mean that the preaching was done by Noah through Christ by the power of the Holy Spirit to the unbelievers that are now locked away in prison because of their rejection of the preaching. In this view Noah is preaching to the people around him while he is building the ark, which took 120 years. Plenty of time to warn people of the coming judgment. And no doubt he had a constant flow of people wondering what in heaven's name was he doing building this ginormous boat. So, God was longsuffering while Noah built the ark and preached, waiting for men to come to repentance, just as He is doing now (2 Peter 3:9). But lest we become confused, let's go back to the three ministries of the Holy Spirit:

BAPTIZING	LEADING	FILLING
ROMANS 6; 1 CORINTHIANS 12	ROMANS 8; GALATIANS 5	ACTS 2; 4:8, 31
INDWELLING	INCREASING	INTOXICATING
PERMANENT	PROGRESSIVE	PERIODIC
FACT	FAITH	FEELING

PRINCIPLE: THE HOLY SPIRIT ONLY FILLS THOSE HE IS LEADING, AND HE ONLY LEADS THOSE HE HAS BAPTIZED.

The filling that we see referenced in the Book of Acts is not the filling of Ephesians 5:18-21. The Ephesians filling was a group worship experience as indicated by the speaking, singing, making melody, giving thanks, and submitting one to another (something that can only be done in a group setting). We get a picture of this in 1 Corinthians 14. In addition to this, the Ephesians passage uses a different Greek word for filling than the one used in the Book of Luke or Acts. And notice the word "holy" is not found in Ephesians 5:18 before "spirit." Whenever we see a filling of the Holy Spirit in Luke or Acts, it always uses the word "Holy" in front of "Spirit." So, the filling of the Holy Spirit seen in Luke and Acts, we would suggest, refers to a special ministry of the Holy Spirit in the life of a believer who is being led by the Spirit. The leading by the Spirit can be all day long. The filling of the Spirit is usually quite short and for a special verbal ministry of some sort. (See a more in-depth discussion of this in Anderson, *Position and Condition*, 285-98.)

Now, having dealt with our relationship with Christ through the baptism of the Holy Spirit (18-20), let's move on to our fellowship with Christ (21-22). Remember, we are saying it is absolutely essential to be baptized by the Holy Spirit to go to heaven (in this dispensation, the Church Age). But it is not necessary to be water baptized to go to heaven. Then why get water baptized? In some countries water baptism into Christianity is the defining point that can lead to martyrdom. Our answer? Faith is the only requirement for salvation from the penalty of sin (the Lake of Fire), but water baptism is one of the requirements for salvation from the power of sin [slavery to our Sin(ful) Nature—see Romans 5-8 in Anderson, *Portraits of Righteousness*].

II. OUR FELLOWSHIP WITH CHRIST 21-22

There is also an antitype which now saves us—baptism (not the removal of the filth of the flesh, but the answer of a good conscience toward God), through the resurrection of Jesus Christ, who has gone into heaven and is at the right hand of

God, angels and authorities and powers having been made subject to Him.

Let it be said at the outset that there is a good chance that all of 3:18-22 is referring to the baptism of the Holy Spirit. After all, it is not the water that saved Noah; it was the ark. The water was the trial. Nevertheless, there are so many that insist on seeing water baptism in vss. 21-22, we will address the significance of water baptism and how it could possible help "save" us.

A lot of the discussion surrounds the word **"saves."** A study of Romans 10:9-10 is helpful here. Here we are told that with the heart one believes unto righteousness and with the mouth one confesses unto salvation. The word "unto" is *eis*, which usually has a goal in mind, that is, "with a view to." So this text really does say that one confesses with the mouth "with a view to" or "with the goal in mind" of salvation. This leaves the obvious dilemma: what if one does not confess with his mouth? Can he go to heaven? If one is honest with the text, he must admit that to be saved one must confess with his mouth. To explain the dilemma as "evidence of salvation" simply circumvents the problem. In Romans 10:10, one absolutely must confess with his mouth to be saved. Of course, this transparent understanding of the text has led most evangelists to the declaration that men and women must respond to an invitation to come to the front and confess Christ with their mouths if they wish to go to heaven.

But for those who can free themselves of the shackles of traditional thinking long enough to explore new solutions to old problems, confession with the mouth is certainly a work. Circumcision was identified as a work by Paul. What are some of the characteristics of a work? Observable by the naked eye; accomplished by physical means; performed by a human agent. All these are true of circumcision, but they are also true of confession with the mouth. If circumcision is a work, then so is confession with the mouth. But that means we must perform a work in order to be saved. Since we do not believe in salvation by works (Ephesians 2:8-10), there must be another explanation. Either confession with the mouth is not a work or it could be that the salvation to which Paul refers in this passage is not reception of eternal life. Perhaps it is in one of the other categories we have already observed to be beyond the scope of the spiritual salvation which gives us eternal life, or perhaps it is in a new category, one which we have yet to observe until now.

One way to find out is to use our concordance again to look up other uses of *sōzō* and *sōtēria* in Romans (Biblical Theology). The first use we find of the verb *sōzō* is in Romans 5:9. It is used again in the next verse. And in both verses we find that the readers have already been justified (v. 9) and reconciled (v. 10), but they have not yet been "saved" (vv. 9 and 10). In both verses, the justification is in the past and the reconciliation is in the past. These past tenses (aorist participles) place the action of the verbs before the action of the main verbs—"shall be saved." But the salvation spoken of is yet in the future. The tense of both verbs is future. These people have been justified and reconciled, but they have not been saved. If they died before receiving the Book of Romans, they would go to heaven because they had been justified and reconciled. But they would not be saved. We cannot escape this truth. Again, the tense of both verbs for being saved in these verses is future. So once again as in Romans 10:10, we are faced with the fact that "saved" here in Romans 5:9-10 might mean something other than the salvation which takes someone to heaven when they die. What could it mean?

We need to look for other clues. Perhaps it would help to ask ourselves what the Romans were to be saved from. Romans 5:9 tells us exactly what they will be saved from: wrath (*orgē*). But what is that? Does not wrath refer to God's judgment on unbelievers for eternity? This is lexically possible, but the key question is to establish the meaning of "wrath" in Romans. So once again, we search in our concordance for the first use of wrath in Romans to see if it gives us any clues. And it certainly does. The first use of wrath in Romans is found in Romans 1:18. There it tells us that the "wrath" of God "is revealed" from heaven against all ungodliness and unrighteousness of men who hold back the truth in unbelief. The important factor to notice is the present tense of "is revealed" (*apokalyptetai*). This wrath is presently being revealed from heaven against the ungodliness and unrighteousness of mankind. This is not referring to something that will take place at the Great White Throne (as a matter of fact, there is no use of *orgē* in the NT which links it directly with the Great White Throne). It is in no way connected with eternal judgment. This is a present time judgment.

Specifically, this wrath is defined in the rest of Romans 1 as three stages of God's giving sinful man over to the control of his sinful nature as he descends the staircase into the basement of depravity. The phrase "God gave them up/over" (*paredōken autous ho theos*) defines these three stages in vv. 24, 26, and 28. The bottom of the basement is to have a mind that is *adokimos*, "disapproved" or "unable to tell right from wrong." It is total control by the sin nature. That is wrath in Romans 1:18ff.

So, let us try it out in Romans 5:9 to see if it makes any sense. "Much more, then, having now been justified by His blood, we shall be saved from wrath [the control of our sinful nature] through Him." Does that make sense? Perhaps. But does it fit the rest of the context? In Romans 5:10, it says that we were reconciled (past tense) through the death of His Son, but we shall be saved (future tense) through His life. If the meaning of wrath in Romans 5:9 is adhered to, then the saving in Romans 5:10 must also refer to being saved from the tyranny of the sin nature in our lives. And this does make sense.

We were saved from the penalty of sin by His death, but we shall be saved from the power of sin by His life. We gained eternal life as He became our substitute in death, but we shall enjoy an abundant life as He becomes our substitute in life. "I am crucified with Christ; nevertheless, I live; yet not I, but *Christ lives in me.* . . ." (Galatians 2:20). The hardest thing for a non-Christian to believe in is the substitutionary death of Christ, but the hardest thing for a Christian to believe in is the substitutionary life of Christ. Romans 5:10 is about His substitutionary life. In this "swing section" of Romans the author is turning away from his focus on justification from the penalty of sin to salvation from the power of sin. And being saved in this section is to be delivered from the tyranny of the sin nature in one's life (the wrath of Romans 1:18).

Could this meaning of "saved" fit in Romans 10? In Romans 5, being saved was an advance in the Christian life over being justified. Being justified delivers one from the penalty of sin; being saved delivers one from the power of sin. Could these definitions work in Romans 10? Maybe. If one looks at v. 9 as an equation, it would look like this: Belief + Confession = Salvation. The verse also makes it clear that belief is a matter of the heart, whereas confession is a matter of the mouth. One is internal, while the other is external. One is spiritual, the other physical. But v. 10 explains that it is the internal transaction of belief which results in righteousness. This righteousness (*dikaiosunē*) is the same righteousness accorded to Abraham in Romans 4:3 (Gen 15:6), *dikaiosunē*. "Abraham believed, and it was reckoned [imputed = *elogisthē*, the aorist tense of *logizomai*] unto him for righteousness." Paul has already established that imputed righteousness is the direct result of faith and faith alone. The verb form for all this is "to justify" (*dikaioō*—can you see this is the same root as *dikaiosunē*?). By faith and faith alone, one is justified or credited with the righteousness of Christ. It is a matter of the heart.

But with the mouth confession is made "with the goal of" (*eis*) salvation. Once again, let us suspend our ingrained presupposition that salvation or being saved must be equivalent to justification or the transaction which would put us in heaven if we died. Let us assume for the sake of argument that this salvation is a step beyond justification, just as it was in Romans 5:9-10. Let us adopt the same definition we discovered in the context of Romans 5, that is, to be saved is to be delivered from wrath, the tyranny of the sin nature in one's life (Romans 1:18ff). If this is so, obviously deliverance from the penalty of sin is a prerequisite for deliverance from the power of sin. In other words, justification must precede sanctification. No one will be sanctified who has not already been justified. With this understanding in mind, Romans 10:9-10 tells us that one believes in his heart with the goal of being justified, and he confesses with his mouth with the goal of being sanctified, or saved, or delivered from the power of the sin nature in his life. We would propose that this understanding makes sense and fits the following context.

Paul himself wants to prove this point, and he calls upon Scripture to achieve his goal. He equates "calling upon the name of the Lord" with confession with the mouth. We know this because of the common understanding that if A = B and B = C, then A = C. In v. 10 he said that "confession with the mouth" (A) leads to "salvation" (B), and in v. 13 he says that being "saved" (B) comes from "calling upon the name of the Lord" (C); therefore, A = B, B = C, and A = C: Confession with the Mouth = Calling upon the Name of the Lord.

But notice from the progression in vv. 14-15a that calling upon the name of the Lord is a separate, distinct, and subsequent act to believing. This becomes transparent if we follow the progression in reverse: 1) After the sending comes the preaching; 2) after the preaching comes the hearing; 3) after the hearing comes the believing; and 4) after the believing comes the calling upon. The acts here are sequential. The calling upon and the believing are not identical acts, nor are they concomitant. After one believes, he can then call upon the name of the Lord (confess with his mouth the Lord Jesus). But this leaves the obvious question of whether one can believe and *not* call upon the name of the Lord.

In order to answer this question, we once again retreat to our concordance to find other uses of "calling upon the name of the Lord." And we discover from its usage in Acts 7:59; 9:14, 21; 1 Corinthians 1:2, and 2 Timothy 2:22, that to "call upon the name of the Lord" is to openly, publicly identify with or to worship Him. Saul of Tarsus found believers because he asked where they were meeting. He was told they were "calling upon the name of the Lord" over at the house of Festus. So, off he went to find them and persecute them. What we discover, then, from Romans 10:9-10 is that calling upon the name of the Lord (confession with the mouth of the Lord Jesus) is open, public identification with Jesus Christ as one's personal Lord and Savior. And Paul explicitly states that this is an integral step in one's deliverance from wrath, or the power of the sin nature in one's life. The power of Satan is in darkness. But when one comes to the light (Ephesians 5:11-14), the darkness is dispersed, and the power of the enemy and his accomplice (our sin nature) is defeated. In the terms used in Romans 5:9 and 10:9-10, the justified believer is then "saved."[99]

The most natural and obvious way to openly identify with Christ ("call on the name of the Lord" in public worship) was to get water baptized. Water baptism was supposed to signify the beginning of a new walk, a new way of life. One who was baptized in Jesus' name was to openly identify and walk with Him, even if it meant death. The promise of the NT to those that were willing to openly identify with Him was to be "saved" from the power of sin in their lives. And I would suggest that Peter is also telling us (if water baptism is in view here) that our boldness to identify with Him through water baptism and a ready answer for the hope that is within us will be a big step in "saving" the meaning of our lives for eternity, which is the main theme of 1 Peter.

---

[99] See Zane Hodges, *Romans: Deliverance From Wrath* (Corinth, Texas: Grace Evangelical Society, 2013) and Joseph Dillow, *Final Destiny: The Future Reign of the Servant Kings* (Grace Theology Press, 2013).

22

"SATAN'S WILL FOR YOUR LIFE"

1 Peter 4:1-6

INTRODUCTION

It was Henry David Thoreau that wrote: "As if you could kill time without injuring eternity." Thoreau put his finger on a vital link between time and eternity, between the temporal and the eternal. So does the Bible. Paul wrote, "Redeem the time, for the days are evil" (Ephesians 5:16). It sounds as though time is a commodity one can purchase at Walmart. Jesus said, "He who would save his life will lose it" (Matthew 16:25). Here it appears that time can be deposited into some sort of savings account that will last forever. That is exactly what Peter is driving at in this letter. Since God is eternal, His concerns are eternal. His focus is not on time, but rather on eternity. It stands to reason, therefore, that His purpose for man is also eternal rather than temporal. But if you were God's enemy how would you try to frustrate His purposes? More specifically, what would you do to try to prevent a person from finding God's will or His highest desire for that person's life and fulfilling that eternal purpose? We hear a lot about God's will for our lives. In this lesson we focus on Satan's will for our lives.

"SAVING THE SAVED"
1 Peter

Salutation	1:1-2
Introduction	1:3-12

Body   "Our Plan of Salvation"

I. Through Personal Sanctification—our Character	1:13-2:10
II. Through Personal Submission—our Conduct	2:11-3:7
III. Through Personal Suffering—Our Courage	3:8-4:19
A. Suffering without Fear	3:8-22
B. Suffering in the Flesh	4:1-11
1. Satan's Will for our Lives	1-6
2. God's Will for our Lives	7-11
C. Suffering for the Faith	4:12-19

Throughout this exposition we have indicated that Peter's purpose in writing this letter is to help us find God's ultimate goal for our lives (1:9), which is to save our time on earth for eternity—to use our time to have an impact on eternity. As opposed to Thoreau, however, we would suggest that killing time will not injure eternity. It just won't have any impact on eternity at all. A life that has no eternal impact is a wasted life, from God's point of view. But through our Character, our Conduct, and our Courage we can save our time forever and have a very definite impact on eternity.

As we enter 1 Peter 4, we find ourselves in the third major section of the letter: our Personal Suffering, which Peter divides into three sections: Suffering without Fear (3:8-22); Suffering in the Flesh (4:1-11); and Suffering for the Faith (4:12-19). We are looking in this lesson at Satan's Will for our Lives. Obviously, he would like us to waste our lives, that is, have no positive eternal impact. Hitler had an eternal impact, but it certainly was not a positive one. So how can Satan induce us to waste our lives? Three ways: Living for Lust (1-2); Perpetuating the Past (3-4); Forgetting the Future (5-6). Let's look at these verse by verse.

I. LIVING FOR LUST—BECAUSE LUSTING IS LIVING 1-2

Therefore, since Christ suffered for us in the flesh, arm yourselves also with the same mind, for he who has suffered in the flesh has ceased from sin, 2 that he no longer should live the rest of his time in the flesh for the lusts of men, but for the will of God.

Though Satan himself is not mentioned in these two verses, "the will of God" is. It is contrasted with "the lusts of men." It is not a big leap to assume that Satan will be working with the lusts of men to frustrate the will of God for our lives. And it might be helpful to say a word about the "will" of God for our lives. This is the word *thelēma*, which usually means "desire." If Peter wanted to speak of a life that has been predetermined, as many teach, he would have used the word *boulēma*, which points to a predetermined decision (more on this in the next section). At this point we will just note the obvious: Satan is trying to thwart God's desire for our lives. Actually, there is a battle going on for the control of our lives. Back in 2:11 Peter wrote, ". . . abstain from fleshly lusts which war against the soul." This is the great conflict between God and the devil concerning God's sovereignty. When we surrender to the Lordship of Christ (Lordship sanctification, not Lordship salvation), we cast our vote for the sovereignty of God instead of Satan. So, returning to the battle imagery, Peter tells us to "arm" (*hoplizō* literally meant to equip for battle) ourselves.

But the armor we are to use to defeat the devil is not a piece of artillery. No, it's our minds. The word for "mind" here is *ennoia*, which might better be translated "insight" (see *BDAG*) as opposed to "attitude" (NIV) or "purpose" (NASB). The right insight is a powerful weapon. What insight? The same as Christ had, that is, the flesh is passing away and the lusts thereof, but the significance of our lives can last forever. Therefore, He was willing to forfeit that which is passing to gain that which is permanent.

Our senses fool us. We think of people as passing away and nations or buildings as things that are permanent. But we all know that nations can topple and buildings can crumble, whereas every person God had ever created will last forever. So, where would you rather invest your time and treasure, into something that is passing or something that is permanent? We know this is Peter's argument because in his very next sentence he mentions "the rest of *his* time," meaning the days he has left on planet earth. The primary focus of this letter is on what we will do with our time on earth, our lives. Save it or lose it—that's what Peter learned from Jesus at Caesarea Philippi (Matt 16:24-27). He isn't talking about living a long life on earth versus a short one, although much sin can lead to an early demise. No, he is saying we can lose the significance of our days on earth or preserve them for all eternity. No one in his right mind would choose the passing over the permanent.

Jesus knew the difference. The devil went after the control of Jesus' life when he tempted Him with the kingdoms of this world (the passing) in place of His kingdom (the permanent). Of course, the devil knew that the price Jesus would have to pay him to get the kingdoms of this world (worship the devil) would cause Him to forfeit His own kingdom because of sin.

Peter contrasts the "lusts of men" with the "will of God." Jesus contrasts the passing and the permanent in the Sermon on the Mount when he tells us to "seek first the kingdom of God and His righteousness" (the permanent) instead of worrying about storing up money or what we will eat, drink, or wear (the passing)—Matthew 6:19-34.

Paul makes the same contrast in 1 Thessalonians 4:3ff when he tells us how to find a life partner.[100] He says:

> [3] For this is the will of God, your sanctification: that you should abstain from sexual immorality; [4] that each of you should know how to possess his own vessel in sanctification and honor, [5] not in passion of lust, like the Gentiles who do not know God; [6] that no one should take advantage of and defraud his brother in this matter, because the Lord *is* the avenger of all such, as we also forewarned you and testified. [7] For God did not call us to uncleanness, but in holiness. [8] Therefore he who rejects *this* does not reject man, but God, who has also given us His Holy Spirit.

It was Bill Gothard decades ago that contrasted the devil's approach to finding a life partner to God's approach.[101] Peter flags the devil's approach with the word "lust." He calls God's approach ("will [*thelēma*] of God") "sanctification."

	SATAN'S WAY	SOCIETY'S WAY	GOD'S WAY
BODY	Physical Intimacy	Dating	Spiritual
SOUL	Emotional	Engagement	Emotional
SPIRIT	Spiritual	Marriage	Physical Intimacy

---

[100] *Skeuos* is the Greek word used in 1 Thessalonians 4:4 dealing with sanctification and the opposite sex. Many interpreters see the word as meaning one's own sexual organ(s) and translate it "vessel." But there is good support for the word meaning your life partner, which makes a lot more sense to me.

[101] Bill Gothard, Institute in Basic Life Principles, *Basic Seminar Textbook*, 182.

Is it any surprise that Satan's approach to finding a life partner is the inverse of God's approach? During the dating phase God wants us to get involved on the spiritual level first. Share how we met Christ; significant steps in spiritual growth; perhaps go to church together; concerts; retreats. I met my wife at a Christian retreat and then saw her subsequently at meetings for Campus Crusade for Christ. After all, the basis for unity in a marriage or a church is not Christian love. I can love a Catholic or a Jew. But I can't work with them if we don't believe the same thing. That's why Paul exhorts the Ephesians to strive to keep the unity based on what they believed: "*There is* one body and one Spirit, just as you were called in one hope of your calling; [5] one Lord, one faith, one baptism; [6] one God and Father of all, who *is* above all, and through all, and in you all" (Ephesians 4:4-6). When a believer is married to an unbeliever, they can stay married, but without spiritual unity they miss out on the deepest unity a man and wife can enjoy.

Now the western culture is not one where marriages are arranged by the parents, which may be a better system. But since we start with dating, if there is spiritual unity, the emotional sparks may or may not begin to fly. An engagement may take place that leads to marriage. Then comes the physical intimacy, a final expression of the spiritual and emotional intimacy that has already taken place.

The devil would flip this. He wants us to get involved on the physical level first. In fact, one college freshman was meeting with me recently and said, "Dr. Anderson, I would like to help protect you." Protect me? What are you talking about? "Well, when we set up this meeting you asked me if I want to hook up at Starbucks. Remember?" Well, yes. "You may not be aware that in my generation the words 'hook up' have sexual significance. In fact, at my university (a major Texas university) couples 'hook up' before they start dating. They use the sexual experience as an indicator of whether they want to pursue a dating relationship. Instead of waiting until after the marriage ceremony to find out if they are going to be sexually disappointed and stuck in an unsatisfying relationship for the rest of their lives, they just walk through that door the first time they go out." Naturally,

I was at a loss for words and was reminded of why I stopped pastoring in my sixties—I could no longer relate to the generation under me. They are educated in a different way, they process data in a different way, and they are tempted in a different way from my generation. And all the more reason we need young Christian leaders that can relate to the millennials.

As most of us have experienced in one arena or another, feelings follow actions. That's why John tells the Ephesians who had lost their first love (Christ) to go back to doing the works they were doing when they were on fire for Christ. They may well regain their emotional attachment to Christ when they do the things they were doing when they were new believers. God knows this principle. But so does Satan. So, if he can get a couple physically involved, their feelings will often follow suit. Before long they (or at least the girl) will be in love. Then comes engagement. Finally, they may look up a preacher or go to their own pastor and ask him to put his spiritual stamp of approval on their union.

A not-so-surprisingly high percentage of couples that follow the devil's order for finding a life partner wind up in the divorce courts. Apparently, the guilt of physical involvement before marriage often leaves the wife with the impression that she trapped her husband into marriage through sexual promiscuity. She tests his love by becoming frigid or cold in the bedroom. He becomes more demanding, thus verifying her doubts. The downward spiral into the black hole of divorce has begun. Communication breaks down. Extra-marital affairs may puncture the relationship before an actual divorce occurs.

Now we have developed just one area of "lust" high-lighted by 1 Thessalonians 4:1-6. But 1 John 2:15-18 points to three areas that are specifically poisonous: lust of the flesh, lust of the eyes, and the pride of life.

> [15] Do not love the world or the things in the world. If anyone loves the world, the love of the Father is not in him. [16] For all that *is* in the world—the lust of the flesh, the lust of the eyes, and the pride of life—is not of the Father but is of the world.

¹⁷ And the world is passing away, and the lust of it; but he who does the will of God abides forever.

Some say the three main areas of temptation for males can fit into these three arenas of temptation: sex (lust of the flesh), material things (lust of the eyes), and power (pride of life). Obviously, many lusts fit into these arenas of temptation besides sex, material things, and power. Eve, for example, was seduced by something from each area in her fall in the Garden of Eden: "So when the woman saw that the tree *was* good for food [lust of the flesh], that it *was* pleasant to the eyes [lust of the eyes], and a tree desirable to make *one* wise [pride of life], she took of its fruit and ate" (Genesis 3:6).

When I met Miles, he had just been through God's woodshed. A high performer, very energetic, and quite competitive, Miles had always done well—didn't matter what it was. And so, he was doing well in business handling some of the repos from the S&L debacle of the mid-80's. He ran a large office and had a seven-figure income. But the cares of this world had lured him further and further from his first love—Jesus. Then a rogue wave wiped him out. He said to himself, "I won't make that mistake again. The cares of this world are not going to suck me dry."

After hearing his story, I asked Miles, who had been an elder and Sunday School teacher in his former church, if he would like to go a little deeper in the Scriptures. He joined a small group I was teaching on how to interpret the Bible. The students had to write their own commentary on a book of the Bible we would choose. They had to learn the Greek alphabet, to use dictionaries of NT Greek, how to use a concordance, and the basic use of tenses in the NT Greek. The course took about four months. I was teaching them how to find what E. D. Hirsch calls the *intrinsic genre* of the book, or the basic thread that weaves its way throughout the book and tells you the main point the author is making.

Well, Miles might well be the most dedicated Bible student I have ever had or known. I have taught this approach to Bible study to about four hundred people over a fifty-year period, but Miles is the only one I know that gets up and gets started at five every morning to spend two hours looking for clues to the *intrinsic genre* of a book of the Bible like Sherlock Holmes, master detective. As the economy improved, Miles had the opportunity to chase dollars once again. But, no, he was quite satisfied with his five-figure income. He wanted his energies directed in the spiritual direction. His studies were just part of his program. I had lunch with him recently. He is still going at it, and it has been twenty-five years. He refuses to let the lusts of this world crowd out the Word of God from his life. May his tribe increase.

Satan's will for your life? Live for lust. But also perpetuate the past—because you can't really change.

II. PERPETUATE THE PAST—BECAUSE YOU CAN'T REALLY CHANGE 3-4

For we have spent enough of our past lifetime in doing the will of the Gentiles—when we walked in lewdness, lusts, drunkenness, revelries, drinking parties, and abominable idolatries. In regard to these, they think it strange that you do not run with them in the same flood of dissipation, speaking evil of you.

A. Bondage to our Past 3

Let's not overlook the word **"lifetime."** It is *chronos* in Greek, obviously the word that is the basis for our word "chronology," the study of events in their order of sequence in time. Peter does not want his readers to lose the significance of their "lifetime," their time on earth. He implores us not to waste any more time chasing after the "will of the Gentiles." We might expect him to use the word *thelēma* (desire) here since the following list we might associate with our desires or lusts. But, no, Peter uses the word *bulēma*, the word for a "predetermined choice."

We witness the predetermined choice of "the Gentiles" (used for unbelievers) today in the agendas being pushed by certain groups in America that are the opposite of God's desires. For example, on January 22, 2019, legislators in the State of New York passed a bill more expansive than the provisions coming out of *Roe v. Wade* of 1973. Now abortions do not have to be performed by medical doctors. They can be licensed nurse practitioners, physicians' assistants, or midwives. There are no restrictions up through the 24th week of pregnancy and allowed after the 24th week if the baby is deemed unviable or the mother's life or health is at risk. However, "health" now can be interpreted by the courts to include age, emotional status, economic status, and social status. The above are understood to be judgment calls, and no criminality is attached to the abortion if the court does not agree with the judgment call of the practitioner.[102]

This kind of action is not the result of overriding desire, passion, or lust. It is the work of those making a "predetermined choice" to undergird the federal right to abortion coming out of *Roe v. Wade*. This bill was passed by a vote of thirty-eight to twenty-four. So, thirty-eight legislators made a predetermined choice (vote) to support abortion without restriction, which opens the door to more harvesting of organs.

Interesting that when it speaks of "God's will" the word *thelēma* (desire) is used. That is because God has many wonderful desires for us, but He will not force His desires upon us, as some theologies teach.[103] But when Peter speaks of the "will of the Gentiles" he uses

---

[102] https://www.snopes.com/fact-check/new-york-abortions-birth/, accessed January 24, 2019.

[103] Here, the universalists have a point. They argue, against the Calvinists, that if God forces His will on us as the Calvinists teach (see R. C. Sproul on John 6:44 and their whole discussion on irresistible grace), then all men will go to heaven because God "desires all men to be saved . . ." (1 Timothy 2:4). But Calvinists think God only chose (elected) a small minority of humankind to be with Him forever. In the Calvinistic system there is a breakdown somewhere. There is a chink in God's armor when it comes to His omnipotence (He is not powerful enough to force all

"*boulēma*," meaning the Gentiles were not swept away by a sea of emotions into their vile deeds. No, they made a predetermined choice to go in that direction. And they are aggressive; they want to take as many people as possible into their *cul de sac* of carnality.

According to Robert S. McGee one of the four great lies the devil whispers in our ears is that "I am what I am; I cannot change."[104] Many traumatic experiences in our past can act as a ball and chain to keep us from moving forward in our Christian walk. Bob was a depressed pastor. He told me he began masturbating when he was just twelve. The older boys were doing it, so why shouldn't he? He continued this behavior almost daily until he got married. To his surprise, even though frequency was not an issue in his marriage, he continued to masturbate. This did not seem right to him, especially since he usually used some form of pornography to help him. The images acted like wallpaper in the halls of his mind, and his feelings of guilt increased. He used every spiritual principle he knew to overcome this stronghold in his life. He tried counseling, though he was deathly afraid and ashamed to admit to another man his issue. Meanwhile, after each incidence the devil whispered, "See, you'll never change. Where's the power of the Holy Spirit in your life? What makes you think you are really a Christian, anyway? Well, one thing is for sure: you are a world-class hypocrite. You present one picture to your congregation, but God and His holy angels see a completely different picture. You're really a piece of pond scum." Finally, when he couldn't kick his habit after years of trying, he left the ministry. Better to quit than to perpetuate his hypocrisy.

Of increasing concern are the suicides among teenage girls over

---

men to be saved), or His omnibenevolence (He really does not love all men the same in contradiction to James 2). They can't have their cake and eat it too.

[104] Robert S. McGee, *The Search for Significance* (Houston, TX: REVISION, 1987), 83.

body shaming, especially through social media. Though girls that perceive themselves to be somewhat overweight or underweight are only ten percent more likely to attempt or think about suicide, those who perceive themselves to be significantly overweight or underweight are fifty percent more likely to attempt or contemplate suicide.[105] Other research revealed this:

> Some believe that making overweight people feel ashamed of their weight or eating habits actually helps motivate them to lose weight. However, nothing could be further from the truth. Psychologists have done a lot of research on this, and the evidence is very clear. Fat shaming does not motivate people, but makes them feel terrible about themselves and actually causes them to eat more and **gain** more weight.[106]

As the media constantly bombards women with the "perfect" shape and size, young girls can look in the mirror shortly after puberty and make a judgment as to what they will have to do to measure up to society's standard of beauty. If their body structure is such that they "have no chance" of ever reaching this self-imposed perfection, they feel they can never change. The problems are only compounded by the cyber-bullying from their peer group where people will say cruel things over the internet they wouldn't normally say to someone's face.

This leads to the second problem with the past: bondage to our peers.

---

[105] https://www.cbsnews.com/news/body-image-issues-and-teen-suicide/, accessed January 26,2019.

[106] https://www.healthline.com/nutrition/fat-shaming-makes-things-worse/, accessed January 26, 2019.

B. Bondage to our Peers 4

Wherein lies the power of "peer pressure"? Is it not in our fear of being thought **"strange"** and being "made fun of." Perhaps peer pressure is never greater than during the early teenage years when we are pulling away from the nest of our homes but have not yet established a nest of our own. We are leaving the love and security of our homes to seek the same with our own life partner. It is during this transitional time we find ourselves most vulnerable to the opinions of our peers. They become our surrogate source of security and significance.

Here Peter uses the word *xenizō*, which comes from the noun for "foreigner, stranger, or alien." We want to fit in, be one of the guys or girls, certainly not ostracized or ridiculed. The word Peter uses for **"speaking evil"** is *blasphēmeō*. The NASB translates this "malign"; the NIV says "heap abuse." Isn't that what ridicule or making fun of someone is, heaping abuse?

I just had the misfortune of watching a Netflix docuseries on Ted Bundy, the notorious serial killer from Seattle. Mega-sickening. You even have to ask yourself, "Why am I watching this?" The only answer I could come up with is the fascination of trying to figure out what on earth could cause a personality to become so twisted. His parents doted on him until his stepfather's death. He was in Scouts and church. Always had a smile on his face in family pictures. But when some of his classmates were interviewed, they painted a picture of Bundy as a reject from society. He wanted to be class president, but he was not popular. He wanted to be an athlete, but he was awkward and uncoordinated. He wanted a girlfriend, but his first prolonged attempt wound up in rejection. Apparently, the pressure to "fit in" backfired when people dubbed him "strange." His anger at society and attractive girls in particular exploded in a maniacal rage. Add an element of demonic activity and Bundy was ascribed superhuman powers because of his ability to stay one step ahead of the police and even jump from a second story jail window (25 ft.) and walk away in his first escape in Aspen, CO. Bundy described a dark entity within that kept him from changing and being a better person.

Satan's will for our lives? 1) Live for Lust; 2) Perpetuate the Past; and lastly, 3) Forget the Future.

III. FORGET THE FUTURE—BECAUSE THERE IS NO ACCOUNTABILITY 5-6

They will give an account to Him who is ready to judge the living and the dead. For this reason the gospel was preached also to those who are dead, that they might be judged according to men in the flesh, but live according to God in the spirit.

Because of the double use of "dead," "living/live," and "judge/judged" it can be easy to get confused. Let go through this slowly: "They (the unbelievers of v. 4) will give an account to Him who is ready to judge the living (alive physically) and the dead (those who have died physically). For this reason the gospel was preached also to those who are dead (spiritually dead, that is, unbelievers) that they (the unbelievers) might be judged according to men in the flesh (judged by their contemporaries while still alive in their flesh) but live (spiritually) according to God in the spirit (in other words they become believers). Peter is giving a strong reminder of future accountability.[107]

In my experience as a pastor I never ran into anyone with an intellectual problem with Christianity that held water. There are no sound arguments against Christianity. But what I discovered about people that claim to reject Christ on intellectual grounds is that they have a moral problem. Once the laws of morality have been broken the lawbreaker must get rid of the Lawmaker or he stands self-condemned. Their "intellectual" problems are just their attempt to remove accountability.

A family called me over to talk about church membership. The family consisted of a husband and wife and three boys between the

---

[107] For an extended discussion of the options here see Paul J. Achtemeier, *1 Peter*, Hermeneia (Minneapolis: Fortress Press, 1996), 286-91.

ages of eight and twelve. I went around the horn listening to their testimonies, starting with the youngest. Last was the patriarch. I said, "Fred, how did you come to Christ?" He replied, "Well, my story is real simple: I just don't believe." You can imagine my shock. "But you come to church every Sunday." "Yes, well I do that to support the family." "Well, that's a good thing. But I notice you go to sleep within five minutes after I start my message." "I'm not sleeping. I am thinking of all the ways I could refute your message."

Fred was a lawyer who relished in arguing. He claimed to have all sorts of intellectual problems with a faith he called "pretty far-fetched." To my further surprise he said he wanted to go on one of my trips to Israel. When I lead a tour of Israel, I provide a tome of material (about a thousand pages). He is the only one that went on the trip and read all this material (twice). Surely, I thought, with all this evidence for Christ right in front of him this guy will finally believe. But, no, he did not cross the line. That's when I surmised, he had a moral problem, not an intellectual one. And sure enough, it wasn't long after the trip that his wife discovered he had been having an affair with someone at work for years.

Our text tells us that we will all give an "account" someday for the time we have had on earth. The word for **"account"** is *logon,* which is associated with the verb *logizomai,* an accounting term (see Romans 14:12; Philippians 4:17; and Hebrews 13:17). There will be future accountability. But the devil doesn't want us to think about that. It could have an impact on how we live now. On a trip to India I asked a former Hindu about the appeal of Hinduism. How could anyone be attracted to a system of karma that might have them return in the next life as a roach? I'll never forget his reply: "Oh, it's very attractive. You see, it is the ultimate system of non-accountability because you always get another chance. If you mess up in your current life, there is always the next one to do better." The Bible says, ". . . it is appointed for men to die once, and after this the judgment" (Hebrews 9:27). But what if the Bible is wrong? Then we can get rid of final accountability in another life. Can you see why the devil's main tactic to undermine Christianity is to undermine our faith in the Bible?

"Dead" here refers to those who are alive in the flesh but dead (separated from God) in their spirits. Unbelievers will judge those that come to Christ but fear not. We need not be concerned about the judgment of men, but rather the judgment of God. We don't hear much about the judgment of God in today's pulpits. What a contrast to the epic poem by Dante, the *Divine Comedy*. In the first part of this poem Dante depicts hell as nine concentric circles within the earth. A sign over the Gate of Hell concludes: "Abandon all hope, you who enter here." Virgil, Dante's guide, introduces him to the suffering of the uncommitted, those who took no sides or stands in life but were wholly committed to their own self-interests. "Naked and futile, they race around through the mist in eternal pursuit of an elusive, wavering banner (symbolic of their pursuit of ever-shifting self-interest) while relentlessly chased by swarms of wasps and hornets who continually sting them. Loathsome maggots and worms at the sinners' feet drink the putrid mixture of blood, pus, and tears that flows down their bodies."[108]

The second and third part of *The Divine Comedy* deal with purgatory and paradise. Written in the 14th Century, I think we can safely conclude that Dante had a very strong view of future accountability, that is, judgment by God. But Dante grew up in the shade of the papacy. What about Protestant America in its early years? Some would argue that the most famous sermon ever preached on American soil was by Jonathan Edwards ("Sinners in the Hands of an Angry God") in the middle of the 18th Century. This single paragraph is typical of the whole sermon:

> Therefore natural men are held in the hand of God over the pit of hell; they have deserved the fiery pit, and are already sentenced to it; and God is dreadfully provoked, His anger is

---

[108] https://en.wikipedia.org/wiki/Inferno_(Dante), accessed February 14, 2019.

as great towards them as to those that are actually suffering the executions of the fierceness of His wrath in hell, and they have done nothing in the least to appease or abate that anger, neither is God in the least bound by any promise to hold them up one moment: the devil is waiting for them, hell is gaping for them, the flames gather and flash about them, and are eager to grab hold of them, and swallow them up; the fire pent up in their own hearts is struggling to break out; and they have no interest in any Mediator, there are no means within reach that can be any security to them. In short, they have no refuge, nothing to take hold of; all that preserves them every moment is the mere arbitrary will, and uncovenanted, unobliged patience, of an incensed God.[109]

The preaching of Edwards was a powerful poker stirring the fireplace of the Great Awakening (1730's). Others might argue that the sermon by R. G. Lee (1926), "Pay Day Some Day," is the most famous because it was delivered by Lee 1275 times and heard by over a million people in person. From the title of the sermon to its conclusion Lee offers no way of escaping accountability before a righteous Judge. These words sum it up:

The certainty of "Payday Someday" for all who regard not God or man is set forth in the words of an unknown poet:

You'll pay. The knowledge of your acts will weigh
Heavier on your mind each day.
The more you climb, the more you gain,
The more you'll feel the nagging strain.
Success will cower at the threat
Of retribution. Fear will fret
Your peace and bleed you for the debt;

---

[109] http://www.biblebb.com/files/edwards/je-sinners.htm, accessed February 14, 2019.

Conscience collects from every crook
More than the worth of what he took,
You only thought you got away
But in the night you'll pay and pay.[110]

But almost a century after "Payday Someday" most churches have very little to say about final accountability. I once read these words from Edward's sermon in my own church:

The God that holds you over the pit of hell, much as one holds a spider, or some detestable insect, over the fire, detests you, and is dreadfully provoked: His wrath towards you burns like fire; He looks upon you as worthy of nothing else, but to be thrown into the fire; His eyes are too pure than to bear to have you in His sight; you are ten thousand times more abominable in His eyes, than the most hateful venomous snake is in ours. You have offended Him infinitely more than ever a stubborn rebel did his prince: and yet, it is nothing but His hand that holds you from falling into the fire every moment. It is to be ascribed to nothing else, that you did not go to hell last night; that you were allowed to awake up again in this world, after you closed your eyes to sleep. And there is no other reason to be given, why you have not dropped into hell since you arose this morning, but that God's hand has held you up. There is no other reason to be given why you have not gone to hell, since you have sat here in this church, provoking His pure eyes by your sinful wicked manner of attending His solemn worship. Yes, there is nothing else that is to be given as a reason why you do not this very moment drop down into hell.[111]

---

[110] http://www.ministers-best-friend.com/Most-Famous-Sermon-Payday-Someday-by-NewtonStein.html, accessed February 13, 2019.

[111] http://www.biblebb.com/files/edwards/je-sinners.htm, accessed February 13, 2019.

They laughed. I don't relate this to degrade my church members. It's just that Edwards' words sound so over the top in our dot.com, tech savvy age. But credit him for this: Edwards preached accountability. The devil would have us discount or even deny accountability. The pendulum has swung away from the wrath of God to the love of God. Surely there is a biblical balance Satan does not want us to acknowledge. But the future is supposed to impact the present. Isn't this what Peter (2 Peter 3:10-14) was telling us:

> But the day of the Lord will come as a thief in the night, in which the heavens will pass away with a great noise, and the elements will melt with fervent heat; both the earth and the works that are in it will be burned up. Therefore, since all these things will be dissolved, what manner *of persons* ought you to be in holy conduct and godliness, looking for and hastening the coming of the day of God, because of which the heavens will be dissolved, being on fire, and the elements will melt with fervent heat? Nevertheless we, according to His promise, look for new heavens and a new earth in which righteousness dwells. Therefore, beloved, looking forward to these things, be diligent to be found by Him in peace, without spot and blameless . . .

The **FUTURE** should impact the **PRESENT**.

CONCLUSION

What is Satan's Will for Your Life? According to this text, you should Live for Lust, because Lusting is Living; you should Perpetuate the Past, because you can't really change; and you should Forget the Future, because there is no future accountability. In a nutshell, the devil wants us to lose (waste) our lives, to never discover the reason we were created, the wonderful purpose God has for our lives.

There are three things that never come back: the spoken word, the neglected opportunity, and time past. Save it or lose it.

23

"GOD'S WILL FOR YOUR LIFE"

1 Peter 4:7-11

INTRODUCTION

Most of the people I know in America believe we only live once. There are pockets of those who believe in reincarnation, but I couldn't point to any of them. I don't know what the percentage is, but some portion of those who believe we only have one life to live would like to invest their life and do something that is permanent rather than something that is passing. After all, if we invest our lives into something that's passing away, then the significance, or perhaps I should say the insignificance of our lives will pass away as well.

If we want to be good investors it behooves us to be able to distinguish the permanent from the passing. But trying to distinguish the temporal from the eternal is rather like trying to tell the difference between a false diamond and the real thing. It takes a trained eye to tell the difference. As the late Haddon Robinson observed:

> We easily fall into the trap of feeling that human beings are part of the passing. They live for less than a century, and

they're gone. What really matters, we suppose, are their causes to which they give their lives. Civilizations, cultures, nations, and governments were here when we arrived, and they'll go on when we die. They count greatly. In God's view of things, though, that kind of thinking is all mixed up. It is men, not causes, who will exist somewhere forever.[112]

As C. S. Lewis warns us in *The Weight of Glory*: "There are no ordinary people. You have never talked to a mere mortal . . . it is immortals whom we joke with, work with, marry, snub, and exploit—immortal horrors or everlasting splendors."[113] So it's people, not causes or cultures, who last forever. Therefore, a simple observation tells me the most lasting and secure investment I can make with my life must somehow be connected with people.

But what else lasts forever? Well, what about God? Isn't He eternal? Of course. Therefore, if I invest my life in the things of God, I am investing in the eternal. Perhaps that is why Jesus said, "Seek first the kingdom of God and His righteousness" (Matthew 6:33a). And there is one more thing that is permanent, isn't there? God's Word: "All flesh is as grass and the glory of man as the flower of the grass. The grass withers and its flower falls away, but the Word of the Lord endures forever" (1 Peter 1:24-25).

So, what is God's Will for Your Life? Well, if Satan's will is to Live for Lust, to Perpetuate the Past, and to Forget the Future, then you can probably get God's Will for Your Life by inverting these three: Focus on the Future, Perpetuate Prayer, and Live for Love. And that is precisely what we have in 1 Peter 4:7-11.

---

[112] Haddon Robinson, Sermon on 1 Corinthians 13, Believers Chapel, 1971.

[113] C. S. Lewis, *The Weight of Glory* (New York: HarperCollins, 1980).

"SAVING THE SAVED"

1 Peter

I. FOCUS ON THE FUTURE—BECAUSE IT WILL GIVE YOU COURAGE FOR TODAY   7a

But the end of all things is at hand.

Peter immediately transitions from Satan's will for our lives to God's will for our lives by turning our focus from this world, which is passing away (1 John 2:17), to the end of this world as we know it. **"Is at hand"** (NKJ, KJV) = *ēggike* = "come near" in the perfect tense. The general thrust of the perfect tense is to speak of action completed in the past with present results. The side note in the NASB says "has come near." It is as though the consummation of the age is just sort of hovering over us and could take place at any time.

Theologians call this concept "imminency." That is, the end could take place today; the "end" is imminent. There is no prophecy which must be fulfilled before the end could take place. It seems that God has wished for every generation to live as though He could come at any moment. Some say a Jewish temple needs to be built for the

311

prophecy concerning the antichrist of 2 Thessalonians 2:4 to take place: "who opposes and exalts himself above all that is called God or that is worshiped, so that he sits as God in the temple of God, showing himself that he is God." But the word for temple used here (*naos*) does not have to refer to the temple that was on the temple mount in Jerusalem before Titus had it torn down. The same word was used for pagan shrines or temples (Acts 17:24) found around the Mediterranean world. It was definitely a place of worship. The Jews will be sacrificing in a place of worship, and the antichrist will stop this worship, but this worship does not have to be on the old temple mount. "The Great Synagogue" across from the Leonardo Hotel in downtown Jerusalem was built according to the layout of Herod's temple.[114] It holds 850 men and 550 women. Sacrificing could begin here. This could be the place where the antichrist exalts himself and stops their worship.

Any time is a good time for the Lord to return, but can you think of a better time? Perhaps before WWII? With the steady degradation of the human race in terms of moral values, we wonder just how much longsuffering the Lord has as He waits for men to come to repentance.

A focus on the future will change your life. That's why the next word in v. 7 is **"therefore."** When we live with a focus on the future and the accountability of that day, it can't help but affect the way we live today. In Matthew 24-25 Jesus is talking about "end" (24:3, 6, 13, 14) times. In the midst of this discourse He contrasts a wise and faithful servant to an evil one. The defection of the evil servant began when he lost sight of the imminent return of his master, who had gone on an extended trip. He said, "My master is delaying his coming." Immediately after losing his focus on the imminent return of his master, the evil servant "begins to beat *his* fellow servants, and to eat and drink with the drunkards." Our focus or lack thereof on the

---

[114] https://en.wikipedia.org/wiki/Great_Synagogue_(Jerusalem), accessed February 19, 2019.

future return of our Master to whom we will give an account affects how we live today.

A focus on the future return of Christ can also give us courage to face the debilitating discouragements of today. G. Campbell Morgan, who underwent much physical suffering during the last decade of his life, claimed a focus on the imminent return of Christ was like a light at the end of a dark tunnel for him that helped him endure his current suffering. It gave him courage. So, our text says something about the future. It also says something about prayer.

II. PERPETUATE PRAYER—BECAUSE IT REDEEMS THE TIME   7b

... therefore, be serious and watchful in your prayers.

I can't see the word **"serious"** here without thinking of my Afrikaner friend from South Africa. He had a great career with British Petroleum and retired near Guadalajara, Mexico. He told me his grandparents fought in the Boer War against the British, and he was raised in the Dutch Reformed church. He said they were not allowed to laugh or smile in church. If one felt a smile coming on, he would have to step outside until the smile dissipated. After all, the business of the church is serious stuff, the stuff of heaven and hell— no laughing matter.

The word translated "serious" in the NKJ is probably better translated "be of sound judgment" (NASB) or "be clear-minded" (NIV). It's the word *sōphronizō*, which means "to be balanced" (literally, not drunk; able to walk a straight line). So, prophecy is important; that is, live as though He could come today. But one must keep a balanced perspective: plan as though you were going to live to be eighty (Psalm 90). Our time on earth (our life) is our greatest possession. After mentioning the length of a healthy life (seventy or eighty years) the psalmist points to the brevity of our life: "for soon it is cut off and we fly away." He immediately concludes his thoughts on time by saying, "So teach us to number our days that we may gain a heart of wisdom."

Paul also connects time and wisdom when he writes in Ephesians 5:15-17: "See then that you walk circumspectly, not as fools but as wise, redeeming the time, because the days are evil. Therefore, do not be unwise, but understand what the will of the Lord *is*." This is Paul's rendition of Matthew 16:24-27. When we redeem our time on earth, we are saving our lives (our time on earth) for eternity. And one of the best ways to do that is through prayer.

The word for **"watchful"** is *nēphō*, which carries with it the idea of attentiveness, alertness. As opposed to the disciples, who quickly fell asleep in the Garden of Gethsemane when they should have been on guard and watchful, Peter again learns from a rebuke from the Lord. This whole letter came out of the rebuke at Caesarea Philippi (Matthew 16:24-27). But the rebuke in Matthew 26:41 may still be in his mind as Peter urges his followers to watchful **"in their prayers."** This is an interesting dimension of prayer we don't hear much about. He seems to say that we should be praying for the return of the Lord and that part of our prayer time should have a prophetic focus.

While Betty and I were in seminary, we were looking for a means of support. Betty had a part time job as a secretary for a mission organization, but we needed something that paid more. The opportunity came to help a Christian man that was a quadriplegic. We went to the interview. He was an amazing man with a wonderfully positive attitude. I personally can't imagine being a quadriplegic, but this guy was something else. His greatest joy was telling us about his prayer ministry. He redeemed the time of his life through prayer. He had a prayer hotline and prayed eight hours a day or more for people from around the world who called in with their requests. That was about fifty years ago. To this day I have not met a more faithful prayer warrior than that quadriplegic. Was his life a waste? Only if you don't believe in prayer.

So, what is God's will for our lives in this passage? So far, we have seen that we should Focus on the Future, Perpetuate Prayer, and finally, we should Live for Love.

III. LIVE FOR LOVE—BECAUSE LOVING IS LIVING   8-11

A. Love for Each Other   8

> And above all things have fervent love for one another, for
> "love will cover a multitude of sins."

"Above all things" (*pro pantōn* = before all things) tells us that
on a horizontal level love for one another is God's highest priority
for us. That shouldn't come as any surprise since Jesus told us
the highest commandment is to love God (vertical), but the next
highest is to love our neighbor (horizontal). As pastors are fond of
saying, "The ministry would be great if it weren't for people." Far
easier to love things than people. Things usually don't hurt us. Some
have more love for cars than people. Others love houses more than
people. I probably could have been accused of loving sports more
than people at one time in my life. But it only makes sense that
we should love people more than things. After all, they last; things
don't.

I had lost track of a couple of my friends from seminary days,
so I tried reconnecting this year. Both of them were outstanding
athletes, one of them Olympic caliber. The other was the starting
center fielder for UCLA's baseball team. He had a cannon for an arm
and could really hit the ball. The other had two NCAA championship
rings from his days playing basketball for John Wooden at UCLA
and a gold medal from the Olympics in Mexico City. When I got
ahold of Tim Crater's wife, Cherry, she informed us that Tim (the
baseball player) had recently died of ALS. When I got ahold of Doug
McIntosh (the basketball player), he had just left his pulpit because
he is dying of cancer. The days of glory through athletics is decades
in the past for those guys, but the ministry they have had in the lives
of the people they have loved will live on forever.

Though I was always just a wannabe athlete, as I sit here typing
and counting my artificial joints (knee, hip, shoulder) and steel in
my wrist and ankle, I think about all the time I invested in sports
and realize I misplaced my affections earlier in my life. Of course,

there is nothing wrong with sports—unless my affection for them is greater than my affection for people. Peter says our highest horizontal priority is to love one another.

Peter also says something about the extent of love we are to have for one another (see 1:22): **"fervent"** (NKJ; NASB)/"deeply" (NIV)/"earnestly"(ESV) = *ektenē* = the taut muscles of the strenuous and sustained effort of an athlete. The root idea is "to be stretched or strained." The verb is used by Xenophon to describe a horse made to go full gallop. So, it suggests being stretched to the limit. You can expect your love for one another to be stretched to the limit. Hurt from other believers is one of the top three causes of people dropping out of church and out of the Christian life in general. When the flesh is in charge, born-again people are capable of doing most everything an unbeliever can do.

One day as I was browsing around the public library I saw a psychology book with an interesting title: *The Sociopath Next Door*. I have always pictured a sociopath as some social misfit that has committed serious enough crimes that they belong in prison. Not according to this book. It claims that fifteen percent of the people in our everyday lives are sociopaths. They describe a sociopath as usually a gifted, often even charismatic character that compulsively runs over people without any remorse in order to reach his or her goals for power and influence. Ooops, if that description is correct, I had hired a sociopath and turned him loose in our church. Over a period of years, he would lie, misrepresent, slander, and manipulate in order to eliminate people in his path. His influence was such that even when the powers that be caught him in lies, they chose not to fire him. I blame myself for the number of people he hurt and the pain he created—worse hire I ever made. He stretched my love to the limit.

How do you love someone like that? It helped me to understand that he was sick. I find it easier to forgive and love a person for their misdeeds when I know they are sick. Quite often, according to the book, the sociopath is not even aware of the psychological forces driving him to do his nefarious deeds. When I think of the person as "sick," it is easier to pray, "Father, forgive him; he doesn't know what he is doing."

We can think of a hundred more examples, can't we? But bottom line, we have to realize what Peter warns us of in the next chapter: the devil is a roaring lion seeking whom he can devour. Our enemy is not a flesh and blood brother or sister. It's the devil that would use slights and wounds from our fellow Christians to knock us out of the Christian race. In order to defeat him we must realize that our love for each other will be stretched to the limit at times.

And why should we love each other fervently? Because love **"covers a multitude of sins."** This phrase is used in James 5:20 and Proverbs 10:12 to mean "prevent" a multitude of sins. In other words, love can keep us from committing sins and will help us forgive sins that have been committed. When we are sinned against, love can keep us from retaliation and revenge. That's on our side. But love towards the one that sinned against us can also short circuit the revenge cycle in that we don't give any cause to the one that sinned against us to keep pouring gasoline on the fire.

In 1993 I was in Kenya while the "Black Hawk Down" debacle was going on across the border in Somalia. Directly to the west of Kenya was Uganda where Idi Amin committed his atrocities. And a year after I was in Kenya the Rwandan genocide occurred just south of Uganda where the Hutu dominated government of Rwanda killed approximately 800,000 Tutsi refugees. I asked the missionary I was staying with if that kind of thing could happen in Kenya, long considered the most civilized of the nations in E. Africa. He said, "Sure. The hatred and cycle of revenge within these tribes began hundreds of years ago." Hundreds of years ago, I thought to myself. You have to be kidding. No, the hatchet of revenge is always sharp. When one tribal member is killed by another tribal member, the tribe of the victim is honor bound to avenge his death. But that just keeps the cycle going because the victims of revenge are honor bound to avenge the revenge.

Love can break the cycle. But we are to love more than just our brothers. We are also to love strangers.

B. Love for Strangers 9

Be hospitable to one another without grumbling.

When we see the word **"hospitable,"** we usually think of opening our homes to invite people over for meals and fellowship, maybe even to spend a week or so with us. That certainly is one form of hospitality. But the Greek word translated "hospitable" in this passage is a compound word made up of two Greek words: *philo* + *zenoi* = emotional love + strangers. This kind of love involves the emotions more so than the usual uses of *agapē,* the word usually thought of as a selfless, divinely sourced love as in one of the fruits of the Spirit (Galatians 5:22). I would suggest that it means we should *feel* for the strangers in our midst. Empathize with them. Can you remember when you were the outsider in a group, a stranger? It is a lonely feeling. If Facebook's wild success has proven nothing else, it has proven that we humans are communal beings. We long to be connected. In fact, when it comes to church, it is said that people will visit a church for a whole variety of reasons, but they will only stay when they feel connected.

Strangers long to be strangers no more. Romans 12:13 actually tells us to be "given" (NKJ) to hospitality. The word there for "given" is *diōkō,* which means "to hasten or run after" (*BDAG*) the love of strangers (*philozenian*). It is as though we are to run around the church looking for anyone who looks like a stranger. Make them welcome. Help them get connected. In one church I pastored, due to its rapid growth there were all kinds of strangers popping up each Sunday. 1 Timothy 3:2 lists this love of strangers as a qualification for being an elder. In other words, the church leaders were to set the example when it came to pursuing strangers. So, in this particular church we declared the foyer to be the "Stranger Zone." Before and after each service a couple of elders were assigned to reach out to any strangers they saw. These elders volunteered to avoid their friends until all the strangers had been greeted and offered a helping hand. That's actually pretty hard to do since we only see most of our church friends at church and we want to talk to them. So, it was a sacrifice for these elders to volunteer for this service. It would have been easy to grumble. But our passage (1 Peter 4:9) tells us to love strangers without grumbling.

Let us remember that the first thing God labeled as "not good" is loneliness. His plan to overcome loneliness is through one's physical family and one's spiritual family. The Great Commission of the church is to go into the world to make disciples of all nations (Matthew 28:19-20); but the Great Mission of the church is to go into the church itself to overcome loneliness.

Love for each other; love for strangers; and finally, love for the Body.

C. Love for the Body   10-11

> As each one has received a gift, minister it to one another, as good stewards of the manifold grace of God. If anyone speaks, let him speak as the oracles of God. If anyone ministers, let him do it as with the ability which God supplies, that in all things God may be glorified through Jesus Christ, to whom belong the glory and the dominion forever and ever. Amen.

Sometimes people ask me about my "call to the ministry." I usually pause a second and then ask, "OK. But you tell me about your call to the ministry first." Of course, they kind of look at me cross-eyed because they assume that "the ministry" means full-time professional ministry. Actually, beyond the twelve apostles (Matthias substituting for Judas—Acts 1:25-26) and Paul, the only call to the ministry we find is right here in 1 Peter 4:10-11.

Let us first notice the words **"each one."** There is no reason to take this statement as hyperbolic (gross exaggeration for effect). Peter is telling us that every single believer has received a gift that is to be used for ministry. There's your call. If you are a believer, you have been given a gift. These gifts are listed in Romans 12, 1 Corinthians 12, Ephesians 4, Hebrews 2, and right here. You have one or more of these gifts. Peter says we are to be **"good stewards"** of these gifts. The word for "steward" (*oikonomia*) is often associated with a manager of goods or money as in Luke 16:1, 3. It is even used of a treasurer (*BDAG*). We are left with the impression that the gift we have is quite valuable and shouldn't be ignored or wasted. The Lord speaks of a time of accountability when He will ask us what we have done with the gift(s) He has given us. He even implied that if we have buried our gift in the sand, it will be taken from us and given to someone who has been faithful with their gift(s) to be used in the Millennial Kingdom to serve the Master (Matthew 25:25-30).

Using these gifts is one way we show our love for the Body of Christ, the church universal and local. To use one's gift is to serve. Serving is loving. In our consumer Christianity most folks go to church to be served instead of to serve. But Jesus Himself said He did not come to be serve but to serve and give His life a ransom for many. Of course, when we serve others, we find happiness (John 13:17 and James 1:25), the by-product of serving others.

Sometimes lives are transformed when a person discovers his or her spiritual gift. My wife is the oldest of six sisters. She had a verbally abusive father who made fun of her when she was just a little girl trying to learn the piano. He would say things like, "Can't you do any better than that?" after she had done her best on a recital piece. All the girls grew up with scars (father wounds). These emotional scars left Betty with a lack of confidence and low self-esteem. After we had been married about seven years a book came out called *Total Woman* written by a former Miss America and dealt with ways wives could make themselves appealing to their husbands. Lots of women were talking about the book. Betty told me she thought she was the "subtotal woman."

But then Betty discovered her spiritual gift—administration. It revamped her life. For over forty years she has used that gift to run anything from Pioneer Girls to Eagle Forum in our county. In fact, she is so well known in our county that I am known as "Betty's husband." She loves using her gift and finds great fulfillment in doing so. So, within a year of discovering her gift she announced to me that she was now the total woman! I couldn't agree more (except I think she is also part angel).

Since Peter has introduced the subject of spiritual gifts, he decides to whet our appetites with some instruction on the subject. In just one verse (11) he speaks of the Placement of Spiritual Gifts (11a), the Power for Spiritual Gifts (11b), and the Purpose of Spiritual Gifts (11c).

1. Placement of Spiritual Gifts   11a

> If anyone speaks, let him speak as the oracles of God. If anyone ministers, . .

There are three categories of spiritual gifts: speaking, serving, and signs.

a. **Speaking Gifts.** The speaking gifts listed in Romans 12 and 1 Corinthians 12 include: evangelism, teaching, encouragement, and preaching (prophecy was 90% forth-telling and 10% fore-telling). Moses was a prophet, but almost all he said was forth-telling (preaching the Word). The "oracles" = *logia* = used of Scripture in Romans 3:2 and Hebrews 5:12. Those who spoke were to minister the Word of God, not the words of men.

b. **Serving Gifts.** These include: giving, leading, mercy, faith, and service, shepherding,[115] missionary,[116] administration, and helping.

---

[115] The word often translated as "pastors" is *poimenas*, which literally speaks of "shepherds." The term "pastor" came from the *pastoral* setting of a shepherd and his sheep. The common rendering "pastor-teacher" as a spiritual gift came from a misunderstanding of what is known as Grandville-Sharp's Rule, which equates two nouns joined by "and" when preceded by one article (the). However, it never applies to plural nouns, as we have in Ephesians 4:11: pastors and teachers. Pastoring and teaching were different gifts, although in rare cases the same individual might have both gifts.

[116] There were three types of "apostles" found in the NT: the office (such as

c. **Sign Gifts.** These were given for confirmation at the beginning of a work of God. They were called "signs, wonders, and miracles" in Hebrews 2:4. They included: tongues, the interpretation of tongues, healings, a word of knowledge, a word of wisdom, discerning of spirits, and miracles. 1 Corinthians 13:8ff cannot be used to say tongues have passed away.[117] However, church history says the sign gifts ceased,[118] at least in the Mediterranean world. But whether they ceased or not isn't the question. They always could come back and someday will be here for sure (during the Tribulation Period—2 Thessalonians 2:9). The pertinent question is if they have come back today?[119]

---

the twelve), the gift of being sent forth (like Barnabas, a church planter—Acts 14:14), and a messenger (like Epaphroditus). The word simply meant "sent from." A good equivalent today would be "missionary," which means "one who is sent."

[117] "That which is perfect" does not refer to the canon of Scripture, which is not found in the near or far context. But the return of Christ is in the near context (v. 12). "Perfect" = *teleios* = complete, mature. It is talking about going from childhood to manhood, from part knowledge to full, complete knowledge when Christ returns.

[118] Montanus (150AD) was accused of heresy because he reinstituted the sign gifts. He couldn't reinstitute them if they had not ceased.

[119] Because we live in the "latter rain" in which the Holy Spirit is moving around the world (more have heard the gospel in the last hundred years than in all the prior centuries since the cross put together) we would expect the sign gifts to be present just as they were during the days of the early church, the "early rain" (James 5:7). However, so far, I have yet to validate any instances of raising people from the dead or healing people with one's shadow or leading people to Christ by speaking in their language without prior knowledge of that language. I have had the privilege of witnessing and taking part through prayer in many healings, but that is not the same as having the gift of healing. So, though I firmly

2. Power for Spiritual Gifts   11b

. . . let him do it as with the ability which God supplies, . . .

The word **"ability"**(NKJ)/"Strength"(NIV) = *ischuos* = "to be able." The emphasis is on the strength one actually possesses within himself (*TDNT*)[120]. But who has the strength for ministry? Supernatural works require supernatural power. We can minister through human power or what is often called the energy of the flesh, but nothing supernatural will be accomplished. It is the Holy Spirit living in us that supplies the power for spiritual ministry.

"Supplies"(NKJ)/"Provides"(NIV) = *chorēgeō* = "to lead a chorus" or "to pay the expenses for training a chorus." It came to mean "to defray the expenses of something, to provide, to supply in abundance." Do we let God provide the expenditure of energy in His service, or do we insist on footing the bill? Christ said, "Without me you can do nothing" (John 15:5). That doesn't mean we can't brush our teeth in the morning or drive to work. The context is bearing spiritual fruit. He says we cannot do this on our own. We have to abide in the vine (Jesus). There is great comfort for the minister in these promises. There will be times in ministry when we feel like we cannot go on, or when we go for long periods of time without seeing fruit. But Jesus promises if we abide in Him, we will "bear much fruit." That does not mean we will see all that fruit. Adoniram Judson saw very little fruit in his lifetime. But he laid the groundwork for countless converts to Christ in Burma (Myanmar) after his death.

---

believe in faith-healing (James 5:15ff), I have real questions about those who claim to be faith-healers.

[120] Theological Dictionary of the New Testament 10-Volume Set, vol.3 (Wm. B. Eerdmans Publishing Co., 1965), 397.

3. Purpose of Spiritual Gifts   11c

> ... that in all things God may be glorified through Jesus
> Christ, to whom belong the glory and the dominion forever
> and ever. Amen.

Who gets the glory? God gets the glory. He gives the gifts, and
He gives the strength to minister the gifts. It's not our ability, and it's
not our strength. When one forgets this, his service gets an asterisk
in heaven for self-seeking. Daniel 12:3 tells us that those who turn
many to righteousness will shine "like the stars" forever and ever. It
never says we are stars. There is only one Superstar in heaven. But
we will shine "like" the stars. What shines like stars? Well, moons
and planets, if they are reflecting the light of the sun. A moon has
no light of its own; it simply reflects light. We too will be moons in
heaven or the New Jerusalem reflecting the light of the SON. Light
is a composite of all the colors of the prism. In a way, His light is
a composite of His attributes. As we become more like Christ, we
reflect more of His character (His light).

And guess what? There are no half-moons in heaven. Everyone is
a full moon. The only difference between moons will be the amount
of light they reflect based on their faithfulness while on earth. The
more we use our spiritual gift(s) while on earth, the more light we
will reflect. Obviously, He gets all the glory because the glory of God
is an open, public manifestation of His character qualities. We are
reflecting His character before the whole universe. To Him be the
glory and the dominion forever and ever. Amen.

CONCLUSION

Only that which is done for eternity will last for eternity.
Obviously, some people don't believe in eternity, so why live for
eternity, something that does not exist. But if we do believe there is
another life after this one, could there be a connection between the
two? Apparently, Paul thought so. After motivating his readers to
persevere through suffering in Romans 8:17, he makes this statement:

"For I consider the sufferings of this present time not worthy to be compared to the glory that will be revealed in us." Perhaps it was because of being caught up to the third heaven (2 Corinthians 12:2) where he saw things no man still alive in the flesh had ever seen that Paul was so convincing about what awaits faithful believers. He knew something we have yet to learn.

A man in New York City had a wife that had a cat. She doted on the cat. She loved the cat. She stroked it, combed its fur, fed it, and pampered it. The man detested the cat. He was allergic to cat hair; he hated the smell of the litter box; he couldn't stand the scratching on the furniture; and he couldn't get a good night's sleep because the cat kept jumping on the bed. When his wife was out of town for the weekend, he put the cat in a bag with some rocks, dumped it in the Hudson river, and uttered a joyful good-bye to the cat. When his wife returned and could not find her cat, she was overwhelmed with grief.

Her husband said, "Look, honey, I know how much that cat meant to you. I'm going to put an ad in the paper and give a reward of five hundred dollars to anyone who finds the cat." No cat showed up, so a few days later he said, "Honey, I'll tell you what I'll do. I'll buy another ad and raise the ante. We'll increase the reward to one thousand dollars."

A friend saw the ad and exclaimed. "You must be nuts; there isn't a cat on earth that is worth a thousand dollars." The man replied, "Well, when you know what I know, you can afford to be generous."[121]

If we only knew what Peter and Paul knew, it might affect how we invest our lives today. And that's why they wrote. They wanted to pass their knowledge along to us. Why live for the passing when we can live for the permanent?

---

[121] Haddon Robinson, *The Solid Rock Construction Company* (Grand Rapids: Discovery House, 1989), 55.

24

"LIFE IS UNFAIR, BUT GOD ISN'T"

1 Peter 4:12-19

INTRODUCTION

Yes, it's true: life is unfair. As one wag puts it, "Some people get the gold mine . . . others get the shaft."

Arthur Ashe, the famous black tennis player, might well have spoken those words. Ashe underwent heart bypass surgery in 1983. At that time, hospitals were not checking blood samples for HIV, the virus that causes AIDS. Through a blood transfusion, Ashe contracted that much dreaded disease. He did not suspect he was infected until 1988, when he had to have brain surgery after his right arm became paralyzed. The surgery revealed a parasitic infection that quickly led to a diagnosis of AIDS. Ashe had not planned to reveal his illness until the time came when he would be noticeably changed by the disease physically. But USA Today demanded he confirm or deny the rumor that he had AIDS in 1992. The tennis star, ranked seventh in world before he was forced to retire, bravely held a press conference and announced that he was indeed an AIDS victim.

Like anyone else, Arthur Ashe was tempted to aim his rage at God, but he conquered that temptation. Speaking at the Niagara County Community College in the fall of 1992, he testified to the place Jesus Christ held in his life:

> I've had a religious faith, growing up in the south and black and having the church as a focal point of my life. And I was reminded of something Jesus said on the cross: "My God, my God, why have you forsaken me?" Remember, Jesus was poor, humble, and of a despised minority. I wasn't poor in that my father was a policeman, but we certainly weren't rich. And Jesus asked the question, in effect, of why the innocent must suffer. And I'm not so innocent–I mean, I'm hardly a perfect human being–but you ask yourself, "Why me?" And I think, "Why not me?" Why should I be spared what some others have been afflicted with? And I have to think of all the good of my life, of having a great wife and daughter, and family and friends, and winning Wimbledon and the U.S. Open and playing for and coaching the Davis Cup team, and getting a free scholarship to UCLA—all kinds of good things. You could also ask about this, "Why me?" Sometimes there are no explanations for things, especially for the bad.

What an extraordinary testimony. There are no explanations for many of the bad things that happen–at least no explanation understandable by our limited brains. But we need to admit that sometimes innocent people suffer. Life is sometimes very unfair. But what about God? If God is sovereign over life, surely, He is unfair as well. Surely, the syllogism is true:

1. Major Premise: Life is unfair.

2. Minor Premise: God is sovereign over life.

3. Conclusion: Therefore, God is unfair.

Rather than believe in a God that is unfair, many simply conclude there is no God. The wreckage caused to the faith of many who suffer these situations sits beside the road of life like abandoned vehicles flagged to be hauled off to the junk yard. Why does unjust suffering all too often eat away at the foundation of faith until the whole superstructure implodes? Isn't it the illogic of it all? "How can a loving God allow . . . ?" Or worse yet, "How can an all-knowing, all-powerful, loving God *cause* . . . ?"

But maybe there is something wrong with the syllogism. Maybe the syllogism does not give us the full picture. Maybe we don't have all the facts. Perhaps we don't know "the rest of the story," as the late Paul Harvey would say. How many times do we judge people, including God, without all the facts? Though still limited, Peter is trying to give us the "rest of the story." In fact, that is the main point of this lesson: This life is unfair, but we haven't heard the rest of the story."

"SAVING THE SAVED"
1 Peter

For many, this would be the climax of the letter. Here Peter hits undeserved suffering head-on. He wants to motivate his readers to persevere in the midst of their trials. He recognizes that most of us want the product of Christianity (Christ-likeness) without the process of Christianity (Christ's life); we want the goal without the gore. We want to become like Jesus without going through what He endured. But we don't get the product without the process. Peter motivates them with a Promise of Joy (12-14) and a Promise of Judgment (15-17).

I. THE PROMISE OF JOY   12-14

A. Prevalence of Unfair Suffering   12

> Beloved, do not think it strange concerning the fiery trial which is to try you, as though some strange thing happened to you;

This section (12-19) takes us back to his introduction (1:3-12) with many of the same concepts: fiery trials, suffering, revelation of future glory, judgment of Christians, and the *salvation of their time on earth* (*sōzō* [save] + *psychē* [your life] in 18 and 19). **"Fiery"** (*pyrōsei*)—used in Proverbs 27:21 of a furnace to refine gold, as in 1:6-9. **"Trial"** (*pros peirasmon* = for a test)—he's saying they should not be surprised at the furnace in their lives because it is for a test, that is, there is a purpose.

Undoubtedly, no blow has hit the belly of Judaism harder than the Holocaust. My wife and I recently watched the series "Against All Odds" with Michael Greenspan, a thirteen-part series that chronicles the restoration of the Jews to Israel in the 20th Century. The series was to investigate whether genuine miracles had taken place to establish this modern homeland for the Jews. Greenspan went as a skeptic with an open mind. As he interviewed Jew after Jew, it struck me how many of them were either agnostic or atheistic based on the Holocaust. Either there is no God, or they wanted to have nothing to do with a God that would torture and kill His chosen people. Talk about a fiery furnace, literally—a bunch of them.

I too have wondered from time to time about the good that could come out of the Holocaust. My favorite scholar was a little Jewish man (Moshe Weinfeld), who used to head up the Bible department at Hebrew University in Jerusalem (meaning he was considered numero uno among Jewish Bible scholars). He once invited me to come to his apartment after he was retired to discuss one of our favorite subjects. I was awestruck by this little genius of a man and asked him how he escaped the Holocaust since he came from Poland. He said his parents hid the family in Russia and then came to Israel in 1948. Knowing that 20% of the Nobel Prizes have been awarded to Jewish people, I wondered how many more potential winners had been burned up in those fiery furnaces at Auschwitz. What plan or purpose did God have?

Then Greenspan said something that must have stared me in the face for decades. After leading over twenty tours of Israel, it had never occurred to me that without the Holocaust there would be no Israel. I knew that Harry Truman cast the deciding vote for the United Nations to recognize the State of Israel in 1948, but for some reason it had never occurred to me that without the world's sympathy for the suffering of the Jews at the hands of Hitler, there very well may never have been the support needed for Israel to become a homeland for the Jews. And again, in the Yom Kippur War of 1973, it was a phone call at 3AM from Golda Meyer to Richard Nixon that initiated the biggest airlift of foreign aid since the Marshall Plan. Even though Nixon was in the middle of Watergate and on the way out, his decision to help Israel at the last hour is credited with saving the State. It was still the ripple effect from the Holocaust.

Yes, there may be a furnace in your life, but God has a purpose for the furnace. And Peter says we shouldn't think of this furnace as something **"strange"** (*xenos*—foreign or alien). This experience of unjust suffering is not alien or foreign; it is the *normal* Christian life. As James points out, we are to count it all joy *when* we fall into various trials, not *if* (Jas 1:2). Remember, most of us want the product without the process, Christ-likeness without Christ's suffering. *But you don't get the product without the process.*

I once had to fire an employee for embezzling $18,000 from our school. Later in the year I went off to Germany to write my first book, *Maximum Joy*. When I got back a number of families had left the church. I discovered that while I was gone this disgruntled ex-employee had spread slanderous accusations (none of which was true) throughout the church and even beyond. When the elders tried to meet with him, he retained a lawyer. Finally, the elder board dismembered him (literally, I was hoping). It was one of the five biggest trials of my life. When a pastor's integrity is shattered, there's nothing left. For months I used to slice and dice this guy when I took my walks in the evening. I kept telling the Lord how unfair all this was. Then one night He stopped me in my tracks and said (not audibly), "So, you think you are suffering undeservedly, right?" "Right, Lord. Don't you agree?" He confirmed my feelings and said, "Well, you have preached for decades that the Christian life is not about how big a splash you make in the ocean. You always told everyone the goal of the Christian life was to become like Christ, as much as possible." Yes, well, isn't that right? "Right. You got that right. But let me ask you this. What percentage of my Son's suffering was deserved?" Hmmm, like zero percent? "Right. Now, . . . how are you going to become like my Son without going through what He went through?" Boom. The light bulb came on. I wanted the Product without the Process. Suddenly, I found genuine joy in the midst of unfair suffering. The things I suffered there were in line with God's purpose for my life all along.

Now, let's not get confused. Did God cause the guy to slander me? Did God cause the Holocaust? Heavens no. The devil is behind a lying tongue. He is the father of lies. And Hitler? If the devil possessed anyone in the 20th Century, it had to be Hitler. He presents himself as a messianic figure in *Mein Kampf*. And the Third Reich— how long? A thousand years. Remind you of anything? No, God is not the efficient moral cause behind the evil in the universe, unless you believe in the micro-managing God of Augustinian-Calvinism, which was spawned by the determinism of the Stoics, Neo-Platonists, and Manicheans.[122] No, but God is so great and so sovereign, He can even use the sinfulness of mankind for our ultimate good and His ultimate glory.

No, there is nothing strange about unfair or undeserved suffering. It is prevalent. It's also paradoxical.

B. The Paradox of Unfair Suffering   4:13

> . . . but rejoice to the extent that you partake of Christ's sufferings, that when His glory is revealed, you may also be glad with exceeding joy.

The paradox: My joy increases as my sharing in His sufferings increases.

Inexplicably, but not surprisingly, the NIV completely omits a key Greek term in its translation: *katho*—"to the degree" (NASB) or "to the extent" (NKJ). To the degree or extent that we partake of Christ's sufferings. . . . "Partake" (*koinōneite*) comes from the word we often translate as "fellowship" or "share." The NASB translates it "share," while the NIV says "participate." So, *my joy is directly proportionate to my sharing in His sufferings (all of which were undeserved).*

Isn't this the same thing we read in the Sermon on the Mount. After telling us nine things that can bring us happiness, the Beatitudes, Jesus tells us how to be super happy: be persecuted and falsely accused for Christ sake and you can be exceedingly happy because great will be your reward in heaven. Here Peter is saying almost the same thing. In fact, the same two verbs are used to express this truth: *chairō* (rejoice) and *agalliaō* (exceeding joy). The next verse (14) talks about our present happiness, a beatitude if you will, but in this verse he talks about the exceeding joy that will be ours when we see how He is glorified in the next life by our sufferings.

---

[122] See Ken Wilson, *The Foundation of Augustinian-Calvinism* (Regula Fedei Press, 2019).

But my present joy is by faith (1:8), and that is hard. My future joy is by sight (when His glory is revealed), and that joy is "overjoyed" (NIV) or "exceedingly" (NKJ). In other words, we can be happy now (v. 14) and delirious later. What a paradox? Because there is a future world where the first will be last and the last first, much of the biblical perspective on this life is counterintuitive. Take Philippians 1:29, for example: "For to you it has been granted on behalf of Christ, not only to believe in Him, but also to suffer for His sake." That word for "granted" is the verb form of the word we translate "grace." If grace is an undeserved favor from God, then this verse tells us it is an undeserved favor from God to suffer on behalf of Christ. Are you kidding me? I get the faith for salvation from the penalty of sin part—that's by grace. But are you telling me that by this same grace we get the privilege to suffer for Christ? Now that is counterintuitive.

Not all will choose to suffer for Him, and He doesn't force any of us to do so. It's like Jimmy Doolittle challenging his best pilots to enter a suicide mission to bomb Tokyo after the preemptive strike on Pearl Harbor by the Japanese. He made it clear that they would not have enough gas to bomb Tokyo and get back to the carrier. They would have to fly on as far as their gas would take them into China. Many would not return, if any. Wanna sign up? No one was forced to go. Only those who were willing to die for their country. They wouldn't be discharged from the military should they choose not to go. Jesus does the same thing (Luke 14:25-33). Don't enter the battle if you are not willing to say good-bye to everything you have, which could include your own life. Count the cost before you volunteer. But, make no bones about it, this is not a draft call. It is a call for volunteers. No one will be kicked out of the family if he or she does not volunteer. But they may well forfeit the most joyful and fulfilling life anyone can live, both now and forever.

But what if I'm not up to it? I'd like to volunteer, but some of the stories I have heard of suffering overwhelm me. I don't think I have the strength to do it. Great. Glad you realized that because Peter talks about not only the prevalence and the paradox of unfair suffering, but he also points to the power source for us to endure.

C. The Power for Unfair Suffering   4:14

> If you are reproached for the name of Christ, blessed are you,
> for the Spirit of glory and of God rests upon you. On their part
> He is blasphemed, but on your part He is glorified.

Here is that word we saw in the Beatitudes: *makarioi* = happy or fortunate. But why are they fortunate? "For" (= because) the Spirit of divine glory rests on you" (my translation).[123] Isaiah 11:2 used these same terms to say that the Spirit of the Lord rested on Christ:

> **There shall come forth a Rod from the stem of Jesse,**
> **And a Branch shall grow out of his roots.**
> **The Spirit of the Lord shall rest upon Him,**
> **The Spirit of wisdom and understanding,**
> **The Spirit of counsel and might,**
> **The Spirit of knowledge and of the fear of the Lord.**

It is comforting to know that the same Spirit that enabled Christ to endure suffering will rest on us as it did Him. So, as we share in Christ's suffering, we shall also share in His enablement. George Matheson, the great poet, developed this kind of wisdom—the hard way. When his eyesight vanished, so did his fiancée. Twenty years later he wrote the immortal hymn, "Oh, Love, That Will Not Let Me Go." But he also penned these very meaningful words that are sometimes overlooked:

> My God, I have never thanked you for my thorns. I have
> thanked you a thousand times for my roses, but not once for
> my thorns. I have been looking forward to a world where I
> shall get compensation for my cross, but I have never thought
> of my cross as itself a present glory. Teach me the glory of my

---

[123] "The Spirit of glory and of God" is a special construction in the Greek NT known as a hendiadys, which, in this case, means that one of the nouns following "of" describes the other. Usually the second describes the first, i.e., "the Spirit of **divine** glory."

cross: teach me the value of my thorn. Show me that I have climbed to you by the path of pain. Show me that my tears have made my rainbow.[124]

What a beautiful thought: *my tears have made my rainbow.*

So, one motivation Peter offers is the Promise of Joy in the midst of suffering: the prevalence of unfair suffering, the paradox of unfair suffering, and the power for unfair suffering. If we can find joy in unfair suffering, then we should be able to live a joyous life in general. Otherwise, we will live "under" the circumstances, instead of "over" them. Now, as a second motivation to endure unfair suffering, Peter offers the Promise of Judgment (15-17).

II. THE PROMISE OF JUDGMENT   4:15-19

Future accountability is used throughout Scripture to motivate us to more godly living. Peter introduces that subject here by talking about different categories of suffering (15), the consequences for sufferers (17-18), and our commitment in the midst of suffering (19). Let's go through these in order:

A. Categories of Suffering   15-16

1. Deserved Suffering   15

But let none of you suffer as a murderer, a thief, an evildoer, or as a busybody in other people's matters.

Peter may be reviewing the sections on Conduct (2:13-3:12) in his mind and contrasting good conduct with the other option, bad conduct: instead of respect for secular authorities, we could plot assassinations/*murders*; instead of respectfully obeying our unfair bosses, we could steal (*thief*) from them (2:18-25); instead of turning

---

[124] George Matheson, *Dynamic Preaching* (October, 1995), 24.

away from evil to do good (3:11), we could be *evildoers*; instead of refraining our tongues from evil (3:10), we could be *busybodies*.

The suffering we reap from this kind of evil is deserved; we should not get mad at God because of it. He has written to us about it because He loves us. If we rob a bank, get caught, and go to prison, we are getting what we deserve. We certainly can't blame God for our suffering. No, it's not deserved suffering that challenges our faith; it is undeserved suffering, which Peter introduces next.

2. Undeserved Suffering   16

> Yet if anyone suffers as a Christian, let him not be ashamed, but let him glorify God in this matter.

There is such a thing as undeserved suffering of the innocent. When the Israelites let their sons "pass through the fire" (Ezekiel 20:26, a euphemism for sacrificing their first-born sons to Moloch), the little babies were innocent suffers. They had done nothing to cause their own deaths. But the undeserved suffering Peter addresses in this passage is suffering directly and specifically because of our Christian faith. The little girls used as suicide bombers by Boko Haram in Nigeria were originally kidnapped because they were attending a Christian school. The missionaries beheaded by ISIS would still be alive if they were Buddhists. But let's get closer to home.

A young businessman is doing well at work. He is offered a job making more money, but the price he would pay would be travel. He knew he had a problem with sexual impurity when he traveled. His way to "flee fornication" was simply not to travel. But when he refused to do so, he never went any further with his company. The price he paid was earning less money and having less prestige in the company. Like Daniel, he did not want to defile his conscience or worse by eating any of the king's meat or drinking his wine (Daniel 1:8).

A Navy pilot loves flying his F-14 and military life. Flew in the Gulf War. But in the world of macho Top Guns he stuck out. Because of his Christian values he would not run around with the "boys" and do the things they were doing. When the military downsized under Clinton, he was the first to be weeded out. Why? According to him, it was because of his Christian values.

There are a hundred more examples, aren't there? But they all have one thing in common: the undeserved suffering stems directly from their Christian faith. Peter tells those who so suffer not to **"be ashamed."** If we are not ashamed now, we won't be ashamed later (1 John 2:28).

B. Consequences for Sufferers   17-18

1. The House of God   17a, 18a

> For the time has come for judgment to begin at the house of God; and if it begins with us first . . . Now if the righteous one is scarcely saved, . . .

Way back in 1:17 Peter said a time of judgment was coming in which the work of each would be judged without partiality. Believers are judged before unbelievers. We see the Judgment Seat of Christ in 1 Corinthians 3, 2 Corinthians 5, Romans 14, Revelation 4, 5, and Luke 14:14. This occurs before the Tribulation Period begins. Then believers martyred by the antichrist during the Tribulation and the Old Testament saints are raised from the dead and judged for their rewards (Daniel 12:1-3). The Gentile believers alive at the end of the Tribulation are judged (the sheep—Matthew 25) along with the remnant of Jews that invite Jesus to return as their Messiah (Ezekiel 20:34-44). Notice all these groups are made up of believers. Finally, one more group of believers must be judged before unbelievers are looked at. It is those who believe in Jesus during the Millennium, His 1,000-year reign on earth (Revelation 20:4-7) before the Great White Throne (Revelation 20:10). Finally, all unbelievers since Adam until the end of the Millennium are judged at the Great White Throne. But we are getting ahead of ourselves. We need to discuss the word "saved."

If "saved" means "go to heaven," then we get there by being

"**righteous**." The verse referenced here is Proverbs 11:31: "If the righteous will be recompensed on the earth . . ." This is a direct quote from the LXX (the Greek translation of the OT by the Jews done between 250 and 150 BC). Both the LXX and Peter use the word "saved" (*sōzetai*). The Jews that translated the Hebrew into Greek chose *sōzetai* to translate the Hebrew word *yeshulam*, which is the verb form of *shalom*. The English translations have "rewarded" (NAS) or "due" (NIV) or "recompensed" (NKJ). None of these has anything to do with going to heaven. Notice "**on earth**." The verse is not talking heaven at all. It is about rewards for the righteous who are living. Bottom line, "saved" means the same thing it did when Peter mentioned the "salvation of our lives" back in 1:9. As we endure unjust suffering, there are credits in heaven and our lives are being saved for God's glory forever and ever.

2. The House of Satan   17b, 18b

> . . . what will be the end of those who do not obey the gospel of God? . . . Where will the ungodly and the sinner appear?"

The "end" is *telos*, meaning the end result, the final consequences. There will be a judgment for unbelievers. It too will be for their works (Revelation 20:11-15). Their judgment will be after the Millennium. The "ungodly" and "sinner" are paralleled to "those who do not obey the gospel" in 17b.[125] This judgment is usually called the Great White Throne judgment, since that is how it is described in Revelation 20:11. These people do not get there by their works. They get there because of their unbelief. Their eternal destiny is already determined by their lack of faith: the Lake of Fire (Revelation 20:14). But they are judged for their works to determine their rewards (negative). With the Judgment Seat of Christ, though there will be shame for those who have wasted their lives (1 John 2:28), the overall emphasis will

---

[125] For the use of "disobey" (ἀπειθούντων) for "disbelieve" see Roman 15:31, John 3:36, Acts 14:2 and 19:9.

be positive because all the negative is burned up. The positive is left over (1 Corinthians 3:9-14). However, with the Great White Throne all their good deeds are burned up like "filthy rags"(Isaiah 64:6). The emphasis is negative because that is what is left over. They are rewarded accordingly.

Having set forth the categories of suffering and the consequences for sufferers, Peter calls for a commitment.

C. COMMITMENT IN SUFFERING   19

> Therefore, let those who suffer according to the will of God commit their souls to Him in doing good, as to a faithful Creator.

"**Therefore**" leads to Peter's conclusion on what he has said about suffering. This is to those suffering undeservedly because they are doing "**the will of God.**" Again, the subject is clearly unfair or undeserved suffering that actually comes from seeking and doing God's will.

"**Souls**" (*psychas*) is the same word we had in 1:9 when Peter said the goal (*telos*—the end) of our faith is the salvation of our **lives** (see that passage for a discussion of and why this entire letter is coming out of Peter's memory of his embarrassment in Matthew 16:20-27). This book is about saving the significance of our time on earth (our life) for all eternity. The life lived for one's own kingdom and pleasure is like a drop of rain falling on hot cement—here for a moment; gone forever. But the life lived for His kingdom and His righteousness is like a drop of rain falling into a stream that flows into a river and out into the ocean to abide forever.

Peter's call to commit our lives *to Him* in doing good is much like his passage in 1 Peter 2:18-25 where the one suffering unfairly is challenged by the example of Christ who "committed Himself to Him who judges righteously." That passage ends by reminding us that Jesus is "the Shepherd and Overseer" of our "lives" (*psychōn*). Peter wants his readers to commit the rest of their lives (time on earth =

psyche) to the One Who created them (gave them their time on earth) by doing good. And note that the word for "good" here is *agathos*, a good that is not necessarily observable from the outside.

Doug McIntosh (see p. 315) grappled with this truth about the same time I did, during our second year in seminary. Doug and I played on a seminary basketball team and ministered to College and Career, High School and Junior High at Scofield Memorial Church in Dallas, respectively. One big difference between Doug and me was our basketball ability. Though I walked on and made the travel squad at Rice University, I did not letter. Doug, on the other hand, played for the great John Wooden at UCLA, had two national championship rings, a gold medal from the Mexico Olympics (1968), and his solo picture on the front of *Sports Illustrated*. Get the picture. Doug was really good. He had chosen to forego the newly formed American Basketball Association to come to seminary in 1967. But after winning his gold medal at the 1968 Olympics he had a lot of offers from teams looking for talent. He had a choice to make. His kingdom or God's kingdom (not to imply the two are necessarily mutually exclusive). Lots of money; no money. More fame; no fame.

Doug wanted his time on earth to count for eternity. Though he probably could have done that while playing professional basketball, he felt he could maximize his time for God's glory by teaching and preaching the Bible full time. So, he said no to the basketball opportunities and helped start a church in North Atlanta. I spoke with Doug this past summer. He had just stepped down from his pulpit after forty-seven years of preaching because he was dying of cancer. Regrets? Never.

CONCLUSION

"Scarcely" (4:18a—NKJ) is a puzzling word. Does this mean a righteous man scarcely gets into heaven? The Greek word is *molis*, which is "with difficulty" (NAS) or "hard" (NIV) or "only rarely, scarcely" in *BDAG*. We have already proposed that this has nothing to do with getting into heaven or it implies that people get in as a result of their own righteousness. But if the "saved" means to save one's time on earth for God's eternal glory, then "scarcely" or "only rarely" takes on a new meaning. It would be: rare is the Christian who understands the significance of "saving his life" for eternity and is willing to pay the price to do it. Fortunately, many do understand that "saving one's life" for eternity is the end game (1:9) and are willing to pay the price to do just that. And sometimes that which is required is undeserved, unjust suffering.

There are times in the midst of this kind of suffering we need to read verses like Matthew 5:11-12 again: "Blessed are you when they revile and persecute you, and say all kinds of evil against you falsely for My sake. Rejoice and be exceedingly glad, for great *is* your reward in heaven." This verse is telling us "the rest of the story." Just thinking about the reward we receive for unjust suffering can bring rejoicing and exceeding happiness. But that takes faith, doesn't it? In the midst of our suffering we find ourselves in a fog so thick we can't see the sun. Things are dark, and we feel lost and alone. But Jesus says there is more.

During the days of the Napoleonic Wars, Napoleon and Wellington were slugging it out at the Battle of Waterloo. It seemed as though all England was standing on the Cliffs of Dover waiting for news of the outcome of the battle. Finally, a message came across the English Channel, letter by letter. There was no telephone or television or internet or drones. They depended on semaphores to send their messages one letter at a time. The message read: W-E-L-L-I-N-G-T-O-N D-E-F-E-A-T-E-D. And then a fog set in. Doom and gloom swept through the hearts of the English around the country. But eight hours later the fog lifted and they saw the rest of the message: W-E-L-L-I-N-G-T-O-N D-E-F-E-A-T-E-D T-H-E E-N-E-M-Y. Now a tsunami of joy flooded their hearts. They had seen the complete message.

Right now, many of us live in the fog. We see no rhyme nor reason for our suffering. If we are not careful, doom and gloom will suck the life right out of us faster than mosquitoes suck blood. But at the resurrection the fog will lift, and we will get the rest of the message, the rest of the story. Then we will see that the sufferings of this present time are not worthy to be compared with the glory which shall be revealed in us. (Romans 8:18).

25

"STAIR STEPS TO HUMILITY"

1 Peter 5:1-7

INTRODUCTION

Young people set out to take life by the throat. Peter was such a young man. He had big plans. He'd tell you about it too, if you gave him half a chance. But life has a way of humbling most of us. It doesn't seem to matter what I take pride in; the Lord finds a way to humble me. A recent example.

After driving for almost sixty years I prided myself in never having had a car wreck that was my fault. I had been hit but had never been the hitter. Now Betty and I belong to a small group of believers who meet regularly for Bible study and prayer. Sometimes we eat out at a restaurant. This was one of those times. We were in Betty's car, so I let her drive to and from the dinner. As we got into the car to come home from the restaurant, she got her iPhone out. I said, "Betty, please don't do that while we are driving. I'm in the suicide seat here. My life is at stake." She proceeded to drive with one hand and fumble with her phone with the other. With a slight increase in the decibels for the sake of emphasis I observed, "Betty, what you are doing is illegal in some states. We could die, not to mention the people we might take with us." Finally, to my great relief she put the phone away.

Well, we had left my car at another house and went by there to exchange cars on our way to yet another destination. We left our home with me driving and stopped at a four-way stop. Turned left. Drove two blocks and stopped at another four-way stop. I looked at my phone briefly to punch into my favorite station on Pandora. I began to leave the intersection and BOOM: my first wreck.

Apparently, another car was at the stop sign perpendicular to mine and pulled into the intersection just before I did. Could my looking down at my iPhone have anything to do with the fact I did not see that car? Perish the thought. I was only going a couple of miles an hour. No tickets were issued and there was minimal damage, but I couldn't keep from laughing internally at the irony of the situation. I had just been mildly rough on my wife for driving while looking simultaneously at her iPhone. Fifteen minutes later I have the first car wreck of my life for doing the same thing! In all seriousness, small though that might seem to be, it is but one of fifty examples I could probably come up with where the Lord is still trying to teach me humility. Obviously, I have a long way to go.

But this leads to another question. Why is the Lord so concerned about humility in a letter about "saving the saved"? It almost seems out of place to focus on humility in the conclusion of this letter. The same man that once might have taught a seminar on assertiveness training, now teaches us how to be "clothed with humility." I wonder why?

"SAVING THE SAVED"
1 Peter

Salutation		1:1-2
Introduction		1:3-12
Body	"Our Plan of Salvation"	
I. Through Personal Sanctification—our Character		1:13-2:10
II. Through Personal Submission—our Conduct		2:11-3:7
III. Through Personal Suffering—Our Courage		3:8-4:19
Conclusion	"Our Posture for the Plan"	5:1-11
A. Humility among the Saints		1-5
B. Humility before the Sovereign		6-11

From the outline above we can see that we have finished the body of the letter, which tells us three ways to make our lives count for eternity: Through Personal Sanctification, Through Personal Submission, and Through Personal Suffering. But Peter tops off the letter in his conclusion with a focus on Humility among the Saints and Humility before the Sovereign. I am calling humility the correct posture we should have as we live out the three ways to make our lives count forever. In the section on Humility among the Saints we see the Humility of the Shepherds (1-4) and the Humility of the Sheep (5).

I. HUMILITY OF THE SHEPHERDS   1-4

A. Responsibilities of Shepherding   1-2a

The elders who are among you I exhort, I who am a fellow elder and a witness of the sufferings of Christ, and also a partaker of the glory that will be revealed: Shepherd the flock of God which is among you, serving as overseers . . .

"Elders" (*presbeuterous*) means "elders." Wasn't that helpful? The Hebrew term behind this came from "grey hair." Why should elders of a church be older men? Three reasons:

1. Older men are less feisty (see 1 Timothy 3 and Titus 1 for *not violent, not pushy, not quarrelsome, not self-willed, not quick-tempered*). Feistiness causes church splits (see 1 Kings 12 and how the younger men versus the older men split the kingdom). Why? Testosterone. They say love makes the world go around. I challenge that. I can't explain all the wars and senseless killing on this planet with love; but I can with testosterone. Younger men are quicker to fight.

2. Knotty family problems are best solved by fathers who have solved knotty family problems; that is, they have raised a teenager or two. The church is a family with knotty family problems. If a man has navigated the treacherous teenage years successfully, he can probably do the same thing in a church family.

3. It's hard to be a good elder and a good father of young children at the same time. Either the church or the family will suffer.

Peter identifies himself as a fellow elder and then reminds us of this principle of suffering before glory. We saw this in his introduction: "the sufferings of Christ and the glories that would follow" (1:11). This was such a peculiar thing (Christ suffering before glory) that the angels got on their hands and knees, so to speak (*parakyptō*—BDAG), to inspect closely and carefully the entire matter. We have to remember the angels had never suffered. Now Peter picks up this idea of suffering before glory once again. It reminds us (1:9) that to receive back (*komizō*—as in a commission) the end (*telos* = goal) of our faith, which is the salvation (preservation) of our lives (*psychas*) forever. It's the difference between that drop of water falling on the hot pavement and the drop of water falling into the ocean of time to be preserved for eternity. Or to use the words of Abraham Lincoln, "And in the end, it's not the years in your life that count. It's the life in your years."

The responsibilities of the elder mentioned in this passage is to "shepherd" (*poimanate*) and to "oversee" (*episcopountes*). To "shepherd" means just that: to pastor, to feed, to water, to protect, to guide. From this description a strong case can be made that pastors should be elders. Paul uses similar wording when describing the responsibilities of the Ephesian elders (Acts 20:28): "Therefore take heed to yourselves and to all the flock, among which the Holy Spirit has made you overseers, to shepherd the church of God which He purchased with His own blood." To shepherd is to pastor. In fact, the only time we have "pastor" mentioned as a noun is in Ephesians 4:12, where it is listed as a spiritual gift. The NT knows no such thing as the office of "pastor." The offices are elders, deacons, and perhaps deaconesses. The office of pastor, foreign to the NT, probably was a carryover from the model of the high priest in the Mosaic Law. In 1 Peter 5 and Acts 20 it is the elders of the church that are to do the pastoring. However, it is also important to understand that these elders that pastored the flock were paid for it (1 Timothy 5:17-18 and below).

The "overseeing," when viewed from the perspective of a shepherd and his sheep, was to watch over every area where the sheep gather or roam. 1 Peter 2:25 identifies Jesus as the Shepherd and Overseer of our lives, which implies that men are just under shepherds. Beware when an under shepherd tries to usurp the place of the Chief Shepherd as Diotrophes did in 3 John 9. He loved the preeminence, John says, using a word (*prōteuōn*—preeminence) found only one other place in the NT: Colossians 1:18 where it says Jesus "is the head of the body, the church, who is the beginning, the firstborn from the dead, that in all things He may have the preeminence."

So much for the responsibilities of the shepherds. What about the rules for shepherding?

B. Rules for Shepherding   2b-3

> . . . not by compulsion but willingly, not for dishonest gain but eagerly; nor as being lords over those entrusted to you, but being examples to the flock . . .

1. **Voluntarily**—not out of a sense of compulsion. God's army is not a collection of draftees. In Romans 12:1 God invites people to present their bodies as a living sacrifice for service. He does not command them. In Psalm 110:3 we read, "Your people shall be volunteers in the day of Your power; in the beauties of holiness, from the womb of the morning, You have the dew of your youth." The scene is Armageddon when the Messiah calls for volunteers to fight the final battle against the Antichrist and his forces. The army of Israel was led by its priest dressed in their off-white, linen robes. The Messiah's army will also be led by believer-priests wearing the white robes of the imputed righteousness of Christ. They will be so numerous they will look like the dew of the morning.

2. **Passionately** = *pro* + *thumos* = **very** + **passion** = **very passionately**—they are not to serve with money as their primary motive. The laborer is worthy of his hire and the teaching elder is to be given a double stipend (1 Timothy 5:17-18), but the elder is not to be motivated primarily by money (1 Timothy 3:3—"not greedy for money"). We can all pick out examples of ministers that seem bent on getting rich from the ministry. However, we could go to the other end of the spectrum as well. I heard of a ministry that claimed to have started ten thousand churches in a five-year span in a country in the 10/40 window. I knew some missionaries in that area of the world. I asked, "Tell me about those churches." They said, "Oh, those are just ma and pa shops. You only need $200 a month to live in that country. They start a church to set up a family

business for the sake of financial security." Hmmm. Paul actually went out of his way to not even handle the money being collected for the starving saints in Israel (2 Corinthians 8-9). He wanted to avoid any appearance of financial motive associated with his ministry. He defended his right to receive a "salary" from his work, but to keep from having his ministry maligned, he made tents to support himself.

3. **Examples** = *typoi* = **types**—of what? Of those who are willing to endure suffering before glory (see vv. 1, 4, 9, and 10), of which Jesus was the supreme *type* (2:21-25). Here is where you see the humility of the elders. They were not "being lords" over the flock entrusted to them. They weren't to think of themselves as lords but as servants ("serving . . . as overseers"). The word for "being lords" is *katakurieuontes* = *kata* (down) + *lord*. It carries with it the idea of subjugating those under authority. People like this have trouble being **under** authority and being **in** authority. The word for "example" (*typos*) originally meant the "mark" caused by a blow; it came to refer to a "stamp, model, mold, figure, pattern, or type." May others see the "mark" of Christ imprinted or stamped into our lives, which will help them endure suffering before glory.

C. Rewards for Shepherding   4

. . . and when the Chief Shepherd appears, you will receive the crown of glory that does not fade away.

There are a number of words here that point to the Judgment Seat of Christ: "appears . . . receive . . . crown . . . doesn't fade away." "Appears" (*phaneroō*) is a term for His second coming. That is when the judgment takes place for believers (1 Corinthians 3, 2 Corinthians 5, Romans 14). This is when how much of our lives is going to count for eternity is determined and measured by our rewards. But unlike most rewards on earth these rewards in heaven are not to glorify us but rather to glorify the Chief Shepherd. That should motivate anyone that is grateful for what Christ has done for us. The more rewards, the more glory—for Him.

"Receive" is the same word we saw in 1:9—*komizō*, the Greek word from which we get "commission." It is to receive what is earned. And the word for "crown" (*stephanos*) is the victor's crown, the laurel wreath from an Olympic victory, not the royal crown (*diadem*) that a potentate would wear. And finally, "doesn't fade away" (*amarantinon*) takes us back to the inheritance of 1:4, which does not fade away. Crowns are part of our inheritance.

II. HUMILITY OF THE SHEEP 5-7

> Likewise, you younger people, submit yourselves to your elders. Yes, all of you be submissive to one another, and be clothed with humility, for "God resists the proud, but gives grace to the humble."

A. Submission to Church Elders 5a

> Likewise, you younger people, submit yourselves to your elders.

The fact that "younger people" are singled out here contrasts them with the elders with respect to age. In fact, the word for "younger people" (*neoteroi*) is masculine in gender. Many translations actually translate it "young men" (NIV84, NASB). "Elders" are mentioned just a few words later. If elders could also be young men, the sentence would make no sense. It is just more evidence that elders were in fact elders (by age).

The word "submit" (*hypotassō*) is a compound word made up of "under" (*hypo*) and "to place" (*tassō*). So, submission meant "to place yourself under" the authority of someone. In this case it refers to the elders of the church. It takes some humility to be in submission. In fact, I might suggest that the mother of submission is humility. The opposite of submission is independence, and independence is quite often a sign of pride. It says, "I am an authority unto myself. I don't need you or anyone else telling me what to do."

I might suggest that the first step in order to shield oneself against satanic influence is to place oneself under the authority of church elders; in other words, join a local church. Solo acts are a perfect target for Satan. They are half-way under his influence already because their solo act is a demonstration of independence and pride. Someone will say that they do not respect the elders. Well, you often hear people say we should respect the office of the President of the United States. Even in this book Peter's readers were told to "honor the king" (2:17). The king at the time of Peter's writing was Nero, one of the more dastardly of the Roman Emperors, probably the man responsible for the martyrdom of Peter. Certainly, as a person Nero was not worthy of honor. But the answer is that we are to honor the position, not the person. Sometimes we can do both. Sometimes not. But we can always honor the position.

It is the same for anyone in a position of authority. Peter told the Christian wife to be in submission to her husband even if he is disobedient to the Word (3:1). That means the husband could be a Christian or a non-Christian, but in either case he is not obedient to God's Word. The wife is to respect the position, not necessarily the person. So, the husband, the boss, the government leader, yes, and even elders are worthy of submission because of their position, not necessarily their person.

Let us not forget that one of the two questions about God coming out of Lucifer's rebellion was, "Is God worthy of ruling the universe?" His sovereignty was challenged. When we submit to divinely ordained human authorities, we are submitting to God Himself (Ephesians 5:22). When we do that, we are answering that question about God's sovereignty in the affirmative. Thus, we are fulfilling one of the reasons for the creation of the human race. In other words, submission to authority is a BIG DEAL. As already developed in the second major section of the body of this letter, it is one way to "save the saved," make our lives count for eternity.

Someone will surely ask, "But what if one or more of the elders is not biblically qualified?" Well, how do you know they are unqualified? One of the more neglected verses in the NT regarding church elders is 1 Timothy 5:19, which says, "Do not receive an accusation against an elder except from two or three witnesses." I'd like to put the emphasis on the words "**do not receive**." We are not even supposed to listen to an accusation against an elder if there aren't at least two witnesses. Just an accusation, when made public, will cast doubt in the minds of listeners concerning the one accused. It's blood sport to castigate the character of spiritual leaders, or any leader, as far as that goes.

Consider the Cavanaugh hearings.[126] What if before the accusation was seriously entertained or considered worthy of investigation witnesses were required? There would not have been any Cavanaugh hearings. Two little girls and an innocent wife could have been spared a lot of pain. Judge Cavanaugh could have been spared a lot of pain. The whole nation could have been spared a lot of pain. I rarely have to stay at home because of sickness, but it was one of those days. The Cavanaugh hearings were on, so I watched. I'd have to say it was my lowest day as an American citizen. I came to tears twice; my response was visceral; I wanted to vomit.

Is it any wonder that one of the seven things the Lord hates the most is "a false witness who speaks lies (Proverbs 6:19) or that one of the ten commandments is to not "bear false witness against your neighbor" (Exodus 20:16)? Judge Cavanaugh feels his life has been forever tainted by the accusations made against him. There is an element within our fallen nature that latches onto the prurient and disgusting. It revels in it like a bunch of maggots in a feeding frenzy on a rotting corpse. Without any evidence whatsoever, some will always believe the lie. A good name is one of our most valuable possessions.

---

[126] Allegations of sexual misconduct were made against Brett Cavanaugh in 2018 after he had been nominated to the Supreme Court of the United States by President Trump.

Our reputation is like a vase. Once broken, a vase can be repaired, but the world will always keep its eye on the place where the crack was. Just like our justice system is supposed to be (presumed innocent), so an elder should get the benefit of the doubt in the absence of two or three witnesses. The enemy loves to scatter the flock by shooting the shepherds.

B. Submission to Church Members   5bc

> Yes, all of you be submissive to one another, and be clothed with humility, for "God resists the proud, but gives grace to the humble."

We have a command here to be clothed with humility toward one another (NIV, NAS) or to be clothed with humility by being subject to one another (NKJ). Either way, the net result will be the same: we need each other. The word for "humility" (*tapeinō* + *phrosunēn*) comes from an attitude of dependence stemming from one's realization of his own condition of depravity and need. The message is: "I need you." To admit that requires some humility. It is hard for most of us to admit we need others. Pride says, "I don't need you." That's independence, and that kind of independence is satanic.

When we try to go it alone, we not only expose ourselves to the darts of the devil, but we also find that God Himself will come out in battle array against us. The word "resists" (*anti* + *tassō* = against + to set, to place) means God sets or places Himself against the proud person. He gets in my way, when I am proud. He blocks my plans, which are usually to fulfill my own desires instead of His.

The word for "proud" (*hyper* + *phanois* [phantom; fantasy] = above + to appear). Pride is "to appear above" others, but it is a fantasy, an appearance lacking reality. The accoutrements of the world that we use to buttress this appearance are usually external things that have nothing to do with our internal value, which is the same for all people regardless of race, gender, social standing, or ability.

Instead of being proud, Peter urges us to "be clothed with humility." Surely Peter has Palm Sunday and the Upper Room in mind as he writes this. On Palm Sunday the Chief Shepherd came riding into Jerusalem on a donkey; in the Upper Room He "took a towel and girded Himself," that is, He clothed Himself with humility. The Savior served. Peter was especially humbled by having his feet washed by Jesus. That was the job of Peter and John, the appointed servants for the feast, who should have been by the entrance washing the feet of the invited guests as they entered the room. Although by His example and teaching Jesus showed His disciples the need for clean hearts and humble hearts (the greatest among you shall be the servant), He also told them they would not understand at that time what He was doing. He did say the time would come when they would understand. By the time Peter is writing this letter he fully understands. He chooses to clothe himself with humility. Why?

Peter explains that God resists the proud but gives grace to the humble. So humility has a double effect: 1) God stops blocking our plans; and 2) God opens His storeroom of grace. "Grace" (*charis*) usually refers to an undeserved favor or blessing. God gives undeserved favors or blessing to the humble.

C. Submission before God   6-7

> Therefore, humble yourselves under the mighty hand of God,
> that He may exalt you in due time, casting all your care upon
> Him, for He cares for you.

"**Therefore**" brings us to an obvious conclusion to this subject of humility. If God is going to resist the proud and give undeserved blessings to the humble, is there any other conclusion than to humble ourselves. But how do we do that?

"**Humble**" (*tapeinōthēte*) means to make an all-out declaration of dependence on God. It speaks of one's inner realization of unworthiness, knowing one's true condition of need and total dependence on God's grace to live this life. I would suggest this inner realization comes from two angles: 1) By becoming increasingly aware of my own depravity; and 2) By getting closer and closer to Jesus. And one leads to the other. The closer I get to Jesus, the more aware I am of my own depravity. When I see my own sinful condition next to His holy position, pride looks for a place to hide.

Of course, you have to be careful here or you will become proud of your humility. Sickening, isn't it? We will probably never expunge pride while in the flesh since it is part and parcel of our sinful nature. Trying to completely eradicate pride is like trying to eradicate our sinful nature. Not going to happen. But we can make choices that help such as our all-out declaration of dependence on the Lord and speaking His love language that bring us closer to Him. Remember, the closer we get to Jesus, the more we are impressed with Him and the less we are impressed with ourselves. He must increase; we must decrease.

Peter's mention of future exaltation for the humble is one more example of the counterintuitive thinking he learned from the Master. "But many who are first shall be last, and the last first" (Matthew 19:30). "He who exalts himself shall be humbled, but he who humbles himself shall be exalted" (Matthew 23:13; Luke 14:11, 18:14; James 4:10). Although this exaltation could come in this life, it most assuredly will come in the next. The promise of Jesus concerning the first and the last in Matthew 19 comes in answer to Peter's question about what the disciples would receive in recompense for all they had given up to follow Jesus. The answer points to the next life, specifically the twelve thrones ruling over the twelve tribes of Israel when Jesus sets up His Millennial Kingdom. Again, at that time we will find out how much of our life on earth has been "saved" to glorify God forever.

But sometimes sacrificing the "good life" to follow Jesus is uncomfortable. If we have a family, worry and concern for their well-being must be addressed. That's when Peter's next words bring comfort to the uncomfortable. **"Casting"** (*epiriptō*) speaks of throwing clothes on a horse so you can ride it. So, this means to let the Lord carry our load. **"Care"** (*merimnan*) refers to anything we might worry or be concerned about. To carry around our own cares is another act of independence.

I have a wonderful lady who works for our school, Grace School of Theology. Her husband has worked for Hewitt-Packard (formerly

Compaq) most of his career. But as they approached their fifties, her husband wanted to work more directly for the kingdom of God. But they didn't have a lot of savings and leaving the security of HP was a big deal. When they talked to me about it, I just mentioned the obvious: "You can't walk on water until you get out of the boat." One of the problems with getting out of the boat is discomfort. We are much more comfortable sitting in the boat. But we will never experience the thrill of walking on water in the boat. Well, wouldn't you know it, they decided to get out of the boat. But the ministry they went with did not fulfill some promises given before he signed up, specifically dealing with finances. He worked for several months before any funding came in, and when it did, it wasn't what he had been promised. Yesterday she came in my office and began crying. I thought the financial pressure had gotten to them, but she said, "We got out of the boat, and now I have no idea how the Lord will take care of us, but I know He will. I have never been so thrilled in my life. Here I am in my fifties, and this is the most excited I have ever been." She's walking on water. Delusional thinking? People that stay in the boat will never know.

CONCLUSION

In 1863 Abraham Lincoln signed the Emancipation Proclamation, perhaps the most significant piece of legislation of the 19th century. But also in 1863 Lincoln made another proclamation: Proclamation of a Day of National Humiliation, Fasting and Prayer, 1863:

> We have been the recipients of the choicest bounties of heaven; we have been preserved these many years in peace and prosperity; we have grown in numbers, wealth, and power as no other nation has ever grown. But we have forgotten God. We have forgotten the gracious hand which preserved us in peace and multiplied and enriched and strengthened us, and we have vainly imagined, in the deceitfulness of our hearts, that all these blessings were produced by some

superior wisdom and virtue of our own. Intoxicated with unbroken success, we have become too self-sufficient to feel the necessity of redeeming and preserving grace, too proud to pray to the God that made us.[127]

Over 150 years have gone by since that proclamation, but if those words described America in 1863, how much more so do they reflect America today. We have grown in numbers, wealth, and power as no other nation has ever grown. But we too have forgotten God, even more so than in the days of Lincoln. Actually, "forgotten" is too tepid a word to describe our national relationship with God. No, not passively forgotten, but purposefully excommunicated: out of our schools, out of our courtrooms, yes, and in some cases, out of our churches.

Will you notice what Lincoln observes to be the essence of pride: self-sufficiency. Independence from God. In this passage we see the folly of taking credit for what God has given us or accomplished through us. The wise man or woman, or the wise church or political leader will humble himself to make an all-out declaration of dependence upon God to accomplish anything that will last forever. As Jesus said, "Without me you can do nothing" (John 15:5). By that he does not mean I can't brush my teeth or dress myself without God. It means we can do nothing that will last for eternity without Christ. "Only one life twill soon be past; only what's done for Christ will last."

---

[127] www.abrahamlincolnonline.org/lincoln/speeches/fast.htm, accessed 7/10/ 2019.

26

"THE LION'S ROAR"

1 Peter 5:8-9

INTRODUCTION

I n 1970 Time magazine contained an article about Anton LaVey, the founder of the Church of Satan in San Francisco. I wanted to find out how someone could join such a church, so I sent off for an application to join. It wasn't long before I received a six-page document explaining their philosophy and how to join. On the first page it said:

> As a Satanist you'll receive a suitably inscribed membership card of a striking appearance, and have the opportunity to meet other Satanists near you or anywhere in the world, study for the Satanic Priesthood, if you so desire, overcome any obstacle through the practice of ceremonial magic, gain your desires through the ability to control people and events, and perform and participate in authentic Satanic rituals... We Satanists are winners, not losers. The die has been cast. The Satanic Age is upon us... Satan represents indulgence instead of absence! Satan represents a vengeance,

instead of turning the other cheek! Satan represents all of these so-called sins, as they all lead to physical or mental gratification! . . . The Satanic Age is upon us! Want to take advantage of it and . . . LIVE ("evil" spelled backwards).

At the time such open, unapologetic adulation for Satan was shocking and newsworthy. My, how times have changed. In 2017 I read an article about a witches and warlock conference at Randolph Air Force Base in San Antonio, TX. It was reported that 360 participants showed up. I was incredulous and asked someone living near-by if he thought it was true. "Sure," he said. "It's the fruit of the Harry Potter Series. White magic is in."

Someone has suggested that Satan's most cunning deceit in the 20th Century was to simply make people think he does not exist. Perhaps that's why we hear so little about the devil and hell in pulpits today. People see no objective proof of Satan and hell, so it is assumed they don't exist. As C. S. Lewis might have said, "The only joy in hell is the rejoicing among the demons when one sinner says in his heart, 'There is no hell.'"

What does 1 Peter say about the devil? Is he, or isn't he—that is the question. We want to look at Respect for the Devil (8a), the Roar of the Devil (8b), and Resisting the Devil (9).

Be sober, be vigilant; because your adversary the devil walks about like a roaring lion, seeking whom he may devour. [9] Resist him, steadfast in the faith, knowing that the same sufferings are experienced by your brotherhood in the world.

I. RESPECT FOR THE DEVIL   8a

Be sober, be vigilant . . .

Peter calls for a balanced approach regarding the devil. "Sober" (NKJ, NAS) is *nēpsate*, which means "to be well-balanced, free from excess, rashness, or passion." In other words, let's have a balanced approach here to Satan. "Be vigilant" (*grēgorēsate*) literally meant "to keep one's eyes open"; figuratively, it means "to stay alert and watchful."

But what is a balanced, alert approach to Satan? First of all, we should not look for a demon under every bush. For some people the devil or his demons cause everything sinful in their lives. Subtly, this can lead to a "devil made me do it" response to sin, thus minimizing our personal responsibility. The Scriptures speak of three enemies the believer faces: the world (1 John 2:15ff), the flesh (Galatians 5:17-21), and the devil. And James 1:14-15 tells us temptation comes from within us, from our own desires. These temptations are coming from our sinful nature. So, yes, the devil or demons can tempt us as they did Jesus in the wilderness. He was not tempted by His sinful nature because He did not have one. The devil tempted Him. But he used the world as his accomplice. The lust of the eye, the lust of the flesh, and the pride of life are three areas where the world tempts us. We need to remember all three enemies we face lest we try to blame everything on the devil. That is one imbalanced approach.

Another is to discount the devil and his demons. Sometimes the devil comes out in the open. While teaching at Jordan Evangelical Theological Seminary in Amman, Jordan, I met a blond-haired, blue-eyed Kurd, unusual to say the least in the Arab world. I was sitting by him at lunch and asked him how he came to be a student at the seminary. He said he was living in the Kurdish region of Iraq but had decided to leave Iraq to become a professional warlock in Germany. His sister had preceded him to become a professional witch in Germany. They were both Zoroastrians and worshipped Shatan (Satan).

To get out of the country they had to buy a black-market passport. He got all the money he had in the world together (about $5,000) and bought the passport. Unfortunately, the fake passport was a fake, fake passport. He couldn't get out of the country and was penniless. So, he decided to commit suicide. But a professor from JETS had passed through his town about a year before and preached the gospel at a rally. This young man heard the good news but did not receive it at that time. But it was a message of hope. So he decided to become a refugee from his country in order to go to Amman to seek out this professor. He found him and trusted Christ. He decided to give his life to serve Jesus.

But this Kurdish man was having trouble concentrating in class. His professor pulled him aside to see what was going on. He said he brought three spirit friends with him from Iraq. When he was in class his spirit friends went over into a corner and mocked and laughed at the professor when he was lecturing. So, the professor asked him if he had any vestiges from Zoroastrianism with him. Answer was yes. He carried around a small amulet his mother had given him. So, the professor and a couple of witnesses took the young man to the edge of the city and destroyed the amulet while claiming victory over the three spirit friends. The young man never saw his spirit friends again.

Such things happen, but they are not the normal Christian life. More commonly the devil hides in the background and is not easily spotted. We are told (2 Corinthians 11:14-15) that Satan transforms himself into an angel of light and his ministers into ministers of righteousness. When we think about an angel of light, we probably think of some glowing figure floating around and looking down on us. But the word angel (*angelos*) just means "messenger." And we often use the word "light" in terms of new knowledge or understanding. I've seen the "light," so to speak. We saw from the garden of Eden that the primary tactic of the devil is to undermine or cause us to doubt the Word of God. A full-frontal attack on the veracity of God's Word began with The Enlightenment (18th Century). New knowledge, "light," became the foundation of this assault on the Bible. By the end of the 19th Century not a single seminary in Europe considered the Bible to be inspired by God. Anyone who still believed the Bible was uneducated and ignorant.

If only the scientists were attacking the Scriptures, the fallout might not have been as great, but when the spiritual intelligentsia (seminary professors) joined the attack, millions of people lost their faith. Today Europe is a spiritual wasteland, at least with respect to Christianity. While vacationing in Switzerland with my wife, we went up and down a tram with a couple from France who headed up a Bible College. They told me there were more witches and warlocks in France than pastors. How did we get here? It did not begin with the devil riding through Paris on a red dragon waving his pitchfork. No. It was the slow steady drip of intellectual cynicism that caused people to doubt whether the Bible came from God. After all, if it's just the product of man, it must contain errors. And why should I hold what some guy or guys wrote thousands of years ago to a completely different culture as my authority for living my life?

So, yes, we should have a healthy respect for the devil. But what about the roar of the devil mentioned by Peter?

II. ROAR OF THE DEVIL 8b

> . . . because your adversary the devil walks about like a roaring lion, seeking whom he may devour.

Just who is Satan? Is he a myth, just the personification of evil? Is he a serpent (Genesis 3)? Is he an angel (Isaiah 14:12-15)? Is he a dragon (Revelation 12:7-9)? Here are three important facts we need to know about Satan from Scripture: 1) Satan is a real person, not an animal or a reptile; 2) Satan is a fallen angel as are the demons who followed him (Revelation 12); 3) Satan is not omnipotent, omnipresent, or omniscient.

But Satan is our "Adversary" (NKJ; NAS) "Enemy" (NIV) = *antidikos* = an opponent in a court room (Rev 12:10; Job 1:6ff). He is an unscrupulous lawyer who wants you to spend your life in a prison of sin where the prison warden is your sinful nature. Satan is not a lion, but he walks around "like" a roaring lion. But remember, the roar of the lion is only a scare tactic designed to paralyze the prey with fear. What does his roar sound like?

1. The Bible is the product of men, not God.

2. Religion is the opium of the people.

3. Miracles are myths.

4. You'll never change, you miserable piece of pond scum.

5. A loving God could never allow this kind of suffering.

What is the goal of a lion? It's to "devour" its prey. Here devour is *kata* (down) + *pinō* (to drink): to swallow. In other words, the lion wants to swallow you, eat you alive and not leave a trace; nothing left of your life when it is over; gone forever. This is the opposite, of course, of what God desires for our lives. He created us with a purpose and with a unique set of abilities and gifts and sphere of influence. No one else has your parents, your siblings, your children, your spouse, your neighbors, your place at work, and so on. This means you have the opportunity to have an eternal impact that no one else on earth has had, does have, or ever will have. Just you. But you only get one shot at it. The devil wants you to miss it. Peter wants you to save it. "Saving the Saved"—that's what this letter is all about.

I admire the man who came into my office yesterday. The lion had all but devoured him. Seventeen years ago (he's now forty-eight) his wife left him (no immorality on his part, no abuse, no biblical justification). After much wrestling he decided to turn away from the security of a plush job and devote himself to serving the Lord. He said the Lord's call on his life was almost audible. He was so convinced. He applied to two well-known seminaries, but both of them turned him down saying they thought his divorce was too fresh (two years old). He felt the sting of rejection from the seminaries, but more so from God. It was as though God had rejected him. So, he went back to his old company. In time he remarried and had a child. But God's call on his life continued to whisper his name. He sold his company and was financially independent. He offered to work at his church for nothing. They didn't have a place for him. More rejection.

When this discouraged man came into my office, he had all but given up. He had ruptured his Achilles tendon and it became infected so that he was bedridden for about a year and had gained about seventy pounds. But he was determined not to waste his life. Under a doctor's care he lost most of the weight. Then he told me his wife had given him a fifty-dollar bill and told him to apply to our school. Maybe in the process of getting more spiritual education he could find God's place for him. Now, that's a pretty long story to make one point: he desperately wanted his life to count forever. He told me that over and over during our time. Do you want your life to count forever? The lion doesn't.

So, how can we resist the lion? We looked at having respect for the devil and the roar of the devil. How do we resist him?

III. RESISTING THE DEVIL   9

Resist him, steadfast in the faith, knowing that the same sufferings are experienced by your brotherhood in the world.

Much of 1 Peter 5 sounds like James 4. James 4 urges us to humility before God, as does this passage in 1 Peter 5. The same for resisting the devil. James 4:7 promises us that if we resist the devil, he will flee from us. What a wonderful promise. But do we know how to resist him? The word "resist" is another of those compound words in Greek, made up of two Greek words: *anti* + *istēmi* = against + to stand (the word from which we get antihistamine, a drug to resist allergies). Resisting means to take a stand against something. But how do you do that? In the name of Jesus.

The Lion of Hades is no match for the lion of Judah. But woe be to the Christian that thinks he can battle of the devil in his own strength. We are no match for the most gifted of God's creatures. But Jesus is. A minister friend of mine pastored a church in College Station, TX, the home of Texas A&M. One afternoon a couple of women that were not part of his church wanted to see him. One introduced herself as the yoga instructor of the other. She said her student was drifting in and out of trances during her class. The instructor wondered if a local church could help her student. It seemed to be a spiritual problem. While they were visiting, the youth pastor of the church walked into the pastor's office. The yoga student was immediately flung up against a wall of the office and spoke in a low, guttural, male voice: "Why does he get a second chance and we don't?" was the question coming out of the girl's mouth.

The pastor immediately recognized he had a case of demon possession on his hands. He said over the next three days they cast out twenty-seven demons from this student, who had come from India. They named themselves as they came out. As I heard this story, I had no doubt of its veracity since this pastor was one of my own disciples. I asked him, "Were you ever afraid?" He said, "At first I was nervous, but when I used the name of Jesus they were kind of like puppy dogs; they whimpered when they came out."

Neither this pastor nor I am given to sensationalism. In fact, we would normally be very skeptical of stories like this one. However, since I have known this pastor for decades and have never heard anything like this from him before or since, I have no doubt the story is true. I share it for only one reason. I think it is a good modern illustration of the power of Jesus' name. Yes, we are to have a healthy respect for the devil. Going up against him in our own strength is worse than a sixth-grade kid trying to beat Mike Tyson in his prime. But when we go in Jesus' name, we can't be touched. It's like Sonny Liston trying to hit Cassius Clay—not gonna happen.

Peter tells us to be **"steadfast."** This word (*stereoi*) in its verb form meant "to strengthen, to become strong." It was used in the Acts 3 passage where Peter and John told the lame man to rise up and walk. It says: "Immediately his feet and ankle bones received strength (*stereoō*). Then he went running, and leaping, and praising God." I like this word because it speaks of an aggressive stand against the devil, not a passive one. Early on in my ministry I ran into an attack from the devil that almost knocked me out. Arrogantly, I had gone up against the devil in my own strength, but I was no match. My beloved wife, Betty, saw the attack coming. When it came she began taking notes, literally. She wrote down a legal pad full of symptoms of a demonic attack. While I seemed helpless, Betty decided to fight.

She called up the seminary from which I graduated to find help. No one there, according to her, knew anything about spiritual warfare. After all, I made an "A" in demonology, but I didn't know squat about how to resist the devil. Betty exhausted our contacts here in Texas. Discouraged, she didn't know which way to go. Finally, she was directed to someone in California that educated her in spiritual warfare. She has never been the same. She and a couple of friends applied what she had learned in their fight against the devil, and I was delivered from a power I had never experienced before. Most of what I now know about spiritual warfare I learned from my wife. That's why I blame her and Jesus for anything good in my life.

This much I can tell you. Like David and Goliath, they take the battle to the enemy. "So it was, when the Philistine arose and came and drew near to meet David, that David hurried and ran toward the army to meet the Philistine" (1 Samuel 17:48). When David saw the Philistine coming, he didn't retreat into a deer blind; he hurried and ran to meet him. And he did not expect to win the battle "with sword and spear," for "the battle was the Lord's" and He would give Goliath to the Israelites. Just so, Christ's warriors are "*stereo*," strong, fortified for spiritual battle by the Lord Himself. When they stand fast in Jesus' name, the demons whimper away like little puppy dogs.

When Peter talks about the **"same sufferings,"** he's talking about the undeserved sufferings he has referenced throughout this letter. As noted, one of Satan's primary tools is to paralyze his prey by getting him to focus on underserved suffering. In one of my early trips to Israel I had a window seat, my wife was next to me, and next to her was a Jewish man. While I was trying to go to sleep, I could overhear my wife talking to this Jewish man. Slowly, but surely, the subject came around why she was going to Israel, and she began to talk about Jesus. The guy couldn't get away so she had a captive audience. I began to pray. This poor man had no idea what he was getting into. He said he had completely given up on the God of Israel. When Betty asked why, he simply said he couldn't believe in a God that would allow his people to be slaughtered as they were in the Holocaust. He quoted Karl Marx by saying that religion was the opium of the people.

Betty had never heard that expression. She hesitated for moment and then replied, "You're right . . . and it's wonderful." Before long both of them had tears rolling down their cheeks. The man opened up. Four of his family members had been killed by Hitler. The idea of a loving God was beyond his comprehension. But he could see the love of a Gentile woman in Betty's eyes and hear it in her voice. We don't know the outcome of those shared moments, but we pray that light penetrated the steel wall of undeserved suffering and that we will meet that gentleman again in another life.

Finally, we need to say something about the word **"experienced"** (*epi* + *teteisthai* = on top of + to complete, finish, mature, perfect). This is translated "undergoing" in the NIV and "are being accomplished" in the NAS. The second half of this word (*teteisthai*) is the same verb used in Hebrews 2:10 where it says the Captain of our salvation was "made perfect" through suffering. With the little word "on top of" (*epi*) we get the picture of the final touches of a Grand Master on his painting. We are portraits of righteousness. In an oil painting the artist puts one layer of paint after another until he is satisfied with his work. The final touches may be a completely different color than the original, base layer. It seems the Lord, the Great Artist, uses our suffering for His final touches on our portrait.

I had lunch today with a man almost seventy that has seen nothing but trials for about five years: bankruptcy, closed doors for ministry, a home condemned because of toxic mold, a wife at death's door with leukemia, and on it goes. With tears flowing down his cheeks in a public restaurant I tried, with difficulty, to explain the "final touches" on his portrait. These "touches" of suffering are the final test of our faith. Will we weaken, flounder, turn back? Not this couple. They have already been to the grave and back a couple of times in the last two years. But as the Lord has given them more years to serve, this brother said his wife was overwhelmed with opportunities to share her story of faith at banquets, retreats, and so on. In her book, *In our Weakness, God is Strong*, Carmen Pate says:

In this book, you will see me in my darkest moments. In excerpts from my daily hospital blog, written through the battle for my life—an aggressive relapse of Acute Lymphoblastic Leukemia, I pray you would also see the power of God working through my weakness to minister to those around me. Ernest Hemingway's complete quote reads: "Life breaks all of us, but many are made stronger in the broken places." That has been my experience, and my desire is that you, too, would be made stronger in the broken places. I will forever be amazed by his grace![128]

CONCLUSION

Yes, the devil is a roaring lion seeking whom he may devour. And what better prospects than our youth. Get them off track when they are young, and they can waste their entire lives, never knowing the reason why God created them. I watched a Grizzly bear attack on YouTube the other day. This bear was going full speed (35 mph) after a young elk. It was able to split the yearling elk away from the herd of mature animals and take it down. Our teenagers make the mouth of the lion drool. It's when they are off on their own, unprotected by their parents or other adults that they are most vulnerable.

Judy was a really cute fifteen-year-old adoptee from Korea. She had a loving home here in Houston, caring parents, and a really good brain. But a guy several years older slipped a noose around her emotions and began to drag her away from her values and faith. Soon she was swallowing drugs like M&Ms. Suddenly, she was gone. After hiring an investigator, she was located in a motel in San Antonio. Her father jumped in a car and went after her. He found her, yanked her out of the clutches of her "boyfriend," and brought her home. The next task was to get her off the drugs. Her parents had the means, so they found a recovery center in the hinterlands of Utah. She was at church the Sunday before being sent away. I saw her in the foyer, went up to her, picked her up (I'm over a foot taller than she), lifted

---

[128] Carmen Pate, *In our Weakness, God is Strong* (Houston: Grace Theology Press, 2019), 3.

her up to my ear and said, "Judy, just remember, no one yet has out-sinned God's grace."

As I remember, the program was three weeks or a month. Her emotions traveled the full gamut of anger, resentment, remorse, rebellion, catharsis, and resolve to be a better person. When she came back home, she told me those words about God's grace were the only thing that kept her going. She now has a very productive job in a major city, an adoring husband, and a young child. Yes, the devil tried to swallow her whole, but God's grace won again.

27

"TRUE GRACE"

1 Peter 5:10-14

INTRODUCTION

Back in 1997 a survey was taken by *Time* magazine and written up in an article entitled, "Does Heaven Exist?" eighty-one percent of the people surveyed believed in the existence of heaven, a place where people live forever with God after they die on earth. And only six percent of the people surveyed believed we can get into heaven by the good things we do. You would think, then, that the rest of the people believed we get to heaven by our faith in God. Wrong. Only thirty-four percent believed we get into heaven by faith alone. Most of them (57%) thought we get into heaven by faith in God *and* the good things we do. Are you one of those fifty-seven percent? Maybe you are and don't know it. The question we want to answer in this lesson is, "What is *true* grace?"

Every group that identifies with Jesus Christ believes in grace. How could you not? Just the word "grace" (*charis*) occurs 154 times in the New Testament. It's everywhere. The Roman Catholics believe in grace. In fact, Augustine wrote about free grace more than any church father. Catholics believe that without grace nobody goes to heaven. Of course, they also believe there are certain things we can do to obtain grace from God, which they call the sacraments. When the Protestant Reformation split off from the Roman Catholic Church, its two main branches, Calvinism and Arminianism, both laid hold of grace as their crowbar to pry open the gates of heaven. In fact, many modern Calvinists call the five points of Calvinism "The Five Graces." And in Methodism, which is an expression of Arminianism, they talk about a second act of grace, which is "entire sanctification." Yes, every Christian group within the reach of Catholicism and Protestantism believes in grace. But do they all believe the same thing about grace? They didn't in the first century. That's why at the end of this letter Peter speaks of Silvanus as standing in the "true grace." Apparently, there was an untrue grace. Can there be such a thing as true grace versus false grace? Apparently, Peter thought so.

In the circles I run in we talk a lot about "free" grace. Often people who run in different Christian circles ask me why we call it free grace. After all, isn't grace by definition free? Unmerited favor from God–isn't that what grace is? Well, apparently the Holy Spirit knew there would be confusion on this issue. That's why in Ephesians 2:8-9 Paul further explained what grace meant by saying: "For by grace you have been saved through faith, and that not of yourselves; *it is* the gift of God, ⁹ not of works, lest anyone should boast." The word for "gift" (*dōron*) meant something given that's absolutely free—works excluded. Apparently, the Holy Spirit knew that our enemy the devil would try to distort the meaning of grace to turn it into something very costly. Some add conditions to get grace like the sacraments or conditions to prove you had received grace like living a good life until you die (the fifth point of Calvinism). So, in our final lesson on 1 Peter we want to talk about true grace. I think we can all agree this is pretty important if indeed we are saved by grace. It behooves us to understand what God means by grace.

"SAVING THE SAVED"
1 Peter

IV. GOD OF ALL GRACE   10

But may the God of all grace, who called us to His eternal glory by Christ Jesus, after you have suffered a while, perfect, establish, strengthen, and settle you.

The mention of **"all grace"** certainly raises a question as to the boundaries of grace. What does Peter mean by "all" grace? May we suggest the Scriptures identify grace before justification, through justification, and after justification:

1. Grace before Justification—God makes it rain on the just and the unjust. We call this "common" grace because all men experience it regardless of their relationship with God.

2. Grace through Justification—"For by grace are you saved . . . " This is how we become part of God's eternal family.

3. Grace after Justification—God ... gives grace to the humble. This would be grace for sanctification. As James 4:1-10 indicates, after we become believers we still wrestle with our sinful nature, which creates various lusts with in us, which in turn spawn arguing and fighting in our private lives, our public lives, in our church lives. In order to overcome our sinful natures we need more grace. The grace that justified us can also sanctify us. But God resists the proud and gives grace to the humble.

Now comes an interesting contrast in the text, the contrast between eternal glory and temporal suffering. Peter is coming full circle. Here is the same word (*oligon*) we had back in 1:6 with reference to their temporal suffering. It is for "a little while." He reminds them that their current suffering, painful as it may be, is leading them to a purer, stronger faith, which ultimately will bring more glory to God forever and ever. Let us remember that the glory of anything is an open, public, manifestation of the attributes or character qualities of that which is being glorified. If we talk about the glory of Arnold Schwarzenegger, in our mind we see Arnold posing for a Mr. Universe contest. His muscles are sleek and bulging. It looks like the veins in his arms and legs are going to burst. His enormous physical attributes are openly displayed or manifested for the world to see.

Now let's turn away from Arnold to God. The glory of God is an open, public display of His attributes or character qualities. Just this week a sixty-year-old minister told me the Christian life did not click for him until he understood the glory of God. In other words, we glorify God when we openly display His communicable attributes and character. When we display the love of Christ, we glorify Jesus. When we display the fruit of the Spirit, we are bringing glory to God because we are openly manifesting His character by the power of the Holy Spirit. When we see that the purpose of our lives is to bring glory to God by being a reflection of Him to the world and to each other, it can completely reshape our response to undeserved suffering or any kind of suffering, for that matter. Remember in 2:21 Peter said we are called to undeserved suffering with Christ setting the example. And 1:11 told us that suffering precedes glory.

The end of verse 10 is especially encouraging. Peter uses four words, each of which can be understood as part of a process of restoring a broken bone to its usefulness:

1. *Katartizō* = "perfect" (NKJ)/ "restore" (NIV) = to set a broken bone (Galatians 6:1)

2. *Stērizō* = "establish" = to put a splint on the broken bone

3. *Sthenoō* = "strengthen"—put a wrap around the splint

4. *Themelioō* = give it time to heal; literally meant "to establish" or make secure.

Perhaps we are bent out of joint because of our suffering, or maybe the lion has taken a big chomp and broken a bone or two. God offers complete healing. He doesn't always restore us to the same position or work we were doing before the lion's charge, but he certainly wants to restore us to usefulness. Why else go to the trouble to restore a broken bone?

I can never forget breaking my shoulder and humerus bone on my left arm while riding in the middle of the Baja Peninsula. Three friends and I wanted to ride dirt bikes along a trail used for what was called the Baja 1000, a thousand-mile dirt bike race. I had a lot of dirt bike experience riding with my son in the national forests north of Houston. However, I had never ridden on sand. The first time we hit some sand in our Baja ride I fell and broke bones. With a broken shoulder and broken left arm it made for an interesting ride back to Tijuana to find a doctor. At one point I was getting about a half a mile behind my friends, and it was slowly getting dark. I couldn't use the clutch with the hand on my broken arm, so the only way I could shift gears was to use my left foot. The pain was so intense that every time I hit a bump, I yelled out loud. I'm sure the group in front of me was glad not to listen to all my whining and yelling. I have a very low pain threshold.

But my yelling did attract someone. As it was getting dark, about twelve Federales (Mexican police) stepped out from behind a hill and stopped me. Although I've studied lots of languages, I have never studied Spanish and don't speak it. They kept asking me questions I couldn't answer. As it was getting even darker and I was getting nowhere with the Federales, I could see them taking me off to a dark and dank Mexican prison, or worse yet, just disposing of me behind one of these hills. Fortunately, I saw a light coming at some distance, so I knew my friends were backtracking to see where I was.

When the Federales saw I had backup, they just asked for some cigarettes, which we didn't have, so they left us alone. When I finally got to a doctor in Tijuana, he confirmed by x-ray that I had broken my shoulder and my humerus bone. He gave me some heavy painkillers, and I got back to San Diego and got a ticket back to Houston. When I saw a doctor in Houston, I was black and blue from my neck all the way to my left elbow. He said that the shoulder was too messed up to help, but the humerus break was clean enough, meaning not frayed, that it didn't need any work from him at all. He put it in a sling and said it would heal by itself.

By this he meant that nature would begin making a paste that it would lay around the break, kind of like you put a metal sleeve on a broken pipe to fix the pipe. He said it would take about four weeks for the paste to be laid down thickly enough to heal the break. Then it would be a couple more weeks for the paste to harden. He said when the process was over, although the bone wouldn't be as good as new, it would be restored to usefulness, and I wouldn't be able to tell the difference.

Just as God does that in the natural, physical world, He does so in the spiritual world. In nature it only takes six weeks for a bone to be healed; in the spiritual world it may take longer, depending on what kind of break the bone has suffered. But if you are alive and breathing, God is not finished with you. He still wants to use you, and He is right there to restore you, to set the bone, strengthen the bone and then give it time to fully heal. And if we understand 1:6-8 correctly, your faith will be even stronger (purified) after you have been restored, established, strengthened and healed.

II. GOD OF ALL GLORY   11

To Him be the glory and the dominion forever and ever. Amen.

Throughout our explanation of 1 Peter we have stressed that how much of the "saved" is "saved" will show up at the Judgment Seat of Christ. That's where we will find out how much of our time on earth will count for eternity and how much will be burned up or wasted. This letter is about how to keep from wasting our lives. It is about how to "save our lives" (*sōtērian psychōn*). The rewards we receive at this judgment seat measure the amount of our lives that count forever. But often I hear that living one's life to receive rewards is this selfish thing. That could be true. It all depends upon our motive.

Here we see that Peter is not at all confused about this issue. The motive for living a life that counts is to glorify God, because **"to Him be the glory and the dominion forever and ever."** If we think the rewards we receive are for our own glory, we indeed are quite mixed up and have selfish motives. But when we realize that we cast our crowns before His feet because He alone is worthy to wear them (Revelation 4:10-11) because whatever we do of eternal value was done through Him in His power (John 15:5), then our motives are not selfish at all. We are motivated by the opportunity to glorify God forever and ever.

As mentioned before Daniel 12:3 says that those who are wise shall shine like the brightness of the firmament, and those who turn many to righteousness like the stars for ever and ever." This is a beautiful picture of rewards. It doesn't say the faithful will be stars. This says they will shine *like* the stars. What shines like a star? Planets and moons. They have no light of their own. They simply reflect the light of the nearest star. Light comes from the star. And so, there is only one Superstar in heaven. We are simply moons. As such, we reflect His light. If we think of light in the physical universe as a composite of all the colors of the spectrum, then we might think of His light as a composite of His character qualities. When we reflect His light, we are making an open, public display of His character qualities, that is, we are bringing glory to God.

There's nothing selfish about this. The more we become like Him on earth, the more we will reflect His character forever and, thus, the more we glorify Him forever and ever. If we go back to the moon analogy, the more faithful we are on earth the greater our capacity to reflect His glory. In other words, some moons will be larger than others. But there will not be any jealousy. Jealousy is one of the rotten fruits coming from our sinful nature. We leave our sinful natures when we get our glorified bodies at the rapture or the resurrection. And there's no sense of lack. There will be no half-moons in heaven. Every faithful believer will be a full moon.

This is what we call a theocentric view of human existence. In this view the reason for our existence revolves around God. In other words, it's all for His glory. Passage after passage reinforces the theocentric view:

1. Romans 11:36—For of Him and through Him and to Him are all things, to whom be **glory** forever. Amen.

2. Romans 16:27—to God, alone wise, *be* **glory** through Jesus Christ forever. Amen.

3. 1 Corinthians 10:31—Therefore, whether you eat or drink, or whatever you do, do all to the **glory** of God.

4. Galatians 1:5—to whom *be* **glory** forever and ever. Amen.

5. Ephesians 3:21—to Him *be* **glory** in the church by Christ Jesus to all generations, forever and ever. Amen.

6. Philippians 4:20—Now to our God and Father be **glory** forever and ever. Amen.

7. 1 Timothy 1:17—Now to the King eternal, immortal, invisible, to God who alone is wise, be honor and **glory** forever and ever. Amen.

8. Jude 25—to God our Savior, who alone is wise, be **glory** and majesty, dominion and power, both now and forever. Amen.

And why not? Revelation 4 and 5 peel back the curtains of heaven for a bit of theodicy (justifying the ways of God with man). The Tribulation Period predicted in Daniel 9 and 12 is going to begin in Revelation 6. It will be a time of trouble such as the world has never seen (Daniel 12:1). The majority of all humans alive at the beginning of this tumultuous time will be dead before it's over. The question begs: how can a just and loving God be so cruel as to wipe out potentially billions of people? The answer is twofold: 1) it is right because of God's act of creation; we belong to Him by virtue of creation; and 2) it is right because of God's act of redemption; He paid the price to redeem all of us from this fallen planet; we belong to Him by virtue of redemption. All glory and honor go to the One that created us and redeemed us.

Glory to the Father, and to the Son, and to the Holy Ghost: as it was in the beginning, is now and ever shall be, world without end. Amen, Amen.

III. GOD OF TRUE GRACE   12-14

> By Silvanus, our faithful brother as I consider him, I have written to you briefly, exhorting and testifying that this is the true grace of God in which you stand. She who is in Babylon, elect together with you, greets you; and so does Mark my son. Greet one another with a kiss of love. Peace to you all who are in Christ Jesus. Amen.

The mention of **"true grace"** certainly implies there are teachings about grace that are not true. Apparently, there was another kind of grace being taught in **"Babylon"** (v.13—Rome, the center of false teaching), a false grace. Only a proper understanding of grace can "assure" the heart (Hebrews 13:9). The Hebrews passage makes an interesting contrast between external legalism and internal assurance.

He says, "For *it is* good that the heart be established by grace, not with foods which have not profited those who have been occupied with them." Most approaches to God through Christ offer some form of performance on our part in order to assure ourselves of our eternal relationship with God. Hence, the multiplicity of various forms of legalism taught in our churches today. Unfortunately, trying to gain assurance that we will always be loved by God through keeping a set of rules is a dead man walking. We will never measure up. With our failures, seeds of doubt assail our hearts. The only possible way to have a firm assurance of our eternal salvation is through grace. Only grace incorporates our failures. Only Grace picks us up when we fall.

The Gospel of Grace is polluted by teachers that want us to pay a price before the cross or after the cross. They either "front-end" load or "back-end" load[129] the gospel, which says, "by *grace* are you saved through faith, and that not of yourselves; it is the *gift* of God. . . ." What are some of these front-end loads and back-end loads?

Front-End Loads:

1. Baptism—yes, but only baptism of the Holy Spirit (1 Corinthians 12:13)

2. Repentance—yes, but only that I am sinful and Jesus is the Savior. This presumes you interpret repentance to mean "change of mind." Some of us think it is a fellowship issue, not a relationship issue. You believe for an eternal relationship with God and you repent for temporal fellowship with God.

3. No gross moral sins (sexual, chemical, covetous, reviler, swindler, etc.). One of many problems here are the

---

[129] For those not familiar with this terminology, a "front-end" load is a commission charged by a brokerage firm when you buy a mutual fund. A "back-end" load is a commission they charge you when you sell the mutual fund.

addictions out there. Asking an addict to be cured of his addiction in order to go to heaven might be asking him to do something only the power of the Holy Spirit can do. We firmly believe Jesus cleans His fish *after* He catches them.

4. Confession of Jesus as Lord—yes, for salvation from the power of sin, not the penalty of sin. Confession with the mouth is an observable, physical act like circumcision. There is no physical act required to receive the imputed righteousness of Christ (Romans 4:2).

5. Surrender—yes, but I surrender my sins, so to speak, for justification/salvation; I surrender my life for discipleship or service (Romans 12:1).

Back-End Loads:

1. Good fruit—yes, but some fruit is internal (the fruit of the Spirit of Galatians 5:22-23) and cannot be externally observed. True grace never says there will be no fruit in the life of one regenerated by the Holy Spirit. But "fruit inspecting" in order to determine whether one is in the "family" or not will always lead to doubt since the questions of how much is enough and what about rotten fruit and how consistent must I be, et cetera, will always plague the pilgrim.

2. No gross moral sins—the claim here is that a genuinely born-again person cannot continue in sin (a mistranslation of 1 John 3:9). But what about the carnal Christian in 1 Corinthians 5:5? This incestuous brother has continued in sin to the point that that apostle turns him over to Satan for the destruction of the flesh that his spirit will be saved in the day of the Lord Jesus. By the way, 1 John 3:9 does not limit its claim to gross moral sins. So where would you put pride, one of the seven sins that are an abomination to

the Lord and listed in God's hate list even above murder (Proverbs 6:16-19)? Ever known anyone with an ongoing problem with pride?

3. No habitual sins—but what about Moses? He killed the Egyptian at forty, broke the tablets at eighty, and struck the rock at a hundred and twenty. Looks like he had an ongoing problem with anger.

4. No blasphemy—but what about Hymenaus and Alexander who had made shipwreck of their faith and had to be taught not to blaspheme (1 Timothy 1:19-20)? The word for teaching here is *paideuō*, a word consistently used for child-training. This implies they were believers that needed divine discipline for the sin of blasphemy.

5. No apostasy—but 2 Timothy 2:13 says, "If we stop believing, nevertheless, He is faithful; He cannot deny Himself" (translation mine). Interestingly enough, almost all the English translations start off with: "If we are faithless" or "if we are unfaithful." The problem with these translations is that they are turning a verb into an adjective. The Greek says: "*ei apistouomen.*" That second word is a verb, not an adjective. It literally means, "If we do not believe" or, "If we stop believing." So why do so many translate it as an adjective? Because their Reformed theology does not allow for apostasy. They claim a genuine believer cannot deny the faith or stop believing, so they turn the verb into an adjective (faithless). This is actually one of the strongest verses in the Bible supporting eternal security. A child of God can actually stop believing, but God won't cast him away. This is a great comfort to so many parents whose children have been seduced by the great lies of the lion.

There are many other "front-end" loads and "back-end" loads various groups attach to the gospel. I have listed here just a few examples. It all goes back to what is true grace versus false grace. Anything added on to the simple message of faith alone in Christ alone is false grace. Of course, some Reformed theologians like D. A. Carson get around the problem of adding onto the simple gospel by redefining faith.[130] Carson now says that the very essence of faith includes works. So rather than contrasting faith and works as Paul did in Romans and Galatians, Carson now includes works as part of grace. He says perseverance is of the very essence of saving faith. In other words, if you don't persevere faithfully to the end of your life, you never had saving faith to begin with. And I would suggest that as long as you have to have works as part of your faith to go to heaven, whether the works are generated by man or God, there will be no firm assurance of one's salvation. Of course, we all want good works generated by God, not by the flesh. Ephesians 2:10 says that's why we were regenerated, that is, for the purpose that we might walk in good works. But there's a big difference between the purpose for something and the cause of something. The good works are not the cause of being born again; good works are the purpose for which we were born again.

CONCLUSION

Carmen Pate gained a national reputation as president of Concerned Women for America. She also did radio work four D. James Kennedy and Kirby Anderson of Probe Ministries. At a recent banquet for Right to Life she was the keynote speaker and shared her story. What most people have never known about Carmen is that she suffered through an abortion, not once but twice. At the time she had an executive position within a major US corporation. She was afraid that having children out of wedlock would jeopardize her career. In

---

[130] D. A. Carson, "Reflections on Assurance," in *Still Sovereign*, eds. Thomas R. Schreiner and Bruce A. Ware (Grand Rapids: Baker Books, 2000), 267.

her description of what she went through in the clinics where she had the abortions, you can feel her anguish, pain, and guilt. She had bought the lie that her babies were just pieces of tissue and would feel no pain.

After years of depression she came to believe that what she had done was definitely wrong before God. For years she lived a life of legalism, trying to make up to God for what He had created in her womb and she had taken away. But no matter how many acts of goodness or deeds of kindness she did, Carmen could not break loose from the ball and chain of guilt that followed her relentlessly during the day and mercilessly during the night. Then one day she discovered God's grace, true grace. She accepted the fact that she couldn't do anything to win God's love and acceptance. She learned that He loved and accepted her right where she was without conditions either before or after she received His gift of forgiveness through the blood of Christ.

And from that day forward she has been eager to serve the loving God that forgave her, not because she has to, but because she wants to. She's not living a "have-to" life; she's living a "thank You" life. In her address Carmen said that statistics show that one third of adult women in America have had an abortion. Of those millions of women nearly all of them suffer post-abortive anguish and guilt. She began going to post-abortive clinics where suffering women are told to write letters to their aborted babies and to name their aborted babies, to talk to their aborted babies. According to Carmen, these women may have found a temporary salve for their guilt but not a lasting healing. Only when they were introduced to God's marvelous grace, true grace do they find comfort for their souls.

Grace, grace, God's grace,
Grace that is greater than all my sin.
Grace, grace, God's grace,
Grace that will pardon and cleanse within.

EPILOGUE

I recently heard a talk by Cliff Robinson, one of the executive vice presidents of Chick-fil-A. In the speech he made the connection between Decision, Directions, and Destinies. In essence, he said Decisions determine Directions, which in turn determine Destinies. He gave the example of a unique feature of Chick-fil-A: they close all their fast-food restaurants on Sunday. Robinson claimed this practice began with a Decision to put people ahead of profits. It would seem intuitively obvious that a store open seven days a week could make more money than one open six days a week.

But the leadership of the company, mainly Truitt Cathy, observed that his people were tired a lot. So, the Decision to put people ahead of profits started the company in a new Direction. They wanted to give their people some rest so they wouldn't be so tired. Why not give them one day off every week? Being a committed Christian, Cathy thought giving them Sunday off might encourage some of them to go to church. That original Decision to put the needs of people before the desire for profits changed the Direction of the company. The end game (Destiny) of the company was the result of their new Direction. The desired Destiny was a group of fiercely competent and loyal employees, which is exactly what they got.

I submit to you it is no different in the Christian life. Our Decisions determine our Directions, which in turn determine our Destinies. Let's suppose we think the end game (the Destiny) of Christianity is to go to heaven when we die. That understanding could well lead to the Decision to do what is necessary to reach our destiny, heaven. Now, we will pursue the path in life (Direction) that will lead us to heaven. If we are taught that keeping seven sacraments is the right Direction to get us there, by God's grace that is what we will do, but no more. If we think all we have to do (Direction) to go to heaven when we die (Destiny) is to believe in Jesus as my personal Savior from my sins, then we might make a Decision to do that very thing, but potentially no more. Why should I do more if my Destiny is guaranteed.

Of course, this kind of thinking is one of reasons so many Christian groups resist the doctrine of eternal security. If you tell people believing in Jesus guarantees them eternal life in heaven, then you are also telling them their future sins are already forgiven. As the Council of Trent (RCC—1545-63) accused the Reformers, such teaching will breed license. Tell the people their future sins are already forgiven, and they will live like hell.

But what if some of the early leaders of the Church, namely Augustine, got it all wrong? That is, what if our ultimate Destiny is not simply to spend eternity with God. Maybe the end game is more inclusive than that. In fact, when we read Romans 8:29, predestination is mentioned, but it does not mention predestination to a place; it talks about predestination to a person: "predestined to be conformed to the image of His Son." Uh, oh. That's a different end game (Destiny) than entrance to heaven. Well, what does it mean to be conformed to the image of Christ? That is a question about Direction.

If my desired Destiny one weekend is to visit my daughter in Austin and I live in Houston, I might look on the map for directions. But suppose for some reason Maps has a malfunction and gives me the directions to San Antonio? If I follow those directions, my ultimate Destiny will be San Antonio instead of Austin. Directions determine Destiny. Just so, the Directions to the Destiny of conformity to the image of Christ are different than the Directions to the Destiny of heaven. Not that the two are mutually exclusive. Let's say my ultimate Destiny is to go deer hunting in Kerrville, TX, but the Directions to Kerrville lead right through Austin. Then the Directions to Kerrville will be the same as the Directions to Austin, at least until we get to Austin. But they go on. There is more.

So it is in 1 Peter. We suggest the theme verse for the book is 1:9, "Receiving the end of your faith, the salvation of your *psychē*," where *psyche* does not refer to your soul but rather your life, your time on earth (*à la* Matthew 16:24-27). This is a different end game than going to heaven when we die. It is a different Destiny. Oh, it includes going to heaven, but there is so much more. We don't want to stop in Austin; we want to go through Austin on the way to Kerrville. We certainly want to go to heaven when we die, but we also want to live out the purpose for which we were created so that our time on earth will last forever, will have an impact on eternity. 1 Peter tells us how to do that. It gives us Directions. But before we can follow the Directions, we have to make a Decision. The Decision is that we want to go beyond Austin to Kerrville. We want more than just landing on the moon like a tiny pebble. We want to hit the moon like a meteor and leave a nice crater that the Holy Trinity can point to forever to their glory.

Now in this epilogue I want to point out that this theme of making one's life count for eternity is not found in just 1 Peter. We find the same thing in James. And why not. He grew up with Jesus. He and Jesus would use words the same way. In fact, realizing this commonality between the vocabulary of James and Jesus could do much to solve the problem so many have with the theology of James and the theology of Paul. Some say James teaches salvation by faith plus works (James 2:14-26), whereas Paul teaches salvation is by faith alone (Romans 4:1-4). Wayne Grudem says James 2:14-26 is a section on how to go to heaven. [131] But Bible Methods 101 says to find out the meaning of a word, look for its other uses by the same author, especially the first use. The first use of "save" in James is in 1:21 where it says, "Therefore, lay aside all filthiness and overflow of

---

[131] Wayne Grudem, *Free Grace Theology: 5 Ways it Diminishes the Gospel* (Wheaton, IL: Crossway), 134-40.

wickedness, and receive with meekness the implanted word which is able to save your *psychas*." The "saving" of the *psychas* here is exactly what Peter talks about in 1 Peter 1:9. And this comes straight from Jesus in Matthew 16:24-27. If James 1:21 is about going to heaven, then the only way to get there is by cleaning up our act and become a humble Bible student.

But no, James is talking to people who are already "born again" in 1:21. How do we know? Because it is addressed to the "beloved brethren" of 1:19. Who are these "beloved brethren"? Is it a mixed audience of believers and unbelievers? Of course not, because it is the same "beloved brethren" of 1:16. Of these "beloved brethren" James says they have been "brought . . . forth by the word of truth," obviously a reference to spiritual birth, not physical birth. But the verse also says, "us" and "we." Who are the "us" and the "we"? It is the beloved brethren, of course, but it also includes the writer of the book, James. Do we think James will be in heaven when we get there? If James is there, his readers will be there, "the beloved brethren." Hence, 1:21 is directed to those who are already "saved" in the sense of going to heaven when they die, just like those born again in 1 Peter 1:3. And thus the "saved" of James 2:14 most likely has the same meaning as 1:21. It is how to save the saved. In other words, it is about the Judgment Seat of Christ where we will find out how much of our lives will count for eternity.

But this concept of saving the saved is not limited to just 1 Peter and James. It may also play a key role in Hebrews. One of the two most discussed warnings in Hebrews is in 10:26-39. The language of this passage is so severe that people reading it interpret the warning to be about eternal damnation. Admittedly, phrases like "certain fearful expectation of judgement," "fiery indignation," "fearful thing to fall into the hands of the living God," and "perdition" would seem to point to an eternal condemnation. But as we go on in the passage, reward language starts popping out. They were willing to suffer the loss of their temporal possessions in exchange for "an enduring possession . . . in heaven." They can look forward to "great reward." Finally, the author includes himself when he says, "We are not of those who draw back to perdition, but of those who believe to the saving of the soul."

The word for "perdition" is *apōleia*. If you are persuaded the passage is a warning against eternal condemnation, then "perdition" is certainly a good translation. But there are many passages where *apōleia* does not mean eternal condemnation, not the least of which is Deuteronomy 4:26 where we find a temporal warning to the unfaithful Israelites after they enter the land. If they become idolatrous, they will *apōleia apoleisthe* (putting *apoleian* side by side is for emphasis): be utterly destroyed. So, this language is even stronger than the *apōleia* of Hebrews 10:39. It is *apōleia* squared. But it is not a warning about hell. It is a temporal warning about being put out of the land (see also Deuteronomy 2:12 where *apōleian* is used of a temporal judgement and as a contrast to "possession" just as in Hebrews 10:39).

One good way to help understand the warning of *apōleia* in 10:39 is to look at its contrast: "the saving of the soul." The word "soul" is the same as used by Jesus, Peter, and James: *psychē* ("life, time on earth"). But the word for "saving" is not *sōzō*, the word used by Jesus, Peter, and James. No. This is the word *peripoiēsis*, which means "possession." Can you see why the Holy Spirit used this word instead of *sōzō*? It is because the word "possession" would have jumped out at his readers more so than *sōzō*. Why? Because they are Jewish Christians. No NT book has had more references to the OT than the book of Hebrews. Anything that would grab the attention of the Jews would be important to help dissuade them from shrinking back into Judaism. This would be especially true in a book that has so many references to Kadesh-Barnea. Why?

Well, what were the Jews supposed to do when they entered the land? Right! They were to "possess" the land: 1:8, 21, 38, 39; 2:5, 9 (2x), 19 (2x), 24, 31; 3:18, 20 (2x), 28; 4:1, 5, 14, 22, 26, 38. And so on. It's all over the place in Deuteronomy. But note well: they could go into the land without possessing the land. So also, the Christian can go into the kingdom without possessing the kingdom. And in Hebrews 10:39 "possessing" one's life is equivalent to "saving" one's life in the passages where "saving the life" occurs in Jesus, Peter, and

James. We are suggesting the author to the Hebrews selected the word for "possession" because it had a special meaning to his Jewish Christian readers.

Thus, perhaps we should look at the word "salvation" through new lenses in Hebrews. For example, in its very first use, the writer speaks of his readers as those "who will inherit salvation" (1:14). When it uses the word "inherit," it uses the same word Moses uses in Deuteronomy for both "inherit" and "possess": *klēronomeō*. Could it be that this inheritance in Hebrews is a reward for possessing one's life? Some regard Hebrews 2:10 as the theme verse of the whole book. But notice the very next verse:

> For it was fitting for Him, for whom *are* all things and by whom *are* all things, in bringing many sons to glory, to make the captain of their salvation perfect through sufferings. For both He who sanctifies and those who are being sanctified *are* all of one, for which reason He is not ashamed to call them brethren . . .

Verse 10 and 11 are connected by "for" (*gar*), which tells us v. 11 is either giving us the reason why v. 10 is true or an explanation of v. 10. The whole context is one of perfecting (sanctifying) the "sons" who have the opportunity to endure some of the same sufferings as their Captain. Could it be, then, the entire book is about faithful sons sharing in the rewards (inheritance) of their Captain?[132] The first ten chapters are about the "Superiority of the Faithful Son," while the final chapters are about the "Search for Faithful Sons." You might say the readers of Hebrews are not in danger of losing their "place" in heaven; rather, they are in danger of losing their "piece" of heaven. Entrance is not the issue; ownership is.

While the "saving of your life" may not be the major *motif* of the

---

[132] The author wrote his dissertation in defense of such a view: *The King-Priests of Psalm 110 in Hebrews*, Studies in Biblical Literature 21, Hemchand Gossai, Gen. Ed. (New York: Peter Lang, 2001).

NT, it is certainly a *leit motif* (subtheme) and one we don't hear much about in our churches. Peter tells us right up front (1:9) that the goal of our faith is to "save" our time on earth, our "lives," for eternity. He suggests three ways to do that: through our Sanctification, our Submission, and our Suffering. The list is not exhaustive, but it is a pretty good start.

Decisions determine our Direction, and our Direction determines our Destiny. If we think our ultimate Destiny is to go to heaven when we die, our Direction in life may be much different than if we believe our ultimate Destiny is to save our time on earth for eternity by being conformed to the image of Jesus Christ. If you agree that our ultimate Destiny is the later, you need to Decide now what Direction your life will take.

> Only one life,
> 'twill soon be past;
> Only what's done
> For Christ will last.[133]

---

[133] An excerpt from a poem by C.T. Studd.

SCRIPTURE INDEX

Scripture index created by Gracelife.org Scripture Indexing Tool:
https://www.gracelife.org/resources/bibletools/